MAKERS OF THE WESTERN TRADITION

Portraits from History
Volume 1

FIFTH EDITION

MAKERS OF THE WESTERN TRADITION

Portraits from History
Volume 1

FIFTH EDITION

J. Kelley Sowards, editor

Wichita State University

St. Martin's Press

New York

Senior editor: Don Reisman
Project editor: Beverly Hinton Beers
Production supervisor: Katherine Battiste
Text design: Nancy Sugihara
Photo researcher: Inge King
Cover design: Edward A. Butler
Cover art: Edward A. Butler

Library of Congress Catalog Card Number: 89-63936

5432

fedc

For information, write:
St. Martin's Press, Inc.
175 Fifth Avenue
New York, NY 10010

ISBN: 0-312-03601-9

Acknowledgments

AKHENATON: Prichard, J., ed., *Ancient Near Eastern Texts Relating to the Old Testament, 3rd edition with supplement.* Copyright 1954 Princeton University Press. © 1969 renewed by Princeton University Press. "Hymn to Aton" reprinted by permission of Princeton University Press. Reprinted with permission of Charles Scribner's Sons, an imprint of Macmillan Publishing Company from *The Dawn of Conscience* by James H. Breasted. Copyright 1933 James Henry Breasted; copyright renewed © 1961 Charles Breasted, James Breasted, Jr., and Astrid Breasted Horman. Redford, D. *Akhenaten: The Heretic King.* Copyright © 1984 Princeton University Press. Excerpts from pp. 4, 57–60, 62–63, 137, 140–44, 166–67, 169–70, 175–78, 232–35 reprinted by permission of Princeton University Press.

Acknowledgments and copyrights are continued at the back of the book on pages 314–316, which constitute an extension of the copyright page.

To Oliver, Elliott, Meredith, Sam, and Peter,
my darling grandchildren

Preface

Are men and women able to force change upon history by their skill and wits, their nerve and daring? Are they capable of altering its course by their actions? Or are they hopelessly caught up in the grinding process of great, impersonal forces over which they have no real control?

Historians, like theologians, philosophers, and scientists, have long been fascinated by this question. People in every age have recognized great forces at work in their affairs, whether they perceived those forces as supernatural and divine, climatological, ecological, sociological, or economic. Yet obviously at least a few individuals—Alexander, Charlemagne—were able to seize the opportunity of their time and compel the great forces of history to change course. Still others—Socrates, Martin Luther, Galileo—were able, solely by the power of their thought or their vision, to shape the history of their period and of all later time more profoundly even than the conquerors or military heroes.

The purpose of this book is to examine the careers and the impact of several figures who significantly influenced the history of Western civilization, or who embodied much that is significant about the periods in which they lived, and at the same time to introduce the student to the chief varieties of historical interpretation. Few personalities or events stand without comment in the historical record; contemporary accounts and documents, the so-called original sources, no less than later studies, are written by people with a distinct point of view and interpretation of what they see. Problems of interpretation are inseparable from the effort to achieve historical understanding.

The readings in this book have been chosen for their inherent interest and their particular way of treating their subject. Typically, three selections are devoted to each figure. The first selection is usually an autobiographical or contemporary biographical account; in a few instances, differing assessments by contemporaries are included. Next, a more or less orthodox interpretation is presented; it is often a selection from the "standard work" on the figure in question. The final selection offers a more recent view, which may reinforce the standard interpretation, revise it in the light of new evidence, or dissent from it completely. In some cases, two very different recent views are set side by side.

A book of this size cannot hope to include full-length biographies of all the individuals studied. Instead, each chapter focuses on an important interpretive issue. In some chapters, the figure's relative historical importance is at issue; in others, the significance of a major point mooted in the sources; in still others, the general meaning of the figure's career, as debated in a spread of interpretative positions. In every chapter, it is hoped, the problem examined is interesting and basic to an understanding of the figure's place in history.

The fifth edition, like the previous ones, is based on responses to a questionnaire by colleagues across the country who used the fourth edition in their classes. Their comments about which chapters or selections appealed to students and which did not, their suggestions about which figures ought to be deleted and which added or substituted, and their candid observations were extremely helpful in the revision.

Volume 1 contains one entirely new chapter, on Christopher Columbus. In addition, two chapters—those on Akhenaton and Peter Abelard—have been brought back from earlier editions. The chapter on Akhenaton is substantially revised and updated. Volume 2 contains three new chapters, on Voltaire, Simone de Beauvoir, and Margaret Thatcher; two chapters—those on Cecil Rhodes and Sigmund Freud—contain new selections.

All the selections in the readings were carefully reviewed, and the chapter reading lists were updated.

J. K. S.

Contents

xii *Contents*

MAKERS OF THE WESTERN TRADITION

Portraits from History
Volume 1

FIFTH EDITION

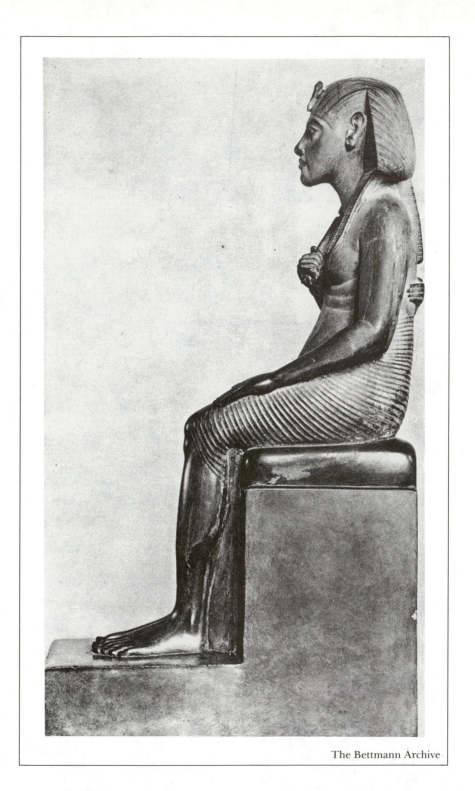

AKHENATON:
THE HERETIC KING

c. 1377 B.C.	Reign began
c. 1372 B.C.	Founded new capital of Akhetaton
c. 1360 B.C.	Died

With the enormous distance in time that separates us from ancient Egypt and the Near East, the scale of individual human size is reduced nearly to the point of oblivion. Even the greatest kings and conquerors, high priests, viziers, queens and "chief wives" tend to be reduced to lists of properties and exploits, names without substance or dimension.

For Egypt in particular the problem is compounded by the fact that the Egyptian culture tended to stress timelessness and eternity rather than history or individuals. The Egyptians had no continuous chronology. The names of successive pharaohs and their identifying epithets were often run together, overlapped, and sometimes blandly falsified in records and inscriptions or deliberately obliterated— probably for political purposes. The great modern British Egyptologist Sir Alan Gardiner, speaking of this maddening anonymity of Egyptian history, notes however that "in one case only, that of Akhenaten towards the end of Dyn. XVIII, do the inscriptions and reliefs bring us face to face with a personality markedly different from that of all his predecessors."[1]

This is the famous "heretic king," the most intriguing figure in Egyptian history.

[1]Sir Alan Gardiner, *Egypt of the Pharaohs* (Oxford: Oxford University Press; 1st ed., 1961; 1972), p. 55. The reader will note the first of several variations in the spelling of Akhenaton in this passage. Hieroglyphics did not write the vowels and there were consonant sounds we do not have. Hence considerable latitude in rendering names is to be expected.—ED.

A Hymn to Aton

There is no contemporary biographical account of this remarkable ruler, nor should we expect to find one. But what is more intriguing, conscious efforts apparently were made to obliterate every trace of him and of his reign. His name was systematically hacked out of official inscriptions and omitted from king lists. Even the genealogical lines, so important to Egyptian royal continuity, were altered. But a handful of inscriptions did remain, the most substantial being the Long Hymn to Aton, *from the tomb of one of Akhenaton's successors, Eye. Part of this inscription follows below. Although the authorship of the hymn is not recorded it is quite possible that Akhenaton himself wrote it. Yet it is not about him. It is about the god Aton, the disk of the sun, to whom Akhenaton subordinated all the other myriad of Egyptian gods, "sole god, like whom there is no other!" This was the apostasy of "the heretic king." This was the offense that seems to have created the animus toward Akhenaton, nearly unique in Egyptian history.*

Thou appearest beautifully on the horizon of heaven
Thou living Aton, the beginning of life!
When thou art risen on the eastern horizon,
Thou hast filled every land with thy beauty.
Thou art gracious, great, glistening, and high over every land;
Thy rays encompass the lands to the limit of all that thou hast made:
As thou art Re, thou reachest to the end of them;
(Thou) subduest them (for) thy beloved son.
. . . .

When thou settest in the western horizon,
The land is in darkness, in the manner of death.
Every lion is come forth from his den;
All creeping things, they sting.
Darkness *is a shroud*, and the earth is in stillness,
For he who made them rests in his horizon.

At daybreak, when thou arisest on the horizon,
When thou shinest as the Aton by day,
Thou drivest away the darkness and givest thy rays.
. . . .

All the world, they do their work.
All beasts are content with their pasturage;

4

Trees and plants are flourishing.
The birds which fly from their nests,
Their wings are (stretched out) in praise to thy *ka*.
All beasts spring upon (their) feet.
Whatever flies and alights,
They live when thou hast risen (for) them.
The ships are sailing north and south as well,
For every way is open at thy appearance.
The fish in the river dart before thy face;
Thy rays are in the midst of the great green sea.

. . . .

How manifold it is, what thou hast made!
They are hidden from the face (of man).
O sole god, like whom there is no other!
Thou didst create the world according to thy desire,
Whilst thou wert alone:
All men, cattle, and wild beasts,
Whatever is on earth, going upon (its) feet,
And what is on high, flying with its wings.

The countries of Syria and Nubia, the *land* of Egypt,
Thou settest every man in his place,
Thou suppliest their necessities:
Everyone has his food, and his time of life is reckoned.
Their tongues are separate in speech,
And their natures as well;
Their skins are distinguished,
As thou distinguishest the foreign peoples.
Thou makest a Nile in the underworld,
Thou bringest it forth as thou desirest
To maintain the people (of Egypt)
According as thou madest them for thyself,
The lord of all of them, wearying (himself) with them,
The lord of every land, rising for them,
The Aton of the day, great of majesty.

. . . .

Thou art in my heart,
And there is no other that knows thee
Save thy son Nefer-kheperu-Re Wa-en-Re,
For thou hast made him well-versed in thy plans and in thy strength.

The world came into being by thy hand,
According as thou hast made them.
When thou hast risen they live,

When thou settest they die.
Thou art lifetime thy own self,
For one lives (only) through thee.
Eyes are (fixed) on beauty until thou settest.
All work is laid aside when thou settest in the west.
(But) when (thou) risest (again),
[*Everything is*] made to flourish for the king, . . .
Since thou didst found the earth
And raise them up for thy son,
Who came forth from thy body:
the King of Upper and Lower Egypt, . . . Akh-en-Aton. . . . and
the Chief Wife of the King . . . Nefert-iti, living and youthful forever
and ever.

The Dawn of Conscience

JAMES H. BREASTED

*The name of Akhenaton was scarcely known at all in Egyptian studies until
the beginning of this century and the excavations at Tell el-Amarna. The
documents and inscriptions that came to light—including the* Hymn to
Aton—*fascinated Egyptologists, and they began to reconstruct the history of
this king and his age. A leading role was taken by the American
Egyptologist James H. Breasted. Breasted created an engaging portrait of
the young pharaoh, hardly more than a boy, who turned his back upon the
militaristic aggressiveness of his father, Amenhotep III, in favor of a new
and revolutionary religious revelation. Breasted argued that Akhenaton
was not only the first clearly discernible individual in history but the first
person in history to conceive the worship of a single god, in his case Aton,
the disk of the sun. Further, Breasted argued, Akhenaton anticipated the
Hebrew monotheism of Moses and he adduced, as part of his case, the great*
Hymn to Aton *and its clear affinities with the Old Testament, in particular Psalm 104.*

*Breasted's account of Akhenaton and his religious revolution continues in
the following excerpt, taken from his most famous book,* The Dawn of
Conscience.

On a moment's reflection, such fundamental changes as these suggest
what an overwhelming tide of inherited thought, custom, and tradition had been diverted from its channel by the young king who was

guiding this revolution. It is only as this aspect of his movement is clearly discerned that we begin to appreciate the power of his remarkable personality. Before his time religious documents were commonly attributed to ancient kings and wise men, and the power of a belief lay chiefly in its claim to remote antiquity and the sanctity of immemorial custom. Until Ikhnaton the history of the world had largely been merely the irresistible drift of tradition. The outstanding exception was the great physician-architect, Imhotep, who introduced stone architecture and built the first stone masonry pyramidal tomb of the Thirtieth Century B.C. Otherwise men had been but drops of water in the great current. With the possible exception of Imhotep, Ikhnaton was the first individual in history. Consciously and deliberately, by intellectual process he gained his position, and then placed himself squarely in the face of tradition and swept it aside. He appeals to no myths, to no ancient and widely accepted versions of the dominion of the gods, to no customs sanctified by centuries—he appeals only to the present and visible evidences of his god's dominion, evidences open to all, and as for tradition wherever it had left material manifestations of other gods in records which could be reached, he endeavoured to annihilate it. A policy so destructive was doomed to encounter fatal opposition. . . .

Here had been a great people, the onward flow of whose life, in spite of its almost irresistible momentum, had been suddenly arrested and then diverted into a strange channel. Their holy places had been desecrated, the shrines sacred with the memories of thousands of years had been closed up, the priests driven away, the offerings and temple incomes confiscated, and the old order blotted out. Everywhere whole communities, moved by instincts flowing from untold centuries of habit and custom, returned to their holy places to find them no more, and stood dumfounded before the closed doors of the ancient sanctuaries. On feast days, sanctified by memories of earliest childhood, venerable halls that had resounded with the rejoicings of the multitudes, as we have recalled them at Siut, now stood silent and empty; and every day as the funeral processions wound across the desert margin and up the plateau to the cemetery, the great comforter and friend, Osiris, the champion of the dead in every danger, was banished, and no man dared so much as utter his name. Even in their oaths, absorbed from childhood with their mothers' milk, the involuntary names must not be suffered to escape the lips: and in the presence of the magistrate at court the ancient oath must now contain only the name of Aton. All this to them was as if the modern man were asked to worship X and swear by Y. Groups of muttering priests, nursing implacable hatred, must have mingled their curses with the execration of whole communities of discontented tradesmen—bakers who no longer drew a livelihood from the sale of ceremonial cakes at the temple feasts; craftsmen who no longer sold amulets of the old gods at the temple gateway; hack sculptors whose statues of Osiris lay under piles of dust in many a tumbled-down studio; cemetery stone-cutters who found their tawdry tombstones with scenes from the Book of the Dead banished from the necropolis; scribes whose rolls of the same book, filled with the names of the old gods, or even if they bore the word god in the plural, were anathema; actors and priestly mimes who were driven away from the sacred groves on the days when they should have presented to the people the "passion play," and murmuring groups of pilgrims at Abydos who would have taken part in this drama of the life and death and resurrection of Osiris; physicians deprived of their whole stock in trade of exorcising ceremonies, employed with success since the days of the earliest kings, two thousand years before; shepherds who no longer dared to place a loaf and a jar of water under yonder tree, hoping thus to escape the anger of the goddess who dwelt in it, and who might afflict the household with sickness in her wrath; peasants who feared to erect a rude image of Osiris in the field to drive away the typhonic demons of drought and famine; mothers soothing their babes at twilight and fearing to utter the old sacred names and prayers learned in childhood, to drive away from their little ones the lurking demons of the dark. In the midst of a whole land thus darkened by clouds of smouldering discontent, this marvellous young king, and the group of sympathisers who surrounded him, set up their tabernacle to the daily light, in serene unconsciousness of the fatal darkness that enveloped all around and grew daily darker and more threatening.

In placing the movement of Ikhnaton against a background of popular discontent like this, and adding to the picture also the far more immediately dangerous secret opposition of the ancient priesthoods, the still unconquered party of Amon, and the powerful military group, who were disaffected by the king's peace policy in Asia and his lack of interest in imperial administration and maintenance, we begin to discern something of the powerful individuality of this first intellectual leader in history. His reign was the earliest attempt at a rule of ideas, irrespective of the condition and willingness of the people upon whom they were to be forced. . . .

And so the fair city of the Amarna plain arose, a fatuous Island of the Blest in a sea of discontent, a vision of fond hopes, born in a mind fatally forgetful that the past cannot be annihilated. The marvel is that such a man should have first arisen in the East, and especially in Egypt, where no man except Ikhnaton possessed the ability to forget. Nor was the great Mediterranean World which Egypt now dominated any better prepared for an international religion than its Egyptian lords. The imperial imagination of Ikhnaton reminds one of that of Alexander the Great, a thousand years later, but it was many centuries in advance of his own age. . . .

The fall of the great revolutionary is shrouded in complete obscurity. The immediate result of his fall was the restoration of Amon and the old gods whom the Amonite priesthood forced upon Ikhnaton's youthful and feeble son-in-law, Tutenkhamon. The old régime returned. . . . In the great royal lists recording on the monuments the names of all the past kings of Egypt, the name of Ikhnaton never appears; and when under later Pharaohs, it was necessary in a state document to refer to him, he was called "the criminal of Akhetaton."

The Criminal of Akhetaton

DONALD B. REDFORD

It was inevitable that such an unequivocal and highly colored interpretation as Breasted's would attract critics. And it was not simply a matter of interpretation. The Amarna records continued to be studied and refined and new finds were made, there and elsewhere, including the dramatic discovery of the nearly intact tomb of Tutankhamun, Akhenaton's son-in-law. The continuing, patient work of Egyptologists, archaeologists, and historians has produced a rather more complicated story of Akhenaton than Breasted presented—and a considerably darker one. We now know, for example, that he actually reigned alone for only two and a half years at the most; the rest of his reign he shared with regents. This clearly implies that Akhenaton was somehow incompetent to rule, either because of physical or mental incapacity or because he chose not to exercise the powers of his office. We now know that the failure of his religious program was not a matter of the narrow jealousy of the priesthood of Amon, but a general rejection by the whole Egyptian society. It has even been argued that his monotheism may have been only a selfish celebration of his own religious totalitarianism and no true religious movement at all.

The materials for a radically revised assessment of Akhenaton and his reign have been accumulating for more than half a century and Akhenaton now stands revealed not as the clear-eyed visionary of Breasted but as the "heretic king." One of the leading figures in contemporary Akhenaton scholarship is the distinguished field Egyptologist Donald B. Redford. The following account is taken from Redford's book, Akhenaten: The Heretic King.

Possibly in the fifth month of the civil calendar in what had been his father's 38th year (January, 1377 B.C.), Amenophis IV[2] ascended the Horus throne of the living. If sculptors showed uncertainty as to how to treat the strange figure of their new sovereign in art, they but mirrored a general hesitancy and puzzlement about what to expect from this young and unknown ruler. In contrast to the frequent appearance of his brothers and sisters, Amenophis, the second son of Amenophis III—his older brother has died young—is conspicuous by his absence from the monuments of his father. It may well be that he was intentionally kept in the background because of a congenital ailment which made him hideous to behold. The repertoire of Amarna art has made us familiar with the effeminate appearance of the young man: elongated skull, fleshy lips, slanting eyes, lengthened ear lobes, prominent jaw, narrow shoulders, potbelly, enormous hips and thighs, and spindly legs. Of late the experts have tended to identify his problem with some sort of endocrine disorder in which secondary sex characteristics failed to develop, and eunuchoidism resulted.

Be that as it may, it is a fact that Amenophis does not appear on monuments during his father's reign. The only certain reference to him seems to be on a wine-jar seal from Malkata where his name appears in the expression, "the estate of the true(?) king's-son Amenophis." He was, then, old enough to have his own establishment during the last decade of his father's reign, and, as we should expect, was residing at that time with the rest of the court at Thebes. . . .

As we shall see, the changes in cultic iconography and, undoubtedly, the decision to build new structures for a new god belong to the very beginning of Akhenaten's reign. . . .

When Amenophis III died the great complex of Amun at Karnak seemed to have reached a stage of structural completion. . . .

For a few months into the new reign, or perhaps for as much as a single year, sculpting and architectural decoration of a traditional nature proceeded apace. . . . Sometime in the 5th year of his reign, the heretic pharaoh moved the court from Thebes to a new capital in Middle Egypt. Though the change seems to be sudden, it was in fact premeditated. It proved to be the major watershed in the Amarna period. At this point then, let us take stock of the earliest, "Theban" phase of this unusual reign, before moving on toward the denouement of the drama.

Though his intent may have crystalized in his 4th year, Amenophis IV appears to have made no move until his 5th. Then planners, surveyors, and builders appeared at the chosen site, and work began at a feverish pace.

[2]This was the original regnal name assumed by Akhenaton.—ED.

But the king was not quite finished with Thebes. Before departing, and almost by way of a Parthian shot,[3] he unfurled his true iconoclastic colors. Amun was declared anathema. The king changed his name from "Amenophis, the Divine, the Ruler of Thebes" to Akhenaten, which means something like "He who is useful to the Sun-disc," or perhaps "Glorified Spirit of the Sun-disc." Everywhere at Thebes and other cities, in the sun-temples he had built, workmen laid coats of gypsum plaster over the second of the royal cartouches and recut the new name over the old. Undoubtedly it was at the same time that hatchetmen were dispatched to range throughout the temples of the land to desecrate the name "Amun" wherever it appeared on walls, steles, tombs, or objects d'art. Amun's congeners Mut, Osiris, and others suffered too, but to a lesser extent. . . . All efforts were now concentrated on building the new "dream city" of Akhetaten, the "Horizon of the Disc." Sometime during the 5th year, Amenophis IV, or Akhenaten as we shall now call him, arrived at the construction site with his court. No building was as yet complete, and most were probably but a marked layout on the ground; but the king was impatient to live with his father, the sun-disc, in his own special city, and was willing to put up with temporary quarters. The royal family for the rest of that year, and well into the 6th year, made do with a prefabricated dwelling, probably tentlike, which is called "tent (*imw psšt*) of apartments(?)" in the texts.

If people initially treated Amenophis IV with a certain wariness born of fear of an unknown quantity, they were soon to learn that the king lacked the fear-inspiring qualities of his father. The evenhanded policy Amenophis hoped to adopt toward Egypt's dependencies, and which in a moment of foolish candor he had made known even to his least trustworthy vassal, could easily be interpreted as weakness. Perhaps from the outset it was a weakness that the king was rationalizing as fairness. At any rate, Amenophis IV soon found it impossible to enforce his will in Egypt's Levantine sphere of influence. . . .

Even the casual observer will be struck first and foremost by the negative thrust of Akhenaten's reform of the cultus. He excised from the traditional religion much more than he added. The service of the gods was done away with, and their temples allowed to sit idle. In the wake of the desuetude of the cult, the myths of the gods, which provided the hypostasis of many cultic elements, simply disappeared. The sun god Akhenaten championed, of course, enjoyed no mythology; after the early months of the reign he was not even permitted an anthropomorphic depiction. No archetypal symbolism informs the

---

[3]The Asiatic Parthians supposedly were adept at a backward bow shot when they seemed to be retreating.—ED.

artistic style that celebrates the new god, and the very few names and accouterments the sun-disc borrows are entirely from the solar cult of Re and his divine congeners. The marvelously complex world of the Beyond is banished from the minds of men. No truth can come from anyone but the king, and his truth is entirely apodictic: no gods but the sun, no processional temples, no cultic acts but the rudimentary offering, no cult images, no anthropomorphisms, no myths, no concept of the ever-changing manifestation of a divine world. The Roman world might well have called Akhenaten an "atheist," for what he left to Egypt was not a "god" at all, but a disc in the heavens! . . . Roughly at about the same time that the king was laying firm plans for the move to the new site of Akhetaten, a drastic change overcame his cultic program. The decoration of the new temples was all but complete when the king openly broke with Amun. The "king of the gods," tolerated to this point, though his worship had probably languished through lack of priests, now witnessed the formal anathematization of his name and the closing of his temple. The program of defacement that followed was so thorough that we must postulate either a small army of hatchetmen dispatched throughout the realm, or parties of inspectors charged with seeing that local officials did the job. Everywhere, in temples, tombs, statuary, and casual inscriptions, the hieroglyphs for "Amun" and representations of the god were chiseled out; objects sacred to him were likewise defaced. People who bore names compounded with "Amun" were obliged to change them; and the king led the way by discarding the now unacceptable *Amenophis* ("Amun is satisfied") for *Akh-en-aten* ("Effective for the Sun-disc"). Osiris and his cycle of mortuary gods suffered a like anathematization. Funerary practices might be spared, but only if purged of all polytheistic elements. . . .

If any further proof is required of what the king was trying to do, let this one significant omission suffice: the plural word "gods" is never attested after year 5, and occasionally it is found erased in existing inscriptions. For Akhenaten's program, implicitly from the start, and now blatantly and universally, fostered a monotheism that would brook no divine manifestations. The Sun-disc was unique and supreme over all the universe, the only god there was. He did not change his shape or appear in other forms: he was always and only "the living Sun-disc—there is none other than he!"

At Akhetaten the major part of our knowledge about the character of the Disc comes from the great hymn inscribed in the tomb of Ay, quite likely a composition of the king himself. After Akhenaten's aversion to mythology and its symbolism had obliged him to expunge from the genre of hymns all such allusions, the only concepts that could be predicated of the deity were those of universalism, dependence of life on the sun, transcendence, creativity, cosmic regularity, and absolute power. . . .

The doctrine of the sun-disc constituted a strong reaffirmation of divine kingship, as the role Akhenaten assigned himself proves. In the first five years the fragmentary texts from the *talatat*[4] stress the paternity of the Disc and the sonship of the king: the latter is the son of the Sun-disc, the "beautiful child of the Disc" whose "beauty" was "created" by the heavenly luminary. Akhenaten has been granted the kingship by his father, and occupies his thone on earth: heaven and earth are his, his boundaries reach the limits of heaven, and all lands are beneath his feet.

Enough, I hope, has been brought forward in the preceding pages to show that the historical Akhenaten is markedly different from the figure popularists have created for us. Humanist he was not, and certainly no humanitarian romantic. To make of him a tragic "Christ-like" figure is a sheer falsehood. Nor is he the mentor of Moses: a vast gulf is fixed between the rigid, coercive, rarified monotheism of the pharaoh and Hebrew henotheism,[5] which in any case we see through the distorted prism of texts written 700 years after Akhenaten's death. Certain affinities have long since been pointed out between the hymn to the sun-disc and Psalm 104, and the parallels are to be taken seriously. There is, however, no literary influence here, but rather a survival in the tradition of the northern centers of Egypt's once-great empire of the *themes* of that magnificent poetic creation.

If we pass in review the hard facts we have adduced above, and, in the absence of facts the circumstantial evidence, we then catch a glimpse of *this* pharaonic figure. A man deemed ugly by the accepted standards of the day, secluded in the palace in his minority, certainly close to his mother, possibly ignored by his father, outshone by his brother and sisters, unsure of himself, Akhenaten suffered the singular misfortune of acceding to the throne of Egypt and its empire. We have no idea who or what influenced him in his formative years; but he was not brought into contact with his father's court, nor is there any evidence that he spent time at Heliopolis. As a result he nurtured a fear and aversion to his father's coterie of gifted administrators and the noble families from which they had sprung; and his apprehension was extended even to those foreign potentates with whom his father had been on intimate terms. There is evidence to suggest that he was a poor

---

[4]*Talatat* are uniformly sized facing stones that were covered with texts and drawings. They were later removed from the site of El-Amarna and used as fill for other structures or scattered.—ED.

[5]The belief in one god as the specific tribal god of a particular people while not denying the existence of other gods of other peoples.—ED.

judge of character and a prey to sycophancy. Though he was apprehensive about his own lack of resolve, he nonetheless espoused a lenient policy toward his northern provinces which deterred him from acting unhesitatingly in the Asian sphere. Not being gifted as an administrator, Akhenaten was willing to leave the running of everyday affairs, both foreign and domestic, in the hands of military and civilian intermediaries, while he pursued his program of cultic reform.

Akhenaten, whatever else he may have been, was no intellectual heavyweight. He failed to comprehend (or if he did, to appreciate) the true role and potential of cultic mythology, possibly seeing in it a means of concealment rather than revelation of the deity. Maybe he was reacting to the sophisticated cynicism of the age, just as Luther did in the 16th century A.D.; but if so he was surely guilty of identifying the aberrations of the system with its essence. For myths are the building blocks of any religion, even Judeo-Christianity. Though they come to us as the often crass impedimenta from an early and slightly embarrassing stage in our intellectual development, myths nonetheless pose the challenge of reinterpretation on a higher plane and integration one with another to provide a new and consistent view of the supernatural. Ancient Egyptian, like modern, theologians rose to this challenge, and such documents as the Memphite Theology and the New Kingdom hymns to Ptah and Amun are philosophical treatises of the highest achievement. What did Akhenaten substitute for them, once he had declared them anathema? Nothing! If mythology (in the broadest application of the term) is the only means of divine revelation, apart from the vision of the mystic, then what Akhenaten championed was in the truest sense of the word, atheism.

For the icon he devised, that spiderlike disc, could never be viewed as "god." What it was Akhenaten tells us plainly enough: the Disc was his father, the universal king. Significant, it seems to me, is the fact that, on the eve of Amenophis III's passing, the king who sat upon Egypt's throne bore as his most popular sobriquet the title "The Dazzling Sun-disc"; on the morrow of the "revolution" the only object of veneration in the supernal realm is king Sun-disc, exalted in the heavens and ubiquitously termed by Akhenaten "my father." I will not pursue the implications of this, though they appear to me plain enough.

That Akhenaten possessed unusual ability as a poet is, I think, self-evident. For him nature itself, in all its forms, displayed sufficient fascination; the gratification to be had in ruminating on imponderables paled by comparison. Although many images are derivative, the great hymn to the Disc stands out as a major, almost "positivist," statement on the beauty of creation.

I strongly suspect Akhenaten also had a flair for art, sculpture, and design, although this might be harder to demonstrate. The startlingly new expressionism that bursts on the scene in the second year of the reign probably owes more to the monarch's tastes than to those of his artists; and in the light of the well-known drafting ability of Thutmosid kings, it would be difficult to deny that the king also had a hand in working out the details of the new canons. To me it is the art associated with his program that remains Akhenaten's single most important contribution.

Beautiful though they may be, the Amarna reliefs reveal one of the most displeasing characteristics of the way of life Akhenaten held up as a model, refined sloth. Can the king engage in no more strenuous activity than elevating offerings? True, he rides a chariot; how often does he walk? Time and again we glimpse him lounging, completely limp, in a chair or on a stool. He is seen eating and drinking at a table groaning with food, occasionally interrupting his indulgence to lean languidly from the balcony and smile weakly at some sniveling sycophant in the court beneath. Is this effete monarch, who could never hunt or do battle, a true descendant of the authors of Egypt's empire? The court over which he presides is nothing but an aggregation of voluptuaries, bent on personal gratification, and their opportunist followers.

If the king and his circle inspire me somewhat with contempt, it is apprehension I feel when I contemplate his "religion." In Egypt the sun may well be a reliable and beneficent power, but it is nonetheless destructive, and mankind seeks to hide from it. If Re must be worshipped, let there be a refuge of shade close at hand! Both Karnak and Akhetaten become infernos from March to November. Yet the monarch—with relish it would seem!—not only selected these unholy sites for his use, but insisted on the simple open shrine, with no roof and very little shade, in which to honor his father! As one stands on the baking sand of the vast Amarna amphitheater, one cannot help but sense a sinister quality in all of this.

Not content with the subjection of his own body to the rays of his father at every waking moment, the autocratic ruler demanded everyone else follow suit! A fascinating letter found in the Amarna Tablets from the king of Assyria tells us this, and thus opens a new vista on Akhenaten's mental state. Ashuruballit I, eager to open relations with Egypt now that Mitanni had been weakened, sent a delegation to Akhetaten; but they must have returned saying something like this: this pharaoh must be crazy! He holds his audiences, meetings, and ceremonies entirely in the sun, and keeps everyone standing in the heat! This occasioned the following remonstrance from the Assyrian sovereign to Akhenaten: "Why are my messengers kept standing in the open sun? They will die in the open sun. If it does the king good to stand in the open sun, then let the king stand there and die in the open sun. Then will there be profit for the king! But really, why should they die in the open sun? . . . They will be killed in the open sun!." The vignette here sketched is at once comical and outrageous. The regime was plainly, at this stage, intolerable.

For all that can be said in his favor, Akhenaten in spirit remains to the end totalitarian. The right of an individual freely to choose was wholly foreign to him. He was the champion of a universal, celestial power who demanded universal submission, claimed universal truth, and from whom no further revelation could be expected. I cannot conceive a more tiresome regime under which to be fated to live.

Suggestions for Further Reading

For all the antiquity of its subject, the Akhenaton controversy is essentially a modern one, a continuing dispute among Egyptologists about nearly everything connected with the so-called Amarna period of Eighteenth Dynasty Egyptian history and its central figure. The most extreme debunking interpretation of Akhenaton is F. J. Giles, *Ikhnaton: Legend and History* (London: Hutchinson, 1970). Very much in this tradition is Donald B. Redford, *Akhenaten: The Heretic King* (Princeton: Princeton University Press, 1984), excerpted for this chapter. Some of the studies in an earlier work by Redford, *History and Chronology of the Eighteenth Dynasty of Egypt: Seven Studies* (Toronto: University of Toronto Press, 1967) support his view. Dissenting from this view is Cyril Aldred, *Akhenaten: King of Egypt* (London: Thames and Hudson, 1988), a significant revision of Aldred's earlier *Akhenaten: A New Study*. Aldred's interpretation is popularized in Joy Collier, *King Sun: In Search of Akhenaten* (London: Ward Lock, 1970), also published under the title, *The Heretic Pharaoh* (New York: Day, 1970). The chapter on Akhenaton in P. H. Newby, *Warrior Pharaohs: The Rise and Fall of the Egyptian Empire* (London and Boston: Faber and Faber, 1980) is excellent and the final chapter in A. Rosalie David, *Cult of the Sun: Myth and Magic in Ancient Egypt* (London et al.: J. M. Dent, 1980) is a good survey of the controversy. The Pulitzer Prize–winning novelist Allen Drury has written a novel dealing with Akhenaton, *A God against the Gods* (New York: Doubleday, 1976) and one about his successor, Tutankhamun, *Return to Thebes* (New York: Doubleday, 1977). The most famous of all modern novels of ancient Egypt, Mika Waltari, *The Egyptian: A Novel*, tr. Naomi Walford (New York: Putnam, 1949), uses the revolution of Akhenaton as a backdrop for its plot.

For the larger setting of Egyptian history there are a number of excellent books. John A. Wilson, *The Burden of Egypt: An Interpretation of Ancient Egyptian Culture* (Chicago: University of Chicago Press, 1951), republished under the title *The Culture of Ancient Egypt* (Chicago: Phoenix, 1971), while somewhat dated in its research, is still valuable for its insights and is an eminently readable book. Equally readable is Sir Alan Gardiner, *Egypt of the Pharaohs: An Introduction* (London and New York: Oxford University Press, 1972). A somewhat more popularized book is Pierre Montet, *Lives of the Pharaohs* (Cleveland and New York: World, 1968). A good up-to-date historical survey of Egypt, including the Akhenaton period, is Cyril Aldred, *The Egyptians*, rev. and enlarged ed. (London: Thames and Hudson, 1984). John Romer, *People of the Nile: Everyday Life in Ancient Egypt* (New York: Crown, 1982) is lively and interesting as are T. G. H. James, *Pharaoh's People: Scenes from Life in Imperial Egypt* (Chicago: University of Chicago Press, 1984) and *Egypt's Golden Age: The Art of Living in the New Kingdom, 1558–1085 B.C.* (Boston: Museum of Fine Arts, 1982). Finally, to understand more fully the profound nature of Akhenaton's religious revolt, students should read Henri Frankfort, *Ancient Egyptian Religion: An Interpretation* (New York: Columbia University Press, 1948; republished by Harper Torchbooks, 1961), a popular but authoritative essay, and very readable. A more recent work of the same sort is A. Rosalie David, *The Ancient Egyptians: Religious Beliefs and Practices* (London: Routledge and Kegan Paul, 1982).

THE IMAGE OF SOCRATES: MAN OR MYTH?

C. 470 B.C.	Born
C. 431–424 B.C.	Served in Peloponnesian War
406–405 B.C.	Served as a member of Athenian executive council
399 B.C.	Trial and death

By the lifetime of Socrates, in the late fifth century B.C., Greek civilization was almost at an end. This historic civilization was centered in Socrates' own city of Athens, which Pericles proudly called "the school of Hellas." But that magnificent city, which has so captivated our imagination, was widely regarded by its fellow city-states as a threat to their own independence—and with more than a little justification.

This threat led to the great Peloponnesian War, so vividly recounted in the pages of Socrates' contemporary, the historian Thucydides. Athens and its subject states were set against her arch-rival Sparta and Sparta's allies, the Peloponnesian League. It was a long, costly, and enervating war of almost thirty years' duration. And Athens finally lost it. Athens was humiliated, forced to accept its enemies' terms, and stripped of its subject states, its wealth, its navy. The buoyant optimism that had earlier characterized the city was one of the prime casualties of the war, along with confidence in its institutions and even in many of the presuppositions of its public life and private morality. It is in the backwash of these events that we must seek the life, and the death, of Socrates.

Socrates was surely the most famous Athenian of his age. Yet despite that fame, the facts of his life remain stubbornly vague. He was not a public official; hence we do not have archival records to rely on. And though he is a famous figure in literature, he actually wrote

19

nothing himself to which we can refer. There are scattered references to him in Aristotle; a substantial (though prosaic) account in the works of Xenophon, who knew him; and, of course, the principal source of our information about him, the dialogues of the great philosopher Plato, who was Socrates' adoring pupil and disciple and made him the main character in most of his dialogues. And there are references and anecdotes from a considerable number of near contemporary accounts of Socrates that have been preserved, although the original sources are now lost.

What we know about Socrates is this. He was born an Athenian citizen about 470 B.C. His family belonged to the class of small artisans; his mother was a midwife and his father a stone mason. Socrates himself followed his father's trade. Rather late in life he married Xanthippe, and they had three sons, two of them still very young at the time of their father's death. Like most able-bodied Athenians of his time, Socrates was a veteran of the Peloponnesian War and even served with some distinction. On two occasions he seems to have held office on the large civic boards and commissions that carried on the business of the city. But generally he avoided public life. From a number of surviving descriptions and portrait busts we know what Socrates looked like—small and balding, anything but the lofty Greek ideal of physical beauty And we also know that he spent most of his time going about the city, trailed by a delighted and curious crowd of bright young aristocrats, asking often embarrassing questions of people who interested him, usually public officials and individuals of substance and position. This practice was to the detriment of his own family and his own trade. Socrates was a poor man.

The Clouds

ARISTOPHANES

The preceding bare account of Socrates is supplemented—one must almost say contradicted—by a single additional source, The Clouds *of Aristophanes. This work is of considerable value in that it is the only really substantial account of Socrates by a mature contemporary. Even Plato, our principal source of information, was forty years younger than Socrates, knew him only as an old man, and wrote* The Dialogues *many years after Socrates' death.* The Clouds *is, of course, not a biography. It is a play, by the greatest of Greek comic dramatists, in which Socrates is not only one of its chief characters but also the object of its satire.*

Aristophanes was a conservative, and his plays are a catalog of his objections to the management of the war and public policy, the state of literature and philosophy, the subversion of the stern old virtues "of our forefathers," and the "new morality" that he saw about him. In The Clouds *he accused Socrates of being a professional teacher who received, nay extracted, money for his "lessons"—which was not true. He denounced him as a cynical, opportunistic atheist—which was also apparently not the case. He attributed to him an expert competence in natural philosophy—which was highly unlikely. And in what was perhaps the most unfounded of all his charges, he portrayed Socrates as being the chief of the Sophists.*

The Sophists were a school of professional teachers, then very popular in Athens, who taught young men of wealth and position (usually for substantial fees) the techniques of public life, mostly logic and oratorical persuasion. The Sophists also tended to a flexible morality in which success was to be preferred to virtue, victory to either morality or philosophic consistency. It is a more than Socratic irony that Socrates should have been depicted as one of them, for it was squarely against the Sophists and their moral relativism that he had taken his stand. The whole point of his life, the reason he engaged other people in his famous questioning and endured their animosity, the entire "Socratic method" was an attempt to make people understand that there are moral absolutes, unchanging abstract principles of conduct to which they must ultimately resort.

Why Aristophanes portrayed Socrates in this fashion we do not know. Perhaps he genuinely believed that Socrates was a Sophist. Or perhaps he knew the truth but simply did not care, and made use of Socrates' notoriety in Athens to score his own point about the scandalous decline of education and what he regarded as philosophic quackery.

21

*In any event, the play is cruel, mean, and malicious, but it is also out-
rageously funny. And it gives us a view, however hostile, of the historic
Socrates.*

The Clouds *opens in the house of Strepsiades, a foolish old farmer,
whose son Pheidippides's extravagant passion for racehorses has piled up so
many debts that the old man is faced with ruin. One night, unable to sleep,
Strepsiades decides to enroll the boy in the Sophist's school down the street.
He calls it the "Thinkery." But Pheidippides will have nothing to do with
"those filthy charlatans you mean—those frauds, those barefoot pedants with
the look of death. Chairephon and that humbug, Sokrates."*

*The old man then decides to go to the school himself. He kicks on the
door, and a student-doorman answers. As they stand at the door, the student extols the wisdom of his master Socrates, citing a number of examples,
not the least of which is Socrates' resolution of the problem of how the gnat
hums. "According to him, the intestinal tract of the gnat is of puny proportions, and through this diminutive duct the gastric gas of the gnat is forced
under pressure down to the rump. At that point the compressed gases, as
through a narrow valve, escape with a whoosh, thereby causing the characteristic tootle or cry of the flatulent gnat."*

*Strepsiades is suitably impressed. "Why, Thales himself was an amateur
compared to this! Throw open the Thinkery! Unbolt the door and let me see
this wizard Sokrates in person. Open up! I'm MAD for education!" And
Strepsiades enters the school.*

STREPSIADES

　　Look: who's that dangling up there in the basket?

STUDENT

Himself.

STREPSIADES

　　Who's Himself?

STUDENT

　　　　Sokrates.

STREPSIADES

　　　　　SOKRATES!
Then call him down. Go on. Give a great big shout.

STUDENT

Hastily and apprehensively taking his leave.

Er . . . *you* call him. I'm a busy man.

Exit Student.

STREPSIADES

O Sokrates!

No answer from the basket.

Yoohoo. Sokrates!

SOKRATES

From a vast philosophical height.

Well, creature of a day?

STREPSIADES

What in the world are you doing up there?

SOKRATES

Ah, sir,
I walk upon the air and look down upon the sun
from a superior standpoint.

STREPSIADES

Well, I suppose it's better
that you sneer at the gods from a basket up in the air
than do it down here on the ground.

SOKRATES

Precisely. You see,
only by being suspended aloft, by dangling
my mind in the heavens and mingling my rare thought
with the ethereal air, could I ever achieve strict
scientific accuracy in my survey of the vast empyrean.
Had I pursued my inquiries from down there on the ground,
my data would be worthless. The earth, you see, pulls down
the delicate essence of thought to its own gross level.

As an afterthought.

Much the same thing happens with watercress.

STREPSIADES

Ecstatically bewildered.

You don't say?
Thought draws down . . . delicate essence . . . into
watercress. O dear little Sokrates, please come down.
Lower away, and teach me what I need to know!

Sokrates is slowly lowered earthwards.

SOKRATES

What subject?

STREPSIADES

Your course on public speaking and debating techniques.
You see, my creditors have become absolutely ferocious.
You should see how they're hounding me. What's more,
Sokrates, they're about to seize my belongings.

SOKRATES

How in the
world could you fall so deeply in debt without realizing it?

STREPSIADES

How? A great, greedy horse-pox ate me up, that's how.
But that's why I want instruction in your second Logic,
you know the one—the get-away-without-paying argument.
I'll pay you *any* price you ask. I swear it.
By the gods.

SOKRATES

By the gods? The gods, my dear simple fellow,
are a mere expression coined by vulgar superstition.
We frown upon such coinage here.

STREPSIADES

What do *you* swear by?
Bars of iron, like the Byzantines?

SOKRATES

Tell me, old man,
would you honestly like to learn the truth, the *real* truth,
about the gods?

STREPSIADES

By Zeus, I sure would. The *real* truth. . . .

[*At this point the chorus of clouds enters, singing.*]

STREPSIADES

Holy Zeus, Sokrates, who were those ladies that sang
that solemn hymn? Were they heroines of mythology?

SOKRATES

No, old man.
Those were the Clouds of heaven, goddesses of men of
leisure and philosophers. To them we owe our repertoire of
verbal talents: our eloquence, intellect, fustian, casuistry,
force, wit, prodigious vocabulary, circumlocutory skill—

·   ·   ·   ·   ·   ·   ·   ·   ·   ·   ·   ·   ·   ·   ·   ·   ·

[*The leader of the chorus greets them.*]

KORYPHAIOS

Hail, superannuated man!   ·
Hail, old birddog of culture!

To Sokrates.

And hail to you, O Sokrates,
high priest of poppycock!
Inform us what your wishes are.
For of all the polymaths on earth, it's you we most prefer—

·   ·   ·   ·   ·   ·   ·   ·   ·   ·   ·   ·   ·   ·   ·   ·   ·

sir, for your swivel-eyes, your barefoot swagger down the
street, because you're poor on our account and terribly
affected.

STREPSIADES

Name of Earth, what a voice! Solemn and holy and awful!

SOKRATES

These are the only gods there are. The rest are but figments.

STREPSIADES

Holy name of Earth! Olympian Zeus is a figment?

SOKRATES

Zeus?

  What Zeus?

    Nonsense.

      There is no Zeus.

STREPSIADES

         No Zeus?

Then *who* makes it rain? Answer me that.

SOKRATES

        Why, the Clouds,

of course.

   What's more, the proof is incontrovertible.

         For instance,

have you ever yet seen rain when you didn't see a cloud?

But if your hypothesis were correct, Zeus could drizzle

 from an empty sky

while the clouds were on vacation.

STREPSIADES

     By Apollo, you're right. A pretty

 proof.

And to think I always used to believe the rain was just Zeus

pissing through a sieve.

     All right, *who* makes it thunder?

Brrr. I get goosebumps just saying it.

SOKRATES

       The Clouds again,

of course. A simple process of Convection.

STREPSIADES

       I admire you,

but I don't follow you.

SOKRATES

  Listen. The Clouds are a saturate water-solution.

Tumescence in motion, of necessity, produces precipitation.

When these distended masses collide—*boom!*

       Fulmination.

STREPSIADES

But who makes them move before they collide? Isn't that
Zeus?

SOKRATES

Not Zeus, idiot. The Convection-principle!

STREPSIADES

                                   Convection? That's
a new one.
Just think. So Zeus is out and Convection-principle's in.
Tch, tch.
      But wait: you haven't told me who makes it thunder.

SOKRATES

But I just *finished* telling you! The Clouds are water-packed;
they collide with each other and explode because of the
pressure.

STREPSIADES

      Yeah?
And what's your proof for *that*?

SOKRATES

                        Why, take yourself as example.
You know that meat-stew the vendors sell at the Panathenaia?[1]
How it gives you the cramps and your stomach
starts to rumble?

STREPSIADES

                                Yes,
by Apollo! I remember. What an awful feeling! You feel
sick and your belly churns and the fart rips loose like
thunder. First just a gurgle, *pappapax;* then louder,
pappaPAPAXapaX, and finally like thunder,
PAPAPAPAXAPAXAPPAPAXapap!

SOKRATES

Precisely.
First think of the tiny fart that your intestines make.

[1]The quadrennial festival of Athena, the patron goddess of Athens.—ED.

Then consider the heavens: their infinite farting is thunder.
For thunder and farting are, in principle, one and the same.

[*Strepsiades is convinced and is initiated into Socrates' school. But, alas, he is incapable of learning the subtleties Socrates sets out to teach him and is contemptuously dismissed from the school. Then the leader of the chorus suggests that he fetch his son to study in his place. A splendid idea! As Strepsiades drags his son on to the scene, Pheidippides protests.*]

PHEIDIPPIDES

But Father,
what's the matter with you? Are you out of your head?
Almighty Zeus, you must be mad!

STREPSIADES

"Almighty Zeus!"
What musty rubbish! Imagine, a boy your age
still believing in Zeus!

PHEIDIPPIDES

What's so damn funny?

STREPSIADES

It tickles me when the heads of toddlers like you
are still stuffed with such outdated notions. Now then,
listen to me and I'll tell you a secret or two
that might make an intelligent man of you yet.
But remember: you mustn't breathe a word of this.

PHEIDIPPIDES

A word of what?

STREPSIADES

Didn't you just swear by Zeus?

PHEIDIPPIDES

I did.

STREPSIADES

    Now learn what Education can do for *you:*
Pheidippides, there is no Zeus.

PHEIDIPPIDES

There is no Zeus?

STREPSIADES

No Zeus. Convection-principle's in power now.
Zeus has been banished.

PHEIDIPPIDES

                 Drivel!

STREPSIADES

                     Take my word for it,
it's absolutely true.

PHEIDIPPIDES

              Who says so?

STREPSIADES

                   Sokrates.
And Chairephon too. . . .

PHEIDIPPIDES

Are you so far gone on the road to complete insanity
you'd believe the word of those charlatans?

STREPSIADES

                      Hush, boy.
For shame. I won't hear you speaking disrespectfully
of such eminent scientists and geniuses. And, what's more,
men of such fantastic frugality and Spartan thrift,
they regard baths, haircuts, and personal cleanliness
generally as an utter waste of time and money—whereas
you, dear boy, have taken me to the cleaner's so many times,
I'm damn near washed up. Come on, for your father's sake,
go and learn.

[*Some time later*]
Enter Strepsiades from his house, counting on his fingers.

STREPSIADES

Five days, four days, three days, two days, and then
that one day of the days of the month
I dread the most that makes me fart with fear—
the last day of the month, Duedate for debts,
when every dun in town has solemnly sworn
to drag me into court and bankrupt me completely.

And when I plead with them to be more reasonable—
"But PLEASE, sir. Don't demand the whole sum now.
Take something on account. I'll pay you later."—
they snort they'll never see the day, curse me
for a filthy swindler and say they'll sue.
                                        Well,
let them. If Pheidippides has learned to talk,
I don't give a damn for them and their suits.
                                        Now then,
a little knock on the door and we'll have the answer.

He knocks on Sokrates' door and calls out.

Porter!
        Hey, porter!

Sokrates opens the door.

SOKRATES

                    Ah, Strepsiades. Salutations.

STREPSIADES

Same to you, Sokrates.

He hands Sokrates a bag of flour.

                            Here. A token of my esteem.
Call it an honorarium. Professors always get honorariums.

Snatching back the bag.

But wait: has Pheidippides learned his rhetoric yet—. . . .

SOKRATES

Taking the bag.

He has mastered it.

STREPSIADES

                O great goddess Bamboozle!

SOKRATES

Now, sir, you can evade any legal action you wish to.

[*But instead of help with his creditors, Strepsiades gets a very different kind of treatment from his son.*]

With a bellow of pain and terror, Strepsiades plunges out of his house, hotly pursued by Pheidippides with a murderous stick.

STREPSIADES

OOOUUUCH!!!

HALP!

For god's sake, help me!

Appealing to the Audience.

Friends!
Fellow-countrymen! Aunts! Uncles! Fathers! Brothers!
To the rescue!

He's beating me!

Help me!

Ouuch!

O my poor head!

Ooh, my jaw!

To Pheidippides.

—You great big bully,
Hit your own father, would you?

PHEIDIPPIDES

Gladly, Daddy.

STREPSIADES

You hear that? The big brute *admits* it.

PHEIDIPPIDES

Admit it? Hell,
I *proclaim* it. . . .
Would a logical demonstration
convince you?

STREPSIADES

A logical demonstration? You mean to tell me
you can *prove* a shocking thing like that?

PHEIDIPPIDES

Elementary, really.
What's more, you can choose the logic. Take your pick.
Either one.

STREPSIADES

Either *which?*

PHEIDIPPIDES

Either *which?* Why,
Socratic logic or pre-Socratic logic. Either logic.
Take your pick.

STREPSIADES

Take my pick, damn you? Look,
who do you think paid for your shyster education anyway?
And now you propose to convince *me* that there's nothing
wrong in whipping your own father?

PHEIDIPPIDES

I not only propose it:
I propose to *prove* it. Irrefutably, in fact. Rebuttal
is utterly inconceivable. . . .

[*Pheidippides then "proves" that since his father beat him as a child "for your
own damn good" "because I loved you," then it is only "a fortiori" logic that
the father be beaten by the son, since "old men logically deserve to be beaten
more, since at their age they have clearly less excuse for the mischief that they
do."*]

*There is a long tense silence as the full force of this
crushing argument takes its effect upon Strepsiades.*

STREPSIADES

What?
But how. . . ?
Hmm,
by god, you're right!

To the Audience.

—Speaking for the older generation,
gentlemen, I'm compelled to admit defeat. The kids have
proved their point: naughty fathers should be flogged. . . .

[*But this arrogance is too much, logic or no logic, for Strepsiades.*]

STREPSIADES

O Horse's Ass, Blithering Imbecile,
Brainless Booby, Bonehead that I was to ditch the gods
for Sokrates!

He picks up Pheidippides' stick and savagely smashes the potbellied model of the Universe in front of the Thinkery. He then rushes to his own house and falls on his knees before the statue of Hermes.

—Great Hermes, I implore you!

[Strepsiades and his slave set fire to the Thinkery and he beats the choking, sputtering Socrates and his pallid students off the stage.]

The Apology

PLATO

In 399 B.C., twenty-five years after The Clouds, *Socrates stood before the great popular court of Athens. He was accused of much the same charges that had been leveled at him by Aristophanes, specifically "that Socrates is a doer of evil, who corrupts the youth; and who does not believe in the gods of the state, but has other new divinities of his own." The charges were brought by three fellow Athenians, Meletus, Lycon, and Anytus. Although only one of the accusers, Anytus, was a person of any importance, and he only a minor political figure, the charges carried the death penalty if the court so decided. Indeed, this was the intent of the accusers.*

Socrates, now seventy years old, rose to speak in his own defense; he was not the pettifogging buffoon of The Clouds. *Perhaps that man never really existed. By the same token, did the speaker at the trial ever exist? The trial is Socrates', but the account of it is Plato's.* The Apology, *from* The Dialogues of Plato, *is the "defense" of Socrates at his trial.*

How you, O Athenians, have been affected by my accusers, I cannot tell; but I know that they almost made me forget who I was—so persuasively did they speak; and yet they have hardly uttered a word of truth. But . . . first, I have to reply to the older charges and to my first accusers, and then I will go on to the later ones. For of old I have had many accusers, who have accused me falsely to you during many years; and I am more afraid of them than of Anytus and his associates, who are dangerous, too, in their own way. But far more dangerous are the others, who began when you were children, and took possession of your minds with their falsehoods, telling of one Socrates, a wise man, who speculated about the heaven above, and searched into the earth beneath, and made the worse appear the better cause. The disseminators of this tale are the accusers whom I dread; for their hearers are apt to fancy that such enquirers do not believe in the existence of the gods. And they are many, and their charges against me are of ancient date, and they were made by them in the days when you were more impressible than you are now—in childhood, or it may have been in youth—and the cause when heard went by default, for there was none to answer. And hardest of all, I do not know and cannot tell the names of my accusers; unless in the chance case of a Comic poet. . . .

I dare say, Athenians, that some one among you will reply, 'Yes, Socrates, but what is the origin of these accusations which are brought against you; there must have been something strange which you have been doing? All these rumours and this talk about you would never have arisen if you had been like other men: tell us, then, what is the cause of them, for we should be sorry to judge hastily of you.' Now I regard this as a fair challenge, and I will endeavour to explain to you the reason why I am called wise and have such an evil fame. . . .

. . . I will refer you to a witness who is worthy of credit; that witness shall be the God of Delphi—he will tell you about my wisdom, if I have any, and of what sort it is. You must have known Chaerephon; he was early a friend of mine. . . .Well, Chaerephon, as you know, was very impetuous in all his doings, and he went to Delphi and boldly asked the oracle to tell him whether—as I was saying, I must beg you not to interrupt—he asked the oracle to tell him whether any one was wiser than I was, and the Pythian prophetess answered, that there was no man wiser. Chaerephon is dead himself; but his brother, who is in court, will confirm the truth of what I am saying.

Why do I mention this? Because I am going to explain to you why I have such an evil name. When I heard the answer, I said to myself, What can the god mean? and what is the interpretation of his riddle? for I know that I have no wisdom, small or great. What then can he mean when he says that I am the wisest of men? And yet he is a god, and cannot lie; that would be against his nature. After long consideration, I thought of a method of trying the question. I reflected that if I could only find a man wiser than myself, then I might go to the god with a refutation in my hand. I should say to him, 'Here is a man who is wiser than I am; but you said that I was the wisest.' Accordingly I went to one who had the reputation of wisdom, and observed him— his name I need not mention; he was a politician whom I selected for examination—and the result was as follows: When I began to talk with him, I could not help thinking that he was not really wise, although he was thought wise by many, and still wiser by himself; and thereupon I tried to explain to him that he thought himself wise, but was not really wise; and the consequence was that he hated me, and his enmity was shared by several who were present and heard me. So I left him, saying to myself, as I went away: Well, although I do not suppose that either of us knows anything really beautiful and good, I am better off than he is,—for he knows nothing, and thinks that he knows; I neither know nor think that I know. In this latter particular, then, I seem to have slightly the advantage of him. Then I went to another who had still higher pretensions to wisdom, and my conclusion was exactly the same. Whereupon I made another enemy of him, and of many others besides him. . . .

This inquisition has led to my having many enemies of the worst and most dangerous kind, and has given occasion also to many calumnies. And I am called wise, for my hearers always imagine that I myself possess the wisdom which I find wanting in others: but the truth is, O men of Athens, that God only is wise, and by his answer he intends to show that the wisdom of men is worth little or nothing; he is not speaking of Socrates, he is only using my name by way of illustration, as if he said, He, O men, is the wisest, who, like Socrates, knows that his wisdom is in truth worth nothing. And so I go about the world, obedient to the god, and search and make enquiry into the wisdom of any one, whether citizen or stranger, who appears to be wise; and if he is not wise, then in vindication of the oracle I show him that he is not wise, and my occupation quite absorbs me, and I have no time to give either to any public matter of interest or to any concern of my own, but I am in utter poverty by reason of my devotion to the god.

There is another thing:—young men of the richer classes, who have not much to do, come about me of their own accord; they like to hear the pretenders examined, and they often imitate me, and proceed to examine others; there are plenty of persons, as they quickly discover, who think they know something, but really know little or nothing; and then those who are examined by them instead of being angry with themselves are angry with me: This confounded Socrates, they say; this villainous misleader of youth—and then if somebody asks them, Why, what evil does he practise or teach? they do not know, and cannot tell; but in order that they may not appear to be at a loss, they repeat the ready-made charges which are used against all philosophers about teaching things up in the clouds and under the earth, and having no gods and making the worse appear the better cause. . . .

Turning to the formal charges against him, Socrates dismisses them almost contemptuously, returning to the main charges as he sees them and his lifelong "argument" with his city and its citizenry.

And now, Athenians, I am not going to argue for my own sake, as you may think, but for yours, that you may not sin against the God by condemning me, who am his gift to you. For if you kill me you will not easily find a successor to me, who, if I may use such a ludicrous figure of speech, am a sort of gadfly, given to the state by God; and the state is a great and noble steed who is tardy in his motions owing to his very size, and requires to be stirred into life. I am that gadfly which God has attached to the state, and all day long and in all places am always fastening upon you, arousing and persuading and reproaching you. You will not easily find another like me, and therefore I would advise you to spare me. I dare say that you may feel out of temper (like a person who is suddenly awakened from sleep), and you think that you might easily strike me dead as Anytus advises, and then you would sleep on for the remainder of your lives, unless God in his care of you sent you another gadfly. When I say I am given to you by God, the proof of my mission is this:—if I had been like other men, I should not have neglected all my own concerns or patiently seen the neglect of them during all these years, and have been doing yours, coming to you individually like a father or elder brother, exhorting you to regard virtue; such conduct, I say, would be unlike human nature. If I had gained anything, or if my exhortations had been paid, there would have been some sense in my doing so; but now, as you will perceive, not even the impudence of my accusers dares to say that I have ever exacted or sought pay of any one; of that they have no witness. And I have a sufficient witness to the truth of what I say—my poverty. . . .

The jury returns the verdict of guilty.

There are many reasons why I am not grieved, O men of Athens, at the vote of condemnation. I expected it, and am only surprised that the votes are so nearly equal; for I had thought that the majority against me would have been far larger; but now, had thirty votes gone over to the other side, I should have been acquitted. And I may say, I think, that I have escaped Meletus. I may say more; for without the assistance of Anytus and Lycon, any one may see that he would not have had a fifth part of the votes, as the law requires, in which case he would have incurred a fine of a thousand drachmae.

And so he proposes death as the penalty. . . .

Some one will say: Yes, Socrates, but cannot you hold your tongue, and then you may go into a foreign city, and no one will interfere with you? Now I have great difficulty in making you understand my answer to this. For if I tell you that to do as you say would be a disobedience to the God, and therefore that I cannot hold my tongue, you will not believe that I am serious; and if I say again that daily to discourse about virtue, and of those other things about which you hear me examining myself and others, is the greatest good of man, and that the unexamined life is not worth living, you are still less likely to believe me. Yet I say what is true, although a thing of which it is hard for me to persuade you. Also, I have never been accustomed to think that I deserve to suffer any harm. Had I money I might have estimated the offence at what I was able to pay, and not have been much the worse. But I have none, and therefore I must ask you to proportion the fine to my means. Well, perhaps I could afford a mina, and therefore I propose that penalty: Plato, Crito, Critobulus, and Apollodorus, my friends here, bid me say thirty minae, and they will be the sureties. Let thirty minae be the penalty; for which sum they will be ample security to you. . . .

Socrates is condemned to death.

And now, O men who have condemned me, I would fain prophesy to you; for I am about to die, and in the hour of death men are gifted with prophetic power. And I prophesy to you who are my murderers, that immediately after my departure punishment far heavier than you have inflicted on me will surely await you. Me you have killed because you wanted to escape the accuser, and not to give an account of your lives. But that will not be as you suppose: far otherwise. For I say that there will be more accusers of you than there are now; accusers whom hitherto I have restrained: and as they are younger they will be more inconsiderate with you, and you will be more offended at them. If you think that by killing men you can prevent some one from censuring your evil lives, you are mistaken; that is not a way of escape which is either possible or honourable; the easiest and the noblest way is not to be disabling others, but to be improving yourselves. This is the prophecy which I utter before my departure to the judges who have condemned me.

Friends, who would have acquitted me, I would like also to talk with you about the thing which has come to pass, while the magistrates are busy, and before I go to the place at which I must die. Stay then a little, for we may as well talk with one another while there is time. You are my friends, and I should like to show you the meaning of this event which has happened to me. O my judges—for you I may truly call judges—I should like to tell you of a wonderful circumstance. Hitherto the divine faculty of which the internal oracle[2] is the source has constantly been in the habit of opposing me even about trifles, if I

---

[2]This was Socrates' famous "daimon," more than a conscience, less perhaps than a separate "in-dwelling" god, but, as he claimed, at least a guiding voice.—Ed.

was going to make a slip or error in any matter; and now as you see there has come upon me that which may be thought, and is generally believed to be, the last and worst evil. But the oracle made no sign of opposition, either when I was leaving my house in the morning, or when I was on my way to the court, or while I was speaking, at anything which I was going to say; and yet I have often been stopped in the middle of a speech, but now in nothing I either said or did touching the matter in hand has the oracle opposed me. What do I take to be the explanation of this silence? I will tell you. It is an intimation that what has happened to me is a good, and that those of us who think that death is an evil are in error. For the customary sign would surely have opposed me had I been going to evil and not to good. . . .

Wherefore, O judges, be of good cheer about death, and know of a certainty, that no evil can happen to a good man, either in life or after death. He and his are not neglected by the gods; nor has my own approaching end happened by mere chance. But I see clearly that the time had arrived when it was better for me to die and be released from trouble wherefore the oracle gave no sign. For which reason, also, I am not angry with my condemners, or with my accusers; they have done me no harm, although they did not mean to do me any good; and for this I may gently blame them.

Still I have a favour to ask them. When my sons are grown up, I would ask you, O my friends, to punish them; and I would have you trouble them, as I have troubled you, if they seem to care about riches, or anything, more than about virtue; or if they pretend to be something when they are really nothing,—then reprove them, as I have reproved you, for not caring about that for which they ought to care, and thinking that they are something when they are really nothing. And if you do this, both I and my sons will have received justice at your hands.

The hour of departure has arrived, and we go our ways—I to die, and you to live. Which is better God only knows.

Socrates: A Modern Perspective

MOSES HADAS AND MORTON SMITH

Which Socrates are we to choose? Is it even possible to reconstruct the real man from either the idealized, "gospel"-like account of Plato or the malicious parody of Aristophanes, or from both together? Two distinguished American professors, Moses Hadas (d. 1966) and Morton Smith, do not think so. They state their case in the following selection from their book Heroes and Gods: Spiritual Biographies in Antiquity.

As surely as the figure of Achilles is the paradigm for heroic epic, so surely is Socrates the paradigm for aretalogy.[3] He is manifestly the point of departure for the development of the genre after his time, but he is also the culmination of antecedent development. It is likely that the historical Achilles (assuming there was one) was both more and less than Homer's image of him, but even if he was exactly as the image represents him, without it he could never have served posterity as a paradigm. Nor could Socrates have served posterity except through the image Plato fashioned. It is not, strictly speaking, a developed aretalogy that Plato presents; that is to say, he does not provide a single systematic account of a career that can be used as a sacred text. Indeed, Plato's treatment made it impossible for others to elaborate the image plausibly or to reduce it to a sacred text. But the whole image, full and consistent and unmistakable, is presupposed in every Platonic dialogue which contributes to it. Undoubtedly the historical Socrates was an extraordinarily gifted and devoted teacher, and his image does undoubtedly reflect the historical figure, but the image clearly transcends the man, and the image is the conscious product of Plato's art.

Because of Plato, and only Plato, Socrates' position in the tradition of western civilization is unique. Other fifth-century Greeks have won admiration bordering on adulation for high achievement in various fields, but only Socrates is completely without flaw; the perfect image leaves no opening for impugning his wisdom or temperance or courage or wholehearted devotion to his mission. We might expect that a

---

[3]The worship of, or reverence for, nobility or virtue; from the Greek *areté*, "virtue."—ED.

dim figure out of the imperfectly recorded past, an Orpheus or Pythagoras or even Empedocles, might be idealized, but Socrates lived in the bright and merciless light of a century that could ostracize Aristides, deny prizes to Sophocles, throw Pericles out of office. Perhaps the nearest approach to Plato's idealization of Socrates is Thucydides' idealization of Pericles; some critics have thought that Thucydides' main motive in writing his history was to glorify Pericles. But Thucydides never claimed for Pericles the kind of potency that Plato suggests for Socrates, and on the basis of Thucydides' own history the world has accepted Pericles as a farseeing but not preternaturally gifted or wholly successful statesman. Only in the case of Socrates has the idealized image effaced the reality.

What makes Plato's share in the idealization obvious is the existence of parallel accounts of Socrates that are less reverent. Plato's reports are indeed the fullest: the larger part of his extensive writings purports to be an exposition of Socrates' thought. But there are other witnesses. . . . In the *Clouds* of Aristophanes, Socrates is the central figure, and the boot is on a different foot, for it was produced in 423, when Socrates was not yet fifty and therefore in the prime of his career but not yet shielded by the extraordinary eminence later bestowed upon him. Nor was Aristophanes' comedy the only caricature of Socrates. Also in 423 a comic Socrates figures in a play of Amipsias and two years later in one of Eupolis. These poets, it must be remembered, were dealing with a personality that was familiar to them and also, perhaps more important, to their audiences.

The caricature, certainly Aristophanes' and presumably the others' also, is of course grossly unfair: Socrates did not meddle with natural science or receive pay for his teaching, as the *Clouds* alleges he did: the most carping critic could not question his probity. The very absurdity of the charges and the topsy-turvy carnival atmosphere of the festival eliminated the possibility of rancor; in the *Symposium,* of which the fictive date is a decade after the presentation of the *Clouds,* Plato represents Aristophanes and Socrates as consorting on the friendliest of terms. And yet it is plain that Aristophanes' large audience was not outraged by the frivolous treatment of a saint, and in the *Apology,* which Socrates is presumed to have pronounced at his defense twenty-five years later, the point is made that the caricature had seriously prejudiced the public against Socrates. To some degree, then, the caricature is a significant corrective to later idealization. . . .

Really to know where the truth lies, . . . we should have his actual words or a public record of his deeds, but Socrates wrote nothing and was not, like Pericles, a statesman. The image is therefore not subject to correction on the basis of his own works. Aristophanes also deals harshly with Euripides, but we have Euripides' own plays to read, so that the caricature tells us more of Aristophanes than it does of Euripides. Isocrates wrote an encomium of Evagoras and Xenophon of Agesilaus, but the praise of these statesmen carries its own corrective. Of Socrates we know, or think we know, much more than of those others—what he looked like, how he dressed and walked and talked, and most of all, what he thought and taught. . . .

Actually the only significant datum in the inventory which is beyond dispute is that Socrates was condemned to death in 399 B.C. and accepted his penalty when he might have evaded it. The magnanimity of this act no one can belittle; it is enough to purify and enhance even a questionable career, and it is certainly enough to sanctify a Socrates. For Plato it clearly marked a decisive turn, as he himself records in his autobiographical *Seventh Epistle*. For him it undoubtedly crystallized the image of Socrates that fills the early dialogues. . . . All of Plato's earlier dialogues, and the more plainly in the degree of their earliness, are as much concerned with the personality of Socrates as with his teachings. His pre-eminence in reason, his devotion to his mission, his selfless concern for the spiritual welfare of his fellow men, the purity of his life, even his social gifts, are made prominent. The *Apology,* quite possibly the earliest of the Socratic pieces, is concerned with the man and his personal program, not his doctrines. Here he is made to present, without coyness or swagger or unction, his own concept of his mission to sting men, like a gadfly, to self-examination and to serve as midwife to their travail with ideas. The *Apology* also illustrates the devotion of his disciples to Socrates and the surprisingly large proportion of his jurors who were willing to acquit him. Again, in the short early dialogues, which are mainly concerned with questioning common misconceptions of such abstract nouns as "piety" or "friendship," it is the man as defined by his program, not the abstract doctrine, that is being presented. In the great central group—*Protagoras, Gorgias, Symposium, Republic*—the proportion of doctrinal content is larger, but the doctrine requires the personality of Socrates to make it plausible. The moral significance of education may emerge from the rather piratical dialectic in the *Protagoras,* but the argument takes on special meaning from Socrates' wise and tender treatment of the eager and youthful disciple who is enamored of Protagoras' reputation. That it is a worse thing for a man to inflict than to receive an injury and that a good man is incapable of being injured is the kind of doctrine which absolutely requires that its promulgator be a saint, as Socrates is pictured in the *Gorgias;* on the lips of a lesser man it would be nothing more than a rhetorical paradox. A great weight of individual prestige must similarly be built up to enable a man to enunciate the grand scheme of the *Republic,* and the occasional playfulness of the tone only emphasizes the stature of the individual who enunciates it. People too earth-bound to recognize such stature, like Thrasymachus in Book I, can only find the whole proceeding absurd. And only from a man whose special stature was recognized could the vision of Er be accepted as other than an old wives' tale.

In the *Symposium* more than in other dialogues the individuality of Socrates is underscored. It is not a trivial matter, for establishing the character of Socrates, that he could be welcome at a party of the fashionable wits of Athens, could get himself respectably groomed for the occasion, and engage in banter with his fellow guests without compromising his spiritual ascendancy one whit. We hear incidentally of his absolute bravery in battle and his disregard of self in the service of a friend, of his extraordinary physical vitality that enabled him to stand all night pondering some thought while his fellow soldiers bivouacked around him to watch the spectacle, of how he could lose himself in some doorway in a trance and so make himself late for his appointment until he had thought through whatever was on his mind. The subject of the *Symposium* is love, and love had been conceived of, in the series of speeches praising it, in a range from gross homosexuality to romantic attachment, to a cosmic principle of attraction and repulsion, to Socrates' own concept . . . of an ascent to union with the highest goodness and beauty. . . .

But it is in the *Phaedo* that Socrates comes nearest to being translated to a higher order of being. In prison, during the hours preceding his death, Socrates discourses to his devoted followers on the most timely and timeless of all questions, the immortality of the soul. The *Phaedo* is the most spiritual and the most eloquent of all dialogues; the account of Socrates' last moments is surely the second most compelling passion in all literature. If Plato's object was to inculcate a belief in immortality, there are of course sound practical reasons for giving the spokesman of the doctrine extraordinary prestige. In such an issue it is the personality of the teacher rather than the cogency of his arguments that is most persuasive. . . .

But the saintliness with which Socrates is endowed in the *Phaedo* seems more than a mere device to promote belief in the immortality of the soul. If belief is being inculcated, it is belief in Socrates, not in immortality. Only an occasional reader of the *Phaedo* could rehearse its arguments for immortality years or months after he had laid the book down; the saintliness of Socrates he can never forget. It is his image of Socrates rather than any specific doctrine that Plato wished to crystallize and perpetuate. From the tenor of all his writing it is clear that Plato believed that the welfare of society depended upon leadership by specially endowed and dedicated men. Ordinary men following a prescribed code would not do. Indeed, Plato conceived of his own effectiveness as teacher in much the same way; in the autobiographical *Seventh Epistle* he tells us that no one could claim to have apprehended his teachings merely from study of his writings: long personal contact with a master spirit is essential.

In the centuries after Plato the images of certain saintly figures who, like Socrates, had selflessly devoted themselves to the spiritual improvement of the community and had accepted the suffering, sometimes the martyrdom, these efforts entailed, played a considerable role in the development of religious ideas and practices. In some cases the image may have masked a character negligible or dishonest, and the men who created and exploited the image may have done so for selfish motives; but in some cases, surely, the man behind the image was a devoted teacher whose disciples embroidered his career in good faith into a kind of hagiology[4] that they then used for moral edification. Whatever the motivation, there can be little doubt that the prime model for the spiritual hero was Socrates. . . .

Suggestions for Further Reading

Socrates is a maddeningly elusive historical figure: he exists only in the works of others. Luis E. Navia, *Socratic Testimonies* (Lanham, Md.: University Press of America, 1987), is a convenient outline of the sources of historical information we do have for Socrates and of the major critical problems in Socratic studies. Because of the lack of historical sources there is a nearly irresistible urge to create a "historical Socrates," which has produced a number of biographical or semibiographical works on him. The preeminent modern account is A. E. Taylor, *Socrates* (New York: Anchor, 1953 [1933]), in which the great British Platonist argues that the striking figure of Socrates as derived from Plato's dialogues is essentially an accurate historical account. The book is clear and readable as well as authoritative. An almost equally good account is Jean Brun, *Socrates,* tr. Douglas Scott (New York: Walker, 1962), in which the author, writing for young people, simplifies and sorts out the leading elements in the traditional view of Socrates—i.e., the Delphic dictum "Know thyself," Socrates' "in-dwelling Daimon," and the Socratic irony. At the other extreme are Alban D. Winspear and Tom Silverberg, *Who Was Socrates?* (New York: Russell and Russell, 1960 [1939]), and Norman Gulley, *The Philosophy of Socrates* (London and New York: Macmillan and St. Martin's, 1968). Winspear and Silverberg argue—not entirely convincingly—for a complete revision of the tradition and make Socrates evolve in the course of his career from a

---

[4]Veneration of a saint or saints.—ED.

democratic liberal to an aristocratic conservative. And Gulley argues for the rejection of Plato's view of Socrates as a skeptic and agnostic in favor of a more constructive role for Socrates in ancient philosophy. Laszlo Versényi, *Socratic Humanism* (New Haven, Conn.: Yale University Press, 1963), while not going as far as Gulley, does advocate a separation between the often paired Socrates and Plato in favor of tying Socrates more closely to the sophists, especially Protagoras and Gorgias. Students should find especially interesting Alexander Eliot, *Socrates: A Fresh Appraisal of the Most Celebrated Case in History* (New York: Crown, 1967). It is less a fresh appraisal than a popular and extremely readable review of Socrates' background, life, and the evidence brought to his trial. The second part of the book is what the author calls "a free synthesis" of all the Platonic dialogues touching on the trial and death of Socrates—essentially a new, dramatic dialogue account in fresh, modern English. On the matter of "the case" of Socrates—i.e., his trial and the evidence and testimony presented—two essays in Gregory Vlastos (ed.), *The Philosophy of Socrates: A Collection of Critical Essays* (South Bend, Ind.: University of Notre Dame Press, 1980 [1971]), Kenneth J. Dover, "Socrates in the *Clouds*" and A. D. Woozley, "Socrates on Disobeying the Law," are of considerable interest. On the two dialogues most pertinent to the trial and death of Socrates, *The Apology* and *The Crito*, two books are recommended. R. E. Allen, *Socrates and Legal Obligation* (Minneapolis, Minn.: University of Minnesota Press, 1980) is a clear and penetrating analysis of the dialogues as is Richard Kraut, *Socrates and the State* (Princeton, N.J.: Princeton University Press, 1984), which also makes the case for Socrates' conscious civil disobedience: it is the best modern treatment of Socrates before the law. Thomas C. Brickhouse and Nicholas D. Smith, *Socrates on Trial* (Princeton, N.J.: Princeton University Press, 1989) judiciously surveys all the evidence for the trial. On the other hand, I. F. Stone, *The Trial of Socrates* (New York: Anchor, 1989) is a muckraking attempt to portray Socrates as an antidemocratic reactionary—an outrageous book, but an interesting one. Mario Montuori, *Socrates: Physiology of a Myth*, tr. J. M. P. and M. Langdale (Amsterdam: J. C. Gieben, 1981) is an account paralleling that of Hadas and Smith in the chapter, but more detailed.

　　Of somewhat larger scope is the important scholarly work of Victor Ehrenberg, *The People of Aristophanes: A Sociology of Old Attic Comedy* (New York: Schocken, 1962 [1943]), a study not only of the characters in the plays but also of the audiences; see especially ch. 10, on religion and education, for Socrates. Of larger scope still is T. B. L. Webster, *Athenian Culture and Society* (Berkeley and Los Angeles: University of California Press, 1973), a superb analysis of the linkage between the culture of Athens and its society—the background to an understanding of the place of Socrates in that society and culture. For this sort of analysis, students may prefer Rex Warner, *Men of Athens* (New York: Viking, 1972), a brilliant popularization which sees Socrates as the end product as well as the victim of fifth-century Athenian culture. J. W. Roberts, *City of Sokrates: A Social History of Classical Athens* (London: Routledge and Kegan Paul, 1984), however, is the best modern historical treatment of Socrates' Athens.

The standard work on the system of Athenian government is A. H. M. Jones, *Athenian Democracy* (Oxford, England: Oxford University Press, 1957), which should be updated by reference to W. R. Connor, *The New Politicians of Fifth Century Athens* (Princeton, N.J.: Princeton University Press, 1971).

THE "PROBLEM" OF ALEXANDER THE GREAT

356 B.C.	Born
336 B.C.	Became king of Macedonia
334 B.C.	Began conquest of Persia
333 B.C.	Battle of Issus
331 B.C.	Battle of Gaugamela and death of Darius, the Persian king
326 B.C.	Battle of Hydaspes in India
323 B.C.	Died

If Alexander had simply been a successful conqueror, no matter how stupefying his conquests, there would really be no "Alexander problem." But, from his own lifetime, there lingered about Alexander the sense that there was something more to him, that he was "up to something," that he had great, even revolutionary, plans. The conviction of manifest destiny that Alexander himself felt so strongly contributed to this, as did his instinct for the unusual, the cryptic, the dramatic in political and religious, as well as in strategic and military, decisions. But most of all, his death at age thirty-three, in the year 323 B.C.—his conquests barely completed and his schemes for the future only hinted at or imperfectly forecast—led the ancient writers to speculate about the questions, "What if Alexander had lived on?" "What plans would his imperial imagination have conceived?" and to sift and resift every scrap of information available—and to invent a few that were not!

The problem of the ancient sources themselves has added greatly to the difficulty of interpretation. And this is surely ironic. For Alexander's own sense of his destiny made him unusually sensitive to the need for keeping records of his deeds. A careful log or journal was maintained, but it exists today only in the most useless fragments, if indeed the "fragments" in question even came from that record. Alexander's staff included at least two scholar-secretaries to keep records.

One was Callisthenes, the nephew of Alexander's old friend and tutor Aristotle. The other was the scientist-philosopher Aristobulus. Callisthenes subsequently fell out with Alexander and was executed for complicity in a plot in 327 B.C. But, while nothing of his work remains it was clearly the basis for a strongly anti-Alexandrian tradition that flourished in Greece, especially in Athens. This hostile tradition is best represented in Cleitarchus, a Greek rhetorician of the generation following Alexander, who never knew him but who became "the most influential historian of Alexander."[1] The account of Aristobulus, who was apparently much closer and more favorable to Alexander than was Callisthenes or Cleitarchus, is also lost. Ptolemy, one of Alexander's most trusted generals and later founder of the Hellenistic monarchy in Egypt, wrote a detailed memoir based in part on Alexander's own *Journal,* but this did not survive either.

Later ancient writers like Diodorus, Plutarch, Curtius, and Justin did know these sources and used them. But of the accounts of Alexander surviving from antiquity, the best one is that of the Greek writer Arrian, of the second century—thus over four hundred years removed from his sources! Furthermore, while Arrian's account is our fullest and most detailed and is based scrupulously on his sources, it is terribly prosaic: we miss precisely what we most want to have, some sense of the "why" of Alexander. Despite Arrian's devotion to his subject, he tends to tell the story—mainly the military side of it at that—without significant comment. And where we would like to have him analyze, he moralizes instead.

Modern scholars have continued to be fascinated by the puzzle of what Alexander was "up to," and none more than William W. Tarn (d. 1957). Tarn was one of those brilliant English "amateurs" of independent means and equally independent views who have contributed so uniquely to scholarship in a score of fields. He was a lawyer by profession, but he devoted most of his scholarly life—more than half a century—to Greek history. Tarn practically invented Hellenistic scholarship, that is, the study of the post-Alexandrian period in the history of Greek civilization. He authored numerous books and studies, beginning with his "Notes on Hellenism in Bactria and India," which appeared in the *Journal of Hellenic Studies* for 1902, through his first important book, *Antigonos Gonatas* (1913), to *Hellenistic Civilization* (1928), *Hellenistic Military and Naval Developments* (1930), *The Greeks in Bactria and India* (1938), and chapters in the first edition of the *Cambridge Ancient History* (1924–1929).

Because the springboard of the Hellenistic age was Alexander,

[1] N. G. L. Hammond, *Alexander the Great: King, Commander and Statesman* (Park Ridge, N.J.: Noyes Press, 1980), p. 2.

Tarn devoted special attention to him. He adopted the stance of a scholar-lawyer, in a sense, taking Alexander as his "client" and setting out to make a case for the defense. And Alexander was badly in need of such defense. The trend of modern scholarship before Tarn had been to view Alexander as an archtyrant, arbitrary and megalomaniac, a drunken murderer, and the oppressor of Greek political freedom and philosophic independence—a view derived ultimately from the Callisthenes-Cleitarchan tradition of antiquity.

Tarn was brilliantly successful in turning opinion around in his defense of Alexander, so much so that the "traditional" view of Alexander today is still essentially that created by Tarn. His authority has been so great that it has even affected the way in which we interpret the ancient sources themselves, whether they seem to be "for" or "against" Tarn's case.

The Ancient Sources:
Arrian, Eratosthenes, and Plutarch

In the first selection of this chapter, we present the five "proof texts" on which Tarn built his defense of Alexander: one from Arrian, one from Eratosthenes (preserved in Strabo), and three from Plutarch.

This passage, from The Life of Alexander the Great *by Arrian, took place near the end of Alexander's incredible journey of conquest. In 324* B.C. *Alexander assembled his Macedonian troops at Opis in Mesopotamia and announced that he proposed to discharge and send home, with lavish rewards, all those who were disabled or overage. But, instead of gratitude, a smoldering resentment surfaced, and the entire Macedonian force began to clamor to be sent home. Arrian attributes the resentment to Alexander's "orientalizing," his adoption of Persian dress and customs, and his attempt to incorporate Persians and other peoples in his army. This had offended the Macedonians' stubborn pride and sense of exclusiveness, and they now threatened a mutiny. Alexander was furious. After having the ringleaders arrested, he addressed the Macedonians in a passionate, blistering speech, reminding them of their own accomplishments, as well as his, and of what he had done for them. Alexander's speech had a profound effect upon the Macedonians, as did the plans, immediately put into effect, for reorganizing the army in the event that they defected. But instead of deserting, the Macedonians repented.*

Alexander, the moment he heard of this change of heart, hastened out to meet them, and he was so touched by their grovelling repentance and their bitter lamentations that the tears came into his eyes. While they continued to beg for his pity, he stepped forward as if to speak, but was anticipated by one Callines, an officer of the mounted Hetaeri, distinguished both by age and rank. "My lord," he cried, "what hurts us is that you have made Persians your kinsmen—Persians are called 'Alexander's kinsmen'—Persians kiss you. But no Macedonian has yet had a taste of this honour."

"Every man of you," Alexander replied, "I regard as my kinsman, and from now on that is what I shall call you."

Thereupon Callines came up to him and kissed him, and all the others who wished to do so kissed him too. Then they picked up their weapons and returned to their quarters singing the song of victory at the top of their voices.

To mark the restoration of harmony, Alexander offered sacrifice to the gods he was accustomed to honour, and gave a public banquet which he himself attended, sitting among the Macedonians, all of whom were present. Next them the Persians had their places, and next to the Persians distinguished foreigners of other nations; Alexander and his friends dipped their wine from the same bowl and poured the same libations, following the lead of the Greek seers and the Magi. The chief object of his prayers was that Persians and Macedonians might rule together in harmony as an imperial power. It is said that 9,000 people attended the banquet; they unanimously drank the same toast, and followed it by the paean of victory.

After this all Macedonians—about 10,000 all told—who were too old for service or in any way unfit, got their discharge at their own request.

Eratosthenes of Cyrene, who lived about 200 B.C., was head of the great Library of Alexandria and one of the most learned individuals of antiquity. But his works exist only in fragments and in citations in the writings of others, such as the following, from The Geography *by the Greek scientist Strabo, of the first century B.C.*

Now, towards the end of his treatise—after withholding praise from those who divide the whole multitude of mankind into two groups, namely, Greeks and Barbarians, and also from those who advised Alexander to treat the Greeks as friends but the Barbarians as enemies—Eratosthenes goes on to say that it would be better to make such divisions according to good qualities and bad qualities; for not only are many of the Greeks bad, but many of the Barbarians are refined—Indians and Arians, for example, and, further, Romans and Carthaginians, who carry on their governments so admirably. And this, he says, is the reason why Alexander, disregarding his advisers, welcomed as many as he could of the men of fair repute and did them favours—just as if those who have made such a division, placing some people in the category of censure, others in that of praise, did so for any other reason than that in some people there prevail the law-abiding and the political instinct, and the qualities associated with education and powers of speech, whereas in other people the opposite characteristics prevail! And so Alexander, not disregarding his advisers, but rather accepting their opinion, did what was consistent with, not contrary to, their advice; for he had regard to the real intent of those who gave him counsel.

Two of the Plutarch passages are from his essay "On the Fortune of Alexander," which is one of the pieces comprising the collection known as the Moralia.

Moreover, the much-admired *Republic* of Zeno, the founder of the Stoic sect, may be summed up in this one main principle: that all the inhabitants of this world of ours should not live differentiated by their respective rules of justice into separate cities and communities, but that we should consider all men to be of one community and one polity, and that we should have a common life and an order common to us all, even as a herd that feeds together and shares the pasturage of a common field. This Zeno wrote, giving shape to a dream or, as it were, shadowy picture of a well-ordered and philosophic commonwealth; but it was Alexander who gave effect to the idea. For Alexander did not follow Aristotle's advice to treat the Greeks as if he were their leader, and other peoples as if he were their master; to have regard for the Greeks as for friends and kindred, but to conduct himself toward other peoples as though they were plants or animals; for to do so would have been to cumber his leadership with numerous battles and banishments and festering seditions. But, as he believed that he came as a heaven-sent governor to all, and as a mediator for the whole world, those whom he could not persuade to unite with him, he conquered by force of arms, and he brought together into one body all men everywhere, uniting and mixing in one great loving-cup, as it were, men's lives, their characters, their marriages, their very habits of life. He bade them all consider as their fatherland the whole inhabited earth, as their stronghold and protection his camp, as akin to them all good men, and as foreigners only the wicked; they should not distinguish between Grecian and foreigner by Grecian cloak and targe, or scimitar and jacket; but the distinguishing mark of the Grecian should be seen in virtue, and that of the foreigner in iniquity; clothing and food, marriage and manner of life they should regard as common to all, being blended into one by ties of blood and children.

After dwelling on the wisdom of Alexander in affecting a mixed Graeco-Macedonian and Persian costume, Plutarch continues.

For he did not overrun Asia like a robber nor was he minded to tear and rend it, as if it were booty and plunder bestowed by unexpected good fortune. . . . But Alexander desired to render all upon earth subject to one law of reason and one form of government and to reveal all men as one people, and to this purpose he made himself conform. But if the deity that sent down Alexander's soul into this world of ours had not recalled him quickly, one law would govern all mankind, and they all would look toward one rule of justice as though toward a common source of light. But as it is, that part of the world which has not looked upon Alexander has remained without sunlight.

The passage from the famous "Life of Alexander" in Plutarch's Lives *deals with an incident early in Alexander's career, after his conquest of Egypt—his journey across the desert to the oracle of Ammon at Siwah.*

When Alexander had passed through the desert and was come to the place of the oracle, the prophet of Ammon gave him salutation from the god as from a father; whereupon Alexander asked him whether any of the murderers of his father had escaped him.[2] To this the prophet answered by bidding him be guarded in his speech, since his was not a mortal father. Alexander therefore changed the form of his question, and asked whether the murderers of Philip had all been punished; and then, regarding his own empire, he asked whether it was given to him to become lord and master of all mankind. The god gave answer that this was given to him, and that Philip was fully avenged. Then Alexander made splendid offerings to the god and gave his priests large gifts of money. . . . We are told, also, that he listened to the teachings of Psammon[3] the philosopher in Egypt, and accepted most readily this utterance of his, namely, that all mankind are under the kingship of God, since in every case that which gets the mastery and rules is divine. Still more philosophical, however, was his own opinion and utterance on this head, namely that although God was indeed a common father of all mankind, still, He made peculiarly His own the noblest and best of them.

Alexander the Great
and the Unity of Mankind

W. W. TARN

We turn now to the thesis that W. W. Tarn built in defense of Alexander. He had begun to develop his characteristic view in a number of journal articles and anticipated it in fairly complete form in his contributions to the

[2]Alexander had come to the throne of Macedonia upon the murder of his father, Philip II, in 336 B.C.—ED.

[3]This is the only reference in antiquity to such a person.—ED.

1927 edition of the Cambridge Ancient History. *He was later to state it most completely in his monumental two-volume* Alexander the Great *(Cambridge: Cambridge University Press, 1948). But the most succinct statement of the Tarn thesis is that contained in his Raleigh Lecture on History, read before the British Academy in 1933. It is entitled "Alexander the Great and the Unity of Mankind."*

What I am going to talk about is one of the great revolutions in human thought. Greeks of the classical period, speaking very roughly, divided mankind into two classes, Greeks and non-Greeks; the latter they called barbarians and usually regarded as inferior people, though occasionally some one, like Herodotus or Xenophon, might suggest that certain barbarians possessed qualities which deserved consideration, like the wisdom of the Egyptians or the courage of the Persians. But in the third century B.C. and later we meet with a body of opinion which may be called universalist; all mankind was one and all men were brothers, or anyhow ought to be. Who was the pioneer who brought about this tremendous revolution in some men's way of thinking? Most writers have had no doubt on that point; the man to whom the credit was due was Zeno, the founder of the Stoic philosophy. But there are several passages in Greek writers which, *if* they are to be believed, show that the first man actually to think of it was not Zeno but Alexander. This matter has never really been examined; some writers just pass it over, which means, I suppose, that they do not consider the passages in question historical; others have definitely said that it is merely a case of our secondary authorities attributing to Alexander ideas taken from Stoicism. I want to consider to-day whether the passages in question are or are not historical and worthy of credence; that is, whether Alexander was or was not the first to believe in, and to contemplate, the unity of mankind. This will entail, among other things, some examination of the concept which Greeks called Homonoia, a word which meant more than its Latin translation, Concord, means to us; it is more like Unity and Concord, a being of one mind together, or if we like the phrase, a union of hearts; ultimately it was to become almost a symbol of the world's longing for something better than constant war. For convenience of discussion I shall keep the Greek term Homonoia.

Before coming to the ideas attributed to Alexander, I must sketch very briefly the background against which the new thought arose, whoever was its author; and I ought to say that I am primarily talking throughout of theory, not of practice. It may be possible to find, in the fifth century, or earlier, an occasional phrase which looks like a groping after something better than the hard-and-fast division of Greeks and barbarians; but this comes to very little and had no importance for history, because anything of the sort was strangled by the idealist philosophies. Plato and Aristotle left no doubt about their views. Plato said that all barbarians were enemies by nature; it was proper to wage war upon them, even to the point of enslaving or extirpating them. Aristotle said that all barbarians were slaves by nature, especially those of Asia; they had not the qualities which entitled them to be free men, and it was proper to treat them as slaves. His model State cared for nothing but its own citizens; it was a small aristocracy of Greek citizens ruling over a barbarian peasantry who cultivated the land for their masters and had no share in the State—a thing he had seen in some cities of Asia Minor. Certainly neither Plato nor Aristotle was quite consistent; Plato might treat an Egyptian priest as the repository of wisdom, Aristotle might suggest that the constitution of Carthage was worth studying; but their main position was clear enough, as was the impression Alexander would get from his tutor Aristotle.

There were, of course, other voices. Xenophon, when he wanted to portray an ideal shepherd of the people, chose a Persian king as shepherd of the Persian people. And there were the early Cynics. But the Cynics had no thought of any union or fellowship between Greek and barbarian; they were not constructive thinkers, but merely embodied protests against the vices and follies of civilization. When Diogenes called himself a cosmopolite, a horrible word which he coined and which was not used again for centuries, what he meant was, not that he was a citizen of some imaginary world-state—a thing he never thought about—but that he was not a citizen of any Greek city; it was pure negation. And the one piece of Cynic construction, the ideal figure of Heracles, labouring to free Greece from monsters, was merely shepherd of a *Greek* herd till after Alexander, when it took colour and content from the Stoics and became the ideal benefactor of humanity. All that Xenophon or the Cynics could supply was the figure of an ideal shepherd, not of the human herd, but of some national herd.

More important was Aristotle's older contemporary Isocrates, because of his conception of Homonoia. The Greek world, whatever its practice, never doubted that in theory unity in a city was very desirable; but though the word Homonoia was already in common use among Greeks, it chiefly meant absence of faction-fights, and this rather negative meaning lasted in the cities throughout the Hellenistic period, as can be seen in the numerous decrees in honour of the judicial commissions sent from one city to another, which are praised because they tried to compose internal discord. There was hardly a trace as yet of the more positive sense which Homonoia was to acquire later—a mental attitude which should make war or faction impossible because the parties were at one; and Isocrates extended the applica-

tion of the word without changing its meaning. He took up a suggestion of the sophist Gorgias and proposed to treat the whole Greek
world as one and the futile wars between city and city as faction
fights—to apply Homonoia to the Greek race. For this purpose he
utilized Plato's idea that the barbarian was a natural enemy, and decided that the way to unite Greeks was to attack Persia; "I come," he
said, "to advocate two things: war against the barbarian, Homonoia
between ourselves." But somebody had to do the uniting; and Isocrates bethought him of the Cynic Heracles, benefactor of the Greek
race, and urged King Philip of Macedonia, a descendant of Heracles,
to play the part. But if Philip was to be Heracles and bring about the
Homonoia of the Greek world, the way was being prepared for two
important ideas of a later time; the essential quality of the king must
be that love of man, φιλανθρωπία,[4] which had led Heracles to perform his labours, and the essential business of the king was to promote Homonoia; so far this only applied to Greeks, but if its meaning
were to deepen it would still be the king's business. The actual result
of all this, the League of Corinth[5] under Philip's presidency, was not
quite what Isocrates had dreamt of.

This then was the background against which Alexander appeared.
The business of a Macedonian king was to be a benefactor of Greeks
to the extent of preventing inter-city warfare; he was to promote
Homonoia among Greeks and utilize their enmity to barbarians as a
bond of union; but barbarians themselves were still enemies and
slaves by nature, a view which Aristotle emphasized when he advised
his pupil to treat Greeks as free men, but barbarians as slaves.

I now come to the things Alexander is supposed to have said or
thought; and the gulf between them and the background I have
sketched is so deep that one cannot blame those who have refused to
believe that he ever said or thought anything of the sort. There are
five passages which need consideration: one in Arrian; one from
Eratosthenes, preserved by Strabo; and three from Plutarch, one of
which, from its resemblance to the Strabo passage, has been supposed
by one of the acutest critics of our time to be taken in substance from
Eratosthenes,[6] and as such I shall treat it. The passage in Arrian says
that, after the mutiny of the Macedonians at Opis and their reconciliation to Alexander, he gave a banquet to Macedonians and Persians, at
which he prayed for Homonoia and partnership in rule between
these two peoples. What Eratosthenes says amounts to this. Aristotle

---

[4]Literally "philanthropy."—ED.

[5]The league Philip formed after defeating the Greek states at Chaeronea in 338
B.C.—ED.

[6]The reference is to the German scholar E. Schwarz.—ED.

told Alexander to treat Greeks as friends, but barbarians like animals; but Alexander knew better, and preferred to divide men into good and bad without regard to their race, and thus carried out Aristotle's real intention. For Alexander believed that he had a mission from the deity to harmonize men generally and be the reconciler of the world, mixing men's lives and customs as in a loving cup, and treating the good as his kin, the bad as strangers; for he thought that the good man was the real Greek and the bad man the real barbarian. Of the two Plutarch passages, the first says that his intention was to bring about, as between mankind generally, Homonoia and peace and fellowship and make them all one people; and the other, which for the moment I will quote without its context, makes him say that God is the common father of all men.

It is obvious that, wherever all this comes from, we are dealing with a great revolution in thought. It amounts to this, that there is a natural brotherhood of all men, though bad men do not share in it; that Homonoia is no longer to be confined to the relations between Greek and Greek, but is to unite Greek and barbarian; and that Alexander's aim was to substitute peace for war, and reconcile the enmities of mankind by bringing them all—all that is whom his arm could reach, the peoples of his empire—to be of one mind together: as men were one in blood, so they should become one in heart and spirit. That such a revolution in thought did happen is unquestioned; the question is, was Alexander really its author, or are the thoughts attributed to him those of Zeno or somebody else? . . .

"To try to answer that question," Tarn follows with a long and complex analysis of Homonoia and kingship in Graeco-Roman history, leading to the universalism of the late Roman empire.

The belief that it was the business of kings to promote Homonoia among their subjects without distinction of race thus travelled down the line of kingship for centuries; but the line, you will remember, had no beginning. . . . It must clearly have been connected with some particular king at the start, and that king has to be later than Isocrates and Philip and earlier than Diotogenes and Demetrius.[7] It would seem that only one king is possible; we should have to postulate Alexander at the beginning of the line, even if there were not a definite tradition that it *was* he. This means that Plutarch's statement, that Alexander's purpose was to bring about Homonoia between men

[7]Isocrates (436–338 B.C.), the Athenian orator; Philip II of Macedonia (355–336 B.C.); Diotogenes, an early Hellenistic author of uncertain date; Demetrius (336–283 B.C.), an early Hellenistic ruler.—ED.

generally—that is, those men whom his arm could reach—must be taken to be true, unless some explicit reason be found for disbelieving it; and I therefore now turn to the Stoics, in order to test the view that the ideas attributed to him were really taken from Stoicism. . . . We have seen that it was the business of kings to bring about Homonoia; but this was not the business of a Stoic, because to him Homonoia had already been brought about by the Deity, and it existed in all completeness; all that was necessary was that men should see it. . . .

This is the point I want to make, the irreconcilable opposition between Stoicism and the theory of kingship, between the belief that unity and concord existed and you must try and get men to see it, and the belief that unity and concord did not exist and that it was the business of the rulers of the earth to try and bring them to pass. . . . Consequently, when Eratosthenes says that Alexander aspired to be the harmonizer and reconciler of the world, and when Plutarch attributes to him the intention of bringing about fellowship and Homonoia between men generally—those men whom his arm reached— then, wherever these ideas came from, they were not Stoic; between them and Stoicism there was a gulf which nothing could bridge. This does not by itself prove that Alexander held these ideas; what it does do is to put out of court the only alternative which has ever been seriously proposed, and to leave the matter where I left it when considering the theory of kingship, that is, that there is a strong presumption that Alexander *was* their author. . . .

Before leaving Stoicism, I must return for a moment to Zeno's distinction of the worthy and the unworthy; for Alexander, as we saw, is said to have divided men into good and bad, and to have excluded the bad from the general kinship of mankind and called them the true barbarians. Might not *this* distinction, at any rate, have been taken from Stoicism and attributed to him? The reasons against this seem conclusive, apart from the difficulty of discarding a statement made by so sound and scientific a critic as Eratosthenes. First, no Stoic ever equated the unworthy class with barbarians; for to him there were no barbarians. . . . Secondly, while the unworthy in Zeno, as in Aristotle, are the majority of mankind, Alexander's "bad men" are not; they are, as Eratosthenes says, merely that small residue everywhere which cannot be civilized. One sees this clearly in a story never questioned, his prayer at Opis, when he prayed that the Macedonian and Persian races (without exceptions made) might be united in Homonoia. And thirdly, we know where the idea comes from: Aristotle had criticized some who said that good men were really free and bad men were really slaves (whom he himself equated with barbarians), and Alexander is in turn criticizing Aristotle; as indeed Eratosthenes says, though he does not quote this passage of Aristotle. The matter is not important, except for the general question of the credibility of Eratosthenes, and may conceivably only represent that period in Alexander's thought when he was outgrowing Aristotle; it does not conflict, as does Zeno's conception of the unworthy, with a general belief in the unity of mankind. . . .

There is just one question still to be asked; whence did Zeno get his universalism? Plutarch says that behind Zeno's dream lay Alexander's reality; and no one doubts that Alexander was Zeno's inspiration, but the question is, in what form? Most writers have taken Plutarch to mean Alexander's *empire;* but to me this explains nothing at all. One man conquers a large number of races and brings them under one despotic rule; how can another man deduce from this that distinctions of race are immaterial and that the universe is a harmony in which men are brothers? It would be like the fight between the polar bear and the parallelepiped. The Persian kings had conquered and ruled as large an empire as Alexander, including many Greek cities; why did Darius never inspire any one with similar theories? It does seem to me that what Plutarch really means is not Alexander's empire but Alexander's ideas; after all, the frequent references in antiquity to Alexander as a philosopher, one at least of which is contemporary, must mean *something*. Zeno's inspiration, then, was Alexander's idea of the unity of mankind; and what Zeno himself did was to carry this idea to one of its two logical conclusions. Judging by his prayer at Opis for the Homonoia of Macedonians and Persians, Alexander, had he lived, would have worked through national groups, as was inevitable in an empire like his, which comprised many different states and subject peoples; Theophrastus,[8] who followed him, included national groups in his chain of progress towards world-relationship. But Zeno abolished all distinctions of race, all the apparatus of national groups and particular states, and made his world-state a theoretic whole. His scheme was an inspiration to many; but in historical fact it was, and remained, unrealizable. But Alexander's way, or what I think was his way, led to the Roman Empire being called one people. I am not going to bring in modern examples of these two different lines of approach to world-unity, but I want to say one thing about the Roman Empire. It has been said that Stoic ideas came near to realization in the empire of Hadrian and the Antonines, but it is quite clear, the moment it be considered, that this was not the case; that empire was a huge national state, which stood in the line of kingship and was a partial realization of the ideas of Alexander. When a Stoic *did* sit on

---

[8]The philosopher-scientist who followed Aristotle as head of his school.—ED.

the imperial throne, he was at once compelled to make terms with the national state; to Marcus Aurelius, the Stoic world-state was no theoretic unity, but was to comprise the various particular states as a city comprises houses. And there is still a living reality in what he said about himself: "As a man I am a citizen of the world-state, but as the particular man Marcus Aurelius I am a citizen of Rome."

I may now sum up. We have followed down the line of kingship the theory that it was the business of a king to promote Homonoia among his subjects—all his subjects without distinction of race; and we have seen that this theory ought to be connected at the start with some king, who must be later than Philip and earlier than Demetrius; and there is a definite tradition which connects the origin of the theory with Alexander. We have further seen that the intention to promote Homonoia among mankind, attributed in the tradition to Alexander, is certainly not a projection backwards from Stoicism, or apparently from anything else, while it is needed to explain certain things said by Theophrastus and done by Alexarchus.[9] Lastly, we have seen the idea of the kinship or brotherhood of mankind appearing suddenly in Theophrastus and Alexarchus; their common source can be no one but Alexander, and again tradition supports this. Only one conclusion from all this seems possible: the things which, in the tradition, Alexander is supposed to have thought and said are, in substance, true. He did say that all men were sons of God, that is brothers, but that God made the best ones peculiarly his own; he did aspire to be the harmonizer and reconciler of the world—that part of the world which his arm reached; he did have the intention of uniting the peoples of his empire in fellowship and concord and making them of one mind together; and when, as a beginning, he prayed at Opis for partnership in rule and Homonoia between Macedonians and Persians, he meant what he said—not partnership in rule only, but true unity between them. I am only talking of theory, not of actions; but what this means is that he was the pioneer of one of the supreme revolutions in the world's outlook, the first man known to us who contemplated the brotherhood of man or the unity of mankind, whichever phrase we like to use. I do not claim to have given you exact proof of this; it is one of those difficult borderlands of history where one does not get proofs which could be put to a jury. But there is a very strong presumption indeed that it is true. Alexander, for the things he *did,* was called The Great; but if what I have said to-day be right, I do not think we shall doubt that this idea of his—call it a purpose, call it a dream, call it what you will—was the greatest thing about him.

---

[9]A minor Macedonian princeling, following Alexander, who set up his small state apparently on the model of Alexander's ideas.—Ed.

The New Alexander

N. G. L. HAMMOND

*Despite Tarn's enormous scholarly reputation and his lordly dismissal of
critics, his own interpretive view of Alexander was bound to be challenged,
and it has been. Tarn massively overstated his case. As Mary Renault put
it, "the defence was pushed too far."[10] And Ernst Badian, probably Tarn's
most effective critic among this generation of scholars, has called the Alexander of Tarn's vision a "phantom" that "has haunted the pages of scholarship" for "a quarter of a century."[11] In reaction against Tarn's view of
Alexander not only as a stunning conqueror but as a conqueror of stunning
philosophic profundity as well, scholars have again depicted him "as a ruth-
less murderer, an autocratic megalomaniac, even a bisexual profligate."[12]
Even more careful and moderate scholars like R. D. Milns hold that such
an idea as the kinship of mankind was quite beyond Alexander and must be
attributed to "later thinkers and philosophers."[13]*

*Now the reaction seems to be moving back toward the Tarn view. The
"new" Alexander is more anchored in his own times and mores, and none
of the more recent authorities attribute to Alexander the "great revolution in
thought" that Tarn did. But the Alexander we see today is considerably
more cerebral and innovative both in thought and action. This new image
of Alexander is nowhere better represented than in the work of the distinguished Cambridge classicist N. G. L. Hammond,* Alexander the Great:
King, Commander and Statesman, *from which the following excerpt is
taken.*

We have the advantage of hindsight. We can see that it was Alexander's leadership and training which made the Macedonians incompa-
rable in war and in administration and enabled them as rulers of the
so-called Hellenistic kingdoms to control the greater part of the
civilised world for a century or more. In a reign of thirteen years he
brought to Macedonia and Macedonians the immense wealth which

[10]Mary Renault, *The Nature of Alexander* (New York: Pantheon, 1975), p. 23.

[11]Ernst Badian, "Alexander the Great and the Unity of Mankind," *Historia* 7 (1958),
425.

[12]Hammond, *Alexander the Great,* p. 5.

[13]R. D. Milns, *Alexander the Great* (London: Robert Hale, 1968), p. 265.

maintained their strength for generations. All this was and is an unparalleled achievement. Moreover, as king of Macedonia he did not
drain his country unduly in his lifetime, since Antipater had enough
men to defeat the Greeks in 331 B.C. and 322 B.C. Yet the system he
was creating—quite apart from any further conquests he had in mind
in 323 B.C.—was certain to put an immense strain on present and
future Macedonians. They were spread dangerously thin at the time
of his death, and the prolonged absence of so many Macedonians
abroad was bound to cause a drop in the birth-rate in Macedonia
itself. Of course Alexander expected his Macedonians to undertake
almost superhuman dangers and labours, and it was their response to
his challenge that made them great. But the dangers and labours
were being demanded for the sake of a policy which was not Macedonian in a nationalistic sense, which the Macedonians did not wholly
understand, and which they never fully implemented. Philip's sin-
glemindedness made him the greatest king of Macedonia. Alexander's wider vision made him at the same time something more and
something less than the greatest king of Macedonia. . . .

As constitutionally elected king, Alexander had sole right of command and an inherited authority. From the age of twenty onwards he
appointed his deputies without let or hindrance, issued all orders,
and controlled all payments, promotions, and discharges. His authority as a commander was almost absolute, his discipline unquestioned,
and his position unchallenged. As religious head of the state, he
interceded for his men and was seen daily to sacrifice on their behalf.

Unique in his descent from Zeus and Heracles, he was acclaimed
"son of Zeus" by the oracle at Didyma, the Sibyl at Erythrae, and the
oracle of Ammon (the last at least in the opinion of his men), and he
fostered the idea of divine protection by having the sacred shield of
Athena carried into battle by his senior Bodyguard (it saved his life
against the Malli; [Arrian] 6.10.2). Before engaging at Gaugamela
Alexander prayed in front of the army, raising his right hand towards
the gods and saying, "If I am really descended from Zeus, protect and
strengthen the Greeks." That prayer, apparently, was answered. In
the eyes of most men—and most men then had faith in gods, oracles,
and omens—Alexander was favoured by the supernatural powers. To
those who were sceptical he had extraordinarily good luck.

The brilliance of Alexander's mind is seen most clearly in his major
battles. . . . For example, he saw at once the advantages and disadvantages of Darius' position on the Pinarus river and he anticipated the
effects of his own detailed dispositions and orders to a nicety. "He
surpassed all others in the faculty of intuitively meeting an emergency," whether in besieging Tyre or facing Scythian tactics or storm-
ing an impregnable fortress. He excelled in speed and precision of

thought, the calculation of risks, and the expectation of an enemy's reactions. Having himself engaged in every kind of action and having grappled with practical problems from a young age, he had a sure sense of the possible and extraordinary versatility in invention. Unlike many famous commanders, his mind was so flexible that at the time of his death he was creating an entirely new type of army.

A most remarkable quality of Alexander's was the concern for his men. No conqueror had so few casualties in battle, and the reason was that Alexander avoided "the battle of rats" by using his brains not just to win, but to win most economically. He made this his priority because he loved his Macedonians. He grew up among them and fought alongside them, both as a youth admiring his seniors and as a mature man competing with his companions. He honoured and rewarded courage and devotion to duty in them, paying a unique tribute to the first casualties by having bronze statues made by the leading sculptor, and he felt deeply with them in their sufferings and privations. He aroused in them an amazing response. He not only admired courage and devotion to duty in his own men but in his enemies, whom he treated with honour. In return he won the respect and loyalty of Asians of many races whom he had just defeated in battle. . . . Some commanders may have rivalled him in the handling of his own race. None have had such a capacity for leading a multiracial army. . . .

We have already touched upon his statesmanship in enhancing the prestige of the Macedonian monarchy and advancing the power of the Macedonian state. He reduced the harshness of customary law, (for instance, he no longer required the execution of the male relatives of a convicted traitor), and he was concerned for the welfare and the birth rate of Macedonia. He provided tax reliefs for the dependants of casualties, brought up war orphans at his own expense, and sought to avoid conflicts between the European and Asian families of his Macedonians by maintaining the latter in Asia. He increased the number of young Macedonians when he legitimised the soldiers' children by Asian women, and he sent the 10,000 veterans home in the expectation of their begetting more children in Macedonia. . . .

While Philip invented and inaugurated the Greek League, it was Alexander who demonstrated its efficacy as a *modus operandi* for the Macedonians and the Greeks and used their joint forces to overthrow the Persian Empire. By opening Asia to Greek enterprise and culture Alexander relieved many of the social and economic pressures which had been causing distress and anarchy in the Greek states. At the same time he was personally concerned with affairs in Greece, as we see from the large number of embassies which came to him in Asia rather than to his deputy, Antipater, in Macedonia. . . .

Alexander's originality is seen most clearly in Asia. He set himself an unparalleled task when he decided in advance not to make the Macedonians and the Greeks the masters of the conquered peoples but to create a self-sustaining Kingdom of Asia. Within his kingdom he intended the settled peoples to conduct their internal affairs in accordance with their own laws and customs, whether in a Greek city or a native village, in a Lydian or a Carian state, in a Cyprian or a Phoenician kingdom, in Egypt, Babylonia, or Persis, in an Indian principality or republic. As his power extended, he did not introduce European administrators at a level which would inhibit native self-rule (as so-called colonial powers have so often done); instead he continued native administrators in office and raised the best of them to the highest level in civil affairs by appointing them as his immediate deputies in the post of satrap (e.g., Mazaeus at Babylon) or nomarch (e.g., Doloaspis in Egypt). . . .

What is important is the effectiveness of Alexander's system: native civilians and armed forces alike lodged complaints with Alexander, the accused were tried legally and openly, and those found guilty were executed forthwith, in order "to deter the other satraps, governors, and civil officers" and to make it known that the rulers were not permitted to wrong the ruled in Alexander's kingdom. In the opinion of Arrian, who lived at the zenith of the Roman Empire and had a standard of comparison, it was this system which "more than anything else kept to an orderly way of life the innumerable, widely diffused peoples who had been subjugated in war or had of their own will joined him" (6.27.5). In the same way rebels, sometimes in the form of native pretenders, were put on trial; and, if found guilty, they were executed, often in the manner native to the particular area (Arrian 6.30.2). Where the rights of his subjects were at stake, he showed no mercy or favouritism for any Macedonian, Greek, Thracian, Persian, Median, or Indian. . . .

What Alexander sought in his senior administrators was summed up in the word "excellence" (*arete*). He assessed it by performance in his own army and in that of his enemy; for he approved courage and loyalty, wherever he found it. But a particular kind of excellence was needed where conquerors had to accept the conquered as their equals in administering the kingdom of Asia. The Macedonians justifiably regarded themselves as a military élite, superior to Greeks and barbarians, and closer to their king than any foreigner; and the Greeks despised all Asians as barbarians, fitted by nature only to be slaves. Yet here was Alexander according equal status, regardless of race, not only to all his administrators but also to all who served in his army! Resentment at this was the chief factor in the mutiny of the Macedonians at Opis. On that occasion Alexander enforced his will. He celebrated the concept of equal status in an official banquet, at which the Macedonians sat by their king, with whom they were not reconciled; next were the Persians; and after them persons of "the other races." All the guests were men who ranked first in reputation or in some other form of excellence (*arete*). . . .

When Alexander encountered nomadic or marauding peoples, he forced them, often by drastic methods of warfare, to accept his rule and to adopt a settled way of life. Many of his new cities were founded among these peoples so that "they should cease to be nomads," and he encouraged the concentration of native villages to form new urban centres. For he intended to promote peace, prosperity, and culture within these parts of his kingdom too, and the cities and centres were means to that end. Strongly fortified and well manned, they were bastions of peace, and the young men in them were trained by Macedonian and Greek veterans to join Alexander's new army and maintain his peace. They were sited to become markets for agricultural produce and interregional exchange, and their citizens, especially in the new cities by the deltas of the Nile, the Euphrates, and the Indus, learnt the capitalistic form of economy, which had brought such prosperity to the Greek states in the fifth and fourth centuries.

The cultural model for the new cities was the Macedonian town, itself very strongly imbued with Greek ideas and practices. The ruling element from the outset was formed by Macedonian and Greek veterans; and the Asians, although free to practise their own religion and traditions, were encouraged to learn Greek and adopt some forms of Greco-Macedonian life. According to Plutarch (*Mor.* 328e) Alexander founded 70 new cities, which started their life with 10,000 adult male citizens as the norm, and he must have envisaged a fusion of European and Asian cultures developing within and spreading out from these arteries into the body of the kingdom. . . .

The effects of a statesman's ideas, especially if he dies at the age of thirty-two, are rarely assessable within his lifetime. Yet before Alexander died his ideas bore fruit in the integration of Asians and Macedonians in cavalry and infantry units; the training of Asians in Macedonian weaponry; the association of Asians and Macedonians in each file of the army; the settling of Macedonians, Greeks, and Asians in the new cities; the spread of Greek as a common language in the army and in the new cities; the development of Babylon as the "metropolis" or capital of the kingdom of Asia; the honouring of interracial marriage; and the raising of Eurasian children to a privileged status.

Peace reigned in this kingdom of Asia, and its people now had little to fear from their neighbours. Urbanisation, trade, water-borne commerce, agriculture, flood-control, land-reclamation, and irrigation were developing fast, and exchange was stimulated by the liberation of hoarded treasure. The gold and silver coinage of Alexander, uniform in types and weights, was universally accepted because it was of real, bullion value. In the eastern satrapies especially the gold darics and silver shekels of the Persian treasuries continued to circulate, and in the western satrapies local currencies were provided by the Greek, Cyprian, and Phoenician cities. . . .

The skill with which Alexander changed the economy of Asia into that system of commercial exchange which the Greeks had invented and we call capitalism, and at that within so few years, is one of the most striking signs of his genius. . . .

The fulfilment of Alexander's plans was impaired by his early death and by the strife between the generals which ensued. Yet even so, within the span of thirteen years, he changed the face of the world more decisively and with more longlasting effects than any other statesman has ever done. He first introduced into Asia the Greco-Macedonian city within the framework of a monarchical or autocratic state, and this form of city was to be the centre of ancient and medieval civilisation in the southern Balkans, the Aegean, and the Near East. For the city provided that continuity of Greek language, literature, and culture which enriched the Roman world, fostered Christianity, and affected Western Europe so profoundly. The outlook and the achievements of Alexander created an ideal image, an apotheosis of kingship which was to inspire the Hellenistic kings, some Roman emperors, and the Byzantine rulers. And his creation of a state which rose above nationalism and brought liberators and liberated, victors and defeated into collaboration and parity of esteem puts most of the expedients of the modern world to shame. . . .

That Alexander should grow up with a sense of mission was certainly to be expected. For he was descended from Zeus and Heracles, he was born to be king, he had the career of Philip as an exemplar, and he was advised by Isocrates, Aristotle, and others to be a benefactor of Macedonians and Greeks alike. His sense of mission was inevitably steeped in religious associations, because from an early age he had been associated with the king, his father, in conducting religious ceremonies, and he was imbued with many ideas of orthodox religion and of ecstatic mysteries. Thus two observations by Plutarch (*Mor.* 342 A and F) have the ring of truth. "This desire (to bring all men into an orderly system under a single leadership and to accustom them to one way of life) was implanted in Alexander from childhood and grew up with him"; and on crossing the Hellespont to the Troad Alexander's first asset was "his reverence towards the gods." Already by then he planned to found a Kingdom of Asia, in which he would rule over the peoples, as Odysseus had done, "like a kindly father" (*Odyssey* 5.11). He promoted the fulfilment of that plan "by founding Greek cities among savage peoples and by teaching the principles of law and peace to lawless, ignorant tribes." When he had completed the conquest of "Asia" through the favour of the gods and especially that of Zeus Ammon, he went on to establish for all men in his kingdom "concord and peace and partnership with one another" (*Mor.* 329 F).

This was a practical development, springing from a religious concept and not from a philosophical theory (though it led later to the philosophical theory of the Cynics, who substituted for Asia the whole inhabited world and talked of the brotherhood of all men), and it came to fruition in the banquet at Opis, when he prayed in the presence of men of various races for "concord and partnership in the ruling" of his kingdom "between Macedonians and Persians."

What distinguishes Alexander from all other conquerors is this divine mission. He had grown up with it, and he had to a great extent fulfilled it, before he gave expression to it at the banquet at Opis in such words as those reported by Plutarch (*Mor.* 329 C). "Alexander considered," wrote Plutarch, "that he had come from the gods to be a general governor and reconciler of the world. Using force of arms when he did not bring men together by the light of reason, he harnessed all resources to one and the same end, mixing the lives, manners, marriages and customs of men, as it were in a loving-cup." This is his true claim to be called "Alexander the Great": that he did not crush or dismember his enemies, as the conquering Romans crushed Carthage and Molossia and dismembered Macedonia into four parts; nor exploit, enslave or destroy the native peoples, as "the white man" has so often done in America, Africa, and Australasia; but that he created, albeit for only a few years, a supranational community capable of living internally at peace and of developing the concord and partnership which are so sadly lacking in the modern world.

Suggestions for Further Reading

As is often the case, the classical sources for the biography of Alexander are among the most lively and entertaining works about him, especially Plutarch and Arrian. Plutarch's "Life of Alexander" from his *Parallel Lives of Noble Greeks and Romans* (available in several editions) is, like the rest of the biographical sketches in this famous book, a gossipy and charming account, containing most of the familiar anecdotes associated with Alexander. Arrian's work, the most substantial of the ancient sources, despite a certain stuffiness and lack of analytical daring, is solidly based on more contemporary sources now long lost—particularly Ptolemy's journal and the work of Aristobulus. And it contains the best and most detailed account of Alexander's conquests. See the excellent modern translation by Aubrey de Sélincourt, *Arrian's Life of Alexander the Great* (Harmondsworth, England: Penguin, 1958).

The views of W. W. Tarn summarized in the excerpted passage above from his Raleigh Lecture on History, "Alexander the Great and the Unity of Mankind," are spelled out in greater detail in the chapters he wrote on Alexander and his age—chs. 12–15 of the *Cambridge Ancient History,* vol. 6 (Cambridge, England: Cambridge University Press, 1927), and in his larger *Alexander the Great,* 2 vols. (Cambridge, England: Cambridge University Press, 1948), based on the account in *Cambridge Ancient History* but expanded and updated.

Tarn's most bitter critic is Ernst Badian, who chose to challenge Tarn in particular for the views expressed in his Raleigh Lecture. Badian's article, with the same title, "Alexander the Great and the Unity of Mankind," appeared in *Historia,* 7 (1958), 425–444, and is reprinted in *Alexander the Great: The Main Problems,* ed. G. T. Griffith (New York: Barnes and Noble, 1966). This article is highly specialized, closely reasoned, and contains long passages in Greek; but it is very important and, despite the difficulties of the text, the argument can be clearly followed even by the nonspecialist. Peter Green, *Alexander the Great* (New York: Praeger, 1970), is a modern general account of Alexander's career in the same critical tradition as Badian. Two other modern works that deal more with the conquests than the conqueror are Peter Bamm, *Alexander the Great: Power as Destiny,* tr. J. M. Brownjohn (New York: McGraw-Hill, 1968), and Sir Mortimer Wheeler, *Flames over Persepolis: Turning Point in History* (New York: Morrow, 1968), the latter of particular interest because of Wheeler's expert knowledge of Near Eastern and Indian archaeology.

There is another relatively recent book that stresses the continuing work in archaeology, including the dramatic finds at Vergina in Macedonia: Robin Lane Fox, *The Search for Alexander* (Boston: Little, Brown, 1980). The most balanced and readable modern general account, however, may still be A. R. Burn, *Alexander the Great and the Hellenistic Empire* (London: The English Universities Press, 1947), although the more recent R. D. Milns, *Alexander the Great* (London: Robert Hale, 1968) is also recommended.

Finally, Alexander is the subject of two first-rate historical novels by Mary Renault, *Fire from Heaven* (New York: Pantheon, 1969), and *The*

Persian Boy (New York: Pantheon, 1972), the first carrying the story through Alexander's childhood to his accession to the throne of Macedonia, the second recounting his conquests as narrated by the Persian boy-eunuch Bagoas, Alexander's companion and lover. Renault has also produced a nonfiction account, fully as readable as her novels, and based on the meticulous research she prepared for them, *The Nature of Alexander* (New York: Pantheon, 1975).

JULIUS CAESAR: THE COLOSSUS THAT BESTRODE THE NARROW WORLD

c. 100 B.C.	Born
69 or 68 B.C.	Elected quaestor
62 B.C.	Elected praetor
59 B.C.	Elected consul; First Triumvirate with Crassus and Pompey
58–50 B.C.	Conquest of Gaul
49–45 B.C.	Civil war
44 B.C.	Assassinated

Unlike Alexander, who conquered the world "as a boy" and was dead at thirty-three, Julius Caesar reached a mature age without achieving astonishing success. He did have considerable experience as a political faction leader, but in the judgment of most of his contemporaries he was not likely to be a world conqueror of Alexander's stamp. And yet, in 49 B.C., when Caesar was fifty years old, a series of events began to unfold that would make him one of the great conquerors of world history and set him alongside Alexander in the estimation of scholar and schoolboy alike.

For ten years, Caesar had been building a military reputation with his successful campaigns in Gaul, Britain, and along the Rhine frontier, but always with an eye on events in the city of Rome and the Roman senate, where he had a personal interest in the fierce contest among cliques and factions that dominated senatorial politics in the last years of the Roman Republic. As the year 49 B.C. approached, Caesar's proconsular authority in Gaul was running out. He demanded that he be permitted to stand *in absentia* for the consulship for the following year—neither an unprecedented nor unreasonable demand. Caesar attempted to negotiate with his old ally, the great general Pompey, perhaps to prolong their alliance. But Pompey, his own military reputation threatened by Caesar's growing prestige, and relentlessly pressured by Caesar's enemies in the senate, refused him and joined with the senate in demanding that Caesar surrender his military command and return to Rome as a private citizen to stand for the consulship. But to do so would have meant his death or proscription. Thus, in January of 49 B.C., Caesar took the fateful step into open revolution, leading a token force across the Rubicon, the little stream that separated his Gallic province from peninsular Italy.

For nearly a century the Roman constitution had been progressively subverted by a succession of extralegal expedients to legitimize the authority of one strong man after another, one faction after another—whether the prolonged consulships of Marius, the perpetual dictatorship of Sulla, or the triumviral authority that Caesar himself had held with Pompey and Crassus. Such practices, as well as a pervasive disenchantment with the self-serving senatorial oligarchy, had created broad support in Rome and in Italy for a policy of change, even revolutionary change. Caesar's popular reputation attracted that support as he marched south toward Rome. Even Pompey's legions in Spain declared for Caesar. Pompey and his remaining allies fled to Greece, where they were pursued by Caesar under vast emergency authority readily granted by an overawed senate, and were defeated at Pharsalus. In the next four years, Caesar moved through Asia Minor and Syria, Egypt, North Africa, and Spain and encircled the Mediterranean with his conquests, giving the final rough form to the greatest empire of antiquity.

It was at this point that the plot to assassinate Caesar was formed. It was carried out on the Ides of March of the year 44 B.C.

Caesar and Alexander beg for comparison, despite the many dissimilarities in their lives. Plutarch, the greatest of ancient biographers, paired them in his *Parallel Lives of Noble Greeks and Romans,* and almost every other ancient writer who speculates upon the meaning of Caesar's career suggests comparison with Alexander. The obvious basis for the comparison is, of course, the military parallel and the fact that Caesar, like Alexander, seized his time and wrenched it so violently that the direction of world events was fundamentally changed. But equally important, both men were cut off before their schemes for a civil order could be realized. There was about Caesar, as about Alexander, an aura of things to come, of unfulfilled dreams even more astounding than his conquests. Thus the question again intrigues us, "What would Caesar have accomplished had he lived on?"

In one important respect Caesar differs radically from Alexander—in our sources of information about him. As we saw in the last chapter, all the contemporary works that dealt with the career of Alexander have been lost, and the best surviving account of him was written some four hundred years after he died. Not so with Caesar. He lived during the most heavily documented period in ancient history, a time when we know more about the people and events at the center of the world's stage than we will know again for more than a thousand years. We have Caesar's own considerable volume of writings. We have the works of his great senatorial contemporary Cicero. We have the writings of poets and essayists and narrative historians. But despite the abundance of material and the wealth of detail about Julius Caesar, a clear and convincing picture of the man—what he was and what he might have become—eludes us, precisely because, as Shakespeare's Cassius says in *Julius Caesar,* ". . . he doth bestride the narrow world like a colossus," because his dominating personality, his overweening ambition, and his striking accomplishments made it nearly impossible for his contemporaries to be objective about him. His own writings are propagandistic, and the writings of Cicero, his often bitter and vindictive opponent, and Sallust, his partisan, are obviously biased. The accounts of both Pollio and Livy exist in epitomes or in traces in others' works. For our best account of Caesar, we must reach down into the imperial period that followed his own brilliant "golden age of Latin literature," to one of the writers of "the silver age," the biographer Suetonius.

The Life of Caesar

SUETONIUS

The choice of Suetonius is a good one on a number of counts. Although he has been charged with a journalistic style and mentality and with too great a fondness for scandal, rumor, and portent, the late imperial Historia Augusta, *for what it is worth, refers to him as having written* vere, *"truly," and a great modern Roman historian calls him "far and away the best authority" on Caesar.[1] Unlike his contemporary Plutarch, Suetonius was not a moralist using biography as a source of example. Nor was he a deliberate partisan: the factionalism of Caesar's age was long dead. Suetonius was interested only in writing a plain, straightforward account of the characters and events that were his subject. And, like Arrian, he turned to archival sources for his information. The book in which his biography of Caesar appears,* The Lives of the Twelve Caesars, *was begun when Suetonius was still in the imperial civil service of the Emperor Hadrian. It is clear that he had access to archival records, now long lost, as well as to literary sources, and that he followed his sources carefully. His biography of Caesar was apparently a part of the book done before Suetonius left the imperial service in about* A.D. *120 and thus is especially well documented with records and sources.*

And yet, in an important sense, Suetonius was the captive of those very sources he followed so scrupulously. For even though Suetonius was more than a century removed from his sources, the hostility toward Caesar that these records expressed is clearly reflected in Suetonius's writing. Despite his fascination and admiration for Caesar, Suetonius's basic assessment is that Caesar's arrogance and his flaunting of the republican tradition led to his murder: "He abused his powers and was justly slain."

Even after the Civil War and the furious activity of the years 48–44 B.C., *Suetonius tells us, Caesar was full of plans for beautifying the city of Rome, opening libraries, draining the Pomptine marshes, building new highways, constructing a canal through the Isthmus of Corinth, and waging war against both the Dacians and the Parthians.*

---

[1]Sir Ronald Syme, in a review of Matthias Gelzer's "Caesar der Politiker und Staatsmann" in *Journal of Roman Studies*, 34 (1944), 95.

All these enterprises and plans were cut short by his death. But before I speak of that, it will not be amiss to describe briefly his personal appearance, his dress, his mode of life, and his character, as well as his conduct in civil and military life.

He is said to have been tall of stature, with a fair complexion, shapely limbs, a somewhat full face, and keen black eyes; sound of health, except that towards the end he was subject to sudden fainting fits and to nightmare as well. He was twice attacked by the falling sickness during his campaigns. He was somewhat overnice in the care of his person, not only keeping the hair of his head closely cut and his face smoothly shaved, but as some have charged, even having superfluous hair plucked out. His baldness was a disfigurement which troubled him greatly, since he found that it was often the subject of the gibes of his detractors. Because of it he used to comb forward his scanty locks from the crown of his head, and of all the honors voted him by the Senate and people there was none which he received or made use of more gladly than the privilege of wearing a laurel wreath at all times. . . .

It is admitted by all that he was much addicted to women, as well as very extravagant in his intrigues with them, and that he seduced many illustrious women, among them Postumia, wife of Servius Sulpicius, Lollia, wife of Aulus Gabinius, Tertulla, wife of Marcus Crassus, and even Gnaeus Pompey's wife Mucia. . . .

He had love affairs with Queens, too, including Eunoe the Moor, wife of Bogudes, on whom, as well as on her husband, he bestowed many splendid presents, as Naso writes. But his greatest favorite was Cleopatra, with whom he often feasted until daybreak, and he would have gone through Egypt with her in her state-barge almost to Aethiopia, had not his soldiers refused to follow him. Finally he called her to Rome and did not let her leave until he had laden her with high honors and rich gifts, and he allowed her to give his name to the child which she bore. . . .

That he drank very little wine not even his enemies denied. There is a saying of Marcus Cato that Caesar was the only man who undertook to overthrow the state when sober. Even in the matter of food Gaius Oppius tells us that he was so indifferent, that once when his host served stale oil instead of fresh, and the other guests would have none of it, Caesar partook even more plentifully than usual, that he might not seem to charge his host with carelessness or lack of manners.

But his abstinence did not extend to pecuniary advantages, either when in command of armies or when in civil office. For we have the testimony of some writers that when he was Proconsul in Spain, he not only begged money from the allies, to help pay his debts, but also attacked and sacked some towns of the Lusitanians, although they did not refuse his terms and opened their gates to him on his arrival. In Gaul he pillaged shrines and temples of the Gods filled with offerings, and oftener sacked towns for the sake of plunder than for any fault. . . .

He was highly skilled in arms and horsemanship, and of incredible powers of endurance. On the march he headed his army, sometimes on horseback, but oftener on foot, bareheaded both in the heat of the sun and in rain. He covered great distances with incredible speed, making a hundred miles a day in a hired carriage and with little baggage, swimming the rivers which barred his path or crossing them on inflated skins, and very often arriving before the messengers sent to announce his coming. . . .

He joined battle, not only after planning his movements in advance but on a sudden opportunity, often immediately at the end of a march, and sometimes in the foulest weather, when one would least expect him to make a move. It was not until his later years that he became slower to engage, through a conviction that the oftener he had been victor, the less he ought to tempt fate, and that he could not possibly gain as much by success as he might lose by a defeat. He never put his enemy to flight without also driving him from his camp, thus giving him no respite in his panic. When the issue was doubtful, he used to send away the horses, and his own among the first, to impose upon his troops the greater necessity of standing their ground by taking away that aid to flight. . . .

When his army gave way, he often rallied it single-handed, planting himself in the way of the fleeing men, laying hold of them one by one, even seizing them by the throat and turning them to face the enemy; that, too, when they were in such a panic that an eagle-bearer made a pass at him with the point as he tried to stop him, while another left the standard in Caesar's hand when he would hold him back. . . .

At Alexandria, while assaulting a bridge, he was forced by a sudden sally of the enemy to take to a small skiff. When many others threw themselves into the same boat, he plunged into the sea, and after swimming for two hundred paces, got away to the nearest ship, holding up his left hand all the way, so as not to wet some papers which he was carrying, and dragging his cloak after him with his teeth, to keep the enemy from getting it as a trophy.

He valued his soldiers neither for their personal character nor their fortune, but solely for their prowess, and he treated them with equal strictness and indulgence. . . .

He certainly showed admirable self-restraint and mercy, both in his conduct of the civil war and in the hour of victory. While Pompey threatened to treat as enemies those who did not take up arms for the government, Caesar gave out that those who were neutral and of neither party should be numbered with his friends. He freely allowed all those whom he had made Centurions[2] on Pompey's recommendation to go over to his rival. . . . At the battle of Pharsalus he cried out, "Spare your fellow citizens," and afterwards allowed each of his men to save any one man he pleased of the opposite party. . . .

Yet after all, his other actions and words so far outweigh all his good qualities that it is thought he abused his power and was justly slain. For not only did he accept excessive honors, such as an uninterrupted consulship, the dictatorship for life, and the censorship of public morals, as well as the forename Imperator,[3] the surname of Father of his Country, a statue among those of the Kings,[4] and a raised couch in the orchestra of the theater. He also allowed honors to be bestowed on him which were too great for mortal man: a golden throne in the House and on the judgment seat; a chariot and litter in the procession at the circus; temples, altars, and statues beside those of the Gods; a special priest, an additional college of the Luperci, and the calling of one of the months by his name. In fact, there were no honors which he did not receive or confer at pleasure.

He held his third and fourth consulships in name only, content with the power of the dictatorship conferred on him at the same time as the consulships. Moreover, in both years he substituted two Consuls for himself for the last three months, in the meantime holding no elections except for Tribunes and plebeian Aediles, and appointing Praefects instead of the Praetors, to manage the affairs of the city during his absence. When one of the Consuls suddenly died the day before the Kalends of January, he gave the vacant office for a few hours to a man who asked for it. With the same disregard of law and precedent he named magistrates for several years to come, bestowed the emblems of consular rank on ten ex-Praetors, and admitted to the House men who had been given citizenship, and in some cases even half-civilized Gauls. He assigned the charge of the mint and of the public revenues to his own slaves, and gave the oversight and command of the three legions which he had left at Alexandria to a favorite boy of his called Rufio, son of one of his freedmen.

No less arrogant were his public utterances, which Titus Ampius

---

[2]Centurions were "company grade" officers in the Roman legion.—ED.

[3]The title *Imperator*, synonymous with conqueror, was that by which troops would hail a victorious commander. It first assumed a permanent and royal character through Caesar's use of it as a praenomen.—ED.

[4]Statues of each of the seven Kings of Rome were in the Capitol, to which an eighth was added in honor of Brutus, who expelled the last of the Kings. The statue of Julius was afterward raised near them.—ED.

records: that the Republic was a name only, without substance or reality; that Sulla did not know his A. B. C. when he laid down his dictatorship; that men ought now to be more circumspect in addressing him, and to regard his word as law. So far did he go in his presumption, that when a soothsayer once announced to him the direful omen that a victim offered for sacrifice was without a heart, he said: "The entrails will be more favorable when I please. It ought not to be taken as a miracle if a beast have no heart."

But it was the following action in particular that roused deadly hatred against him. When the Senate approached him in a body with many highly honorary decrees, he received them before the temple of Venus Genetrix without rising. Some think that when he attempted to get up, he was held back by Cornelius Balbus; others, that he made no such move at all, but on the contrary frowned angrily on Gaius Trebatius when he suggested that he should rise. This action of his seemed the more intolerable, because when he himself in one of his triumphal processions rode past the benches of the Tribunes, he was so incensed because one of their number, Pontius Aquila by name, did not rise, that he cried: "Come then, Aquila, mighty Tribune, and take from me the Republic," and for several days afterwards, he would promise a favor to no one without adding, "That is, if Pontius Aquila will give me leave."

To an insult which so plainly showed his contempt for the Senate he added an act of even greater insolence. After the sacred rites of the Latin Festival, as he was returning to the city, amid the extravagant and unprecedented demonstrations of the populace, some one in the press placed on his statue a laurel wreath with a white fillet tied to it. When Epidius Marullus and Caesetius Flavus, Tribunes of the Commons, gave orders that the ribbon be removed from the crown and the man taken off to prison, Caesar sharply rebuked and deposed them, either offended that the hint at regal power had been received with so little favor, or, as was said, that he had been robbed of the glory of refusing it. But from that time on he could not rid himself of the odium of having aspired to the title of monarch, although he replied to the Commons, when they hailed him as King, "I am Caesar and not King." At the Lupercalia, when the Consul Antony several times attempted to place a crown upon his head as he spoke from the rostra, he put it aside and at last sent it to the Capitol, to be offered to Jupiter Optimus Maximus. Nay, more, the report had spread in various quarters that he intended to move to Ilium or Alexandria, taking with him the resources of the state, draining Italy by levies, and leaving it and the charge of the city to his friends; also that at the next meeting of the Senate Lucius Cotta would announce as the decision of the Fifteen,[5] that inasmuch as it was written in the books of fate that the Parthians could be conquered only by a King, Caesar should be given that title. . . .

More than sixty joined the conspiracy against him, led by Gaius Cassius and Marcus and Decimus Brutus. At first they hesitated whether to form two divisions at the elections in the Campus Martius, so that while some hurled him from the bridge as he summoned the tribes to vote, the rest might wait below and slay him; or to set upon him in the Sacred Way or at the entrance to the theater. When, however, a meeting of the Senate was called for the Ides of March in the Hall of Pompey, they readily gave that time and place the preference.

Now Caesar's approaching murder was foretold to him by unmistakable signs: . . . when he was offering sacrifice, the soothsayer Spurinna warned him to beware of danger, which would come not later than the Ides of March. . . .

Both for these reasons and because of poor health he hesitated for a long time whether to stay at home and put off what he had planned to do in the Senate. But at last, urged by Decimus Brutus not to disappoint the full meeting, which had for some time been waiting for him, he went forth almost at the end of the fifth hour. When a note revealing the plot was handed him by some one on the way, he put it with others which he held in his left hand, intending to read them presently. Then, after many victims had been slain, and he could not get favorable omens, he entered the House in defiance of portents, laughing at Spurinna and calling him a false prophet, because the Ides of March were come without bringing him harm. Spurinna replied that they had of a truth come, but they had not gone.

As he took his seat, the conspirators gathered about him as if to pay their respects, and straightway Tillius Cimber, who had assumed the lead, came nearer as though to ask something. When Caesar with a gesture put him off to another time, Cimber caught his toga by both shoulders. As Caesar cried, "Why, this is violence!" one of the Cascas stabbed him from one side just below the throat. Caesar caught Casca's arm and ran it through with his stylus, but as he tried to leap to his feet, he was stopped by another wound. When he saw that he was beset on every side by drawn daggers, he muffled his head in his robe, and at the same time drew down its lap to his feet with his left hand, in order to fall more decently, with the lower part of his body also covered. And in this wise he was stabbed with three and twenty wounds, uttering not a word, but merely a groan at the first stroke, though some have written

[5]The college of fifteen priests who inspected and expounded the Sybilline books.— ED.

that when Marcus Brutus rushed at him, he said in Greek, "You too, my child?" All the conspirators made off, and he lay there lifeless for some time, until finally three common slaves put him on a litter and carried him home, with one arm hanging down.

The Heroic Image of Caesar

THEODOR MOMMSEN

Theodor Mommsen (1817–1903) was awarded the Nobel Prize for Literature in 1902, largely for the literary achievement of his monumental, multivolume The History of Rome. *The Nobel citation called him the "greatest . . . master of historical narrative" of his age—a considerable claim in an era that had produced Ranke and Burckhardt, Guizot, Grote, Carlyle, and Macaulay. Still, the assertion may be true. Mommsen, a prolific writer, had gained an immense and well-deserved authority, and his massive* The History of Rome *was profoundly influential. It was Mommsen who at last placed the study of ancient history on a scientific and critical foundation. And he began and directed the first great critical collection of ancient Latin inscriptions.*

Like W. W. Tarn, Theodor Mommsen was trained both in classics and in law. His first academic appointment was as professor of law at Leipzig. Then in 1858 he was appointed to the chair of ancient history at the University of Berlin. Throughout his long life, Mommsen was not only a professor but a passionate political activist. He was involved in the Revolution of 1848 and lost his academic post at Leipzig because of it. In the 1870s he was a prominent member of the Prussian Parliament, frequently clashing with Otto von Bismarck. Like many great historians, Mommsen read the past in terms of present politics. Thus his view of Caesar and the late Roman Republic was colored by his profound disillusionment with German political liberalism and an equally profound hatred for Junker conservatism. Julius Caesar became for Mommsen the archetypal strong man who had swept away the broken pieces of a ruined oligarchy and set the rule of the beneficent Roman Empire firmly on its base. While Mommsen has been rightly criticized for the extravagance of his opinions both on Caesar and on the late Roman Republic, his views, though never quite accepted as the "standard" interpretation, did exert a strong influence on modern scholarship until fairly recently.

Here, from The History of Rome, *is Mommsen's evaluation of Julius*

Caesar. The prose is old fashioned and florid and the judgments are dated, but there is still some power left in the sweep of Mommsen's portrayal of his "perfect man."

The new monarch of Rome, the first ruler over the whole domain of Romano-Hellenic civilization, Gaius Julius Caesar, was in his fifty-sixth year . . . when the battle at Thapsus [46 B.C.], the last link in a long chain of momentous victories, placed the decision as to the future of the world in his hands. Few men have had their elasticity so thoroughly put to the proof as Caesar—the sole creative genius produced by Rome, and the last produced by the ancient world, which accordingly moved on in the path that he marked out for it until its sun went down. Sprung from one of the oldest noble families of Latium—which traced back its lineage to the heroes of the Iliad and the kings of Rome, and in fact to the Venus-Aphrodite common to both nations—he spent the years of his boyhood and early manhood as the genteel youth of that epoch were wont to spend them. He had tasted the sweetness as well as the bitterness of the cup of fashionable life, had recited and declaimed, had practised literature and made verses in his idle hours, had prosecuted love-intrigues of every sort, and got himself initiated into all the mysteries of shaving, curls, and ruffles pertaining to the toilette-wisdom of the day, as well as into the still more mysterious art of always borrowing and never paying. But the flexible steel of that nature was proof against even these dissipated and flighty courses; Caesar retained both his bodily vigour and his elasticity of mind and of heart unimpaired. In fencing and in riding he was a match for any of his soldiers, and his swimming saved his life at Alexandria; the incredible rapidity of his journeys, which usually for the sake of gaining time were performed by night—a thorough contrast to the procession-like slowness with which Pompeius moved from one place to another—was the astonishment of his contemporaries and not the least among the causes of his success. The mind was like the body. His remarkable power of intuition revealed itself in the precision and practicability of all his arrangements, even where he gave orders without having seen with his own eyes. His memory was matchless, and it was easy for him to carry on several occupations simultaneously with equal self-possession. . . .

Caesar was thoroughly a realist and a man of sense; and whatever he undertook and achieved was pervaded and guided by the cool sobriety which constitutes the most marked peculiarity of his genius. To this he owed the power of living energetically in the present, undisturbed either by recollection or by expectation; to this he owed the capacity of acting at any moment with collected vigour, and of applying his whole genius even to the smallest and most incidental enterprise; to this he owed the many-sided power with which he grasped and mastered whatever understanding can comprehend and will can compel; to this he owed the self-possessed ease with which he arranged his periods as well as projected his campaigns; to this he owed the "marvellous serenity" which remained steadily with him through good and evil days; to this he owed the complete independence, which admitted of no control by favourite or by mistress, or even by friend. It resulted, moreover, from this clearness of judgment that Caesar never formed to himself illusions regarding the power of fate and the ability of man; in his case the friendly veil was lifted up, which conceals from man the inadequacy of his working. Prudently as he laid his plans and considered all possibilities, the feeling was never absent from his breast that in all things fortune, that is to say accident, must bestow success; and with this may be connected the circumstance that he so often played a desperate game with destiny, and in particular again and again hazarded his person with daring indifference. As indeed occasionally men of predominant sagacity betake themselves to a pure game of hazard, so there was in Caesar's rationalism a point at which it came in some measure into contact with mysticism.

Gifts such as these could not fail to produce a statesman. From early youth, accordingly, Caesar was a statesman in the deepest sense of the term, and his aim was the highest which man is allowed to propose to himself—the political, military, intellectual, and moral regeneration of his own deeply decayed nation, and of the still more deeply decayed Hellenic nation intimately akin to his own. The hard school of thirty years' experience changed his views as to the means by which this aim was to be reached; his aim itself remained the same in the times of his hopeless humiliation and of his unlimited plenitude of power, in the times when as demagogue and conspirator he stole towards it by paths of darkness, and in those when, as joint possessor of the supreme power and then as monarch, he worked at his task in the full light of day before the eyes of the world. . . . According to his original plan he had purposed to reach his object, like Pericles and Gaius Gracchus, without force of arms, and throughout eighteen years he had as leader of the popular party moved exclusively amid political plans and intrigues—until, reluctantly convinced of the necessity for a military support, he, when already forty years of age, put himself at the head of an army [59 B.C.]. . . .

The most remarkable peculiarity of his action as a statesman was its perfect harmony. In reality all the conditions for this most difficult of all human functions were united in Caesar. A thorough realist, he never allowed the images of the past or venerable tradition to disturb him; for him nothing was of value in politics but the living present and the law of reason, just as in his character of grammarian he set aside historical and antiquarian research and recognized nothing but on the one hand the living *usus loquendi* and on the other hand the rule of symmetry. A born ruler, he governed the minds of men as the wind drives the clouds, and compelled the most heterogeneous natures to place themselves at his service—the plain citizen and the rough subaltern, the genteel matrons of Rome and the fair princesses of Egypt and Mauretania, the brilliant cavalry-officer and the calculating banker. His talent for organization was marvellous; no statesman has ever compelled alliances, no general has ever collected an army out of unyielding and refractory elements with such decision, and kept them together with such firmness, as Caesar displayed in constraining and upholding his coalitions and his legions; never did regent judge his instruments and assign each to the place appropriate for him with so acute an eye.

He was monarch; but he never played the king. Even when absolute lord of Rome, he retained the deportment of the party-leader; perfectly pliant and smooth, easy and charming in conversation, complaisant towards every one, it seemed as if he wished to be nothing but the first among his peers. Caesar entirely avoided the blunder into which so many men otherwise on an equality with him have fallen, of carrying into politics the military tone of command; however much occasion his disagreeable relations with the senate gave for it, he never resorted to outrages. . . . Caesar was monarch; but he was never seized with the giddiness of the tyrant. He is perhaps the only one among the mighty ones of the earth, who in great matters and little never acted according to inclination or caprice, but always without exception according to his duty as ruler, and who, when he looked back on his life, found doubtless erroneous calculations to deplore, but no false step of passion to regret. There is nothing in the history of Caesar's life, which even on a small scale can be compared with those poetico-sensual ebullitions—such as the murder of Kleitos or the burning of Persepolis—which the history of his great predecessor in the east records. He is, in fine, perhaps the only one of those mighty ones, who has preserved to the end of his career the statesman's tact of discriminating between the possible and the impossible, and has not broken down in the task which for greatly gifted natures is the most difficult of all—the task of recognizing, when on the pinnacle of success, its natural limits. What was possible he performed, and never left the possible good undone for the sake of the impossible better, never disdained at least to mitigate by palliatives evils that were incurable. But where he recognized that fate had spoken, he always obeyed. . . .

Such was this unique man, whom it seems so easy and yet is so

infinitely difficult to describe. His whole nature is transparent clearness; and tradition preserves more copious and more vivid information about him than about any of his peers in the ancient world. Of
such a personage our conceptions may well vary in point of shallow-
ness or depth, but they cannot be, strictly speaking, different; to every
not utterly perverted inquirer the grand figure has exhibited the
same essential features, and yet no one has succeeded in reproducing
it to the life. The secret lies in its perfection. In his character as a man
as well as in his place in history, Caesar occupies a position where the
great contrasts of existence meet and balance each other. Of mighty
creative power and yet at the same time of the most penetrating
judgment; no longer a youth and not yet an old man; of the highest
energy of will and the highest capacity of execution; filled with republican ideals and at the same time born to be a king; a Roman in the
deepest essence of his nature, and yet called to reconcile and combine
in himself as well as in the outer world the Roman and the Hellenic
types of culture—Caesar was the entire and perfect man.

Caesar the Politician

RONALD SYME

*The long-time Oxford professor Sir Ronald Syme is probably our leading
ancient historian today. His most important book, and possibly the outstanding work in Roman history in this generation,[6] is* The Roman Revolution. *Syme worked on this book through the late 1930s, against the backdrop of events taking place in Mommsen's Germany, but the vision of one-
person rule was not quite as alluring to him as it had been to Mommsen.
Syme's view of Caesar, however, was not only affected by the rise of Hitler
and the political drift toward World War II. He had before him an impressive accumulation of scholarly research on the darker side of the Caesarian
monarchy. Eduard Meyer's* Caesars Monarchie und das Principat des
Pompejus *(1919) argues that Caesar aspired to the establishment of a
Hellenistic monarchy in Rome. The second volume of Jerome Carcopino's*
Histoire Romaine *(1936) deals with Caesar and maintains that, since his
youth, Caesar's ambition was directed toward monarchy.
Syme also read the important work of Matthias Gelzer—Die* Nobilität

---

[6]Cf. the review, for example, of Michael Ginsburg in *American Historical Review,* 46
(1940), 108.

der Römischen Republik *(1912) and* Caesar der Politiker und Staatsmann *(1921)—which prompted him to examine some of the same ground, the social and political setting in which Caesar lived and died. Syme, like Gelzer, was especially interested in the senatorial oligarchy. The "Roman Revolution" of his title, he argues, occurred when this oligarchy lost its power to a new social group composed of people from all parts of Italy, even the provinces. And he saw Caesar as the political genius who began the revolution that he could not then control.*

Syme insists that Caesar be judged—as he was murdered—"for what he was, not for what he might become," be that an oriental despot or a Helle-nistic monarch. What Caesar was was a Roman aristocrat whose brilliance and luck enabled him to surpass his fellow aristocrats. The key event lead-ing to his assassination was not his arrogance, which was common to his class and station, and not even his high-handedness in subverting the repub-lic; it was the Caesarian dictatorship, prolonged first for ten years and then, in January of 44 B.C., for life, that was intolerable to the senatorial nobility and the cause of his murder.

The following, from The Roman Revolution, *is Syme's analysis of Caesar.*

The conquest of Gaul, the war against Pompeius and the establish-ment of the Dictatorship of Caesar are events that move in a harmony so swift and sure as to appear pre-ordained; and history has some-times been written as though Caesar set the tune from the beginning, in the knowledge that monarchy was the panacea for the world's ills, and with the design to achieve it by armed force. Such a view is too simple to be historical.

Caesar strove to avert any resort to open war. Both before and after the outbreak of hostilities he sought to negotiate with Pom-peius. Had Pompeius listened and consented to an interview, their old *amicitia* might have been repaired. With the nominal primacy of Pompeius recognized, Caesar and his adherents would capture the government—and perhaps reform the State. Caesar's enemies were afraid of that—and so was Pompeius. After long wavering Pompeius chose at last to save the oligarchy. Further, the proconsul's proposals as conveyed to the State were moderate and may not be dismissed as mere manoeuvres for position or for time to bring up his armies. Caesar knew how small was the party willing to provoke a war. As the artful motion of a Caesarian tribune had revealed, an over-whelming majority in the Senate, nearly four hundred against twenty-two, wished both dynasts to lay down their extraordinary commands. A rash and factious minority prevailed.

The precise legal points at issue in Caesar's claim to stand for the

consulate in absence and retain his province until the end of the year
49 B.C. are still matters of controversy. If they were ever clear, debate
and misrepresentation soon clouded truth and equity. The nature of
the political crisis is less obscure. Caesar and his associates in power
had thwarted or suspended the constitution for their own ends many
times in the past. Exceptions had been made before in favour of other
dynasts; and Caesar asserted both legal and moral rights to preferen-
tial treatment. In the last resort his rank, prestige and honour,
summed up in the Latin word *dignitas,* were all at stake: to Caesar, as
he claimed, "his *dignitas* had ever been dearer than life itself." Sooner
than surrender it, Caesar appealed to arms. A constitutional pretext
was provided by the violence of his adversaries: Caesar stood in defence of the rights of the tribunes and the liberties of the Roman
People. But that was not the plea which Caesar himself valued most—
it was his personal honour.

His enemies appeared to have triumphed. They had driven a
wedge between the two dynasts, winning over to their side the power
and prestige of Pompeius. They would be able to deal with Pompeius
later. It might not come to open war; and Pompeius was still in their
control so long as he was not at the head of an army in the field. Upon
Caesar they had thrust the choice between civil war and political
extinction. . . .

Caesar was constrained to appeal to his army for protection. At last
the enemies of Caesar had succeeded in ensnaring Pompeius and in
working the constitution against the craftiest politican of the day: he
was declared a public enemy if he did not lay down his command
before a certain day. By invoking constitutional sanctions against Caesar, a small faction misrepresented the true wishes of a vast majority
in the Senate, in Rome, and in Italy. They pretended that the issue lay
between a rebellious proconsul and legitimate authority. Such ven-
turesome expedients are commonly the work of hot blood and mud-
dled heads. The error was double and damning. Disillusion followed
swiftly. Even Cato was dismayed. It had confidently been expected
that the solid and respectable classes in the towns of Italy would rally
in defence of the authority of the Senate and the liberties of the
Roman People, that all the land would rise as one man against the
invader. Nothing of the kind happened. Italy was apathetic to the
war-cry of the Republic in danger, sceptical about its champions. . . .

Caesar, it is true, had only a legion to hand: the bulk of his army
was still far away. But he swept down the eastern coast of Italy, gathering troops, momentum and confidence as he went. Within two
months of the crossing of the Rubicon he was master of Italy.
Pompeius made his escape across the Adriatic carrying with him several legions and a large number of senators, a grievous burden of

revenge and recrimination. The enemies of Caesar had counted upon capitulation or a short and easy war.

They had lost the first round. Then a second blow, quite beyond calculation: before the summer was out the generals of Pompeius in Spain were outmanoeuvred and overcome. Yet even so, until the legions joined battle on the plain of Pharsalus, the odds lay heavily against Caesar. Fortune, the devotion of his veteran legionaries and the divided counsels of his adversaries secured the crowning victory. But three years more of fighting were needed to stamp out the last and bitter resistance of the Pompeian cause in Africa and in Spain.

"They would have it thus," said Caesar as he gazed upon the Roman dead at Pharsalus, half in patriot grief for the havoc of civil war, half in impatience and resentment. They had cheated Caesar of the true glory of a Roman aristocrat—to contend with his peers for primacy, not to destroy them. His enemies had the laugh of him in death. Even Pharsalus was not the end. His former ally, the great Pompeius, glorious from victories in all quarters of the world, lay unburied on an Egyptian beach, slain by a renegade Roman, the hireling of a foreign king. Dead, too, and killed by Romans, were Caesar's rivals and enemies, many illustrious consulars. Ahenobarbus fought and fell at Pharsalus, and Q. Metellus Scipio ended worthy of his ancestors; while Cato chose to fall by his own hand rather than witness the domination of Caesar and the destruction of the Free State.

That was the nemesis of ambition and glory, to be thwarted in the end. After such wreckage, the task of rebuilding confronted him, stern and thankless. Without the sincere and patriotic co-operation of the governing class, the attempt would be all in vain, the mere creation of arbitrary power, doomed to perish in violence. . . .

Under these unfavourable auspices, a Sulla but for *clementia*, a Gracchus but lacking a revolutionary programme, Caesar established his Dictatorship. His rule began as the triumph of a faction in civil war: he made it his task to transcend faction, and in so doing wrought his own destruction. A champion of the People, he had to curb the People's rights, as Sulla had done. To rule, he needed the support of the *nobiles*, yet he had to curtail their privileges and repress their dangerous ambitions.

In name and function Caesar's office was to set the State in order again (*rei publicae constituendae*). Despite odious memories of Sulla, the choice of the Dictatorship was recommended by its comprehensive powers and freedom from the tribunician veto. Caesar knew that secret enemies would soon direct that deadly weapon against one who had used it with such dexterity in the past and who more recently claimed to be asserting the rights of the tribunes, the liberty of the

Roman People. He was not mistaken. Yet he required special powers: after a civil war the need was patent. The Dictator's task might well demand several years. In 46 B.C. his powers were prolonged to a tenure of ten years, an ominous sign. A gleam of hope that the emergency period would be quite short flickered up for a moment, to wane at once and perish utterly. In January 44 B.C. Caesar was voted the Dictatorship for life. About the same time decrees of the Senate ordained that an oath of allegiance should be taken in his name. Was this the measure of his ordering of the Roman State? Was this a *res publica constituta?*

It was disquieting. Little had been done to repair the ravages of civil war and promote social regeneration. For that there was sore need, as both his adherents and his former adversaries pointed out. From Pompeius, from Cato and from the oligarchy, no hope of reform. But Caesar seemed different: he had consistently advocated the cause of the oppressed, whether Roman, Italian or provincial. He had shown that he was not afraid of vested interests. But Caesar was not a revolutionary. . . .

[He] postponed decision about the permanent ordering of the State. It was too difficult. Instead, he would set out for the wars again, to Macedonia and to the eastern frontier of the Empire. At Rome he was hampered: abroad he might enjoy his conscious mastery of men and events, as before in Gaul. Easy victories—but not the urgent needs of the Roman People.

About Caesar's ultimate designs there can be opinion, but no certainty. The acts and projects of his Dictatorship do not reveal them. For the rest, the evidence is partisan—or posthumous. No statement of unrealized intentions is a safe guide to history, for it is unverifiable and therefore the most attractive form of misrepresentation. The enemies of Caesar spread rumours to discredit the living Dictator: Caesar dead became a god and a myth, passing from the realm of history into literature and legend, declamation and propaganda. . . .

Yet speculation cannot be debarred from playing round the high and momentous theme of the last designs of Caesar the Dictator. It has been supposed and contended that Caesar either desired to establish or had actually inaugurated an institution unheard of in Rome and unimagined there—monarchic rule, despotic and absolute, based upon worship of the ruler, after the pattern of the monarchies of the Hellenistic East. Thus may Caesar be represented as the heir in all things of Alexander the Macedonian and as the anticipator of Caracalla, a king and a god incarnate, levelling class and nation, ruling a subject, united and uniform world by right divine.

This extreme simplification of long and diverse ages of history seems to suggest that Caesar alone of contemporary Roman statesmen possessed either a wide vision of the future or a singular and elementary blindness to the present. But this is only a Caesar of myth or rational construction. . . .

If Caesar must be judged, it is by facts and not by alleged intentions. As his acts and his writings reveal him, Caesar stands out as a realist and an opportunist. In the short time at his disposal he can hardly have made plans for a long future or laid the foundation of a consistent government. Whatever it might be, it would owe more to the needs of the moment than to alien or theoretical models. More important the business in hand; it was expedited in swift and arbitrary fashion. Caesar made plans and decisions in the company of his intimates and secretaries: the Senate voted but did not deliberate. As the Dictator was on the point of departing in the spring of 44 B.C. for several years of campaigning in the Balkans and the East, he tied up magistracies and provincial commands in advance by placing them, according to the traditional Roman way, in the hands of loyal partisans, or of reconciled Pompeians whose good sense should guarantee peace. For that period, at least, a salutary pause from political activity: with the lapse of time the situation might become clearer in one way or another. . . .

At the moment it was intolerable: the autocrat became impatient, annoyed by covert opposition, petty criticism and laudations of dead Cato. That he was unpopular he well knew. "For all his genius, Caesar could not see a way out," as one of his friends was subsequently to remark. And there was no going back. To Caesar's clear mind and love of rapid decision, this brought a tragic sense of impotence and frustration—he had been all things and it was no good. He had surpassed the good fortune of Sulla Felix and the glory of Pompeius Magnus. In vain—reckless ambition had ruined the Roman State and baffled itself in the end. Of the melancholy that descended upon Caesar there stands the best of testimony—"my life has been long enough, whether reckoned in years or in renown." The words were remembered. The most eloquent of his contemporaries did not disdain to plagiarize them.

The question of ultimate intentions becomes irrelevant. Caesar was slain for what he was, not for what he might become. . . .

It is not necessary to believe that Caesar planned to establish at Rome a "Hellenistic Monarchy," whatever meaning may attach to that phrase. The Dictatorship was enough. The rule of the *nobiles,* he could see, was an anachronism in a world-empire; and so was the power of the Roman plebs when all Italy enjoyed the franchise. Caesar in truth was more conservative and Roman than many have fancied; and no Roman conceived of government save through an oligarchy. But Caesar was being forced into an autocratic position. It meant the lasting domination of one man instead of the rule of the law, the constitution and the Senate; it announced the triumph soon or late of new forces and new ideas, the elevation of the army and the provinces, the depression of the traditional governing class. Caesar's autocracy appeared to be much more than a temporary expedient to liquidate the heritage of the Civil War and reinvigorate the organs of the Roman State. It was going to last—and the Roman aristocracy was not to be permitted to govern and exploit the Empire in its own fashion. The tragedies of history do not arise from the conflict of conventional right and wrong. They are more august and more complex. Caesar and Brutus each had right on his side. . . .

Without a party a statesman is nothing. He sometimes forgets that awkward fact. If the leader or principal agent of a faction goes beyond the wishes of his allies and emancipates himself from control, he may have to be dropped or suppressed. . . .

When Caesar took the Dictatorship for life and the sworn allegiance of senators, it seemed clear that he had escaped from the shackles of party to supreme and personal rule. For this reason, certain of the most prominent of his adherents combined with Republicans and Pompeians to remove their leader. The Caesarian party thus split by the assassination of the Dictator none the less survived, joined for a few months with Republicans in a new and precarious front of security and vested interests led by the Dictator's political deputy until a new leader, emerging unexpected, at first tore it in pieces again, but ultimately, after conquering the last of his rivals, converted the old Caesarian party into a national government in a transformed State. The composition and vicissitudes of that party, though less dramatic in unity of theme than the careers and exploits of the successive leaders, will yet help to recall the ineffable complexities of authentic history.

Suggestions for Further Reading

As in the case of Alexander, the ancient sources for the life of Julius Caesar are among the liveliest and most entertaining accounts of him. Students are encouraged to read the rest of Suetonius's sketch beyond what is excerpted in this chapter. They are also encouraged to read Plutarch's Life of Caesar, which, as we have noted, he wrote to be compared with his Life of Alexander. Plutarch and Suetonius between them give us most of the anecdotal matter commonly associated with Caesar. We have in addition, as also noted above, the considerable volume of Caesar's own writings in several attractive modern editions, *The Gallic War,* tr. and ed. Moses Hadas (New York: Modern

Library, 1957), tr. J. Warrington (New York: Heritage, 1955), and tr. S. A. Handford (Baltimore: Penguin, 1965); and *The Civil War*, ed. and tr. Jane F. Mitchell (Baltimore: Penguin, 1967). We also have references to Caesar scattered throughout the works of such contemporaries as Cicero and Sallust.

Caesar has always been a fascinating figure, and there are an impossibly large number of biographies of him. Two can be especially recommended to students. Probably the best brief biography is J. P. V. D. Balsdon, *Julius Caesar and Rome* (London: The English Universities Press, 1967), an authoritative work by an established authority, another in the excellent "Teach Yourself History Library" series. Students may prefer the somewhat larger and more lavish Michael Grant, *Caesar* (London: Weidenfeld and Nicolson, 1974), in the "Great Lives" series; it is interesting and readable as well as authoritative, another book by one of the best modern popularizers of ancient history. Zwi Yavetz, *Julius Caesar and his Public Image* (Ithaca, N.Y.: Cornell University Press, 1983) attempts to assess the various answers to the question of why Caesar was assassinated. Students will find the last chapter, "Public Opinion and the Ides of March," particularly useful as a summary and review of the problem.

There are also many books dealing with Caesar's era and the late Roman republic. One of the best of these, and one that combines the account of the man and the era, is Matthias Gelzer, *Caesar: Politician and Statesman*, tr. Peter Needham (Cambridge, Mass.: Harvard University Press, 1968). Despite its relentlessly prosaic quality, it is an important interpretive work by a great German scholar, stressing Caesar as a political figure of genius and paralleling the views of Sir Ronald Syme, which are represented in this chapter. A somewhat broader account, still considered a standard work by many authorities, is that of F. E. Adcock in chs. 15–17 in vol. 9 of the *Cambridge Ancient History* (Cambridge, England: Cambridge University Press, 1932). Also recommended are R. E. Smith, *The Failure of the Roman Republic* (Cambridge, England: Cambridge University Press, 1955); the somewhat more detailed Erich S. Gruen, *The Last Generation of the Roman Republic* (Berkeley: University of California Press, 1974); and the now famous small study by Lily Ross Taylor, *Party Politics in the Age of Caesar* (Berkeley: University of California Press, 1975 [1949]).

Finally, two special studies are recommended, the attractive small book by F. E. Adcock, *Caesar as Man of Letters* (Cambridge, England: Cambridge University Press, 1956), and Gen. John F. C. Fuller, *Julius Caesar: Man, Soldier, and Tyrant* (New Brunswick, N.J.: Rutgers University Press, 1965), a lively, opinionated, and somewhat debunking book by a great military historian about Caesar as a less-than-brilliant general.

AUGUSTINE:
THE CEREBRAL SAINT

354	Born
383	Went to teach in Rome, then Milan
387	Baptism by St. Ambrose
396	Made Bishop of Hippo
396–410	Struggle with the Donatist heresy
c. 400	The *Confessions*
c. 413–26	*The City of God*
c. 397–428	*De doctrina christiana*
410–430	Struggle with the Pelagian heresy
430	Died

The historian Edward Gibbon capsulized the rise of Christianity in this dramatic sentence: "A pure and humble religion gently insinuated itself into the minds of men, grew up in silence and obscurity, derived new vigor from opposition, and finally erected the triumphant banner of the Cross on the ruins of the Capitol."[1] While modern historians may quarrel with one aspect or another of Gibbon's views, most agree that by the mid-fourth century, Christianity was the dominant spiritual force in the Roman Empire. The public policy of persecution had been replaced by toleration and then endorsement; and since Constantine, every emperor, save only Julian "the Apostate" (361–363), had been at least nominally Christian. The church as an institution had taken form, and its officials were people of importance, from one end of the empire to the other. It was at long last both fashionable and profitable to be Christian; and persons of position and substance adopted the faith.

It is thus not surprising that a bright, well-educated, and ambitious young man of the late fourth century should have been attracted to Christianity. What is unusual is that he wrote a sensitive, detailed

---

[1]*Decline and Fall of the Roman Empire*, Ch. XV.1.

account of the experience of his conversion, entitled the *Confessions*. This work is all the more valuable, for the man who wrote it went on to become the most important theologian of the early church and one of the most influential thinkers in human history—St. Augustine.

The Confessions

ST. AUGUSTINE

The Confessions *is a remarkable book. A modern critic has called it
". . . one of the truest, frankest, and most heart-lifting autobiographies ever
written."[2] For us, however, its "heart-lifting" inspirational quality—and
surely it was written to impart just that quality—will be of less interest than
its fascinating revelation of the process by which a tough-minded intellectual, examining his own life, was brought not only to embrace Christianity
but to make it the very center of his being. No document has ever laid open
that process more candidly or more searchingly than the* Confessions.

*Aurelius Augustinus was born at Tagaste in Roman North Africa in 354,
of a not-uneducated pagan father and a devoutly Christian mother. Signs of
intellectual precocity led his father to send the boy to school at an early age
and at considerable financial sacrifice. He was trained first at the nearby
town of Madaura and then at the great city of Carthage, the capital and the
intellectual and trade center of Roman Africa. Augustine was studying to be
a professional rhetorician. And neither the program nor its aims—the study
of eloquence for the sake of persuasion—had changed in centuries. When he
finished his schooling, Augustine became a teacher of rhetoric. He also became a member of the Manichaeans, a sect particularly strong in North
Africa that taught a form of radical dualism as its principal spiritual-
intellectual doctrine.[3] Though he remained a Manichaean for some nine
years, Augustine was also attracted to astrology; he was impressed with
Cicero's urbane, academic skepticism; he studied Aristotle and Plato and the
fashionable Neoplatonism[4]; and he sampled and rejected the Christian Bible.
Without fully realizing it, he was beginning his search for belief.*

---

[2]Stewart Perowne, *The End of the Roman World* (New York: Crowell, 1967), p. 143.

[3]In its Manichaean form, this represented the philosophical opposition of such
entities as light and darkness, warmth and cold, flesh and spirit, body and soul. And,
though Augustine denounced it, he retained some strong Manichaean influences in
his own thought.—ED.

[4]Plotinus, the greatest of Neoplatonic philosophers, and his popularizer Porphyry
had died only half a century earlier, and their movement still enjoyed great popularity,
especially among intellectuals. It profited from the general ancient reverence for Plato
while emphasizing the more transcendental aspects of his system. The result was the
creation, in Neoplatonism, of something approaching a religion. It had a powerful,
ongoing influence in the history both of philosophy and theology, and even St. Augustine never entirely abandoned some of its tenets.—ED.

By this time Augustine had become a teacher in his native Tagaste, had taken a wife, and had fathered a son. He then obtained a teaching position in Carthage and was becoming a well-known rhetorician and philosopher when, in 383 at the age of twenty-nine, he went to teach in Rome. Within a year, he heard of a position as master of rhetoric to the great city of Milan, which in these declining years of the Roman empire had come to overshadow the old capital as the center of imperial government in the West. It was an important position; Augustine competed for it, delivering a public oration, and was awarded the post.

It was in Milan that Augustine came under the influence of one of the most powerful figures in the early church, St. Ambrose, the Bishop of Milan, who, as Augustine says, "received me as a father." The process of conversion was under way. But it was to be neither an easy nor a painless process. For such a man as Augustine had hard intellectual questions to ask of any faith.

Let St. Augustine himself continue the story.

I began to love him at first not as a teacher of the truth (for I had quite despaired of finding it in your Church) but simply as a man who was kind and generous to me. I used to listen eagerly when he preached to the people, but my intention was not what it should have been; I was, as it were, putting his eloquence on trial to see whether it came up to his reputation, or whether its flow was greater or less than I had been told. So I hung intently on his words, but I was not interested in what he was really saying and stood aside from this in contempt. I was much pleased by the charm of his style, which, although it was more learned, was still, so far as the manner of delivery was concerned, not so warm and winning as the style of Faustus.[5] With regard to the actual matter there was, of course, no comparison. Faustus was merely roving around among Manichaean fallacies, while Ambrose was healthily teaching salvation. But salvation is far from sinners of the kind that I was then. Yet, though I did not realize it, I was drawing gradually nearer.

For although my concern was not to learn what he said but only to hear how he said it (this empty interest being all that remained to me, now that I had despaired of man's being able to find his way to you), nevertheless, together with the language, which I admired, the subject matter also, to which I was indifferent, began to enter into my mind. Indeed I could not separate the one from the other. And as I

[5]A famous Manichaean preacher. Augustine had eagerly anticipated hearing him but was disappointed when he did. From this point, his break with Manichaeanism began.—ED.

opened my heart in order to recognize how eloquently he was speaking it occurred to me at the same time (though this idea came gradually) how truly he was speaking. . . .

By this time my mother had joined me. Her piety had given her strength and she had followed me over land and sea, confident in you throughout all dangers. In the perils of the sea it was she who put the fresh heart into the sailors although as a rule it is for the sailors to reassure the passengers who are inexperienced on the high seas. But she promised them that they would get safely to land because you had promised this to her in a vision. She found me in grave danger indeed, my danger being that of despairing of ever discovering the truth. I told her that, though I was not yet a Catholic Christian, I was certainly no longer a Manichaean; but she showed no great signs of delight, as though at some unexpected piece of news, because she already felt at ease regarding that particular aspect of my misery; she bewailed me as one dead, certainly, but as one who would be raised up again by you; she was in her mind laying me before you on the bier so that you might say to the widow's son: *"Young man, I say unto thee, Arise,"* and he should revive and begin to speak and you should give him to his mother. So her heart was shaken by no storm of exultation when she heard that what she had daily begged you with her tears should happen had in so large a part taken place—that I was now rescued from falsehood, even though I had not yet attained the truth. She was indeed quite certain that you, who had promised her the whole, would give her the part that remained, and she replied to me very calmly and with a heart full of confidence that she believed in Christ that, before she departed from this life, she would see me a true Catholic. . . .

I was not yet groaning in prayer for you to help me. My mind was intent on inquiry and restless in dispute. I considered Ambrose himself, who was honored by people of such importance, a lucky man by worldly standards; only his celibacy seemed to me rather a burden to bear. But I could neither guess nor tell from my own experience what hope he had within him, what were his struggles against the temptations of his exalted position, what solace he found in adversity; nor could I tell of that hidden mouth of his (the mouth of his heart), what joys it tasted in the rumination of your bread. And he on his side did not know of the turmoil in which I was or the deep pit of danger before my feet. I was not able to ask him the questions I wanted to ask in the way I wanted to ask them, because I was prevented from having an intimate conversation with him by the crowds of people, all of whom had some business with him and to whose infirmities he was a servant. And for the very short periods of time when he was not with them, he was either refreshing his body with necessary food or his mind with reading. When he was reading, his eyes went over the pages and his heart looked into the sense, but voice and tongue were resting. Often when we came to him (for no one was forbidden to come in, and it was not customary for visitors even to be announced) we found him reading, always to himself and never otherwise; we would sit in silence for a long time, not venturing to interrupt him in his intense concentration on his task, and then we would go away again. We guessed that in the very small time which he was able to set aside for mental refreshment he wanted to be free from the disturbance of other people's business and would not like to have his attention distracted. . . . But I needed to find him with plenty of time to spare if I was to pour out to him the full flood of agitation boiling up inside me, and I could never find him like this. Yet every Sunday I listened to him rightly preaching to the people the word of truth, and I became more and more sure that all those knots of cunning calumny which, in their attacks on the holy books, my deceivers had tied could be unraveled. . . .

. . . So I was both confounded and converted, and I was glad, my God, that your only Church, the body of your only son—that Church in which the name of Christ had been put upon me as an infant[6]—was not flavored with this childish nonsense and did not, in her healthy doctrine, maintain the view that you, the Creator of all things, could be, in the form of a human body, packed into a definite space which, however mighty and large, must still be bounded on all sides. . . . But it was the same with me as with a man who, having once had a bad doctor, is afraid of trusting himself even to a good one. So it was with the health of my soul which could not possibly be cured except by believing, but refused to be cured for fear of believing something falser. So I resisted your hands, for it was you who prepared the medicines of faith and applied them to the diseases of the world and gave them such potency. . . .

And I, as I looked back, over my life, was quite amazed to think of how long a time had passed since my nineteenth year, when I had first become inflamed with a passion for wisdom and had resolved that, when once I found it, I would leave behind me all the empty hopes and deceitful frenzies of vain desires. And now I was in my thirtieth year, still sticking in the same mud, still greedy for the enjoyment of things present, which fled from me and wasted me away, and all the time saying: "I shall find it tomorrow. See, it will become quite clear

---

[6]Though he had not been baptized as a child, he had apparently been at least nominally Christian, through his mother's influence.—ED.

and I shall grasp it. Now Faustus will come and explain everything. What great men the Academics are! Is it true that no certainty can possibly be comprehended for the direction of our lives? No, it cannot be. We must look into things more carefully and not give up hope. And now see, those things in the Scriptures which used to seem absurd are not absurd; they can be understood in a different and perfectly good way. I shall take my stand where my parents placed me as a child until I can see the truth plainly. But where shall I look for it? And when shall I look for it? Ambrose has no spare time; nor have I time for reading. And where can I find the books? From where can I get them and when can I get them? Can I borrow them from anybody? I must arrange fixed periods of time and set aside certain hours for the health of my soul. A great hope has dawned. The Catholic faith does not teach the things I thought it did and vainly accused it of teaching. The learned men of that faith think it quite wrong to believe that God is bounded within the shape of a human body. Why then do I hesitate to knock, so that the rest may be laid open to me? My pupils take up all my time in the morning. But what do I do for the rest of the day? Why not do this? But, if I do, how shall I find time to call on influential friends whose support will be useful to me? When shall I prepare the lessons for which my pupils pay? When shall I have time to relax and to refresh my mind from all my preoccupations?" . . . As I became more unhappy, so you drew closer to me. Your right hand was ready, it was ready to drag me out of the mud and to wash me; but I did not know. And there was nothing to call me back from that deeper gulf of carnal pleasure, except the fear of death and of judgment to come, and this, whatever the opinions I held from time to time, never left my mind. . . .

As to me, I would certainly say and I firmly believed that you—our Lord, the true God, who made not only our souls but our bodies, and not only our souls and bodies but all men and all things—were undefilable and unalterable and in no way to be changed, and yet I still could not understand clearly and distinctly what was the cause of evil. Whatever it might be, however, I did realize that my inquiry must not be carried out along lines which would lead me to believe that the immutable God was mutable; if I did that, I should become myself the very evil which I was looking for. And so I pursued the inquiry without anxiety, being quite certain that what the Manichees said was not true. I had turned against them with my whole heart, because I saw that in their inquiries into the origin of evil they were full of evil themselves; for they preferred to believe that your substance could suffer evil rather than that their substance could do evil. . . . So I thought of your creation as finite and as filled with you, who were infinite. And I said: "Here is God, and here is what God has created; and God is good and is most mightily and incomparably better than all these. Yet He, being good, created them good, and see how He surrounds them and fills them. Where, then, is evil? Where did it come from and how did it creep in here? What is its root and seed? Or does it simply not exist? In that case why do we fear and take precautions against something that does not exist? Or if there is no point in our fears, then our fears themselves are an evil which goads and tortures the heart for no good reason—and all the worse an evil if there is nothing to be afraid of and we are still afraid. Therefore, either there is evil which we fear or else the fact that we do fear is evil. Where then does evil come from, seeing that God is good and made all things good? Certainly it was the greater and supreme Good who made these lesser goods, yet still all are good, both the creator and his creation. Where then did evil come from? Or was there some evil element in the material of creation, and did God shape and form it, yet still leave in it something which He did not change into good? But why? Being omnipotent, did He lack the power to change and transform the whole so that no trace of evil should remain? Indeed why should He choose to use such material for making anything? Would He not rather, with this same omnipotence, cause it not to exist at all? Could it exist against His will? Or, supposing it was eternal, why for so long through all the infinite spaces of time did He allow it to exist and then so much later decide to make something out of it? Or, if He did suddenly decide on some action, would not the omnipotent prefer to act in such a way that this evil material should cease to exist, and that He alone should be, the whole, true, supreme, and infinite Good? Or, since it was not good that He who was good should frame and create something not good, then why did He not take away and reduce to nothing the material that was evil and then Himself provide good material from which to create all things? For He would not be omnipotent if He could not create something good without having to rely on material which He had not Himself created."

These were the kind of thoughts[7] which I turned over and over in my unhappy heart, a heart overburdened with those biting cares that came from my fear of death and my failure to discover the truth. Yet the faith of your Christ, our Lord and Saviour, professed in the Catholic Church, remained steadfastly fixed in my heart, even though it was on many points still unformed and swerving from the right rule of

---

[7]The long and complex foregoing discussion of "the problem of evil" relates, on the one hand, to Augustine's rejection of Manicheanism, which explained evil by identifying it with matter, and, on the other, to his own important speculations on the problem of free will and predestination.—ED.

doctrine. But, nevertheless, my mind did not abandon it, but rather drank more and more deeply of it every day.

By this time too I had rejected the fallacious forecasts and impious ravings of the astrologers. . . .

But then, after reading these books of the Platonists which taught me to seek for a truth which was incorporeal, I came to see your *invisible things, understood by those things which are made.* I fell back again from this point, but still I had an apprehension of what, through the darkness of my mind, I was not able to contemplate; I was certain that you are and that you are infinite, yet not in the sense of being diffused through space whether infinite or finite: that you truly are, and are always the same, not in any part or by any motion different or otherwise: also that all other things are from you, as is proved most certainly by the mere fact that they exist. On all these points I was perfectly certain, but I was still too weak to be able to enjoy you. I talked away as if I were a finished scholar; but, if I had not sought the way to you in Christ our Saviour, what would have been finished would have been my soul. For I had begun to want to have the reputation of a wise man; my punishment was within me, but I did not weep; I was merely puffed up with my knowledge. Where was that charity which builds from the foundation of humility, the foundation which is Christ Jesus? Humility was not a subject which those books would ever have taught me. Yet I believe that you wanted me to come upon these books before I made a study of your Scriptures. You wanted the impression made by them on me to be printed in my memory, so that when later I had become, as it were, tamed by your books (your fingers dressing my wounds), I should be able to see clearly what the difference is between presumption and confession, between those who see their goal without seeing how to get there and those who see the way which leads to that happy country which is there for us not only to perceive but to live in. For if I had been first trained in your Scriptures and by my familiarity with them had found you growing sweet to me, and had then afterward come upon these books of the Platonists, it is possible that they might have swept me away from the solid basis of piety; or, even if I had held firmly to that healthy disposition which I had imbibed, I might have thought that the same disposition could be acquired by someone who had read only the Platonic books.[8]

---

[8]This is a reference to the Neoplatonic writings that Augustine had again taken up with renewed interest. These works had long been esteemed by the Christians as being an aid to faith. Notice that they are so regarded by Augustine.—ED.

So I most greedily seized upon the venerable writings of your spirit and in particular the works of the apostle Paul. In the past it had sometimes seemed to me that he contradicted himself and that what he said conflicted with the testimonies of the law and the prophets; but all these difficulties had now disappeared; I saw one and the same face of pure eloquence and learned *to rejoice with trembling*. Having begun, I discovered that everything in the Platonists which I had found true was expressed here, but it was expressed to the glory of your grace. . . .

> *Augustine, convinced now on the intellectual plane, retires to a garden with his friend Alypius, who had accompanied him from Africa—and the controversy "in my heart" begins.*

So went the controversy in my heart—about self, and self against self. And Alypius stayed close by me, waiting to see how this strange agitation of mine would end.

And now from my hidden depths my searching thought had dragged up and set before the sight of my heart the whole mass of my misery. Then a huge storm rose up within me bringing with it a huge downpour of tears. So that I might pour out all these tears and speak the words that came with them I rose up from Alypius (solitude seemed better for the business of weeping) and went further away so that I might not be embarrassed even by his presence. This was how I felt and he realized it. No doubt I had said something or other, and he could feel the weight of my tears in the sound of my voice. And so I rose to my feet, and he, in a state of utter amazement, remained in the place where we had been sitting. I flung myself down on the ground somehow under a fig tree and gave free rein to my tears; they streamed and flooded from my eyes, an *acceptable sacrifice to Thee*. And I kept saying to you, not perhaps in these words, but with this sense: "*And Thou, O Lord, how long? How long, Lord; wilt Thou be angry forever? Remember not our former iniquities.*" For I felt that it was these which were holding me fast. And in my misery I would exclaim: "How long, how long this 'tomorrow and tomorrow'? Why not now? Why not finish this very hour with my uncleanness?"

So I spoke, weeping in the bitter contrition of my heart. Suddenly a voice reaches my ears from a nearby house. It is the voice of a boy or a girl (I don't know which) and in a kind of singsong the words are constantly repeated: "Take it and read it. Take it and read it." At once my face changed, and I began to think carefully of whether the singing of words like these came into any kind of game which children play, and I could not remember that I had ever heard anything like it before. I checked the force of my tears and rose to my feet, being quite certain that I must interpret this as a divine command to me to open the book and read the first passage which I should come upon. For I had heard this about Antony[9]: he had happened to come in when the Gospel was being read, and as though the words read were spoken directly to himself, had received the admonition: *Go, sell that thou hast, and give to the poor, and thou shalt have treasure in heaven, and come and follow me.* And by such an oracle he had been immediately converted to you.

So I went eagerly back to the place where Alypius was sitting, since it was there that I had left the book of the Apostle when I rose to my feet. I snatched up the book, opened it, and read in silence the passage upon which my eyes first fell: *Not in rioting and drunkenness, not in chambering and wantonness, not in strife and envying: but put ye on the Lord Jesus Christ, and make not provision for the flesh in concupiscence.* I had no wish to read further; there was no need to. For immediately I had reached the end of this sentence it was as though my heart was filled with a light of confidence and all the shadows of my doubt were swept away.

The Confessions: What Did They Mean?

ETIENNE GILSON

Saint Augustine is one of the world's most complex thinkers. Everything he wrote had multiple levels of meaning that have fascinated critics and commentators since his own time. This is true even of so seemingly simple and straightforward an account as that which we have just presented from the Confessions. *To answer the question, what did the conversion of Augustine mean—and the account of it in the* Confessions*—we turn to an analysis written by the greatest authority on medieval philosophy in this century, the French Catholic scholar Etienne Gilson (d. 1978), from his important work,* Introduction à l'étude de saint Augustin, *translated as* The Christian Philosophy of Saint Augustine. *Gilson begins his analysis at about the point where we picked up the narrative in the* Confessions.

[9]The Egyptian desert hermit, St. Anthony. Augustine and his friends had only recently heard the whole miraculous story of St. Anthony from a mutual friend who had visited them. Thus, it was much in his mind.—ED.

Whatever his idea of God and the extent of his scepticism may have been, Augustine had never lost faith in the existence of a provident God. How, then, could one avoid suspecting that there was a final source of authority? How could anyone help thinking that God willed the authority of Scripture and of the Church which interprets it precisely in order to provide all men with the doctrine of salvation couched in humble language suited to their grasp? Yet it is not merely for the ignorant and simple that the authority of faith can prove salutary; it is salutary for the wise as well. Since the wise man does not always stay on the level of his wisdom, he is happy to find the support of authority available in his moments of weariness. Hence, one can believe before understanding because there are positive reasons for believing. In Catholicism authority does come before reason, but there are reasons for accepting authority; in fact, in one sense, we should never believe anything if we did not first understand that we have to believe it. From this point it was but a short way to taking the last step and bending reason to faith. Augustine finally took the step and accepted the doctrine of salvation contained in the Scriptures, guaranteed by the Church's authority and based on Christ, the Son of God.

To maintain, as some have hoped to do, that Augustine was not a Christian at this time is to contradict all the texts and, while pretending to be critical, to destroy the historical method itself. To imagine that his conversion was perfect and complete from this moment is to fail completely to recognize its character as Augustine himself has revealed it. In his own eyes it did not consist in an instantaneous act; it was a continuing movement that began with his reading of the *Hortensius*,[10] was carried on by his discovery of the spiritual meaning of Scripture and culminated in the act of faith in Christ's Church noted above. He had the faith, he was in the Church, and yet his faith was still unformed, still encumbered with ignorance; and he still had to grasp its content distinctly.

At this period two obstacles still separated him from a faith no longer "unformed and diverging from doctrinal rules" . . . : the first was his unyielding materialism along with the problem of evil of which it made an insoluble enigma; the second was the corruption of his own moral life. He was in search, not of a theory alone, but of a practice as well. The wisdom he sought was a rule of life: adhering to it meant practicing it. Now he was impressed by the fact that the lives of Christians like St. Anthony, the hermit, or St. Ambrose translated an evident wisdom into action. Here was detachment from the goods

---

[10]A book of Cicero, now lost, that was extremely influential in the early thought of Augustine.—ED.

of this world, continence, chastity, the soul's freedom from the body, everything which gave evidence of perfect self-mastery. But Augustine was faced with a dilemma from which he could not free himself. Judging from his own personal experience continence was impossible, but the lives of saints about whom he had read or who were there for him to see showed that it was possible. Consequently, he was not merely a believer who did not have a correct knowledge of the content of his faith, he was also a man who aspired to the Christian life but lacked the power to live it. His final liberation was accomplished in two stages, namely by his contact with Neoplatonism and with St. Paul.

Augustine's introduction to Neoplatonism was brought about by a man filled with appalling pride. He gave him a Latin translation of the books of Plotinus and perhaps of Porphyry as well.[11] The effect of this contact was to reveal philosophical spiritualism to him. In these books he found first doctrine of the divine Word, the creation of the world in the Word and the illumination of men by a divine light which was purely spiritual in nature; but he did not find the Incarnation. Another acquisition which proved decisive for him was the discovery that, since God is immaterial and immutably subsistent truth, He is Being, and compared with Him changing things do not truly deserve the name "beings." Of such things it can neither be said that they are nor that they are not.

A third ray of light for Augustine was the idea that everything is good to the extent that it exists. When the objection is raised that beings are not good because they become corrupt, we forget that they must first be good before they can become corrupt. Evil is the deprivation of being, and if we follow this to its conclusion, the complete deprivation of good would bring about absolute evil and would mean by definition the complete deprivation of being, and this would be nothing. This is to say that evil is only the absence and lack of something. Instead of being an entity, evil is nothing.

One final conclusion follows from this, a conclusion that freed Augustine of his metaphysical anguish once and for all. Since evil is nothing God cannot be its author. Everything that exists is good to the extent that it exists. What is true of material entities is also true of spiritual entities, and what is true of their substances is true of their acts as well, even of evil acts like sins, because these imply some good in so far as they imply being. As soon as he saw this clearly, Augustine was finally given some respite; his distraction subsided, his soul awak-

---

[11]His fellow rhetorician Marius Victorinus. The reference is to Plotinus (205–270), the leading Neoplatonic philosopher, whom Augustine surely read, and to Porphyry (c. 234–c. 305), Plotinus' chief biographer and editor.—Ed.

ened to the knowledge of God. He saw in God an infinite, spiritual substance, and for the first time his view was not that of the flesh but of the spirit.

In its essential features, this was the discovery Neoplatonism brought him. Its importance cannot be exaggerated, provided we do not reduce his conversion to that discovery. In his view, it meant a purification and spiritualization of his Christianity. After Plotinus had made him attentive, he entered into himself and with God's help discovered the spiritual and immaterial nature of the Light of which St. John speaks. In short, Plotinus enabled him to grasp the spiritual nature of the Christian God and the unreal nature of evil. That this vision was indissolubly philosophical and religious is incontestable. He discovered the purely spiritual nature of the Christian God whom he had already accepted through faith. We have here a philosophical vision combined with a religious experience and the two cannot be separated without falsifying arbitrarily the testimony of Augustine himself.

No matter which account of these events we follow, whether that given in the *Contra Academicos* or that of the *Confessions,* we see that the effect, surprising as it seems to us, was to lead Augustine to read St. Paul. The hidden reason for this apparently strange combination was that Augustine was confronted by two pieces of evidence: on the one hand, Christ's admirable life in which he believed through the Scriptures as well as the lives of saints who had imitated Him; and on the other, the clear evidence of Plotinus' philosophy which he had just discovered. Now the good and the true cannot contradict each other, therefore Christian doctrine must be in essential agreement with the thought of Plotinus. It was to test this hypothesis that he took up, tremblingly, the Epistles of St. Paul. One final decisive illumination awaited him there, namely the doctrine of sin and redemption through the grace of Jesus Christ.

In Plotinus Augustine had found the whole prologue of St. John's Gospel with the exception of the one essential fact that the Word became flesh and dwelt amongst us. Reading the Neoplatonists enables us to know the truth but it gives no means of attaining it. By becoming flesh the Word came to give men something more than precepts; He gave them an example capable of bringing souls to themselves and leading them to God. As he read St. Paul he found not only the harmony between the good and true that he had hoped to find, but more important still, he saw that all philosophical truth had already been revealed to men by God and made available by a divine authority which made it unnecessary for their feeble reasons to exhaust themselves in long study. In addition he found the basic cause of his own moral impotence. St. Paul's Christianity makes it possible for the Platonism of the mind to become a thing of the heart, for the Platonism of theory to become practice. To say with Plotinus that spirit is distinct from flesh is in no sense to free the spirit from the flesh. Although Augustine might follow Plotinus in his metaphysical flights towards the intelligible, he was certain to fall back again beneath the weight of his carnal habits until St. Paul showed him the law of sin and the need of grace to set him free from it. Only after this last discovery did he see philosophy in all its grandeur, but from that moment also philosophy was always to mean wisdom, and wisdom was always to imply the life of grace, the acceptance of those things God grants the humble who receive them and denies the proud who claim to provide them for themselves.

The Confessions: How Did They Work?

PETER BROWN

The Confessions *was not only a work tied into the philosophic system of Augustine, it was also a work tied into his responsibilities as a bishop, a servant of the church. In this sense, like so many of Augustine's other works, it was practical in intent. This is the interpretation of the historian Peter Brown, whose* Augustine of Hippo: A Biography *is the best modern biography of Augustine. Brown argues that the book was meant for the* spiritales, *the "men of the spirit" of Augustine's time, and for those whom Augustine hoped to convert to the spirit. For, as Brown sees it, the* Confessions *was a missionary work, among other things, in which Augustine intended to hold up the example of his own life in order to influence the lives of others. The following excerpts are taken from Brown's* Augustine of Hippo.

Wandering, temptations, sad thoughts of mortality and the search for truth: these had always been the stuff of autobiography for fine souls, who refused to accept superficial security. Pagan philosophers had already created a tradition of "religious autobiography" in this vein: it will be continued by Christians in the fourth century, and will reach its climax in the *Confessions* of St. Augustine.

Augustine, therefore, did not need to look far to find an audience for the *Confessions.* It had been created for him quite recently, by the amazing spread of asceticism in the Latin world. The *Confessions* was a book for the *servi Dei,* for the "servants of God," it is a classic document of the tastes of a group of highly sophisticated men, the *spiritales,* the "men of the spirit." It told such men just what they wanted to know about—the course of a notable conversion; it asked of its readers what they made a habit of asking for themselves—the support of their prayers. It even contained moving appeals to the men who might join this new élite: to the austere Manichee and the pagan Platonist, still standing aloof from the crowded basilicas of the Christians. . . .

The *Confessions* is very much the book of a man who had come to regard his past as a training for his present career. Thus, Augustine will select as important, incidents and problems that immediately betray the new bishop of Hippo. He had come to believe that the understanding and exposition of the Scriptures was the heart of a bishop's life. His relations with the Scriptures, therefore, come to form a constant theme throughout the *Confessions.* His conversion to the Manichees, for instance, is now diagnosed, not in terms of a philosophical preoccupation with the origin of evil, but as a failure to accept the Bible. We see Ambrose through the eyes of a fellow-professional: we meet him as a preacher and exegete, facing the Christian people in the basilica, not as the connoisseur of Plotinus.[12] Augustine remembered how, in his early days in Milan, he had seen the distant figure of Ambrose as a bishop, from the outside only. Now a bishop himself, he will ensure that he will not be seen in this way: he will tell his readers exactly how he still had to struggle with his own temptations; and in the last three books of the *Confessions,* as he meditates on the opening lines of the book of *Genesis,* he will carry his readers with him into his thoughts as he, also, sat in his study, as he had once seen Ambrose sit, wrapt in the silent contemplation of an open page. . . .

The *Confessions,* therefore, is not a book of reminiscences. They are an anxious turning to the past. The note of urgency is unmistakable. "Allow me, I beseech You, grant me to wind round and round in my present memory the spirals of my errors. . . ."

It is also a poignant book. In it, one constantly senses the tension between the "then" of the young man and the "now" of the bishop. The past can come very close: its powerful and complex emotions have only recently passed away; we can still feel their contours through the thin layer of new feeling that has grown over them. . . .

Augustine had been forced to come to terms with himself. The

[12]The third-century Alexandrian scholar who really created Neoplatonism. He was a great favorite of St. Ambrose.—ED.

writing of the *Confessions* was an act of therapy. The many attempts to explain the book in terms of a single, external provocation, or of a single, philosophical *idée fixe,* ignore the life that runs through it. In this attempt to find himself, every single fibre in Augustine's middle age grew together with every other, to make the *Confessions* what it is. . . .

The *Confessions* are a masterpiece of strictly intellectual autobiography. Augustine communicates such a sense of intense personal involvement in the ideas he is handling, that we are made to forget that it is an exceptionally difficult book. Augustine paid his audience of *spiritales* the great (perhaps the unmerited) compliment of talking to them, as if they were as steeped in Neo-Platonic philosophy as himself. His Manichaean phase, for instance, is discussed in terms of ideas on which the Platonists regarded themselves as far in advance of the average thought of their age, the ideas of a "spiritual" reality, and of the omnipresence of God. . . .

It is often said that the *Confessions* is not an "autobiography" in the modern sense. This is true, but not particularly helpful. Because, for a Late Roman man, it is precisely this intense, autobiographical vein in the *Confessions,* that sets it apart from the intellectual tradition to which Augustine belonged.

It is more important to realize that the *Confessions* is an autobiography in which the author has imposed a drastic, fully-conscious choice of what is significant. The *Confessions* are, quite succinctly, the story of Augustine's "heart," or of his "feelings"—his *affectus.* An intellectual event, such as the reading of a new book, is registered only, as it were, from the inside, in terms of the sheer excitement of the experience, of its impact on Augustine's feelings: of the *Hortensius* of Cicero, for instance, he would never say "it changed my views" but, so characteristically, "it changed my way of feeling"—*mutavit affectum meum.*

The emotional tone of the *Confessions* strikes any modern reader. The book owes its lasting appeal to the way in which Augustine, in his middle-age, had dared to open himself up to the feelings of his youth. Yet, such a tone was not inevitable. Augustine's intense awareness of the vital role of "feeling" in his past life had come to grow upon him. . . .

Seeing that Augustine wrote his *Confessions* "remembering my wicked ways, thinking them over again in bitterness," it is amazing how little of this bitterness he has allowed to colour his past feelings. They are not made pale by regret: it is plainly the autobiography of a man who, even as a schoolboy, had known what it was to be moved only by "delight," to be bored by duty, who had enjoyed fully what he had enjoyed: " 'One and one is two, two and two is four,' this was a hateful jingle to me: and the greatest treat of all, that sweet illusion—

the Wooden Horse full of armed men, Troy burning and the very ghost of Creusa." . . .

Augustine analyses his past feelings with ferocious honesty. They were too important to him to be falsified by sentimental stereotypes. It is not that he had abandoned strong feeling: he merely believed it possible to transform feelings, to direct them more profitably. This involved scrutinizing them intently. . . .

The *Confessions* are one of the few books of Augustine's, where the title is significant. *Confessio* meant, for Augustine, "accusation of oneself; praise of God." In this one word, he had summed up his attitude to the human condition: it was the new key with which he hoped, in middle age, to unlock the riddle of evil.

Suggestions for Further Reading

St. Augustine was not only an important and influential thinker, he was also a prolific writer, and students are encouraged to read more extensively in his works—certainly to read further in *The Confessions* and at least to try the book generally considered Augustine's most influential work, *The City of God*. Both works are available in a number of editions. For *The City of God*, because of its size and complexity, students may prefer St. Augustine, *The City of God: An Abridged Version*, tr. Gerald G. Walsh, D. B. Zema, Grace Monahan, and D. J. Honan, ed. and intro. V. J. Bourke (New York: Doubleday, 1958). For a further sampling, *An Augustine Reader*, ed. John J. O'Meara (New York: Doubleday, 1973) or *Basic Writings of St. Augustine*, ed. Whitney J. Oates, 2 vols. (New York: Random House, 1948) are recommended.

There is a wilderness of interpretive and explanatory writing about Augustine and his thought, most of it recondite in the extreme, but there are some useful aids. The most readily available and one of the most generally useful is *A Companion to the Study of St. Augustine* ed. Roy W. Battenhouse (New York: Oxford University Press, 1955). A more strictly theological guide of the same sort is Eugène Portalié, *A Guide to the Thought of St. Augustine*, intro. V. J. Bourke, tr. R. J. Bastian (Chicago: Regnery, 1960), the republication and translation of a famous essay from a French dictionary of Catholic theology at the turn of the century. Students can also read from a well-selected series of modern critical essays, *Saint Augustine: His Age, Life and Thought* (Cleveland and New York: Meridian, 1969).

Of a more biographical nature is Frederik van der Meer, *Augustine the Bishop* (London and New York: Sheed and Ward, 1961), a classic work dealing in great detail essentially with Augustine as Bishop of Hippo, the city, its people, the area, and the controversies that involved its famous bishop. Three of those controversies—the Manichaean, the Donatist, and the Pelagian—are examined in considerable detail in Gerald Bonner, *St. Augustine of Hippo: Life and Controversies* (Philadelphia: Westminster Press, 1963). Students may prefer the more general introductory work of Warren Thomas Smith, *Augustine: His Life and Thought* (Atlanta: John Knox Press, 1980) or two other books that are both literary-intellectual biographies: James J. O'Donnell, *Augustine* (Boston: Twayne, 1985) and Henry Chadwick, *Augustine* (Oxford and New York: Oxford University Press, 1986).

There is no lack of books dealing with the historical setting of Augustine and Augustinianism or with late antiquity and the early Middle Ages. Three of the old standard works are still among the best: Ferdinand Lot, *The End of the Ancient World and the Beginnings of the Middle Ages*, tr. Philip and Mariette Leon (New York: Barnes and Noble, 1953 [1931]); Samuel Dill, *Roman Society in the Last Century of the Western Empire* (London: Macmillan, 1898); and M. L. W. Laistner, *Thought and Letters in Western Europe A.D. 500 to 900*, new edition (Ithaca, N.Y.: Cornell University Press, 1957). One of the best recent accounts of the rise of Christianity within late Roman antiquity is R. A. Markus, *Christianity in the Roman World* (New York: Scribners, 1974). Students will find useful (if somewhat heavyweight) a fundamental work of reference, A. H. M. Jones, *The Later Roman Empire 284–602: A Social, Economic, and Administrative Survey*, 2 vols. (Norman: University of Oklahoma Press, 1964). Both more readable and more manageable is Peter Brown, *The World of Late Antiquity* (New York: Harcourt, 1971).

CHARLEMAGNE.

Meissonier.   D.J.Pound.

KING OF FRANCE AND EMPEROR OF THE WEST. A.D. 742.

CHARLEMAGNE
AND THE FIRST EUROPE

742 or 743	Born
768	Joint succession to Frankish throne with his brother Carloman
771	Death of Carloman; beginning of sole rule
774	Conquered Lombard kingdom
772–787	Saxon wars
800	Imperial coronation
814	Died

In the lifetime of St. Augustine, the Roman empire in the West had collapsed. Roman political order was being replaced by regional barbarian kingdoms under their German tribal chiefs, and the West had entered irretrievably upon what an earlier generation of historians was fond of calling "the Dark Ages."

Though the darkness was by no means as pervasive as scholars once thought, the early Middle Ages were a time of great dislocation, surely one of the two or three most important periods of transition in the history of western civilization—for the product of the transition was nothing less than what some historians have called "the first Europe."

It was a Europe no longer classical and imperial, no longer a vast free-trade network of cities governed by a centralized system and ruled by a common law. It was a Europe from which long distance trade had disappeared, to be replaced by an economic localism. It was a Europe of equally localized culture, in which the common classical tradition was maintained by an ever dwindling minority of educated people, with an ever decreasing sophistication. Most, virtually all, of those educated were professional churchmen, for, perhaps most important of all, the first Europe was a Christian Europe.

The great Frankish king Charlemagne (768–814) was, by all accounts and from whatever interpretive viewpoint we choose to see him, the pivotal figure in this first Europe. The Franks were one of the barbarian Germanic tribes that succeeded to the broken pieces of the western empire. By a combination of luck, talent, and timing, they had come to be the leading power among their fellow barbarians. Their position was enhanced by Charlemagne's immediate predecessors, his grandfather Charles Martel and his father, Pepin, who established the claim of his house to the Frankish throne. Frankish supremacy was assured by Charlemagne's dramatic conquests, which brought most of continental western Europe—save only Moslem Spain south of the Ebro River, southern Italy, and the barbarian fringes of the Scandinavian North—under his rule.

Charlemagne's imperial rule was epitomized in his resumption of the ancient imperial title. On Christmas day of the year 800, in the church of St. Peter in Rome, Pope Leo III crowned Charlemagne as "Emperor of the Romans." No one had claimed this exalted title in more than three hundred years, and no barbarian king had ever before presumed to such a dignity. Charlemagne continued to bear his other titles, so we are not sure precisely how he himself saw his imperial role—whether it was an "umbrella" title over his many different dominions, a Christian symbol for "the temporal sword," or simply "a feather in his cap." We do know that it involved him in a delicate and complex negotiation with the other "Emperor of the Romans" in Byzantium, whose rights, however remotely exercised, Charlemagne's act had encroached upon. The assumption of the title, moreover, by virtue of the part played by the pope, was inextricably bound up with the larger role of the church in the secular affairs of the West.

We cannot be sure what Charlemagne's plans for his empire were, although he saw to the imperial succession of his son Louis the Pious. We cannot even be certain of the extent to which Charles was able to realize the plans he did have, for the records of the time simply do not tell us.

But however many unanswered questions remain, the records do contain a precious contemporary account of King Charles, written by his devoted friend, the Frankish noble Einhard.

The Emperor Charlemagne

EINHARD

One of the most obvious signs of the barbarism of early medieval Europe is the scarcity of records. Even more scarce than documentary records are the literary accounts—the biographies, the memoirs, the formal histories—that can give flesh and substance to historical figures. Most, even the greatest, personages of the early Middle Ages remain simply names, with only a handful of facts (and often doubtful "facts" at that) attached to them. Fortunately, this is not the case for Charlemagne. We might wish that Einhard's account had been longer and more detailed, or that he had included more information about Charles's public policy, his political motives, his plans for the empire, and the structure of his reign. But we are lucky to have what we do. Einhard was sensitive about his modest literary gifts. Indeed, he could not even conceive of a formal framework for his account; he simply took Suetonius's biography of Augustus and substituted his own material in the model. But so indebted was Einhard to Charles, his "lord and foster father," and so important were his lord's deeds that he chose to record them rather "than to suffer the most glorious life of this most excellent king, the greatest of all the princes of his day, and his illustrious deeds, hard for men of later times to imitate, to be wrapped in the darkness of oblivion."[1]

Despite its limitations, Einhard's Life of Charlemagne *is an extraordinarily valuable document. It would have been under any circumstances. But its value is enhanced because Einhard was an intimate of the king and his family; he had been raised at Charles's court and later was one of his most trusted councillors. No one was in a better position than Einhard to write on Charles the Great.*

After sketching the background of Charles's dynasty and how the Carolingians (for this is the name historians have given to the house of Carolus Magnus*) succeeded to the Frankish throne, how Charles's father, Pepin, set aside the last of the weak Merovingians with their "vain title of king," Einhard describes in some detail the wars of conquest that earned for Charles the title "Charles the Great"—his pacification of Aquitaine, his conquest of the Lombards and his assumption of the Lombard crown, his long wars with the pagan Saxons along the eastern frontier, his unsuccessful attempt to invade Moslem Spain, his successful quelling of the revolt of*

[1] *The Life of Charlemagne by Einhard* (Ann Arbor: University of Michigan Press, 1960), Preface, p. 16. Translated from the *Monumenta Germaniae* by Samuel Epes Turner.

Bavaria, and his wars against the Avars along the Danube, the Danes,
and other border peoples. Then Einhard continues:

Such are the wars, most skilfully planned and successfully fought,
which this most powerful king waged during the forty-seven years of
his reign. He so largely increased the Frank kingdom, which was
already great and strong when he received it at his father's hands,
that more than double its former territory was added to it. The authority of the Franks was formerly confined to that part of Gaul
included between the Rhine and the Loire, the Ocean and the
Balearic Sea; to that part of Germany which is inhabited by the so-
called Eastern Franks, and is bounded by Saxony and the Danube, the
Rhine and the Saale—this stream separates the Thuringians from the
Sorabians; and to the country of the Alemanni and Bavarians. By the
wars above mentioned he first made tributary Aquitania, Gascony,
and the whole of the region of the Pyrenees as far as the River Ebro,
which rises in the land of the Navarrese, flows through the most
fertile districts of Spain, and empties into the Balearic Sea, beneath
the walls of the city of Tortosa. He next reduced and made tributary
all Italy from Aosta to Lower Calabria, where the boundary line runs
between the Beneventans and the Greeks, a territory more than a
thousand miles long; then Saxony, which constitutes no small part of
Germany, and is reckoned to be twice as wide as the country inhabited
by the Franks, while about equal to it in length; in addition, both
Pannonias, Dacia beyond the Danube, and Istria, Liburnia, and Dal-
matia, except the cities on the coast, which he left to the Greek Emperor for friendship's sake, and because of the treaty that he had
made with him. In fine, he vanquished and made tributary all the
wild and barbarous tribes dwelling in Germany between the Rhine
and the Vistula, the Ocean and the Danube, all of which speak very
much the same language, but differ widely from one another in customs and dress. The chief among them are the Welatabians, the
Sorabians, the Abodriti, and the Bohemians, and he had to make war
upon these; but the rest, by far the larger number, submitted to him
of their own accord.

He added to the glory of his reign by gaining the good will of
several kings and nations. . . . His relations with Aaron, King of the
Persians,[2] who ruled over almost the whole of the East, India ex-
cepted, were so friendly that this prince preferred his favor to that of

[2]This was the famous Harun al-Raschid (786–809), not "King of the Persians" but
the Abbasid Caliph of Baghdad, with whom Charles did indeed enjoy good diplomatic
relations. Harun was most likely interested in a possible alliance against the Byzantine
Empire.—ED.

all the kings and potentates of the earth, and considered that to him alone marks of honor and munificence were due. Accordingly, when the ambassadors sent by Charles to visit the most holy sepulchre and place of resurrection of our Lord and Savior presented themselves before him with gifts, and made known their master's wishes, he not only granted what was asked, but gave possession of that holy and blessed spot. When they returned, he dispatched his ambassadors with them, and sent magnificent gifts, besides stuffs, perfumes, and other rich products of the Eastern lands. A few years before this, Charles had asked him for an elephant, and he sent the only one that he had. The Emperors of Constantinople, Nicephorus, Michael, and Leo, made advances to Charles, and sought friendship and alliance with him by several embassies; and even when the Greeks suspected him of designing to wrest the empire from them, because of his assumption of the title Emperor, they made a close alliance with him, that he might have no cause of offense. In fact, the power of the Franks was always viewed by the Greeks and Romans with a jealous eye, whence the Greek proverb "Have the Frank for your friend, but not for your neighbor." . . .

He liked foreigners, and was at great pains to take them under his protection. There were often so many of them, both in the palace and the kingdom, that they might reasonably have been considered a nuisance; but he, with his broad humanity, was very little disturbed by such annoyances, because he felt himself compensated for these great inconveniences by the praises of his generosity and the reward of high renown.

Charles was large and strong, and of lofty stature, though not disproportionately tall (his height is well known to have been seven times the length of his foot); the upper part of his head was round, his eyes very large and animated, nose a little long, hair fair, and face laughing and merry. Thus his appearance was always stately and dignified, whether he was standing or sitting; although his neck was thick and somewhat short, and his belly rather prominent; but the symmetry of the rest of his body concealed these defects. His gait was firm, his whole carriage manly, and his voice clear, but not so strong as his size led one to expect. His health was excellent, except during the four years preceding his death, when he was subject to frequent fevers; at the last he even limped a little with one foot. Even in those years he consulted rather his own inclinations than the advice of physicians, who were almost hateful to him, because they wanted him to give up roasts, to which he was accustomed, and to eat boiled meat instead. In accordance with the national custom, he took frequent exercise on horseback and in the chase, accomplishments in which scarcely any people in the world can equal the Franks. He enjoyed the exhalations from natural warm springs, and often practiced swimming, in which he was such an adept that none could surpass him; and hence it was that he built his palace at Aix-la-Chapelle, and lived there constantly during his latter years until his death. He used not only to invite his sons to his bath, but his nobles and friends, and now and then a troop of his retinue or bodyguard, so that a hundred or more persons sometimes bathed with him.

He used to wear the national, that is to say, the Frank, dress—next his skin a linen shirt and linen breeches, and above these a tunic fringed with silk; while hose fastened by bands covered his lower limbs, and shoes his feet, and he protected his shoulders and chest in winter by a close-fitting coat of otter or marten skins. Over all he flung a blue cloak, and he always had a sword girt about him, usually one with a gold or silver hilt and belt; he sometimes carried a jeweled sword, but only on great feastdays or at the reception of ambassadors from foreign nations. He despised foreign costumes, however handsome, and never allowed himself to be robed in them, except twice in Rome, when he donned the Roman tunic, chlamys, and shoes; the first time at the request of Pope Hadrian, the second to gratify Leo, Hadrian's successor. On great feastdays he made use of embroidered clothes and shoes bedecked with precious stones, his cloak was fastened by a golden buckle, and he appeared crowned with a diadem of gold and gems, but on other days his dress varied little from the common dress of the people.

Charles was temperate in eating, and particularly so in drinking, for he abominated drunkenness in anybody, much more in himself and those of his household. . . . Charles had the gift of ready and fluent speech, and could express whatever he had to say with the utmost clearness. He was not satisfied with command of his native language merely, but gave attention to the study of foreign ones, and in particular was such a master of Latin that he could speak it as well as his native tongue; but he could understand Greek better than he could speak it. He was so eloquent, indeed, that he might have passed for a teacher of eloquence. He most zealously cultivated the liberal arts, held those who taught them in great esteem, and conferred great honors upon them. He took lessons in grammar of the deacon Peter of Pisa, at that time an aged man. Another deacon, Albin of Britain, surnamed Alcuin, a man of Saxon extraction, who was the greatest scholar of the day, was his teacher in other branches of learning. The King spent much time and labor with him studying rhetoric, dialectics, and especially astronomy; he learned to reckon, and used to investigate the motions of the heavenly bodies most curiously, with an intelligent scrutiny. He also tried to write, and used to keep tablets and blanks in bed under his pillow, that at leisure hours he might accustom his hand to form the letters; however, as he did not begin his efforts in due season, but late in life, they met with ill success.[3]

He cherished with the greatest fervor and devotion the principles of the Christian religion, which had been instilled into him from infancy. Hence it was that he built the beautiful basilica at Aix-la-Chapelle, which he adorned with gold and silver and lamps, and with rails and doors of solid brass. He had the columns and marbles for this structure brought from Rome and Ravenna, for he could not find such as were suitable elsewhere. . . .

He was very forward in succoring the poor, and in the gratuitous generosity which the Greeks call alms, so much so that he not only made a point of giving in his own country and his own kingdom, but when he discovered that there were Christians living in poverty in Syria, Egypt, and Africa, at Jerusalem, Alexandria, and Carthage, he had compassion on their wants, and used to send money over the seas to them. The reason that he zealously strove to make friends with the kings beyond seas was that he might get help and relief to the Christians living under their rule. He cherished the Church of St. Peter the Apostle at Rome above all other holy and sacred places, and heaped its treasury with a vast wealth of gold, silver, and precious stones. He sent great and countless gifts to the popes, and throughout his whole reign the wish that he had nearest at heart was to re-establish the ancient authority of the city of Rome under his care and by his influence, and to defend and protect the Church of St. Peter, and to beautify and enrich it out of his own store above all other churches. Although he held it in such veneration, he only repaired to Rome to pay his vows and make his supplications four times during the whole forty-seven years that he reigned.

When he made his last journey thither, he had also other ends in view. The Romans had inflicted many injuries upon the Pontiff Leo, tearing out his eyes and cutting out his tongue, so that he had been compelled to call upon the King for help. Charles accordingly went to Rome, to set in order the affairs of the Church, which were in great confusion, and passed the whole winter there. It was then that he received the titles of Emperor and Augustus, to which he at first had such an aversion that he declared that he would not have set foot in the Church the day that they were conferred, although it was a great feastday, if he could have foreseen the design of the Pope. He bore very patiently with the jealousy which the Roman emperors showed upon his assuming these titles, for they took this step very ill; and by

---

[3]What is probably meant here is not that Charles literally could not write but that he could not master the precise and beautiful "book hand," the Carolingian Minuscule, developed by Alcuin for the use of the court copyists.—ED.

dint of frequent embassies and letters, in which he addressed them as brothers, he made their haughtiness yield to his magnanimity, a quality in which he was unquestionably much their superior.

It was after he had received the imperial name that, finding the laws of his people very defective (the Franks have two sets of laws, very different in many particulars[4]), he determined to add what was wanting, to reconcile the discrepancies, and to correct what was vicious and wrongly cited in them. However, he went no further in this matter than to supplement the laws by a few capitularies, and those imperfect ones; but he caused the unwritten laws of all the tribes that came under his rule to be compiled and reduced to writing. He also had the old rude songs that celebrate the deeds and wars of the ancient kings written out for transmission to posterity. He began a grammar of his native language. He gave the months names in his own tongue, in place of the Latin and barbarous names by which they were formerly known among the Franks. . . .

Toward the close of his life, when he was broken by ill-health and old age, he summoned Louis, King of Aquitania, his only surviving son by Hildegard, and gathered together all the chief men of the whole kingdom of the Franks in a solemn assembly. He appointed Louis, with their unanimous consent, to rule with himself over the whole kingdom, and constituted him heir to the imperial name; then, placing the diadem upon his son's head, he bade him be proclaimed Emperor and Augustus. This step was hailed by all present with great favor, for it really seemed as if God had prompted him to it for the kingdom's good; it increased the King's dignity, and struck no little terror into foreign nations. After sending his son back to Aquitania, although weak from age he set out to hunt, as usual, near his palace at Aix-la-Chapelle, and passed the rest of the autumn in the chase, returning thither about the first of November. While wintering there, he was seized, in the month of January, with a high fever, and took to his bed. As soon as he was taken sick, he prescribed for himself abstinence from food, as he always used to do in case of fever, thinking that the disease could be driven off, or at least mitigated, by fasting. Besides the fever, he suffered from a pain in the side, which the Greeks call pleurisy; but he still persisted in fasting, and in keeping up his strength only by draughts taken at very long intervals. He died January twenty-eighth, the seventh day from the time that he took to his bed, at nine o'clock in the morning, after partaking of the holy communion, in the seventy-second year of his age and the forty-seventh of his reign.

---

[4]The codes of the two Frankish tribes, the Salian and Ripuarian, that had combined to form the nation.—ED.

A New Portrait
of the Emperor

HEINRICH FICHTENAU

*We turn now from Einhard's contemporary account of Charlemagne to the
description by the modern Austrian medievalist Heinrich Fichtenau. It is
rather more a reconstruction than a description, for in* The Carolingian
Empire: The Age of Charlemagne, *Fichtenau goes beyond Einhard's
account to the other fragmentary records of Charles's age, as well as to the
best of modern Carolingian scholarship. Fichtenau's work is a careful, even
conservative, attempt to set Charlemagne securely in his age. The result is a
distinguished new portrait of the emperor to set beside that of his adoring
friend and subject.*

No man's stature is increased by the accumulation of myths, and
nothing is detracted from genuine historical greatness by the consideration of a man's purely human side. In order to analyse an epoch it is
necessary to analyse the man who was its centre, who determined its
character and who was, at the same time, shaped and determined by
it. It is therefore not mere curiosity but an endeavour to fulfil the
historian's task if we strive to pierce and get behind the myth that has
surrounded the figure of Charles. That myth has been built up over a
period of centuries and has tended to conjure up in place of a tangi-
ble personality, full of vitality, the figure of a timeless hero.

In the case of Charles—and that alone would justify our beginning
with him—we can even form a picture of his bodily physique. The
bodily appearance of his contemporaries, although we know their
names and their works, remains shadow-like for us to-day. But as far
as Charles the Great is concerned, we are not only in possession of his
bodily remains but also have an exact description of his appearance.
It is true that Charles's biographer Einhard borrowed the terms of his
description from Suetonius. Nevertheless it was possible for him to
choose from among the numerous biographies of the ancient emperors which he found in Suetonius those expressions which were most
applicable to his master. Einhard and his contemporaries were especially struck by Charles's bodily size. Ever since the opening of
Charles's tomb in 1861 we have known that his actual height was a

full 6 feet 3½ inches. It was therefore not poetic licence when one of the court-poets, describing the royal hunt, remarked: "The king, with his broad shoulders, towers above everybody else." . . .

It is a pity that Einhard fails us when he describes Charles's personality, for his description is entirely conventional. It had to be conventional, for, although emperors may differ in physical build, they must all have the same virtues, namely the imperial virtues without which nobody can be a real emperor. Thus his description of Charles is couched in Aristotelian and Stoic terms, such as *temperantia, patientia,* and *constantia animi.* And in so far as Einhard attributed *magnanimitas* and *liberalitas* to Charles, we can discern a mingling of ancient and Germanic princely ideals. When the hospitality shown to foreign guests resulted in neglect of considerations of public economy, Stoic *magnanimitas* was imperceptibly transformed into Germanic "loftiness of spirit." For Charles "found in the reputation of generosity and in the good fame that followed generous actions a compensation even for grave inconveniences."

The Stoic traits in Einhard's picture of Charles are, however, by no means insignificant. Many of Charles's counsellors must have drawn his attention to the fact that these traits were ideals that had been appropriate to his imperial predecessors and therefore appropriate for him. People must have appealed again and again to his *clementia,* a Stoic concept subsumed under *temperantia,* when it was a question of preventing the execution of conspirators, of liberating hostages, or of returning property that had been confiscated in punishment for an offence. Stoicism was, after all, allied with Christianity. A Christian ruler had to exercise self-control. If he indulged in *crudelitas* and raged against his enemies he was not far from the very opposite of a good king, the *rex iniquus* or tyrant.

Charles endeavoured in more than one sense to live up to the model of Stoic and Christian self-discipline. He could not tolerate drunkards in his palace. Banquets were held only on important feast days. Fasting, however, he deeply loathed. He often complained that it impaired his health. When he was an old man he conducted a long battle with his physicians who never succeeded in making him eat boiled meat in place of the roast to which he was accustomed. The fact that Einhard incorporated such stories in his biography and that a large number of almost humourous anecdotes, such as were collected later by Notker,[5] were recounted by his own contemporaries, shows that there was a very real difference between the late Roman, and especially the Byzantine, conception of the ruler, on one hand, and the Frankish conception, on the other. Charles did not observe in

---

[5]A late Carolingian monastic chronicler.—ED.

his court the stiff dignity and the ceremonious distance that became an emperor. In this respect he never modelled himself on anyone; he behaved naturally and revealed his true self.

There is no evidence that Charles ever withdrew from the people around him in order to ponder and work out his plans. He always needed the company of people, of his daughters, of his friends, and even of his menial retinue. He not only invited to his banquets everybody who happened to be about; he also gathered people for the hunt and even insisted that his magnates, his learned friends and his bodyguard were to be present when he was having a bath. The author of a poetical description of palace life at Aix-la-Chapelle refers repeatedly to the noisy bustle in the baths. It seems that Charles was happiest among the din of the hunt or in the midst of the building going on at Aix-la-Chapelle.

Charles was the centre of the whole kingdom—not only because it became him as ruler to be the centre, but also because it suited his temperament. Generally receptive, and approaching both science and scholarship with an open mind, he wanted to feel that he was at the centre of everything. It must have been an easy matter for court scholars, like Theodulf of Orléans, to persuade the king that his intellectual faculties were broader than the Nile, larger than the Danube and the Euphrates, and no less powerful than the Ganges. . . . As a rule the courtiers, and Alcuin among them, vied with each other in hiding from the king that there was any difference of quality between the achievements of ancient Christian civilization and their own. A new Rome or Athens was expected to arise in Aix-la-Chapelle, and they were anxious to emphasize their superiority over Byzantium, where government was in the hands of females and theology was riddled with errors. Charles required all the fresh naturalness of his temperament in order to prevent himself from sliding from the realm of practical possibilities into the world of fantastic dreams and illusions in which so many Roman emperors had foundered. . . .

At times Charles's affability, so much praised by Einhard, gave way to surprising explosions of temper. . . . Without a reference to such explosions, however, the portrait of Charles's impulsive and impetuous nature would be incomplete. The king's ire, which made his contemporaries tremble, was quite a different matter. It was part of the Germanic, just as it was of the oriental, conception of a ruler and was contrary to the Stoic ideal. At the beginning of the legend of Charlemagne there stands the figure of the "iron Charles" as his enemies saw him approaching—clad from top to toe in iron, and with an iron soul as well. In confusion they shouted: "Oh, the iron! Woe, the iron!" Not only the king's enemies, however, but also his faithful followers stood in fear of him. Charles's grandson Nithard wrote with

approval that Charles had governed the nations with "tempered severity." Charles was able to control the warring men and the centrifugal
tendencies of his dominions because the fear of his personal severity
made evil men as gentle as lambs. He had the power to make the
"hearts of both Franks and barbarians" sink. No amount of official
propaganda could produce the same effect as the hardness of
Charles's determination. The lack of such determination in Louis, his
successor, was among the factors that led to the decay of the empire.

This side of Charles's character, although necessary for the preservation of the kingdom, was well beyond the boundaries laid down by the
precepts of Stoicism and of Christianity. Charles himself was probably
not aware of this. But Einhard, his biographer, who had much sympathy with both these ideas, felt it deeply. . . . Charles thought of himself
as a Christian through and through, but he never managed to transcend the limits of the popular piety of the Franks. . . . He supported
needy Christians, even outside the borders of the empire. He sent
money to Rome and made four pilgrimages to the papal city. Such were
the religious works of Charles as related by his biographer, Einhard.
The inner life of the Christian, the regeneration of the soul and the
new religious attitude which, at the very time when Einhard was writing, Charles's son, Louis the Pious, was labouring to acquire, are not so
much as mentioned. The reason why Einhard is silent about such
things is scarcely that he could not find the words to describe them in
his model, Suetonius. Charles organized the salvation of his soul as he
was wont to organize his Empire. It would have been contrary to his
nature, and the most difficult task of all, for him to seek the highest
levels of spiritual experience in his own heart. His task as a ruler, as he
saw it, was to act upon the world.

We must remember, however, that the world upon which he acted
bore little resemblance to the sober and dry reality created by modern
commerce and technology. Such modern conceptions were shaped
much later, mostly under the impression of Calvinism. They were
unknown to Charles, who, for instance, first learnt of the pope's
mutilation in distant Rome through a dream. He took it to be one of
his duties as a ruler to observe the course of the stars with the greatest
of attention, for the approach of misfortune for his kingdom could be
foretold from the stars more accurately than from anything else. For
this reason the emperor devoted more time and labour to the study of
astronomy than to any other of the "liberal arts." If the observation of
the stars had been a mere hobby, he would surely have interrupted it
while he was devastating the Saxon country with his army. . . .

Charles the Great was not one of those men who have to fight
against their times and who, misunderstood by their contemporaries,
are appreciated only after their death. He embodied all the tenden-

cies of his own age; he was carried forward by them and, at the same time, moved them forward. It is impossible to describe him except in close conjunction with his friends and the magnates of his land. But for the picture to be complete he must also be shown in the midst of his family. He was surrounded by his children, his wives and the retinue of females, whose numbers and conduct seemed so unbecoming to the puritanism of his successor when he first entered the palace. Such conditions were not peculiar to Charles. It was all part and parcel of Frankish tradition. Charles lived as the head of a clan. The servants were, at least for the purposes of everyday life, included in the clan. As part of the family they enjoyed peace and protection and were, together with their master's blood relations, subject to his authority. Within the framework of the old tribal law, the master ruled his household unconditionally. . . .

In the king's palace there was a constant going and coming. Emigrés from England and from Byzantium rubbed shoulders with foreign ambassadors and all manner of public officials. There must have been, nevertheless, a few fixed key positions in the organization. There was little love lost among the occupants of these positions. For the most part, our sources remain silent on this matter. But now and again we catch a glimpse of the situation. The office of the chamberlain was one of these key positions. It was he who received the people who had come to demand an audience. He decided whether and in what order they were to appear before the king. He also received the annual "donations" of the magnates to the royal treasure which was in his custody. Alcuin considered himself happy to count this man among his friends and emphasized again and again how many envious people and evil counsellors were busy in other places trying to ruin the king.

Alcuin wrote repeatedly that, though the king tried to enforce justice, he was surrounded by predatory men. His judgment was probably no less partisan than that of his opponents who maintained that he himself was ruining the king. . . . Charles's own open and generous nature had never been inclined to inquire too closely into the intrigues and corruptions of his trusted friends and servants.

All things considered, there is little difference between the picture we form of Charles's surroundings and the one we have of his ancestors and of other princes of the period. The only difference was that the imperial household, as in fact the empire itself, was greater, more splendid and therefore also more exposed to danger. As long as its power and splendour were increasing, the cracks in the structure remained concealed. It was the achievement of Charles's own powerful personality to have brought about this rise which, without him, might have taken generations to reach its zenith. His efforts were crowned with success because his whole personality was in tune with the progressive forces active among his people. If this had not been the case, no amount of power concentrated in the hands of the king would have suffered to stamp his countenance upon the age. If this is remembered much of the illusion of well-nigh superhuman achievement, that has inspired both the mediaeval legend of Charlemagne and many modern narratives, is dispelled. What remains is quite enough justification for calling Charles historically great.

A More Somber Light

F. L. GANSHOF

Just as Heinrich Fichtenau represents the tradition of Austrian-German scholarship in modern Carolingian studies, the other great tradition, the Belgian-French, is represented by the Belgian scholar François Louis Ganshof—who has been justly called the dean of Carolingian studies. The passage excerpted below is from an address presented to the Mediaeval Academy of America in 1948. It is in the nature of a summary judgment drawn from a lifetime of patient study and reflection, and has not been materially altered by his continued work of the last thirty years. Ganshof does not really dissent from the portrait created by Fichtenau. But he has always had a penchant for analysis rather than interpretation. He therefore strives to go beyond the limitations of Einhard's biography and other contemporary biographical fragments to describe not so much Charlemagne the man as Charlemagne the statesman. The result is a somewhat somber judgment, dwelling more upon his limitations than his accomplishments. For Ganshof is sharply aware that if Fichtenau sees Charlemagne as the universal father figure of the first Europe,[6] it is of a Europe hardly yet born and due for many turns and reverses before it can realize the promise anticipated in the age of Charlemagne.

We begin just before what Ganshof calls the fifth and last period of Charlemagne's reign.

It would seem that by 792, when Charles was fifty years old, he had acquired experience and wisdom; perhaps, also, the advice of certain counsellors had brought him to understand that moderation is neces-

[6]D. A. Bullough, "*Europae Pater:* Charlemagne and His Achievement in the Light of Recent Scholarship," *English Historical Review*, 85 (1970), 59–105.

sary to consolidate the results of victory. One of the deep causes of the Saxon revolt of 792–793 had been the reign of terror of 785, caused especially by the *Capitulatio de partibus Saxoniæ*,[7] to secure the Frankish domination and the authority of the Christian religion. One must mention, also, the ruthlessness shown by the clergy in exacting payment of the tithe. In 797 a more gentle rule was introduced in Saxony by the *Capitulare Saxonicum* and the results of this new policy were favorable. In the Danube countries the methods used were less rigorous than formerly in Saxony.

A feature which at this period seems to have developed strongly was Charles' special care concerning the interests of the church and their close association with the interests of the state. In the capitulary, where dispositions made by the Synod of Frankfurt in 794 were promulgated, regulations of purely political or administrative character are next to those concerning the life of the church, e.g., the measures taken to extend the right of exclusive jurisdiction of the church over the clerics, and those aiming to render the discipline of the higher clergy more strict by reestablishing over the bishops, chiefs of the dioceses, the superior hierarchical office of the metropolitan.

In matters of dogma the Synod of Frankfurt, under the presidency of Charlemagne, had agreed with Pope Hadrian to condemn adoptianism, a christological heresy. Contrary to the advice of the pope, the synod had condemned the worship of images, which had been restored to honor by the decision of a so called œcumenical council of the Eastern Church. Charlemagne had already got his theologians to criticize this worship in the *Libri Carolini*. In spite of his reverence for the Holy See, Charlemagne appears to be, far more than the pope, the real head of the church in the West. When Leo III ascended the pontifical throne in 795, on the death of Hadrian, Charles stated precisely their respective positions in a letter which leaves no doubt on the subject. The pope became more or less the first of his bishops.

Alcuin and a few other clerics had developed an idea linked with ancient traditions. To protect the church against many corrupt practices and dangers, the realization of the will of God on earth required the reestablishment in the West of an imperial power that would protect faith and church. Charlemagne, in their eyes, fulfilled the necessary conditions to be that Roman Christian emperor; to be, indeed, an emperor quite different in their minds from the historical Constantine and Theodosius. Favorable circumstances occurred. A revolution in Rome overthrew Pope Leo III in 799 and created an

---

[7]"The Capitulary on the Saxon Regions." Capitularies were edicts of the crown which had the effect of law and are among the best evidence we have of Charlemagne's paternalistic style of government.—ED.

extremely difficult situation which remained confused even after Charles had had the pope reestablished on his throne. Charlemagne not only admired in Alcuin the theologian and the scholar to whom he had entrusted the task of revising the Latin text of the Bible, but he also had confidence in his judgment and was strongly under his influence. It was, I believe, owing to Alcuin that he went to Rome with the idea of putting order into the affairs of the church; it was under the same influence that he accepted there the imperial dignity. Pope Leo III crowned him emperor on 25 December 800.

To give even a short account of the immediate and later effects of this great event would be irrelevant here. I shall merely mention the fifth and last period of the reign of Charlemagne, which began on the day following the coronation. It is a rather incoherent stage of his career. One notices this when trying to distinguish what changes in Charlemagne's conduct could be attributed to the influence of his newly-acquired dignity.

He certainly appreciated his new position. He intended to make the most of it towards Byzantium and he exercised a political and military pressure on the eastern emperor until the Byzantine prince recognized his imperial title in 812. However, in matters of government Charles's attitude was not constant. In 802, shortly after his return from Italy, he appeared to be fully aware of the eminent character of his imperial power. He stated that it was his duty to see that all western Christians should act according to the will of God; he ordered all his subjects to take a new oath of allegiance, this time in his quality of emperor, and he extended the notion of allegiance. He started legislating in the field of private law; he stipulated that the clergy must obey strictly canonical legislation or the Rule of St. Benedict; he reformed the institution of his enquiring and reforming commissioners, the *missi dominici,* to make it more efficient. In spite of all this, when (806) he settled his succession, the imperial dignity appeared to have lost, in his eyes, much of its importance. Unless it were to lose its meaning entirely, the empire was indivisible. Yet Charles foresaw the partition of his states between his three sons, according to the ancient Frankish custom, and took no dispositions concerning the *imperialis potestas.* Doubtless those things that had influenced him a few years earlier were no longer effective and the Roman tradition and Alcuin's influence no longer dominated him. Everything was as if the imperial dignity had been for Charles a very high distinction but a strictly personal one. In the very last years of his reign, however, he seemed again to attach more importance to this dignity and most likely some new influences had altered his mind. His two older sons, Charles and Pepin, being dead, he himself conferred the title of emperor on his son Louis in 813.

During the end of the reign, with the one exception of the Spanish "march," which was enlarged and reinforced (Barcelona was taken in 801), no new territorial acquisition was made, in spite of military efforts often of considerable importance. The campaigns against the Northern Slavs, against Bohemia, against the Bretons of Armorica, and against the duke of Benevento only resulted in the recognition of a theoretical supremacy. Actually, fearful dangers became apparent. The Danes threatened the boundary of Saxony and their fleets devastated Frisia; the Saracen fleets threatened the Mediterranean coasts. The general impression left by the relation of these events is the weakening of the Carolingian monarchy. This impression increases when one examines internal conditions of the empire. In the state as in the church abuses increased; insecurity grew worse; the authority of the emperor was less and less respected. The capitularies, more and more numerous, constantly renewed warnings, orders, and interdictions which were less and less obeyed. Charles had grown old. Until then, his personal interferences and those which he directly provoked, had made up for the deficiencies of a quite inadequate administrative organization in an empire of extraordinary size. The physical and intellectual capacities of Charles were declining; he stayed almost continuously at Aachen, his favorite residence after 794, and he hardly ever left the place after 808. The strong antidote present before was now missing; all the political and social defects revealing a bad government appeared. When Charlemagne died in Aachen on 28 January 814, at the age of seventy-two, the Frankish state was on the verge of decay.

I have tried to describe and characterize briefly the successive phases of Charlemagne's reign. Is it possible to grasp his personality as a statesman? Perhaps. A primary fact that must be emphasized is that—even compared with others of his time—Charlemagne was not a cultivated man. In spite of his thirst for knowledge and his admiration of culture, he was ignorant of all that is connected with intellectual life and he had little gift for abstraction.

But he had a sense for realities, and especially those of power. He knew how one gains power, how one remains in power and how one reaches the highest degrees of superior and supreme power. His attitude towards the imperial dignity revealed this. The conception of the clerics, and especially of Alcuin, for whom that dignity was an ideal magistrature infinitely above the royal power, was quite inaccessible to him. He knew or rather he felt, that the real basis of his power was solely his double royal authority[8] and he refused to omit evidence

---

[8]As king of the Franks and of the Lombards.—ED.

of this from his titles after the imperial coronation. For him the imperial dignity magnified and glorified the royal authority; it neither
absorbed nor replaced it.

Charles had also the sense of what was practicable. Save for the
campaign in Spain in 778, he undertook no tasks out of proportion to
his means.

Einhard praises the equanimity of Charlemagne, his *constantia*.
This was, indeed, a remarkable aspect of his personality. In the two
periods of crisis which shook his reign—in 778 and in 792/793—no
danger, no catastrophe, could make him give up the tasks he had
undertaken or alter his methods of government. The moderation
with which he happened to treat his vanquished enemies at certain
times was not in contradiction with the constancy of his character. On
the contrary. Equanimity implies a clear view of one's plans and one
can therefore understand the variations of Charlemagne's attitude
towards the imperial dignity, the full significance of which he never
really understood.

To have a clear line of conduct and keep to it is one thing, but it is
quite another to follow out a complete and detailed program. Charlemagne had, indeed, certain lines of conduct that he followed persistently. The facts presented are sufficient to show this as regards his
foreign policy. It is also true as regards political, administrative, and
juridical institutions. Charlemagne wanted to improve their efficiency so as to bring about a more complete fulfillment of his wishes
and to achieve greater security for his subjects. But one cannot make
out a real program in his actions. He resorted to shifts; he adopted
and improved what was already existing. This is true of the institution
of the *missi,* true also of the royal court of justice, of the royal vassality
and of the "immunity." Occasionally he created something new, but
without troubling about a general scheme. His reforms were empiric
and at times went through several stages of development: as in the
case of the organization of the *placita generalia,*[9] which was roughly
outlined at the beginning of the reign but did not assume a definite
shape until about the year 802, and also the use of writing in recording administrative and juridical matter, prescribed by a series of distinct decisions relating to particular cases.

One must avoid any attempt to credit Charlemagne with preoccupations proper to other times. Because of his efforts to protect *pauperes
liberi homines,*[10] for instance, one cannot attribute to him the inaugura-
tion of a social policy; nor because he promulgated the *capitulare de*

[9]The General Assembly.—Ed.

[10]Impoverished free men.—Ed.

villis[11] can one speak of an economic policy. In both cases he acted on the spur of urgent interests then on hand; free men of modest condition supplied soldiers and the royal manors had to be fit to maintain the court. . . .

This sketch of Charles as a statesman would be distorted if stress was not laid upon his religious concerns. It is indeed hard to draw a line between his religious and his political ideas. His will to govern and to extend his power was inseparable from his purpose to spread the Christian religion and let his subjects live according to the will of God. If something of the "clerical" conception of the empire struck him deeply, it was the feeling that he was personally responsible for the progress of God's Kingdom on earth. But always it was he who was concerned. His piousness, his zeal for the Christian religion were no obstacles to his will to power; in religious matters as in others the pope was nothing more than his collaborator.

One is often tempted to turn Charlemagne into a superman, a far-seeing politician with broad and general views, ruling everything from above; one is tempted to see his reign as a whole, with more or less the same characteristics prevailing from beginning to end. This is so true that most of the works concerning him, save for the beginning and the end of his reign, use the geographical or systematic order rather than a chronological one. The distinctions that I have tried to make between the different phases of his reign may, perhaps, help to explain more exactly the development and effect of Charlemagne's power; they may help us to appreciate these more clearly. Perhaps, also, the features that I have noted bring out the human personality in the statesman and lead to the same results. The account I have given and the portrait I have drawn certainly justify the words which the poet ascribed to Charles in the last verse but one of the *Chanson de Roland:* "Deus" dist li Reis, "si penuse est ma vie." ("O Lord," said the king, "how arduous is my life.")

Suggestions for Further Reading

The almost unique value of Einhard's biography of Charlemagne is dramatized by the scarcity and poor quality of other contemporary sources. Students can become aware of this contrast by looking even briefly at some of these other materials. There is a life of Charlemagne nearly contemporary with Einhard's, authored by a monk of St. Gall—possibly Notker the Stammerer. But unlike the solid and straightforward narrative of Einhard, the monk's account is dis-

[11]The Capitulary on Manors.—ED.

jointed and rambling, filled with legendary matter and scraps of the history of his monastery, and almost totally unreliable. It is available in a good modern edition, *Early Lives of Charlemagne by Einhard and the Monk of St. Gall,* tr. and ed. A. J. Grant (New York: Cooper Square, 1966). Of the same sort are two somewhat later biographies of the brothers Adalard and Wala, abbots of Corbie, by the monk Radbertus of Corbie, although they contain only a few casual bits of information about Charlemagne, despite the fact that the two abbots were Charlemagne's cousins and both had played prominent roles at court: *Charlemagne's Cousins: Contemporary Lives of Adalard and Wala,* tr. and ed. Allen Cabaniss (Syracuse, N.Y.: Syracuse University Press, 1967). The only other narrative source of any value for the reign of Charlemagne is the Royal Frankish Annals, but they are thin and uncommunicative. They can be read as part of *Carolingian Chronicles: Royal Frankish Annals and Nithard's Histories,* tr. Bernhard W. Scholz with Barbara Rogers (Ann Arbor, Mich.: University of Michigan Press, 1970). Several of these accounts and other sorts of documentary materials relating to Charlemagne's reign have been collected in a convenient and well-edited series of selections, *The Reign of Charlemagne: Documents on Carolingian Government and Administration,* ed. H. R. Lyon and John Percival (New York: St. Martin's, 1975).

Because of the stature and importance of Charlemagne and despite the problem of the sources, scholars continue to write about him. Many of their works are specialized scholarly studies. Some can be read profitably by beginning students, such as the several essays in Heinrich Fichtenau, *The Carolingian Empire,* excerpted above, or some of the articles of F. L. Ganshof collected in *The Carolingians and the Frankish Monarchy: Studies in Carolingian History,* tr. Janet Sondheimer (Ithaca, N.Y.: Cornell University Press, 1971). Pierre Riché, *Daily Life in the World of Charlemagne,* tr. Jo Ann McNamara (Philadelphia: University of Pennsylvania Press, 1978), is a fresh and useful work of social history by a great French authority. For a recent and authoritative overview of all Carolingian history, including Charlemagne, see Rosamond McKitterick, *The Frankish Kingdoms under the Carolingians, 751–987* (London and New York: Longman, 1983). There are three excellent modern works, all brief and readable, that treat interesting aspects of Charles's reign: Richard E. Sullivan, *Aix-la-Chapelle in the Age of Charlemagne,* "Centers of Civilization Series" (Norman, Okla.: University of Oklahoma Press, 1963), focuses on the cultural achievements at Charles's capital; Jacques Boussard, *The Civilization of Charlemagne,* tr. Francis Partridge (New York: McGraw-Hill, 1968), presents a favorable revisionist interpretation of the Carolingian culture; and Robert Folz, *The Coronation of Charlemagne: 25 December 800,* tr. J. E. Anderson (London: Routledge and Kegan Paul, 1974), is a close study of this important event, its background and context. One of the most important and most readable of the works on this period is Donald Bullough, *The Age of Charlemagne* (New York: Putnam, 1965).

Of the several biographies of Charlemagne, the best, as well as the most exciting and readable, is Richard Winston, *Charlemagne: From the Hammer to the Cross* (New York: Vintage, 1954). A somewhat briefer and less colorful biography but by an established authority is James A. Cabaniss, *Charlemagne,* "Rulers and Statesmen of the World" (Boston: Twayne, 1972).

Henri Pirenne, *Mohammed and Charlemagne,* tr. Bernard Miall (New York: Barnes and Noble, 1958 [1939]), is the masterwork of a great medieval historian and the chief entry in an important medieval scholarly controversy which continues to be of some interest to students of Charlemagne's reign. It has to do with the question of when and how the Middle Ages actually began. Pirenne says not until Charlemagne. The controversy and its chief figures are represented in *The Pirenne Thesis: Analysis, Criticism, and Revision,* ed. Alfred F. Havighurst (Boston: Heath, 1958). Students are also referred to two more recent works which indicate that the Pirenne controversy is still alive: Bryce Lyon, *The Origins of the Middle Ages: Pirenne's Challenge to Gibbon* (New York: Norton, 1972), and Robert S. Lopez, *The Birth of Europe* (New York: Lippincott, 1967).

PETER ABELARD: "THE KNIGHT OF DIALECTIC"

c. 1079	Born
c. 1112	Studied with Anselm of Laon
1113	Taught in Paris
1118	Affair with and marriage to Heloise
1121	Condemned by Council of Soissons
1141	Condemned by Council of Sens
c. 1142	Died

By the turn of the twelfth century, the Europe of Charlemagne had been transformed. The downward curve of population had steadied and then begun to climb. There were more knights than there were fiefs for them to hold. They had joined the host of William the Bastard, Duke of Normandy, in his chancy adventure against England in the summer of 1066 in return for promises of land, as a decade earlier others had followed the Norman Guiscards and Hautevilles to Sicily. They swelled the armies of Saxon dukes and German kings in their conquests of eastern Europe and of Spanish Christian kings in the *reconquista* of Spain from the Moslems. And they went off to the crusades, the grandest adventure of an expanding Christendom.

Less sanguinary souls had taken to the roads with backpacks and strings of mules. Commerce began to revive, linking together villages and fortresses that would soon become towns and cities. The urban centers swelled with a growing population.

This bulging, booming, changing Europe had need for the skills of the mind. Schools multiplied—there were monastic schools, cathedral schools, guild schools, notarial schools. And men of learning found themselves thrust into the center of things. "The Renaissance of the twelfth century" was at hand, a revolution in learning and teaching, in the subjects to be taught and the methods of teaching them. It was to produce a renewed interest in the Latin classics, revived study of the ancient Roman civil law and the codification of the law of the church. It was to bring a flood of Moslem and Jewish and, ultimately, Greek influences into the processes of Western thought and within a century to create medieval scholasticism, with the medieval university as its institutional setting.

One of the most fascinating, controversial, and important figures of this world of twelfth-century intellectualism was the scholar-teacher-philosopher-theologian-poet Peter Abelard (c.1079–c.1142). Abelard is remembered principally for the arrogant rationalism he expounded among the schoolmen of Paris, Laon, Melun, and Corbeil, and particularly for his logical textbook *Sic et Non;* for his ill-fated romance with Heloise, the fair niece of Canon Fulbert; and for Fulbert's terrible vengeance upon him. But modern scholarship has begun to search beyond the inherited stereotypes of Abelard as the demon lover and the rationalist-out-of-time, neither of which can satisfactorily account for the astonishing reputation that Abelard had among his own contemporaries.

The Story of My Misfortunes

PETER ABELARD

The building of a kind of legendary Abelard began during his own lifetime and resulted, in part, from the appearance of Abelard's autobiography, its stark Latin title Historia suarum calamitatum *somewhat weakly translated as* The Story of My Misfortunes. *This remarkable and candid book had a strange beginning. In 1135 a friend, apparently very close to Abelard—he calls him "most dear brother in Christ and comrade closest to me in the intimacy of speech"—appealed to him for consolation in some sorrow of his own. In response, Abelard wrote him "of the sufferings which have sprung out of my misfortunes" "so that, in comparing your sorrows with mine, you may discover that yours are in truth nought, or at the most but of small account, and so shall you come to bear them more easily."*

After describing his home in Brittany and how he had given up his feudal inheritance and gained the permission of his father to pursue studies, Abelard continues:

I came at length to Paris, where above all in those days the art of dialectics was most flourishing, and there did I meet William of Champeaux, my teacher, a man most distinguished in this science both by his renown and by his true merit. With him I remained for some time, at first indeed well liked of him; but later I brought him great grief, because I undertook to refute certain of his opinions, not infrequently attacking him in disputation, and now and then in these debates, I was adjudged victor. Now this, to those among my fellow students who were ranked foremost, seemed all the more insufferable because of my youth and the brief duration of my studies.

Out of this sprang the beginning of my misfortunes, which have followed me even to the present day; the more widely my fame was spread abroad, the more bitter was the envy that was kindled against me. It was given out that I, presuming on my gifts far beyond the warranty of my youth, was aspiring despite my tender years to the leadership of a school; nay, more, that I was making ready the very place in which I would undertake this task, the place being none other than the castle of Melun, at that time a royal seat. My teacher himself had some foreknowledge of this, and tried to remove my school as far as possible from his own. Working in secret, he sought in every way he could before I left his following to bring to nought the school I had planned and the place I had chosen for it. Since, however, in that very place he had many rivals, and some of them men of influence among the great ones of the land, relying on their aid I won to the fulfillment of my wish; the support of many was secured for me by reason of his own unconcealed envy. From this small inception of my school, my fame in the art of dialectics began to spread abroad, so that little by little the renown, not alone of those who had been my fellow students, but of our very teacher himself, grew dim and was like to die out altogether. Thus it came about that, still more confident in myself, I moved my school as soon as I well might to the castle of Corbeil, which is hard by the city of Paris, for there I knew there would be given more frequent chance for my assaults in our battle of disputation. . . .

To him did I return, for I was eager to learn more of rhetoric from his lips; and in the course of our many arguments on various matters, I compelled him by most potent reasoning first to alter his former opinion on the subject of the universals,[1] and finally to abandon it altogether. Now, the basis of this old concept of his regarding the reality of universal ideas was that the same quality formed the essence alike of the abstract whole and of the individuals which were its parts: in other words, that there could be no essential differences among these individuals, all being alike save for such variety as might grow out of the many accidents of existence. Thereafter, however, he corrected this opinion, no longer maintaining that the same quality was the essence of all things, but that, rather, it manifested itself in them through diverse ways. This problem of universals is ever the most vexed one among logicians, to such a degree, indeed, that even Porphyry,[2] writing in his "Isagoge" regarding universals, dared not attempt a final pronouncement thereon, saying rather: "This is the deepest of all problems of its kind." Wherefore it followed that when William had first revised and then finally abandoned altogether his views on this one subject, his lecturing sank into such a state of negligent reasoning that it could scarce be called lecturing on the science of dialectics at all; it was as if all his science had been bound up in this one question of the nature of universals.

---

[1]This is a reference to the most famous and fundamental of all medieval learned controversies, the Nominalist-Realist controversy over the nature of reality and "universal" properties. The Nominalists traced their position ultimately to Aristotle; the Realists, to Plato.—Ed.

[2]A third-century Neoplatonic philosopher whose works were important in the transmission of medieval Platonism.—Ed.

Thus it came about that my teaching won such strength and authority that even those who before had clung most vehemently to my former master, and most bitterly attacked my doctrines, now flocked to my school. . . .

While these things were happening, it became needful for me again to repair to my old home, by reason of my dear mother, Lucia, for after the conversion of my father, Berengarius, to the monastic life, she so ordered her affairs as to do likewise. When all this had been completed, I returned to France,[3] above all in order that I might study theology, since now my oft-mentioned teacher, William, was active in the episcopate of Châlons. In this field of learning Anselm of Laon, who was his teacher therein, had for long years enjoyed the greatest renown.

I sought out, therefore, this same venerable man, whose fame, in truth, was more the result of long-established custom than of the potency of his own talent or intellect. If any one came to him impelled by doubt on any subject, he went away more doubtful still. He was wonderful, indeed, in the eyes of these who only listened to him, but those who asked him questions perforce held him as nought. He had a miraculous flow of words, but they were contemptible in meaning and quite void of reason. When he kindled a fire, he filled his house with smoke and illumined it not at all. He was a tree which seemed noble to those who gazed upon its leaves from afar, but to those who came nearer and examined it more closely was revealed its barrenness. . . .

It was not long before I made this discovery, and stretched myself lazily in the shade of that same tree. I went to his lectures less and less often, a thing which some among his eminent followers took sorely to heart, because they interpreted it as a mark of contempt for so illustrious a teacher. . . .

Challenged by those "eminent followers" of Anselm, Abelard undertakes to lecture on scripture, at their choice, "that most obscure prophecy of Ezekiel," and carries it off brilliantly—at least in his own opinion.

Now this venerable man of whom I have spoken was acutely smitten with envy, and straightway incited, as I have already mentioned, by the insinuations of sundry persons, began to persecute me for my lecturing on the Scriptures no less bitterly than my former master, William, had done for my work in philosophy. . . .

---

[3]Brittany was not yet a part of the royal domain of "France." He means the vicinity of Paris.—ED.

And so, after a few days, I returned to Paris, and there for several years I peacefully directed the school which formerly had been destined for me, nay, even offered to me, but from which I had been driven out. At the very outset of my work there, I set about completing the glosses on Ezekiel which I had begun at Laon. These proved so satisfactory to all who read them that they came to believe me no less adept in lecturing on theology than I had proved myself to be in the field of philosophy. . . . Thus, I, who by this time had come to regard myself as the only philosopher remaining in the whole world, and had ceased to fear any further disturbance of my peace, began to loosen the rein on my desires, although hitherto I had always lived in the utmost continence. And the greater progress I made in my lecturing on philosophy or theology, the more I departed alike from the practice of the philosophers and the spirit of the divines in the uncleanness of my life. For it is well known, methinks, that philosophers, and still more those who have devoted their lives to arousing the love of sacred study, have been strong above all else in the beauty of chastity.

Thus did it come to pass that while I was utterly absorbed in pride and sensuality, divine grace, the cure for both diseases, was forced upon me, even though I, forsooth, would fain have shunned it. First was I punished for my sensuality, and then for my pride. . . .

Now there dwelt in that same city of Paris a certain young girl named Héloïse, the niece of a canon who was called Fulbert. Her uncle's love for her was equalled only by his desire that she should have the best education which he could possibly procure for her. Of no mean beauty, she stood out above all by reason of her abundant knowledge of letters. Now this virtue is rare among women, and for that very reason it doubly graced the maiden, and made her the most worthy of renown in the entire kingdom. It was this young girl whom I, after carefully considering all those qualities which are wont to attract lovers, determined to unite with myself in the bonds of love, and indeed the thing seemed to me very easy to be done. So distinguished was my name, and I possessed such advantages of youth and comeliness, that no matter what woman I might favour with my love, I dreaded rejection of none. . . .

Thus, utterly aflame with my passion for this maiden, I sought to discover means whereby I might have daily and familiar speech with her, thereby the more easily to win her consent. For this purpose I persuaded the girl's uncle, with the aid of some of his friends, to take me into his household—for he dwelt hard by my school—in return for the payment of a small sum. My pretext for this was that the care of my own household was a serious handicap to my studies, and likewise burdened me with an expense far greater than I could afford. Now, he was a man keen in avarice, and likewise he was most desirous for his niece that her study of letters should ever go forward, so, for these two reasons, I easily won his consent to the fulfillment of my wish, for he was fairly agape for my money, and at the same time believed that his niece would vastly benefit by my teaching. More even than this, by his own earnest entreaties he fell in with my desires beyond anything I had dared to hope, opening the way for my love; for he entrusted her wholly to my guidance, begging me to give her instruction whensoever I might be free from the duties of my school, no matter whether by day or by night, and to punish her sternly if ever I should find her negligent of her tasks. In all this the man's simplicity was nothing short of astounding to me; I should not have been more smitten with wonder if he had entrusted a tender lamb to the care of a ravenous wolf. . . .

The inevitable ensued. Heloise became pregnant, and the child was born. Abelard proposed marriage, but Heloise was reluctant for fear of damaging his career. They finally agreed upon a secret marriage. Then, to protect her from the fury of her uncle and her family, Abelard sent her to the convent at Argenteuil where she had been educated as a young girl.

When her uncle and his kinsmen heard of this, they were convinced that now I had completely played them false and had rid myself forever of Héloïse by forcing her to become a nun. Violently incensed, they laid a plot against me, and one night, while I, all unsuspecting, was asleep in a secret room in my lodgings, they broke in with the help of one of my servants, whom they had bribed. There they had vengeance on me with a most cruel and most shameful punishment, such as astounded the whole world, for they cut off those parts of my body with which I had done that which was the cause of their sorrow. This done, straightway they fled, but two of them were captured, and suffered the loss of their eyes and their genital organs. One of these two was the aforesaid servant, who, even while he was still in my service, had been led by his avarice to betray me.

When morning came the whole city was assembled before my dwelling. It is difficult, nay, impossible, for words of mine to describe the amazement which bewildered them, the lamentations they uttered, the uproar with which they harassed me, or the grief with which they increased my own suffering. Chiefly the clerics, and above all my scholars, tortured me with their intolerable lamentations and outcries, so that I suffered more intensely from their compassion than from the pain of my wound. In truth I felt the disgrace more than the hurt to my body, and was more afflicted with shame than with pain. My incessant thought was of the renown in which I had so much delighted, now brought low, nay, utterly blotted out, so swiftly by an evil chance. I saw, too, how justly God had punished me in that very part of my body whereby I had sinned. I perceived that there was indeed justice in my betrayal by him whom I had myself already betrayed; and then I thought how eagerly my rivals would seize upon this manifestation of justice, how this disgrace would bring bitter and enduring grief to my kindred and my friends, and how the tale of this amazing outrage would spread to the very ends of the earth. . . .

I must confess that in my misery it was the overwhelming sense of my disgrace rather than any ardour for conversion to the religious life that drove me to seek the seclusion of the monastic cloister. Héloïse had already, at my bidding, taken the veil and entered a convent. Thus it was that we both put on the sacred garb, I in the abbey of St. Denis, and she in the convent of Argenteuil, of which I have already spoken. . . .

But even in the monastery Abelard could be neither silent nor humble. His theological writings—in particular a book on the Trinity—led to his being summoned before a council at Soissons. And though the condemnation of his work was far from unanimous, the book was nevertheless condemned, and Abelard himself was forced to cast it into the flames. He was banished to another monastery, which he was eventually permitted to leave. He sought out a lonely spot in the forest near Troyes in Champagne, built a hut, and formed his own monastic congregation. But even here students came to be taught, and his critics revived their charges, this time led by the most formidable religious figure of the century, the great St. Bernard of Clairvaux. And, though Abelard's account ends before that point, Bernard succeeded in having him condemned by the church. But Abelard died in 1142 before the ban could take effect.

A "Renaissance Man"
of the Twelfth Century

CHARLES HOMER HASKINS

The classic modern treatment of Abelard is to be found in Charles Homer Haskins's The Renaissance of the Twelfth Century, *one of the outstanding works of modern medieval scholarship. This book was one of the contributions to the academic controversy in the early part of this century over the status and conception of the Renaissance. That dispute has long been over, but Haskins's charming book survives, as well as his interpretation of Abelard as one of the principal figures in the construction of a medieval Renaissance.*

Haskins begins his account at the point of Abelard's confrontation with St. Bernard. This is where Abelard himself, as we have seen, left off in the history of his own misfortunes.

"Vanity of vanities, saith the preacher," and St. Bernard was first and foremost a preacher, and a fundamentalist preacher at that. Vain above all to him were pride of intellect and absorption in the learning of this world, and his harshest invectives were hurled at the most brilliant intellect of his age, Abaelard, that "scrutinizer of majesty and fabricator of heresies" who "deems himself able by human reason to comprehend God altogether." Between a mystic like Bernard and a rationalist like Abaelard there was no common ground, and for the time being the mystic had the church behind him. With Abaelard we have another type of autobiography, the intellectual, in that long tale of misfortune which he addressed to an unknown friend under the title of *Historia suarum calamitatum*.

Abaelard, it is true, was a monk and an abbot, but he became such by force of circumstances and not from choice. Even when he retires into the forests of Champagne or the depths of Brittany, he has always one eye on Paris and his return thither; indeed, His *Historia calamitatum* seems to have been written to prepare the way for his coming back, to serve an immediate purpose rather than for posterity. It shows nothing of monastic humility or religious vocation, but, on the contrary, is full of arrogance of intellect and joy of combat, even of the lust of the flesh and the lust of the eyes and the pride of life. Its author was a vain man, vain of his penetrating mind and skill in debate, vain of his power to draw away others' students, vain even of his success with the fair sex—so that he "feared no repulse from whatever woman he might deign to honor with his love"—always sure of his own opinions and unsparing of his adversaries. He relies on talent rather than on formal preparation, venturing into the closed field of theology and even improvising lectures on those pitfalls of the unwary, the obscurest parts of the prophet Ezekiel. He was by nature always in opposition, a thorn in the side of intellectual and social conformity. In the classroom he was the bright boy who always knew more than his teachers and delighted to confute them, ridiculing old Anselm of Laon, whose reputation he declared to rest upon mere tradition, unsupported by talent or learning, notable chiefly for a wonderful flow of words without meaning or reason, "a fire which gave forth smoke instead of light," like the barren fig tree of the Gospel or the old oak of Lucan, mere shadow of a great name. In the monastery of Saint-Denis he antagonized the monks by attacking the traditions respecting their founder and patron saint. Always it is he who is right and his many enemies who are wrong. And, as becomes a history of his misfortunes, he pities himself much. Objectively, the facts of Abaelard's autobiography can in the main be verified from his other writings and the statements of contemporaries. Subjectively, the *Historia calamitatum* confirms itself throughout, if we discern between the bursts of self-confidence the intervals of irresolution and despondency in what he tries to present as a consistently planned career. The prolixity and the citations of ancient authority are of the Middle Ages, as are the particular problems with which his mind was occupied, but the personality might turn up in any subsequent epoch—"portrait of a radical by himself"! Yet, just as Heloise's joy in loving belongs to the ages, Abaelard's joy in learning is more specifically of the new renaissance, of which he is the bright particular star. . . .

In Abaelard . . . we have one of the most striking figures of the medieval renaissance. Vain and self-conscious, as we have found him in his autobiography, his defects of temperament must not blind us to his great mental gifts. He was daring, original, brilliant, one of the first philosophical minds of the whole Middle Ages. First and foremost a logician, with an unwavering faith in the reasoning process, he fell in with the dialectic preoccupations of his age, and did more than any one else to define the problems and methods of scholasticism, at least in the matter of universals and in his *Sic et non*. The question of universals, the central though not the unique theme of scholastic philosophy, is concerned with the nature of general terms or conceptions, such as man, house, horse. Are these, as the Nominalists asserted, mere names and nothing more, an intellectual convenience at the most? Or are they realities, as the Realists maintained, having an existence quite independent of and apart from the particular individuals in which they may be for the moment objectified? A mere matter of logical terminology, you may say, of no importance in the actual world. Yet much depends upon the application. Apply the nominalistic doctrine to God, and the indivisible Trinity dissolves into three persons. Apply it to the Church, and the Church ceases to be a divine institution with a life of its own and becomes merely a convenient designation for the whole body of individual Christians. Apply to it the State, and where does political authority reside, in a sovereign whole or in the individual citizens? In this form, at least, the problem is still with us. Practical thinking cannot entirely shake itself free from logic, and conversely, logic has sometimes practical consequences not at first realized. . . . It is not surprising to find that Abaelard, like

Roscellinus before him, ran into difficulties on the subject of the Trinity, being condemned for heresy at Soissons in 1121 and at Sens in 1141. Such conflicts were inevitable with one of Abaelard's radical temper, who courted opposition and combat. . . .

In another way Abaelard contributed to the formation of scholasticism, namely, in his *Sic et non,* or *Yes and No.* True, the method of collecting and arranging passages from the Fathers on specific topics had been used before, as in the *Sentences* of Anselm of Laon, but Abaelard gave it a pungency and a wide popularity which associate it permanently with his name. Like everything he did, it was well advertised. His method was to take significant topics of theology and ethics and to collect from the Fathers their opinions pro and con, sharpening perhaps the contrast and being careful not to solve the real or seeming contradiction. Inerrancy he grants only to the Scriptures, apparent contradictions in which must be explained as due to scribal mistakes or defective understanding; subsequent authorities may err for other reasons, and when they disagree he claims the right of going into the reasonableness of the doctrine itself, of proving all things in order to hold fast that which is good. He has accordingly collected divergent sayings of the Fathers as they have come to mind, for the purpose of stimulating tender readers to the utmost effort in seeking out truth and of making them more acute as the result of such inquiry. "By doubting we come to inquiry, and by inquiry we perceive truth." The propositions cover a wide range of topics and of reading; some are dismissed briefly, while others bring forth long citations. . . . Some . . . , one can almost imagine briefed on either side in modern manuals for the training of debaters. Some such purpose, the stimulating of discussion among his pupils, seems to have been Abaelard's primary object, but the emphasis upon contradiction rather than upon agreement and the failure to furnish any solutions, real or superficial, tended powerfully to expose the weaknesses in the orthodox position and to undermine authority generally.

The Substance of Abelard

DAVID KNOWLES

To Haskins belongs the well-deserved credit, if not for "discovering" Abelard, at least for giving him a setting in which he can be seen with some clarity. More recent scholarship, however, has moved beyond the conception

*of Abelard as an example of the medieval Renaissance man—no matter
how brilliant, fascinating, and attractive—to the larger question of his importance as a substantive figure in medieval intellectual history. Much of
this new scholarship is summarized, and some of it anticipated, by the distinguished British medievalist and ecclesiastical historian Dom David Knowles
in his* The Evolution of Medieval Thought.
We turn now to that summary.

Until very recent years all discussions of Abelard centred upon his
alleged heretical and rationalistic teaching. At the present day, as a
result both of research among unpublished manuscripts and of critical methods applied to his works, he can be seen as a figure of positive
import, as a logician of supreme ability and as the originator of ideas
as well as of methods that were to have a long life. Not only is it now
possible to grasp more fully than before what Abelard taught and
thought, but it has been shown conclusively that throughout his life
he was constantly rewriting and reconsidering his works, and that his
opinions grew more orthodox and more carefully expressed with the
passage of the years. . . .

Of a truth, Abelard was never a rebel against the authority of the
Church, and never a rationalist in the modern sense. He never persisted in teaching what had been censured, even though until censured he may have protested vehemently that he had been misrepresented. Similarly, he never intended that his dialectic should attack or
contradict or replace the doctrines of the Church as formulated by
tradition. In this, full weight must be given to his words in his *Introduction to Theology:* "Now therefore it remains for us, after having laid
down the foundation of authority, to place upon it the buttresses of
reasoning." This is unquestionably a genuine expression of his programme, as are also the celebrated and moving words of his letter to
Héloise after the condemnation of 1141: "I will never be a philosopher, if this is to speak against St Paul; I would not be an Aristotle, if
this were to separate me from Christ. . . . I have set my building on
the corner-stone on which Christ has built his Church . . . if the tempest rises, I am not shaken; if the winds rave, I am not fearful. . . . I
rest upon the rock that cannot be moved." These are not the words of
a deliberate heretic or of a professed rationalist. . . .

Abelard was unquestionably technically unorthodox in many of his
expressions. Though his opponents, and in particular St Bernard, may
have erred in the severity of their attacks and in the universality of their
suspicions, and though recent scholarship has shown that some, at
least, of his expressions can, in their context, bear an orthodox interpretation, and that Abelard became more, and not less, respectful of tradi-

tion as the years passed, yet many of his pronouncements on the Trinity, the Incarnation, and Grace were certainly incorrect by traditional standards and, if carried to their logical issue, would have dangerously weakened the expression of Christian truth. The catalogue of erroneous, or at least of erratic, propositions in his writings drawn up by Portalié sixty years ago cannot be wholly cancelled by explanations of a verbal or logical nature. Error, however, is not always heretical. In the theological controversies of every age there have always been two families among those accused of heresy. There are those who, whatever their professions, are in fact attacking traditional doctrine, and those who, despite many of their expressions have, as we may say, the root of the matter in them . . . and there can be no doubt to which of the families Abelard belongs.

Abelard's genius was versatile, and left a mark on everything he touched. We have already considered his important contribution to logic, and in particular his solution of the problem of universals. In methodology he marked an epoch with his *Sic et non*. This short treatise, composed perhaps in its earliest form *c.* 1122, is perhaps the most celebrated (though not necessarily the most important) of Abelard's contributions to the development of medieval thought; it has in recent years been the occasion of a number of controversies. It consists of a relatively short prologue explaining its purpose and giving rules for the discussion of what follows; then comes a series of texts from Scripture and the Fathers on 150 theological points. The texts are given in groups, and in each case are apparently mutually contradictory. The essence of the work is the exposition of methodical doubt. As Abelard has it, "careful and frequent questioning is the basic key to wisdom," or, as he writes in the same prologue: "By doubting we come to questioning, and by questioning we perceive the truth."

Opinions have been divided as to how far the *Sic et non* is original, how far it is an instrument of scepticism, and what was its influence on the development of scholastic method. It was for long the common opinion that it was completely original, an innovation with resounding consequences as great in its own field as the invention of the spinning-jenny or the mechanical reaper in the world of economics. This view, usually held in conjunction with that which saw in Abelard the first great apostle of free thought, was convincingly refuted by the researches of Fournier and Grabmann, who showed that the juxtaposition of seemingly contradictory authorities was already a method in common use in Abelard's day by compilers of canonical collections, who had not only amassed texts but given rules for criticism and harmonization. Bernold of Constance and Ivo of Chartres in particular had employed this technique, and the *Decretum* and *Panormia* of the latter were shown to have furnished Abelard with some of his quotations from the Fathers.

As regards the primary aim of the *Sic et non,* there have been two views. Many in the past, Harnack among them, have seen in it an attempt to undermine tradition by showing its essentially self-contradictory character, in order to make way for a more rational approach. Others, and among them the greatest names among historians of medieval thought, have strenuously opposed this view, seeing in the *Sic et non* simply an exercise for explaining and harmonizing discrepancies and difficulties in the authorities. This opinion gains additional support from the fact that the work was never used by his opponents as a stick with which to beat Abelard. Such a view might well allow that *Sic et non* was a reaction against the purely traditionalist teaching of the day, and that it was intended to open a wide new field to dialectic, for which only a few samples were given.

As for the influence of the work upon the schools, the verdict of the early historians was summary, and Abelard was hailed as the creator of the scholastic method. . . . As we have seen, all now admit that the borrowing was on Abelard's side. . . .

In theology, the main achievement of Abelard was to discuss and explain, where others merely asserted or proved, and to provide an outline of the whole field of doctrines. It would seem, indeed, that he was the first to use the Latin word *theologia* in the sense that is now current in all European languages; the word had previously borne the connotation familiar in the Greek Fathers and the pseudo-Denis, of the mystical or at least the expert knowledge of God and His attributes. By giving, in versions of increasing length and scope, an "introduction" or survey of Christian teaching, Abelard's writings are an important link in the development of the *summa,* the typical medieval survey of theology.

When thus "introducing" his disciples to theology, Abelard met, as he himself tells us, a genuine demand for an explanation of the mysteries of the faith, and he gave this explanation with opinions that were often original, and which aimed at being reasonable. . . . He was further accused of obscuring the personal union of the divine and human natures in Christ by treating the humanity as something assumed, as it were, as a garment by the divine Son. This, and other questionable propositions, make up an impressive total of erroneous opinions, and although some were due to faulty terminology and others were tacitly dropped from later versions of the same work—for Abelard, resembling other lecturers before and since, was always rewriting and adding precision to his treatises—too much smoke remains to allow the cry of fire to be ignored. Above and through all else was the charge that Abelard left no place in his system for faith. . . .

In yet one more important field, that of ethics, Abelard was destined to leave a durable mark. In his discussion of moral problems in *Scito te ipsum*[4] he showed his originality in such a way as to be one of the founders of scholastic moral theology. Reacting against the view then current which placed moral goodness solely in the conformity of an act to the declared law of God, and which tended to see sin as the factual transgression of the law, even if unknown or misunderstood (e.g. the obligation of certain degrees of fasting on certain days), Abelard placed goodness wholly in the intention and will of the agent, and saw sin not as the actual transgression of the law, but as a contempt of God the lawgiver.... Abelard, in commenting upon the text, "Father, forgive them, for they know not what they do," tended to excuse wholly from sin the agents of the Crucifixion, stressing "they know not what they do" rather than the implicit sin that needed forgiveness. This shocked current susceptibilities, and was one of the charges against him. In another direction his opinions minimized the conception of the law of God and of the absolute ethical goodness of particular actions. Abelard, anticipating with strange exactness the opinions of some fourteenth century "voluntarists," suggested that with God as with man the good depended upon the free choice, and that God might have established canons of morality other than, and even contrary to, those of the Hebrew and Christian revelation.

Look at him how we will, and when full weight has been given to the impression of restlessness, vanity and lack of spiritual depth given by his career and some of his writings, Abelard remains, both as a teacher and as a thinker, one of the half-dozen most influential names in the history of medieval thought.... As a theologian, he was the first to see his subject as a whole, and to conceive the possibility of a survey or synthesis for his pupils, thus taking an important part in fixing the method of teaching. Finally, and perhaps most significantly, he approached theological and ethical problems as questions that could be illuminated, explained and in part comprehended by a carefully reasoned approach, and still more by a humane, practical attitude which took account of difficulties and of natural, human feelings, and he endeavoured to solve problems of belief and conscience not by the blow of an abstract principle, but by a consideration of circumstances as they are in common experience. Abelard failed to become a much-cited authority by reason of his double condemnation and the attacks of celebrated adversaries, but his ideas lingered in the minds of his disciples, and many of them came to the surface, unacknowledged, in the golden age of scholasticism.

[4]"Know thyself."—ED.

Suggestions for Further Reading

Abelard's autobiography, which is excerpted in this chapter and which took the form of a letter to a friend, is available along with seven additional letters exchanged between Abelard and Eloise, in *The Letters of Abelard and Eloise,* tr. C. K. Scott-Moncrieff (New York: Knopf, 1926) and in *The Letters of Abelard and Héloise,* tr. and intro. Betty Radice (Harmondsworth: Penguin, 1974). There are a number of biographical treatments of Abelard. One of the best is a small and elegant book by Etienne Gilson, *Héloise and Abelard,* tr. L. K. Shook (Ann Arbor: University of Michigan Press, 1963 [1951]), in which the great French medievalist retells the familiar story with scholarship and insight. He also includes an appendix in which he argues for the authenticity of the letters. R. W. Southern, the distinguished British medievalist, also deals with the letters and some related topics in a collection of his articles, *Medieval Humanism and Other Studies* (Oxford, England: Blackwell, 1970). Durant W. Robertson, Jr., *Abelard and Heloise* (New York: Dial, 1972) is a good critical biography dealing well with the traditional account and its sources. Régine Pernoud, *Heloise and Abelard,* tr. Peter Wiles (New York: Stein and Day, 1973) is a more conventional retelling of the familiar story, but well-written. There is also a pamphlet by David E. Luscombe, *Peter Abelard* (London: The Historical Association, 1979), which gives a judicious survey of the sources. There is a first-rate historical novel by Helen J. Waddell, *Peter Abelard, A Novel* (New York: Barnes and Noble, 1971 [1933]). J. G. Sikes, *Peter Abelard* (New York: Russell and Russell, 1965 [1932]), is largely about Abelard's thought rather than about his life and is complex and difficult, as is the more recent detailed documentary study of Abelard's influence, D. E. Luscombe, *The School of Peter Abelard: The Influence of Abelard's Thought in the Early Scholastic Period* (Cambridge, England: Cambridge University Press, 1969), but the latter is an important revisionist work, showing Abelard as less the founder of a distinctive school and more a journeyman critic.

It was, of course, largely Abelard's thought that got him in trouble with the church and with St. Bernard of Clairvaux. Their differences are dealt with in Denis Meadows, *A Saint and a Half: A New Interpretation of Abelard and St. Bernard of Clairvaux* (New York: Devin-Adair, 1963); it is less a new interpretation than an attempt to soften the disagreements between them. A sharper treatment of their differences is to be found in A. Victor Murray, *Abelard and St. Bernard: A Study in Twelfth Century "Modernism"* (New York: Barnes and Noble, 1967). For the church itself in Abelard's time, the best brief general survey of the papacy is G. Barraclough, *The Medieval Papacy* (New

York: Harcourt, Brace, 1968). Equally authoritative and readable but more comprehensive for this period is H. Daniel-Rops, *Cathedral and Crusade: Studies of the Medieval Church 1050–1350,* tr. John Warrington (New York: Dutton, 1957). As for the more specific environment of Abelard, the medieval schools, the best and most readable works are still the old classics, Helen Waddell, *The Wandering Scholars* (New York: Holt, 1934 [1927]), Charles Homer Haskins, *The Rise of Universities* (New York: P. Smith 1940 [1923]), and his *Studies in Medieval Culture* (New York: Ungar, 1958 [1929]). Haskins's notions about the Renaissance of the twelfth century are still being debated: see the review of the literature in C. Warren Hollister (ed.), *The Twelfth-Century Renaissance* (New York: Wiley, 1969); Christopher Brooke, *The Twelfth-Century Renaissance* (New York: Harcourt, Brace, 1969), not so much a revision of Haskins's classic work as an updating and extension; and the graceful and learned work of Sidney R. Packard, *12th Century Europe: An Interpretive Essay* (Amherst: University of Massachusetts Press, 1973).

For the relationship of Abelard to medieval learning and scholasticism, further reading in Dom David Knowles, *The Evolution of Medieval Thought* (New York: Vintage, 1962), is recommended, along with another more recent book by David Knowles with Dimitri Obolensky, *The Middle Ages,* "The Christian Centuries" vol. 2 (New York: McGraw-Hill, 1978) and the old standard Gordon Leff, *Medieval Thought* (Harmondsworth, England: Penguin, 1958). Two more straightforward surveys are Meyrick H. Carré, *Realists and Nominalists* (London: Oxford University Press, 1946), and F. C. Copleston, *A History of Medieval Philosophy* (New York: Harper & Row, 1972 [1952]).

Finally, students must remember that the towns and schools of the twelfth century were the products of the economic revolution that was sweeping Europe. The best and most comprehensive treatment of the new medieval economic history is *The Cambridge Economic History of Europe,* 2nd ed., vols. 1–3 (Cambridge, England: Cambridge University Press, 1952–1966). Three additional works may also be recommended, one by the American economic historian Robert S. Lopez, *The Commercial Revolution of the Middle Ages, 950–1350* (Englewood Cliffs, N.J.: Prentice-Hall, 1971), and two by French authorities, R. H. Bautier, *The Economic Development of Medieval Europe,* tr. H. Karolyi (New York: Harcourt, Brace, 1971), and Georges Duby, *The Early Growth of the European Economy,* tr. H. B. Clarke (Ithaca, N.Y.: Cornell University Press, 1974).

ELEANOR OF AQUITAINE AND THE WRATH OF GOD

c. 1122	Born
1137	Married the future Louis VII of France
1147–1149	Second crusade
1152	Divorced from Louis VII and married to the future Henry II of England
1192–1194	Regent during captivity of Richard I
1204	Died

Eleanor of Aquitaine was one of the most remarkable and important figures in medieval history. In her own right, she was duchess of the vast domain of Aquitaine and countess of Poitou, the wife first of Louis VII of France and then of Henry II of England, the mother of "good King Richard" and "bad King John," patroness of poets and minstrels. Tradition remembers her as beautiful and passionate, headstrong and willful. But beyond that intriguing traditional reputation, she is a figure only imperfectly seen and, ironically enough, seen at all largely through the accounts of her enemies.

The sources of medieval history are scanty at best and tend, moreover, to record men's doings in a preponderantly man's world. Even the greatest of medieval women appear in the records of their time as conveyors of properties and channels for noble blood lines, and we know of them only that they were "good and faithful wives"—or that they were not. So it is with Eleanor. We do not even have a contemporary description of her. Troubadour poets sang rapturously of her "crystal cheeks," her "locks like threads of gold," her eyes "like Orient pearls." One even proclaims:

Were the world all mine,
From the sea to the Rhine,

> I'd give it all
> If so be the Queen of England
> Lay in my arms.

In sober fact, we do not know what color her eyes were, nor her hair, whether it was indeed "like threads of gold" or raven black. Even the few pictorial representations we have of her—including her tomb effigy at the Abbey of Fontevrault—are purely conventional.

But Eleanor's part in the great events of her time was real enough. It began with her marriage, at the age of fifteen, to Louis the young king, son of Louis VI (Louis the Fat) of France. Her father, the turbulent Duke William X of Aquitaine, had died suddenly and unexpectedly on pilgrimage to Spain, leaving Eleanor his heir. And, in feudal law, the disposition of both Eleanor and her fiefs was a matter to be decided by her father's overlord, Louis VI of France. Duke William had been Louis's most intractable vassal, and his death was a priceless opportunity not only to put an end to the contumaciousness of Aquitaine but to tie that large and wealthy duchy to the French realm. Louis decided that the interests of his house were best served by the marriage of Eleanor to his son. And so, it was done. There is no record of how either the young bride or the young groom responded, only an account of the brilliant assemblage that gathered to witness the ceremony in Bordeaux and to accompany the couple back by weary stages to Paris. In the course of this journey, the aged King Louis died. His son was now Louis VII, the Duchess Eleanor now queen of France. The year was 1137.

We must not imagine that Eleanor was a very happy bride in those first years of her marriage. Paris was a cold and gloomy northern city, very different from sunny Provence, and the Capetian castles in which she lived were dark and uncomfortable. The king—her husband—had an inexhaustible thirst for devotion and piety and surrounded himself with ecclesiastical advisers, confessors, theologians, and barren, quibbling scholars, so unlike the more robust and charming practitioners of the *gai savoir* (merry learning) with whom Eleanor had grown up at her father's court. Nor was Louis very happy, for he and his young wife had two daughters, Marie and Alix, but no son, no member of what was then considered "the better sex" to be groomed for the Capetian throne.

Then word reached Paris of the fall of Edessa in the distant Latin Kingdom of Jerusalem, one of those fortress principalities to secure the Holy Land dating from the first crusade almost half a century before. The resurgence of Moslem power was clearly seen to threaten the Holy Land, and the call for a second crusade went out. The pious King Louis took the cross—to the consternation of his more realistic advisers. And Eleanor insisted upon accompanying him. Whatever Louis and his fellow crusaders may have thought about this matter, Eleanor's position as a great vassal who could summon a substantial host of warriors from her own lands made her support crucial: and her support was contingent upon her going in person. There is a persistent legend that the queen and her ladies decked themselves out as Amazons in anticipation of their role in the coming military adventure.

But the military adventure itself turned into a military disaster. The second crusade was a dismal failure. The French forces of Louis VII were seriously defeated by the Turks, and the German contingent led by the Emperor Conrad III was almost wiped out. Both the French and the Germans accused the Byzantine Greeks of treachery. There were disagreements among the Western knights, and many of them simply abandoned the crusade and returned home. There were divided counsels among those who remained and mistrust between them and the Christian lords of the Eastern principalities. And there were continued military blunders and defeats. Tempers were short, old quarrels flared, new ones commenced.

In this atmosphere, what had apparently been a growing estrangement between King Louis and Queen Eleanor became an open break. Their troubles were aggravated by what was then considered the boldness and outspokenness of the queen and in particular by her attentions to her handsome uncle, only eight years older than she, Raymond of Poitiers, Prince of Antioch. It may have been no more than an innocent flirtation. But Louis thought otherwise. He brooded not only on his queen's conduct but on what he perceived as her failure to produce a son for him, and his mind turned to divorce, the grounds for which were to be found in consanguinity, a marriage within the prohibited degree of blood relationship, which was the usual legal pretext for the dissolution of feudal marriages no longer bearable or profitable.

Eleanor and the Chroniclers

WILLIAM OF TYRE
AND JOHN OF SALISBURY

Eleanor's role in the second crusade is scarcely mentioned by the chroniclers who recorded the deeds of its other leading figures. Odo of Deuil, a monk of the French royal monastery of St. Denis and the chaplain of Louis VII, wrote the most detailed account of Louis's part in the crusade—De profectione Ludovici VII in orientem—but he makes only four passing references to the queen in the entire narrative. Odo clearly had reason to favor the cause of the king, his master. And, for one reason or another, so did the few other chroniclers who give any account of all of the estrangement between Louis and Eleanor. The most detailed is that of William Archbishop of Tyre. William is generally regarded as the best of all the chroniclers of the crusades, but he was not present at the time of this crisis and we do not know what source he used. In any event, he regarded the behavior of the queen and the resulting breach with her husband as part of a cynical attempt by Raymond of Antioch to turn the crusade to his own advantage. Here is the account of William of Tyre.

For many days Raymond, prince of Antioch, had eagerly awaited the arrival of the king of the Franks. When he learned that the king had landed in his domains, he summoned all the nobles of the land and the chief leaders of the people and went out to meet him with a chosen escort. He greated the king with much reverence and conducted him with great pomp into the city of Antioch, where he was met by the clergy and the people. Long before this time—in fact, as soon as he heard that Louis was coming—Raymond had conceived the idea that by his aid he might be able to enlarge the principality of Antioch. With this in mind, therefore, even before the king started on the pilgrimage, the prince had sent to him in France a large store of noble gifts and treasures of great price in the hope of winning his favor. He also counted greatly on the interest of the queen with the lord king, for she had been his inseparable companion on his pilgrimage. She was Raymond's niece, and eldest daughter of Count William of Poitou, his brother.

As we have said, therefore, Raymond showed the king every attention on his arrival. He likewise displayed a similar care for the nobles and chief men in the royal retinue and gave them many proofs of his great liberality. In short, he outdid all in showing honor to each one according to his rank and handled everything with the greatest magnificence. He felt a lively hope that with the assistance of the king and his troops he would be able to subjugate the neighboring cities, namely, Aleppo, Shayzar, and several others. Nor would this hope have been futile, could he have induced the king and his chief men to undertake the work. For the arrival of King Louis had brought such fear to our enemies that now they not only distrusted their own strength but even despaired of life itself.

Raymond had already more than once approached the king privately in regard to the plans which he had in mind. Now he came before the members of the king's suite and his own nobles and explained with due formality how his request could be accomplished without difficulty and at the same time be of advantage and renown to themselves. The king, however, ardently desired to go to Jerusalem to fulfil his vows, and his determination was irrevocable. When Raymond found that he could not induce the king to join him, his attitude changed. Frustrated in his ambitious designs, he began to hate the king's ways; he openly plotted against him and took means to do him injury. He resolved also to deprive him of his wife, either by force or by secret intrigue. The queen readily assented to this design, for she was a foolish woman. Her conduct before and after this time showed her to be, as we have said, far from circumspect. Contrary to her royal dignity, she disregarded her marriage vows and was unfaithful to her husband.

As soon as the king discovered these plots, he took means to provide for his life and safety by anticipating the designs of the prince. By the advice of his chief nobles, he hastened his departure and secretly left Antioch with his people. Thus the splendid aspect of his affairs was completely changed, and the end was quite unlike the beginning. His coming had been attended with pomp and glory; but fortune is fickle, and his departure was ignominious.

The only other substantial account of the events leading to the divorce of Louis and Eleanor is that of the great twelfth-century ecclesiastic and intellectual, John of Salisbury, in his Historia Pontificalis. *In one respect, John was even further removed from the events than was William of Tyre. He had no direct knowledge of the East at all and was, at this time, in Rome on a mission from the see of Canterbury and attached to the papal court. We do not know what source he used for the events in Antioch. It is likely that he is simply repeating the story as he heard it from members of Louis's retinue, for the hostility against Eleanor that already animated Louis's close supporters is clearly present in John's ac-*

*count. It is also possible that the hostility of the account and its strong
pro-French bias is related to the later time at which John's work was
actually written, about 1163. At this time, John was involved in the
growing bitterness between Thomas Becket, whom he supported, and
Henry II of England, who had just sent John into exile for his support of
Becket. John found refuge in France.*

But in any event, the account in the Historia Pontificalis *is strongly
favorable to Louis, even to the extent of ascribing to Eleanor the initiative in the proposal for the divorce.*

In the year of grace 1149 the most Christian king of the Franks reached
Antioch, after the destruction of his armies in the east, and was nobly
entertained there by Prince Raymond, brother of the late William,
count of Poitiers. He was as it happened the queen's uncle, and owed
the king loyalty, affection and respect for many reasons. But whilst
they remained there to console, heal and revive the survivors from the
wreck of the army, the attentions paid by the prince to the queen, and
his constant, indeed almost continuous, conversation with her, aroused
the king's suspicions. These were greatly strengthened when the
queen wished to remain behind, although the king was preparing to
leave, and the prince made every effort to keep her, if the king would
give his consent. And when the king made haste to tear her away, she
mentioned their kinship, saying it was not lawful for them to remain
together as man and wife, since they were related in the fourth and
fifth degrees. Even before their departure a rumour to that effect had
been heard in France, where the late Bartholomew bishop of Laon had
calculated the degrees of kinship; but it was not certain whether the
reckoning was true or false. At this the king was deeply moved; and
although he loved the queen almost beyond reason he consented to
divorce her if his counsellors and the French nobility would allow it.
There was one knight amongst the king's secretaries, called Terricus
Gualerancius, a eunuch whom the queen had always hated and
mocked, but who was faithful and had the king's ear like his father's
before him. He boldly persuaded the king not to suffer her to dally
longer at Antioch, both because "guilt under kinship's guise could lie
concealed," and because it would be a lasting shame to the kingdom of
the Franks if in addition to all the other disasters it was reported that
the king had been deserted by his wife, or robbed of her. So he argued,
either because he hated the queen or because he really believed it,
moved perchance by widespread rumour. In consequence, she was
torn away and forced to leave for Jerusalem with the king; and, their
mutual anger growing greater, the wound remained, hide it as best
they might.

In the next passage, John is on more familiar ground since he was in Rome, a familiar of the curia and of Pope Eugenius III, and perhaps even a witness to some of the events he describes.

In the year of grace eleven hundred and fifty the king of the Franks returned home. But the galleys of the Emperor of Constantinople lay in wait for him on his return, capturing the queen and all who were journeying in her ship. The king was appealed to to return to his Byzantine brother and friend, and force was being brought to bear on him when the galleys of the king of Sicily came to the rescue. Freeing the queen and releasing the king, they escorted them back to Sicily rejoicing, with honour and triumph. This was done by order of the king of Sicily, who feared the wiles of the Greeks and desired an opportunity of showing his devotion to the king and queen of the Franks. Now therefore he hastened to meet him with an ample retinue, and escorted him most honourably to Palermo, heaping gifts both on him and on all his followers; thereafter he travelled with him right across his territory to Ceprano, supplying all his needs on the way. This is the last point on the frontier between the principality of Capua and Campania, which is papal territory.

At Ceprano the cardinals and officials of the church met the king and, providing him with all that he desired, escorted him to Tusculum to the lord pope, who received him with such tenderness and reverence that one would have said he was welcoming an angel of the Lord rather than a mortal man. He reconciled the king and queen, after hearing severally the accounts each gave of the estrangement begun at Antioch, and forbade any future mention of their consanguinity: confirming their marriage, both orally and in writing, he commanded under pain of anathema that no word should be spoken against it and that it should not be dissolved under any pretext whatever. This ruling plainly delighted the king, for he loved the queen passionately, in an almost childish way. The pope made them sleep in the same bed, which he had had decked with priceless hangings of his own; and daily during their brief visit he strove by friendly converse to restore love between them. He heaped gifts upon them; and when the moment for departure came, though he was a stern man, he could not hold back his tears, but sent them on their way blessing them and the kingdom of the Franks, which was higher in his esteem than all the kingdoms of the world.

Eleanor, the Queen of Hearts

AMY KELLY

Despite "the lord pope's" good offices, his tears and his blessing, even his threat of anathema, the estrangement between Louis and Eleanor continued. Louis was adamant, and finally, in the spring of 1152 at a solemn synod in Beaugency on the Loire, Louis's representatives argued the case of the consanguinity of their lord and his queen, and the Archbishop of Sens proclaimed their marriage invalid. The Archbishop of Bordeaux, the queen's surrogate, sought only the assurance that her lands be restored. But this had already been arranged, as had all the other details of this elaborate royal charade. Eleanor was not even present. She had already returned to Poitou.

But Eleanor was not destined to reign as a dowager duchess in her own domains. Within two months, she married Henry, Duke of Normandy. He was not only the Norman duke but also the heir to the fiefs of his father, Geoffrey Plantagenet, Count of Maine and Anjou. These already substantial lands, when joined to those of his new bride, made Henry lord of a nearly solid block of territories that stretched from the English Channel to the Mediterranean and from Bordeaux to the Vexin, hardly a day's ride from Paris. At one stroke, Henry of Anjou had become the greatest feudatory of France, with lands and resources many times the size of those held by his nominal overlord, King Louis VII. Two years later, another piece of Henry's inheritance came into his hands. His mother, Matilda, was the daughter of the English King Henry I and had never ceased to press the claim of her son to the English throne. The reign of King Stephen was coming to an end, and he had no surviving heirs. At his death in 1154, Henry of Anjou claimed his crown, and there was none to deny him. Eleanor was a queen once more.

But this time, she had a very different king. Henry II was as godless as Louis had been pious, as flamboyant as Louis had been humble. Where Louis was stubborn and persistent, Henry was furiously energetic and decisive. The setting was at hand for one of the classic confrontations of medieval history that was to stretch into the following generation of the kings of both France and England.

As for Eleanor, the sources are once more almost silent. We do know that she and Henry produced a large family. The eldest son, William, born before the succession to England, died in childhood. But in 1155 came Henry; in 1156, their first daughter, Matilda; in 1157 came Richard, to be called the Lion Hearted; in 1158 came Geoffrey; in 1161, Eleanor; in 1165, Johanna; and in 1166, John. We know that through the early years of her marriage to Henry, Eleanor was often with him at court and sometimes presided in his absence, a fact attested by writs and seals. But her marriage was by no means serene. There were long periods of separation during which the king was known to be unfaithful. The incidents of his infidelity had grown more flagrant with the passing years. At about the time of prince John's birth in 1166, Henry was involved with a paramour of spectacular beauty, Rosamond Clifford. Their affair was the object of such celebration by poets, balladeers, and wags alike that Eleanor may have decided that her bed and her dignity could no longer endure such an affront. But there may have been other matters at issue. The queen may have become alarmed at her husband's efforts to substitute his rule for hers in her dower lands.

In any case, about 1170 she returned to Poitou with her favorite son, Richard, whom she installed as her heir for the lands of Poitou and Aquitaine. For the next three or four years she lived in her old capital of Poitiers, separated from her husband. In these years of self-imposed exile, Eleanor not only reasserted her rights to her own lands, but created a center in Poitiers for the practice of the troubadour culture and l'amour courtois that had long been associated with her family.

The following passage, from Amy Kelly's Eleanor of Aquitaine and the Four Kings—*the book that has come to be regarded as the standard work on Eleanor—is a brilliant reconstruction of this period of Eleanor's life.*

When the countess of Poitou settled down to rule her own heritage, she took her residence in Poitiers, which offered a wide eye-sweep on the world of still operative kings. In the recent Plantagenet building program her ancestral city, the seat and necropolis of her forebears, had been magnificently enlarged and rebuilt, and it stood at her coming thoroughly renewed, a gleaming exemplar of urban elegance. The site rose superbly amidst encircling rivers. Its narrow Merovingian area had lately been extended to include with new and ampler walls parishes that had previously straggled over its outer slopes; ancient quarters had been cleared of immemorial decay; new churches and collegials had sprung up; the cathedral of Saint Pierre was enriched; markets and shops of tradesmen and artisans bore witness to renewed life among the *bourgeoisie;* bridges fanned out to suburbs and monastic establishments lying beyond the streams that moated the city. Brimming with sunshine, the valleys ebbed far away below—hamlet and croft, mill and vineyard—to a haze as blue as the vintage. . . .

When Eleanor came in about 1170 to take full possession of her newly restored city of Poitiers and to install her favorite son there as ruling count and duke in her own patrimony, she was no mere game piece as were most feudal women, to be moved like a queen in chess. She had learned her role as *domina* in Paris, Byzantium, Antioch, London, and Rouen, and knew her value in the feudal world. She was prepared of her own unguided wisdom to reject the imperfect destinies to which she had been, as it were, assigned. In this, her third important role in history, she was the pawn of neither prince nor prelate, the victim of no dynastic scheme. She came as her own mistress, the most sophisticated of women, equipped with plans to establish her own assize, to inaugurate a regime dedicated neither to Mars nor to the Pope, nor to any king, but to Minerva, Venus, and the Virgin. She was resolved to escape from secondary roles, to assert her independent sovereignty in her own citadel, to dispense her own justice, her own patronage, and when at leisure, to survey, like the Empress of Byzantium, a vast decorum in her precincts. . . .

The heirs of Poitou and Aquitaine who came to the queen's high place for their vassals' homage, their squires' training, and their courtiers' service, were truculent youths, boisterous young men from the baronial strongholds of the south without the Norman or Frankish sense of nationality, bred on feuds and violence, some of them with rich fiefs and proud lineage, but with little solidarity and no business but local warfare and daredevil escapade. The custom of lateral rather than vertical inheritance of fiefs in vogue in some parts of Poitou and Aquitaine—the system by which lands passed through a whole generation before descending to the next generation—produced a vast number of landless but expectant younger men, foot-loose, unemployed, ambitious, yet dependent upon the reluctant bounty of uncles and brothers, or their own violent exploits. These wild young men were a deep anxiety not only to the heads of their houses, but to the Kings of France and England and to the Pope in Rome. They were the stuff of which rebellion and schism are made. For two generations the church had done what it could with the problem of their unemployment, marching hordes out of Europe on crusade and rounding other hordes into the cloister.

It was with this spirited world of princes and princesses, of apprentice knights and chatelaines, at once the school and the court of young Richard, that the duchess, busy as she was with the multifarious business of a feudal suzerain, had to deal in her palace in Poitiers. . . .

Eleanor found a willing and helpful deputy to assist her in the person of Marie, Countess of Champagne, her daughter by Louis of France. Ma-

rie, now entrusted to Eleanor's tutelage, was a well-educated young woman and apparently well disposed to her mother's plans.

. . . The character of the milieu which Marie appears to have set up in Poitiers suggests a genuine sympathy between the queen and her daughter who had so long been sundered by the bleak fortuities of life. Old relationships were knit up. Something native blossomed in the countess, who shone with a special luster in her mother's court. The young Count of Poitou learned to love particularly his half sister Marie and forever to regard the Poitiers of her dispensation as the world's citadel of valor, the seat of courtesy, and the fountainhead of poetic inspiration. Long after, in his darkest hours, it was to her good graces he appealed. The countess, having carte blanche to proceed with the very necessary business of getting control of her academy, must have striven first for order. Since the miscellaneous and high-spirited young persons in her charge had not learned order from the liturgy nor yet from hagiography, the countess bethought her, like many an astute pedagogue, to deduce her principles from something more germane to their interests. She did not precisely invent her regime; rather she appropriated it from the abundant resources at her hand.

The liberal court of Eleanor had again drawn a company of those gifted persons who thrive by talent or by art. Poets, *conteurs* purveying romance, ecclesiastics with Latin literature at their tongues' end and mere clerks with smatterings of Ovid learned from quotation books, chroniclers engaged upon the sober epic of the Plantagenets, came to their haven in Poitiers. The queen and the countess, with their native poetic tradition, were the natural patrons of the troubadours. It will be seen that the Countess Marie's resources were rich and abundant, but not so formalized as to afford the disciplines for a royal academy nor give substance to a social ritual. The great hall was ready for her grand assize; the expectant court already thronged to gape at its suggestive splendors. . . .

At least one other important source Marie employed. She levied upon the social traditions of her Poitevin forebears. Nostredame relates that in Provence chatelaines were accustomed to entertain their seasonal assemblies with so-called "courts of love," in which, just as feudal vassals brought their grievances to the assizes of their overlords for regulation, litigants in love's thrall brought their problems for the judgment of the ladies. André in his famous work[1] makes

---

[1] André, simply known as the Chaplain, a scholar of this court whose work *Tractatus de Amore* is referred to here, one of the basic works on medieval chivalry and the courts of love.—ED.

reference to antecedent decisions in questions of an amatory nature by "les dames de Gascogne," and the poetry of the troubadours presupposes a milieu in which their doctrines of homage and deference could be exploited. Thus we have in Andre's *Tractatus* the framework of Ovid with the central emphasis reversed, the Arthurian code of manners, the southern ritual of the "courts of love," all burnished with a golden wash of troubadour poetry learned by the queen's forebears and their vassals in the deep Midi, probably beyond the barrier of the Pyrenees. Marie made these familiar materials the vehicle for her woman's doctrine of civility, and in so doing, she transformed the gross and cynical pagan doctrines of Ovid into something more ideal, the woman's canon, the chivalric code of manners. Manners, she plainly saw, were after all the fine residuum of philosophies, the very flower of ethics. . . .

With this anatomy of the whole corpus of love in hand, Marie organized the rabble of soldiers, fighting cocks, jousters, springers, riding masters, troubadours, Poitevin nobles and debutantes, young chatelaines, adolescent princes, and infant princesses in the great hall of Poitiers. Of this pandemonium the countess fashioned a seemly and elegant society, the fame of which spread to the world. Here was a woman's assize to draw men from the excitements of the tilt and the hunt, from dice and games to feminine society, an assize to outlaw boorishness and compel the tribute of adulation to female majesty. . . .

While the ladies, well-accoutered, sit above upon the dais, the sterner portion of society purged, according to the code, from the odors of the kennels and the highway and free for a time from spurs and falcons, range themselves about the stone benches that line the walls, stirring the fragrant rushes with neatly pointed shoe. There are doubtless preludes of music luring the last reluctant knight from the gaming table, *tensons* or *pastourelles,* the plucking of rotes, the "voicing of a fair song and sweet," perhaps even some of the more complicated musical harmonies so ill-received by the clerical critics in London; a Breton *lai* adding an episode to Arthurian romance, or a chapter in the tale of "sad-man" Tristram, bringing a gush of tears from the tender audience clustered about the queen and the Countess of Champagne.

After the romance of the evening in the queen's court, the jury comes to attention upon petition of a young knight in the hall. He bespeaks the judgment of the queen and her ladies upon a point of conduct, through an advocate, of course, so he may remain anonymous. A certain knight, the advocate deposes, has sworn to his lady, as the hard condition of obtaining her love, that he will upon no provocation boast of her merits in company. But one day he overhears detractors heaping his mistress with calumnies. Forgetting his vow in the heat of his passion, he warms to eloquence in defense of his lady. This coming to her ears, she repudiates her champion. Does the lover, who admits he has broken his pledge to his mistress, deserve in this instance to be driven from her presence?

The Countess of Champagne, subduing suggestions from the floor and the buzz of conference upon the dais, renders the judgment of the areopagus. The lady in the case, anonymous of course, is at fault, declares the Countess Marie. She has laid upon her lover a vow too impossibly difficult. The lover has been remiss, no doubt, in breaking his vow to his mistress, no matter what cruel hardship it involves; but he deserves leniency for the merit of his ardor and his constancy. The jury recommends that the stern lady reinstate the plaintiff. The court takes down the judgment. It constitutes a precedent. Does anyone guess the identity of the young pair whose estrangement is thus delicately knit up by the countess? As a bit of suspense it is delicious. As a theme for talk, how loosening to the tongue!

A disappointed petitioner brings forward a case, through an advocate, involving the question whether love survives marriage. The countess, applying her mind to the code, which says that marriage is no proper obstacle to lovers (*Causa coniugii ab amore non est excusatio recta*), and after grave deliberation with her ladies, creates a sensation in the court by expressing doubt whether love in the ideal sense can exist between spouses. This is so arresting a proposition that the observations of the countess are referred to the queen for corroboration, and all wait upon the opinion of this deeply experienced judge. The queen with dignity affirms that she cannot gainsay the Countess of Champagne, though she finds it admirable that a wife should find love and marriage consonant. Eleanor, Queen of France and then of England, had learned at fifty-two that, as another medieval lady put it, "Mortal love is but the licking of honey from thorns."

Eleanor the Regent

MARION MEADE

During the years of Eleanor's dalliance at Poitiers, her husband's larger world had been turned upside down by his quarrel with Thomas Becket. It had not ended even with the martyrdom of that troublesome prelate at the altar of Canterbury in 1170. The question of whether Henry ordered

*Becket's murder or not—and he probably did not—is quite immaterial. For
he bore its consequences. And its principal consequence was to give to the
French king a priceless justification to move against Henry and his fiefs.
What is more, Henry's own sons were as often as not in league with the
French king. With some of them, Henry had been too hard, with others too
soft. And when he favored one, the others feared and plotted against the
favorite of the moment. Even Henry's proposed disposition of his estates and
titles served only to further their quarrels with each other and with him.
These quarrels reached their first climax in the great rebellion of 1173, in
which Henry the young king, Richard, and Geoffrey were in open alliance
with Louis of France against their father. To the alliance flocked rebellious
barons from Scotland to Aquitaine. Henry charged Eleanor with sedition
and with embittering their sons against him. As the rebellion faltered and
then was quelled, Henry was reconciled, however fitfully, with his sons but
not their mother. With Eleanor, Henry was unyielding. She was imprisoned, first at Salisbury Castle, later at Winchester and other places, for the
next sixteen years. One must imagine that the captivity was genteel, but it
was nonetheless real. From time to time, she was released for a holiday visit
to court or to participate in some stormy family council.*

*In the last years of Eleanor's imprisonment, two of her sons, Henry and
Geoffrey, died, but the surviving sons, Richard and John, could still intrigue against their father. They did so in league with a new and more
dangerous Capetian enemy, Philip II Augustus, the able and energetic son
of Louis VII, who had followed him to the throne in 1180. Henry II's final
years were filled with his sons' rebellion, and he died in 1189 shamed by
defeat at their hands. It was only after Henry's death and the succession of
Richard that Eleanor was released from her captivity.*

*With none of her ardor dimmed, the queen, now almost seventy, set about
to serve her favored son, now king at last. While Richard was still on the
Continent, Eleanor assumed the regency and on her own authority
convoked a court at Westminster to demand the oaths of loyalty from the
English feudality to their new king. She then traveled to other centers to
take similar obeisances and to set the affairs of the kingdom in order. Her
son arrived for an undisputed coronation in the summer of 1189.*

*But Richard's thoughts in that triumphal summer season were not upon
the affairs of England or any of his other lands. He had already taken the
cross almost two years before, and the third crusade was about to begin. The
Lion Hearted was to be its greatest hero.*

*The third crusade, despite Richard's heroics, was as unsuccessful as the
second. And, after three years, during which most of his fellow crusaders
had declared their vows discharged and returned to their own lands—
including his Capetian rival, Philip Augustus—Richard started for home.*

*We pick up the story of his return—with its delays and betrayals—and of
Eleanor's role in it from her recent biography, by Marion Meade,* Eleanor

of Aquitaine: A Biography. *Meade's book is broadly revisionist, and the basis of her revisionism is her feminism. Meade observes that "the historical record, written to accommodate men" has judged Eleanor ". . . a bitch, harlot, adultress, and monster" and that this is not surprising "for she was one of those rare women who altogether refused to be bound by the rules of proper behavior for her sex; she did as she pleased, although not without agonizing personal struggle" (p. ix). In Meade's account, as in any other account of Eleanor, there is much latitude for interpretation, given the pervasive silence of contemporary chronicles. Meade further argues that even these are "riddled with lies since monks and historians—in the twelfth century one and the same—have always abhorred emancipated women" (p. xi). Meade intends to redress the balance. And she does so, in no part of her account more forcefully than in the following passage.*

In England, Eleanor was expecting her son home for Christmas. All through November and early December companies of Crusaders had begun arriving in the kingdom; in the ports and marketplaces there were firsthand reports of the king's deeds in Palestine and plans for celebrations once he arrived. But the days passed without news, and newly arrived contingents of soldiers expressed astonishment that they had beaten the king home although they had left Acre after Richard. Along the coast, lookouts peered into the foggy Channel in hope of sighting the royal vessel, and messengers waited to race over the frozen roads toward London with the news of the king's landing. Eleanor learned that Berengaria and Joanna[2] had safely reached Rome, but of her son, weeks overdue, there was an alarming lack of information. She held a cheerless Christmas court at Westminster, her apprehension mounting with each day, her silent fears being expressed openly in the ale houses along the Thames: The king had encountered some calamity, a storm along the Adriatic coast no doubt, and now he would never return.

Three days after Christmas, the whereabouts of the tardy Richard Plantagenet became known, not at Westminster but at the Cité Palace in Paris. On December 28, Philip Augustus received an astounding letter from his good friend Henry Hohenstaufen, the Holy Roman emperor:[3]

---

[2]Berengaria was Richard's wife—a Spanish princess he had married, at Eleanor's urging, on his way to the crusade. Joanna was Richard's sister, the widowed Queen of Sicily, whom he had taken under his protection to Palestine.—ED.

[3]The Plantagenet kings were related by marriage to the great German feudal family, the Welfs, who were the most dangerous rivals to the imperial house of Hohenstaufen. The Angevins, including Richard, had frequently supported the Welfs, hence the emperor's hostility.—ED.

We have thought it proper to inform your nobleness that while the enemy of our empire and the disturber of your kingdom, Richard, King of England, was crossing the sea to his dominions, it chanced that the winds caused him to be shipwrecked in the region of Istria, at a place which lies between Aquila and Venice. . . . The roads being duly watched and the entire area well-guarded, our dearly beloved cousin Leopold, Duke of Austria, captured the king in a humble house in a village near Vienna. Inasmuch as he is now in our power, and has always done his utmost for your annoyance and disturbance, we have thought it proper to relay this information to your nobleness.

Shortly after the first of the new year, 1193, the archbishop of Rouen was able to send Eleanor a copy of the letter, accompanied by a covering note in which he cited whatever comforting quotations he could recall from Scripture to cover an outrage of this magnitude.

Eleanor's most imperative problem—finding the location where Richard was being held prisoner—she tackled with her usual energy and resourcefulness. From all points, emissaries were dispatched to find the king: Eleanor herself sent the abbots of Boxley and Pontrobert to roam the villages of Bavaria and Swabia, following every lead and rumor; Hubert Walter, bishop of Salisbury, stopping in Italy on his way home from the Crusade, changed course and hastened to Germany; even William Longchamp, the exiled chancellor, set out at once from Paris to trace his master. It was not until March, however, that Richard's chaplain, Anselm, who had shared many of the king's misadventures, arrived in England, and Eleanor was able to obtain authentic details [including the fact that Richard was being held in a remote castle of Durrenstein in Austria].

Treachery was rife not only in Germany but in Paris and Rouen; it even percolated rapidly in the queen's own family. Before Eleanor could take steps to secure Coeur de Lion's release, she was faced with more immediate catastrophes in the form of Philip Augustus and his newest ally, her son John. These two proceeded on the assumption that Richard, king of England, was dead. Or as good as dead. But before Eleanor could take her youngest son in hand, he fled to Normandy, where he declared himself the king's heir, an announcement the Norman barons greeted with disdain. John did not wait to convince them, proceeding instead to Paris, where he did homage to Philip for the Plantagenet Continental domains and furthermore agreeing to confirm Philip's right to the Vexin.[4] . . . In the meantime, Eleanor, "who then ruled England," had taken the precaution of

---

[4]The Vexin was an area at the juncture of Normandy, Anjou, and the Ile de France, long disputed by the English and French kings.—ED.

closing the Channel ports and ordering the defense of the eastern coast against a possible invasion, her hastily mustered home guard being instructed to wield any weapon that came to hand, including their plowing tools.

At this point, Eleanor's dilemma in regard to her sons would have taxed the most patient of mothers. John, returning to England, swaggered about the countryside proclaiming himself the next king of England—perhaps he sincerely believed that Richard would never be released alive—and, never known for his sensitivity, constantly regaled Eleanor with the latest rumors concerning the fate of her favorite son. Her actions during this period indicate clearly that she failed to take John seriously. Although he was twenty-seven, she thought of him as the baby of the family, always a child showing off and trying to attract attention. Her attitude was probably close to that of Richard's when, a few months later, he was informed of John's machinations: "My brother John is not the man to subjugate a country if there is a person able to make the slightest resistance to his attempts." With one hand, Eleanor deftly managed to anticipate John's plots and render him harmless; with the other, she worked for Richard's release. After Easter, the king had been removed from Durrenstein Castle and the hands of Duke Leopold and, after some haggling, had been taken into custody by Leopold's suzerain, the Holy Roman emperor. As the emperor's prisoner, Richard found himself the object of high-level decisions. His death, it was decided, would achieve no useful purpose; rather the arrogant Plantagenets, or what remained of them, should be made to redeem their kin, but at a price that would bring their provinces to their knees: 100,000 silver marks with two hundred hostages as surety for payment. The hostages, it was specified, were to be chosen from among the leading barons of England and Normandy or from their children.

Relieved as Eleanor must have felt to learn that her son could be purchased, she could only have been appalled at the size of the ransom. The prospect of collecting such an enormous sum, thirty-five tons of pure silver, seemed impossible after Henry's Saladin tithe[5] and Richard's great sale before the Crusade.[6] Where was the money to be found? Where were two hundred noble hostages to be located? At a council convened at Saint Albans on June 1, 1193, she appointed five officers to assist with the dreaded task. During the summer and fall, England became a marketplace to raise the greatest tax in its history.

---

[5] A tax that Henry had levied for a crusade, hence called after the great Moslem leader Saladin.—ED.

[6] A sale not only of movable property of the crown but that of such protected folk as foreign and Jewish merchants, and what could be extracted from the nobility.—ED.

The kingdom was stripped of its wealth: "No subject, lay or clerk, rich or poor, was overlooked. No one could say, 'Behold I am only So-and-So or Such-and-Such, pray let me be excused.' " Barons were taxed one-quarter of a year's income. Churches and abbeys were relieved of their movable wealth, including the crosses on their altars. The Cistercians, who possessed no riches, sheared their flocks and donated a year's crop of wool. Before long, the bars of silver and gold began slowly to pile up in the crypt of Saint Paul's Cathedral under Eleanor's watchful eyes. But not quickly enough to comfort her. Even more painful was the job of recruiting hostages from the great families, their lamentations and pleadings rising like a sulphurous mist all over the kingdom and providing constant agony for the queen.

From Haguenau, where Richard was incarcerated, came a flood of letters to his subjects and most especially to his "much loved mother." He had been received with honor by the emperor and his court, he is well, he hopes to be home soon. He realizes that the ransom will be difficult to raise but he feels sure that his subjects will not shirk their duty; all sums collected should be entrusted to the queen. . . .

It is said that in her anguish she addressed three letters to Pope Celestine III imploring his assistance in securing Richard's release and in her salutation addressed the pontiff as "Eleanor, by the wrath of God, Queen of England." . . . Why, she demands, does the sword of Saint Peter slumber in its scabbard when her son a "most delicate youth," the anointed of the Lord, lies in chains? Why does the pope, a "negligent," "cruel" prevaricator and sluggard, do nothing?

These letters, supposedly written for her by Peter of Blois, are so improbable that it is surprising that many modern historians have accepted them as authentic. While preserved among the letters of Peter of Blois, who is undoubtedly their author—they are characteristic of his style and use his favorite expressions—there is no evidence that they were written for Eleanor or that they were ever sent. Most likely they were rhetorical exercises. No contemporary of Eleanor's mentioned that she wrote to the pope, and not until the seventeenth century were the letters attributed to her. From a diplomatic point of view, they are too fanciful to be genuine; Eleanor, clearheaded and statesmanlike, was never a querulous old woman complaining of age, infirmities, and weariness of life. On the contrary, her contemporaries unanimously credit her with the utmost courage, industry, and political skill. A second point to notice is that the details of the letters misrepresent the facts of Richard's imprisonment. He was never "detained in bonds," and as both she and the pope knew, Celestine had instantly, upon receiving news of Richard's capture, excommunicated Duke Leopold for laying violent hands on a brother Crusader; he had threatened Philip Augustus with an interdict if he trespassed upon

Plantagenet territories; and he had menaced the English with interdict should they fail to collect the ransom. Under the circumstances, Celestine had done all he could. In the last analysis, the letters must be viewed as Peter of Blois's perception of Eleanor's feelings, a view that may or may not be accurate.

In December 1193, Eleanor set sail with an imposing retinue of clerks, chaplains, earls, bishops, hostages, and chests containing the ransom. By January 17, 1194, the day scheduled for Richard's release, she had presented herself and the money at Speyer, but no sooner had they arrived than, to her amazement, Henry Hohenstaufen announced a further delay. He had received letters that placed an entirely new light on the matter of the king's liberation. As the gist of the problem emerged, it seemed Philip Augustus and John Plantagenet had offered the emperor an equivalent amount of silver if he could hold Coeur de Lion in custody another nine months, or deliver him up to them. These disclosures, and Henry's serious consideration of the counteroffer, provoked horror from the emperor's own vassals, and after two days of argument, Henry relented. He would liberate Richard as promised if the king of England would do homage to him for all his possessions, including the kingdom of England. This request, a calculated humiliation, would have made Richard a vassal of the Holy Roman emperor, a degradation that the Plantagenets were hard put to accept. Quick to realize the meaninglessness, as well as the illegality, of the required act, Eleanor made an on-the-spot decision. According to Roger of Hovedon, Richard, "by advice of his mother Eleanor, abdicated the throne of the kingdom of England and delivered it to the emperor as the lord of all." On February 4, the king was released "into the hands of his mother" after a captivity of one year six weeks and three days.

Seven weeks later, on March 12, the king's party landed at Sandwich and proceeded directly to Canterbury, where they gave thanks at the tomb of Saint Thomas. By the time they reached London, the city had been decorated, the bells were clanging furiously, and the Londoners ready to give a rapturous welcome to their hero and champion. Her eldest son "hailed with joy upon the Strand," Eleanor looked in vain for the remaining male member of her family, but the youngest Plantagenet was nowhere to be found. Once Richard's release had been confirmed, he had fled to Paris upon Philip Augustus's warning that "beware, the devil is loose." . . .

According to the chronicles, "the king and John became reconciled through the mediation of Queen Eleanor, their mother." In the circumstances, it seemed the safest course as well as the wisest. There was no doubt in Eleanor's mind that the boy, now twenty-eight, could not be held responsible for his actions, that he was, as Richard of

Devizes termed him, "light-minded." But at that moment, he was the last of the Plantagenets. With luck, Richard might reign another twenty-five years or more. Who was to say that he would not produce an heir of his own? Thus the queen must have reasoned in the spring of 1194 when her son, after so many adversities, had come home to her.

Suggestions for Further Reading

As we have seen, despite her importance and inherent interest, there are virtually no contemporary source materials for Eleanor. Thus, whether hostile or sympathetic, the treatments of Eleanor have had to be not so much biographies as life-and-times books. This is true even of the best modern works. Two of them, Amy Kelly, *Eleanor of Aquitaine and the Four Kings* (Cambridge, Mass.: Harvard University Press, 1950), and Marion Meade, *Eleanor of Aquitaine: A Biography* (New York: Hawthorn, 1977), are excerpted in this chapter, and students are encouraged to read further in them. Two additional works are also recommended: Curtis H. Walker, *Eleanor of Aquitaine* (Chapel Hill: University of North Carolina Press, 1950), and Regine Pernoud, *Eleanor of Aquitaine*, tr. P. Wiles (New York: Coward-McCann, 1967), both well written, lively, and fast moving. *Eleanor of Aquitaine: Patron and Politician*, ed. Wm. W. Kibler (Austin: University of Texas Press, 1976), is a series of specialized papers on aspects of Eleanor's life and reign.

Of Eleanor's contemporaries, the best, most comprehensive, and up-to-date work on Henry II is W. L. Warren, *Henry II* (London: Eyre Methuen, 1973). Somewhat less intimidating are the smaller but entirely competent Richard Barber, *Henry Plantagenet* (Totowa, N.J.: Rowman and Littlefield, 1964), and John Schlight, *Henry II Plantagenet*, "Rulers and Statesmen of the World" (New York: Twayne, 1973). Probably the best biography of Richard I is Philip Henderson, *Richard Coeur de Lion: A Biography* (New York: Norton, 1959), but students are also encouraged to read James A. Brundage, *Richard Lion Heart* (New York: Scribners, 1974), largely a study of Richard as soldier and crusader, and a tough, realistic work. The standard work on John is Sidney Painter, *The Reign of King John* (Baltimore: Johns Hopkins University Press, 1949). W. L. Warren, *King John* (Berkeley: University of California Press, 1978), is a somewhat revisionist treatment of John showing him as a hard-working monarch and more the victim than the causer of his troubles—but he still is a far from attractive figure. For Eleanor's French royal contemporaries, see R. Fawtier, *The Capetian Kings of France*, tr. Lionel Butler and R. J. Adam (London:

Macmillan, 1960). There are a handful of studies of important nonroyal figures whose lives intertwined with Eleanor's: Sidney Painter, *William Marshall: Knight Errant, Baron, and Regent of England* (Baltimore: Johns Hopkins University Press, 1933); Charles R. Young, *Hubert Walter: Lord of Canterbury and Lord of England* (Durham, N.C.: Duke University Press, 1968); and a number of books on the durable subject of Henry and Becket—the best are Richard Winston, *Thomas Becket* (New York: Knopf, 1967), a tough, skeptical, but solidly source-based work; Dom David Knowles, *Thomas Becket* (London: A. and C. Black, 1970), a scrupulously objective account by a great ecclesiastical historian, but, naturally, most occupied with the arguments of Thomas and the church; and finally, Alfred L. Duggan, *My Life for My Sheep* (New York: Coward-McCann, 1955), a lively novelized account by an experienced historical novelist.

Two special topics relate to Eleanor throughout her life—chivalry and courtly love and the crusades. Both have been much studied and written about. On chivalry and courtly love, see two excellent and well-written background works—John C. Moore, *Love in Twelfth-Century France* (Philadelphia: University of Pennsylvania Press, 1972), and Jack Lindsay, *The Troubadours and Their World of the Twelfth and Thirteenth Centuries* (London: Frederick Muller, 1976), and two equally interesting ones dealing with the actual operation of knightly chivalry as well as its romanticized literary aspects—Sidney Painter, *French Chivalry: Chivalric Ideas and Practices in Medieval France* (Baltimore: Johns Hopkins University Press, 1940), and the more comprehensive Richard Barber, *The Knight and Chivalry* (New York: Scribners, 1970). But the definitive work on chivalry in all its aspects is Maurice Keen, *Chivalry* (New Haven: Yale University Press, 1984). The standard work on the crusades is now *The History of the Crusades* (Philadelphia: University of Pennsylvania, 1955–1962), a great multiauthored work under the general editorship of Kenneth M. Setton: vol. 1, *The First Hundred Years*, ed. M. W. Baldwin, and vol. 2, *The Later Crusades, 1189–1311*, ed. R. L. Wolff. Steven Runciman, *A History of the Crusades*, 3 vols. (Cambridge, England: Cambridge University Press, 1951–1954), may, however, still be the best account. Students may prefer Zoé Oldenbourg, *The Crusades*, tr. Anne Carter (New York: Pantheon, 1966), somewhat less successful than her famous historical novels but still excellent and exciting. For the warfare of the period, students should look at the recent and comprehensive Philippe Contamine, *War in the Middle Ages*, tr. Michael Jones (Oxford: Blackwell, 1984), especially the sections on the Feudal Age and Medieval Society at its prime.

LEONARDO DA VINCI: UNIVERSAL MAN OF THE RENAISSANCE

1452	Born
1472	Admitted to Florentine painters' guild
1482–1499	In service of Ludovico Sforza of Milan
1516	Entered service of Francis I of France
1519	Died

More than any other figure, Leonardo da Vinci is commonly regarded as the exemplar of that uniquely Renaissance ideal *uomo universale*, the universal man.

Leonardo, the spoiled, loved, and pampered illegitimate son of a well-to-do Florentine notary, was born in 1452 at the very midpoint of Florence's magnificent Renaissance century, the Quattrocento. The boy grew up at his father's country home in the village of Vinci. His precocious genius and his talent for drawing led his father to apprentice Leonardo to the artist Verrocchio in Florence. While Verrocchio is best remembered as a sculptor, it should be noted that he was, like most Florentine artists of his time, a versatile master of other artistic crafts, and that his *bottega*—like Ghiberti's earlier or Michelangelo's later—was not only a lively school of craftsmanship and technique but a place where people gathered to gossip and talk over a wide range of subjects. Here the young Leonardo's multiple talents bloomed.

At the age of twenty Leonardo was admitted to the painters' guild and soon after set up his own shop and household. He was well enough received and commissions came his way. But, for reasons that are not entirely clear, he seems not to have been marked for the lavish patronage of the Medici family—as were so many of his fellow artists—or of any other great Florentine houses. The fashion of the moment preferred those artists like Alberti and Botticelli who mingled learned humanism with their art and could converse in Latin with the humanists, poets, and philosophers who dominated the intellectual scene in Florence. But Leonardo knew no Latin. His education consisted only of apprenticeship training and beyond that a hodge-podge of self-instruction directed to his own wide-ranging interests, in some areas profound and original, in others hopelessly limited and naive. It is also possible that Leonardo may simply have set himself apart from the circle of his fellow artists and their patrons. There are hints of alienation and jealousy and even a vaguely worded reference to a homosexual charge against him that was brought before a magistrate and then dropped. But it is most likely that Leonardo's own restless curiosity was already carrying him beyond the practice of his art.

In 1482 Leonardo left Florence for Milan and the court of its lord, Ludovico Sforza, one of the most powerful princes of Italy. In the letter Leonardo wrote commending himself to Ludovico, which has been preserved, he described himself as a military architect, siege and hydraulic engineer, ordnance and demolition expert, architect, sculptor, and painter; he ended the letter, "And if any one of the above-named things seems to anyone to be impossible or not feasible, I am most ready to make the experiment in your park, or in whatever place may please your Excellency, to whom I commend myself with the utmost humility."[1] Humility indeed! The universal man had declared himself.

Leonardo spent the next seventeen years—the most vigorous and productive of his life—at the court of Milan. He painted *The Last Supper* for the Dominican Convent of Santa Maria delle Grazie. He conceived and created the model for what might well have been the world's greatest equestrian statue; but the statue, memorializing Ludovico Sforza's father, the old soldier-duke Francesco, was never cast, and the model was destroyed. In addition, Leonardo created gimcrackery for court balls and fetes—costumes, jewelry, scenery, engines, floats, spectacles. But increasingly he was occupied with studies of a bewildering variety of subjects. The notebooks he kept reveal drawings and notes on the flight of birds and the possibility of human flight; military engineering, tanks, submarines, exploding shells, rapid-firing artillery pieces, and fortifications; bold schemes for city planning and hydraulic engineering; plans for machinery of every sort, pulleys, gears, self-propelled vehicles, a mechanical clock, and a file cutter; detailed studies of plant, animal, and human anatomy that go well beyond the needs of an artist; a complete treatise on painting

---

[1]Quoted in E. G. Holt (ed.), *A Documentary History of Art* (New York: Doubleday, 1957), vol. I, pp. 273–275.

and another on the comparison of the arts. Despite the fact that much of this body of work—including a treatise on perspective that was reputed to be far in advance of other such works—was scattered and lost, some seven thousand pages have survived, all written in a code-like, left-handed, mirror script.

Leonardo's handwriting is of particular interest, for it is indicative of a special side of his nature—almost obsessively secretive, aloof, touchy and suspicious of others. These qualities are part of the traditional image of Leonardo that has been passed down to us, beginning with his earliest biography, by his younger contemporary Vasari.

In Praise of Leonardo

GIORGIO VASARI

Giorgio Vasari (1511–1574) was himself something of a universal man. He was an artist of more than middling ability who worked all over Italy. He was also a respected functionary, the familiar of popes, princes, and dignitaries, as well as artists and scholars. But his most important achievement was his book Lives of the Most Eminent Painters, Sculptors & Architects from Cimabue until our own Time, *the first edition published in Florence in 1550. Wallace K. Ferguson has called it "a masterpiece of art history."[2] In fact, the book is more than a masterpiece of art history, for it virtually created the concept of art history itself.*

Vasari introduces "our present age" with his treatment of Leonardo. But this biography, despite its extravagant praise of Leonardo's genius, is seriously limited. Vasari had access to many of Leonardo's notes, even some that we no longer have. But he was most familiar with the art and artists of Tuscany. It is clear that he had not actually seen several of Leonardo's most important works, in Milan and elsewhere. And much of the information he provided on Leonardo's life was nothing more than current rumor or gossip about him. Vasari, furthermore, was himself a pupil and lifelong admirer of Leonardo's great contemporary Michelangelo (1475–1564), and it was Vasari's thesis that the whole tradition of Italian art reached its fulfillment in Michelangelo. It might be recalled also that Michelangelo despised Leonardo; they had at least one nasty quarrel. And Michelangelo was fond of saying that Leonardo was a technically incompetent craftsman, who could not complete the projects he began. Whether by design or not, this charge became the main line of criticism in Vasari's biography of Leonardo, and it has persisted alongside Leonardo's reputation as an enigmatic genius.

We look now at Vasari's account from Lives of the Most Eminent Painters, Sculptors & Architects.

The greatest gifts are often seen, in the course of nature, rained by celestial influences on human creatures; and sometimes, in supernatural fashion, beauty, grace, and talent are united beyond measure in one single person, in a manner that to whatever such an one turns his attention, his every action is so divine, that, surpassing all other men,

---

[2]In *The Renaissance in Historical Thought: Five Centuries of Interpretation* (Boston: Houghton Mifflin, 1948), 60.

it makes itself clearly known as a thing bestowed by God (as it is), and not acquired by human art. This was seen by all mankind in Leonardo da Vinci, in whom, besides a beauty of body never sufficiently extolled, there was an infinite grace in all his actions; and so great was his genius, and such its growth, that to whatever difficulties he turned his mind, he solved them with ease. In him was great bodily strength, joined to dexterity, with a spirit and courage ever royal and magnanimous; and the fame of his name so increased, that not only in his lifetime was he held in esteem, but his reputation became even greater among posterity after his death.

Truly marvellous and celestial was Leonardo, the son of Ser Piero da Vinci; and in learning and in the rudiments of letters he would have made great proficience, if he had not been so variable and unstable, for he set himself to learn many things, and then, after having begun them, abandoned them. Thus, in arithmetic, during the few months that he studied it, he made so much progress, that, by continually suggesting doubts and difficulties to the master who was teaching him, he would very often bewilder him. He gave some little attention to music, and quickly resolved to learn to play the lyre, as one who had by nature a spirit most lofty and full of refinement; wherefore he sang divinely to that instrument, improvising upon it. Nevertheless, although he occupied himself with such a variety of things, he never ceased drawing and working in relief, pursuits which suited his fancy more than any other. Ser Piero, having observed this, and having considered the loftiness of his intellect, one day took some of his drawings and carried them to Andrea del Verrocchio, who was much his friend, and besought him straitly to tell him whether Leonardo, by devoting himself to drawing, would make any proficience. Andrea was astonished to see the extraordinary beginnings of Leonardo, and urged Ser Piero that he should make him study it; wherefore he arranged with Leonardo that he should enter the workshop of Andrea, which Leonardo did with the greatest willingness in the world. And he practised not one branch of art only, but all those in which drawing played a part; and having an intellect so divine and marvellous that he was also an excellent geometrician, he not only worked in sculpture, making in his youth, in clay, some heads of women that are smiling, of which plaster casts are still taken, and likewise some heads of boys which appeared to have issued from the hand of a master; but in architecture, also, he made many drawings both of ground-plans and of other designs of buildings; and he was the first, although but a youth, who suggested the plan of reducing the river Arno to a navigable canal from Pisa to Florence. He made designs of flour-mills, fulling-mills, and engines, which might be driven by the force of water: and since he wished that his profession should be painting, he studied much in drawing after nature. . . . He was continually making models and designs to show men how to remove mountains with ease, and how to bore them in order to pass from one level to another; and by means of levers, windlasses, and screws, he showed the way to raise and draw great weights, together with methods for emptying harbours, and pumps for removing water from low places, things which his brain never ceased from devising; and of these ideas and labours many drawings may be seen, scattered abroad among our craftsmen; and I myself have seen not a few. . . .

He was so pleasing in conversation, that he attracted to himself the hearts of men. And although he possessed, one might say, nothing, and worked little, he always kept servants and horses, in which latter he took much delight, and particularly in all other animals, which he managed with the greatest love and patience; and this he showed when often passing by the places where birds were sold, for, taking them with his own hand out of their cages, and having paid to those who sold them the price that was asked, he let them fly away into the air, restoring to them their lost liberty. For which reason nature was pleased so to favour him, that, wherever he turned his thought, brain, and mind, he displayed such divine power in his works, that, in giving them their perfection, no one was ever his peer in readiness, vivacity, excellence, beauty, and grace.

It is clear that Leonardo, through his comprehension of art, began many things and never finished one of them, since it seemed to him that the hand was not able to attain to the perfection of art in carrying out the things which he imagined; for the reason that he conceived in idea difficulties so subtle and so marvellous, that they could never be expressed by the hands, be they ever so excellent. And so many were his caprices, that, philosophizing of natural things, he set himself to seek out the properties of herbs, going on even to observe the motions of the heavens, the path of the moon, and the courses of the sun. . . .

He began a panel-picture of the Adoration of the Magi, containing many beautiful things, particularly the heads, which was in the house of Amerigo Benci, opposite the Loggia de' Peruzzi; and this, also, remained unfinished, like his other works.

It came to pass that Giovan Galeazzo, Duke of Milan, being dead, and Lodovico Sforza raised to the same rank, in the year 1494,[3] Leonardo was summoned to Milan in great repute to the Duke, who took much delight in the sound of the lyre, to the end that he might play it: and Leonardo took with him that instrument which he had made with his own hands, in great part of silver, in the form of a horse's skull—a thing bizarre and new—in order that the harmony

---

[3]The date was actually 1482.—Ed.

might be of greater volume and more sonorous in tone; with which he surpassed all the musicians who had come together there to play. Besides this, he was the best improviser in verse of his day. The Duke, hearing the marvellous discourse of Leonardo, became so enamoured of his genius, that it was something incredible: and he prevailed upon him by entreaties to paint an altar-panel containing a Nativity, which was sent by the Duke to the Emperor.

He also painted in Milan, for the Friars of S. Dominic, at S. Maria delle Grazie, a Last Supper, a most beautiful and marvellous thing; and to the heads of the Apostles he gave such majesty and beauty, that he left the head of Christ unfinished, not believing that he was able to give it that divine air which is essential to the image of Christ.[4] This work, remaining thus all but finished, has ever been held by the Milanese in the greatest veneration, and also by strangers as well; for Leonardo imagined and succeeded in expressing that anxiety which had seized the Apostles in wishing to know who should betray their Master. . . .

While he was engaged on this work, he proposed to the Duke to make a horse in bronze, of a marvellous greatness, in order to place upon it, as a memorial, the image of the Duke.[5] And on so vast a scale did he begin it and continue it, that it could never be completed. And there are those who have been of the opinion (so various and so often malign out of envy are the judgments of men) that he began it with no intention of finishing it, because, being of so great a size, an incredible difficulty was encountered in seeking to cast it in one piece; and it might also be believed that, from the result, many may have formed such a judgment, since many of his works have remained unfinished. But, in truth, one can believe that his vast and most excellent mind was hampered through being too full of desire, and that his wish ever to seek out excellence upon excellence, and perfection upon perfection, was the reason of it. "Tal che l'opera fosse ritardata dal desio,"[6] as our Petrarca has said. And, indeed, those who saw the great model that Leonardo made in clay vow that they have never seen a more beautiful thing, or a more superb; and it was preserved until the French came to Milan with King Louis of France, and broke it all to pieces.[7] Lost, also, is a little model of it in wax, which was held to be perfect, together with a book on the anatomy of the horse made by him by way of study.

[4]The head of Christ was finished, along with the rest of the painting. Vasari was repeating gossip and had not seen the work.—ED.

[5]Rather of the Duke's father, Francesco, the founder of the Sforza dynasty.—ED.

[6]"So that the work was retarded by the very desire of it."—ED.

[7]Louis XII of France. The incident of the model's destruction took place during the French occupation of Milan in 1499.—ED.

He then applied himself, but with greater care, to the anatomy of man, assisted by and in turn assisting, in this research, Messer Marc' Antonio della Torre, an excellent philosopher, who was then lecturing at Pavia, and who wrote of this matter; and he was one of the first (as I have heard tell) that began to illustrate the problems of medicine with the doctrine of Galen, and to throw true light on anatomy, which up to that time had been wrapped in the thick and gross darkness of ignorance. And in this he found marvellous aid in the brain, work, and hand of Leonardo, who made a book drawn in red chalk, and annotated with the pen, of the bodies that he dissected with his own hand, and drew with the greatest diligence; wherein he showed all the frame of the bones; and then added to them, in order, all the nerves, and covered them with muscles; the first attached to the bone, the second that hold the body firm, and the third that move it; and beside them, part by part, he wrote in letters of an ill-shaped character, which he made with the left hand, backwards; and whoever is not practised in reading them cannot understand them, since they are not to be read save with a mirror. . . .

With the fall of Ludovico Sforza and the French occupation of Milan in 1499, the artist returned to Florence.

Leonardo undertook to execute, for Francesco del Giocondo, the portrait of Monna Lisa, his wife; and after toiling over it for four years, he left it unfinished; and the work is now in the collection of King Francis of France, at Fontainebleau. In this head, whoever wished to see how closely art could imitate nature, was able to comprehend it with ease; for in it were counterfeited all the minutenesses that with subtlety are able to be painted. . . .

By reason, then, of the excellence of the works of this divine craftsman, his fame had so increased that all persons who took delight in art—nay, the whole city of Florence—desired that he should leave them some memorial, and it was being proposed everywhere that he should be commissioned to execute some great and notable work, whereby the commonwealth might be honoured and adorned by the great genius, grace and judgment that were seen in the works of Leonardo. And it was decided between the Gonfalonier[8] and the chief citizens, the Great Council Chamber having been newly built . . . and having been finished in great haste, it was ordained by public decree that Leonardo should be given some beautiful work to paint; and so the said hall was allotted to him by Piero Soderini, then Gonfalonier of Justice. Whereupon Leonardo, determining to execute this work, be-

---

[8]The title of the chief magistrate of Florence.—ED.

gan a cartoon in the Sala del Papa, an apartment in S. Maria Novella, representing the story of Niccolò Piccinino,[9] Captain of Duke Filippo of Milan; wherein he designed a group of horsemen who were fighting for a standard, a work that was held to be very excellent and of great mastery, by reason of the marvellous ideas that he had in composing that battle. . . . It is said that, in order to draw that cartoon, he made a most ingenious stage, which was raised by contracting it and lowered by expanding. And conceiving the wish to colour on the wall in oils, he made a composition of so gross an admixture, to act as a binder on the wall, that, going on to paint in the said hall, it began to peel off in such a manner that in a short time he abandoned it, seeing it spoiling.[10] . . .

He went to Rome with Duke Giuliano de' Medici, at the election of Pope Leo,[11] who spent much of his time on philosophical studies, and particularly on alchemy; where, forming a paste of a certain kind of wax, as he walked he shaped animals very thin and full of wind, and, by blowing into them, made them fly through the air, but when the wind ceased they fell to the ground. . . .

He made an infinite number of such follies, and gave his attention to mirrors; and he tried the strangest methods in seeking out oils for painting, and varnish for preserving works when painted. . . . It is related that, a work having been allotted to him by the Pope, he straightway began to distil oils and herbs, in order to make the varnish; at which Pope Leo said: "Alas! this man will never do anything, for he begins by thinking of the end of the work, before the beginning."

There was very great disdain between Michelagnolo Buonarroti and him, on account of which Michelagnolo departed from Florence, with the excuse of Duke Giuliano, having been summoned by the Pope to the competition for the façade of S. Lorenzo. Leonardo, understanding this, departed and went into France, where the King, having had works by his hand, bore him great affection; and he desired that he should colour the cartoon of S. Anne, but Leonardo, according to his custom, put him off for a long time with words.

Finally, having grown old, he remained ill many months, and, feeling himself near to death, asked to have himself diligently informed of the teaching of the Catholic faith. . . . [He] expired in the arms of the King, in the seventy-fifth year of his age.[12]

---

[9]A mercenary commander who had worked for Florence.—ED.

[10]Michelangelo was assigned a companion panel and also abandoned his work on it before it was completed.—ED.

[11]Pope Leo X, the former Giovanni Cardinal dei Medici.—ED.

[12]Vasari is inaccurate. In the year Leonardo died, 1519, he actually was sixty-seven.—ED.

Leonardo the Scientist

JOHN HERMAN RANDALL, JR.

From Vasari's time to the present, there has clung to the image of Leonardo da Vinci a kind of Faustian quality, linking him to the origins of modern science. Throughout his life, and increasingly from middle age on, Leonardo was preoccupied with technical studies and scientific experiments, often to the detriment of his art. But the judgments of modern scholars on "Leonardo the scientist" are much more varied and more circumspect than those upon "Leonardo the artist."

We turn first to the views of a distinguished philosopher and historian of science, especially medieval and Renaissance science, the long-time Columbia University Professor of Philosophy, John Herman Randall, Jr. This selection is from his article "The Place of Leonardo da Vinci in the Emergence of Modern Science."

Leonardo was not himself a scientist. "Science" is not the hundred-odd aphorisms or "pensieri" that have been pulled out of his Codici and collected, by Richter, Solmi, and others. "Science" is not oracular utterances, however well phrased; it is not bright ideas jotted down in a notebook. "Science" is systematic and methodical thought. . . .

"Science" is not just the appeal to experience, though it involves such an appeal, as Leonardo stated in answering those critics who had censured him as a mere empiric: "If I could not indeed like them cite authors and books, it is a much greater and worthier thing to profess to cite experience, the mistress of their masters." "Science" is not the mere rejection of authority, the case for which is well put by Leonardo: "He who argues by citing an authority is not employing intelligence but rather memory." . . .

It is true that during Leonardo's youth—the second half of the Quattrocento—the intellectual influence of the non-scientific humanists had been making for a kind of St. Martin's summer of the "authority" of the ancients, and that his life coincides with this rebirth of an authoritarian attitude toward the past. Leonardo's protests were magnificent, and doubtless pertinent. But they are not enough to constitute "science." "Science" is not merely fresh, first-hand observation, however detailed and accurate.

Above all, "science" is not the intuitions of a single genius, solitary and alone, however suggestive. It is cooperative inquiry, such as had prevailed in the Italian schools from the time of Pietro d'Abano (†1315; his *Conciliator* appeared earlier)—and such as was to continue till the time of Galileo—the cumulative cooperative inquiry which actually played so large a part in the emergence of modern science. . . .

In practice, Leonardo always becomes fascinated by some particular problem—he has no interest in working out any systematic body of knowledge. His artist's interest in the particular and the concrete, which inspires his careful, precise and accurate observation, is carried further by his inordinate curiosity into a detailed analytic study of the factors involved. His thought seems always to be moving from the particularity of the painter's experience to the universality of intellect and science, without ever quite getting there. . . .

No evidence has ever been offered that anybody in the sixteenth century capable of appreciating scientific ideas ever saw the Codici of Leonardo. . . . But since the scientific ideas expressed therein were all well-known in the universities of Leonardo's day, and were accessible in much more elaborated form in the books the scientists were reading, there seems to be no "problem" of tracing any presumed "influence" of Leonardo on the development of sixteenth-century scientific thought in Italy.

The *Trattato de la Pittura,* or *Paragone,* was not printed until 1651, but its existence in manuscript form suggests that it had been read much earlier by the Urbino circle. It was put together from various manuscripts of Leonardo by an editor whose identity is not known, but who seems to have been responsible for its systematic organization—an organization which later editors have uniformly tried to improve upon.

With Leonardo's anatomical studies, the story is somewhat different. There is no evidence that Vesalius[13] ever actually saw his drawings; but in view of the marked similarities between them and his own much more systematically planned and organized series of drawings, it is difficult to think that he did not. . . .

Turning now from the things that Leonardo, despite all the adulations of his genius, was clearly not, let us try to state what seems to have been his real genius in scientific matters. During the Renaissance, as a result of the surprising dissolution of the rigid boundaries which had previously kept different intellectual traditions, as it were, in watertight compartments, the many different currents of thought which had long been preparing and strengthening themselves during

---

[13]The Flemish anatomist at the University of Padua who in 1543 published the first modern, scientific descriptive treatise on human anatomy.—ED.

the Middle Ages managed to come together, and to strike fire. The explanation of this phenomenon can ultimately be only sociological—the breaking down of the fairly rigid boundaries that had hitherto shut off one discipline and one intellectual tradition from another. Whatever its cause, the confluence of many different intellectual traditions in the fertile, all-too-fertile mind of Leonardo renders his views an unusually happy illustration of the way in which very diverse intellectual traditions managed during the Renaissance to unite together to create what we now call "modern science."

There is first the "scientific tradition," the careful, intelligent, cooperative and cumulative criticism of Aristotelian physics, which began with William of Ockham.[14] . . . In his reading Leonardo was in touch with this scientific tradition, as Duhem has shown.

There is secondly Leonardo's enthusiasm for mathematics, which goes far beyond its obvious instrumental use. It is very hard to assay the precise sense in which Leonardo thought of mathematics as the alphabet of nature: in this area much work remains to be done. There seems to be in Leonardo no trace of the popular contemporary Pythagoreanism or Platonism. If we examine Leonardo's conception of mathematics as depicted in his drawings, not as inadequately stated in his prose, we find that it differs markedly from the static and very geometrical notion of Dürer.[15] It is movement, not geometrical relations, that Leonardo is trying to capture. There is much in his drawings that suggests a world envisaged in terms of the calculus—like the world of Leibniz[16]—rather than in terms of the purely geometrical vision of the Greek tradition. In his mathematical vision of the world, Leonardo seems to belong to the realm of "dynamic" and "Faustian" attitudes, rather than to the static geometrical perfection of Greek thought.

There is thirdly the tradition of what Edgar Zilsel has called the "superior craftsman"—the man who is not afraid to take an idea and try it out, to experiment with it. . . . As a pupil of Verrocchio [Leonardo] had no fastidious objections to sullying his hands with "experiment." This habit of Leonardo's of descending from the academic cathedra and actually trying out the ideas of which he read had broad repercussions: it is one of the activities of Leonardo that seems to have become generally known, and to have awakened emulation. The consequences of Leonardo's willingness to experiment are to be found in the "practical geometry" of Tartaglia, the greatest of the

---

[14]The important nominalist philosopher of the early fourteenth century.—ED.

[15]The great German artist, a contemporary of Leonardo.—ED.

[16]The great German philosopher and mathematician of the seventeenth century who shares with Newton the discovery of the calculus.—ED.

sixteenth-century Italian mathematicians. Galileo, of course, was in this tradition of the "practical geometers"; he too was an indefatigable inventor. Indeed, Leonardo can fairly claim to belong not to the line of scientists but to the noble tradition of the inventors. . . .

Many of Leonardo's aphorisms treat the matter of the proper intellectual method. He has much to say on the relation between "reason" and "experience," and what he says used to lead commentators to impute to him the anticipation of Francis Bacon's "inductive method"—God save the mark, as though that had anything to do with the method employed by the pioneering scientists of the seventeenth century!

Neither experience alone nor reason alone will suffice. "Those who are enamored of practice without science are like the pilot who boards his ship without helm or compass, and who is never certain where he is going." On the other hand, pure reasoning is without avail: "Should you say that the sciences which begin and end in the mind have achieved truth, that I will not concede, but rather deny for many reasons; and first, because in such mental discourse there occurs no experience, without which there is no certainty to be found."

But Leonardo does not bother to give any precise definition of what he means by his key terms, "experience," "reason," "certainty," or "truth." Certainty depends on "experience," but "there is no certainty where one of the mathematical sciences cannot apply, or where the subject is not united with mathematics." And—maxim for all inventors!—"Mechanics is the paradise of the mathematical sciences, because in it they come to bear their mathematical fruits." . . .

These aphorisms as to the relation between reason and experience are no doubt rhetorically effective. But we have only to compare such vague utterances with the very detailed analyses of precisely the same methodological relation which were being carried out at this very time in the Aristotelian schools of the Italian universities to realize the difference between an artist's insights and the scientist's analysis.

Leonardo was above all else the anatomist of nature. He could see, and with his draughtsmanship depict clearly, the bony skeleton of the world—the geological strata and their indicated past. He could also see everywhere nature's simple machines in operation—in man and in the non-human world alike. . . .

As a genuine contributor, then, to the descriptive sciences, Leonardo reported with his pencil fundamental aspects of nature the great machine—in anatomy, geology, and hydrostatics. As a writer rather than as a graphic reporter, Leonardo shows himself an extremely intelligent reader. But he was clearly never so much the scientist as when he had his pencil in hand, and was penetrating to the mechanical structure of what he was observing.

Leonardo the Technologist

LADISLAO RETI

A substantial group of modern scholars agrees with Randall. Some, however, do not. In the following selection, we will sample the views of one of them, Ladislao Reti, a historian of science and medicine and an authority on Leonardo's scientific and technical manuscripts. Reti not only attaches more importance to Leonardo's scientific work than does Randall; he vigorously denies Randall's charges that Leonardo failed to exhibit a sustained, systematic body of scientific thought; that he stood alone outside the tradition of science; that he failed to develop a methodological terminology; and that he failed to influence the evolution of science beyond his own time. But most of all, Reti disputes Randall's view that science is abstract conception. Rather, he takes the position that science must be the accumulation of particular observations and applications. Reti views "Leonardo the scientist" as "Leonardo the technologist," and he insists that a technologist of such brilliance and inventiveness as Leonardo cannot be so readily dismissed. "The greatest engineer of all times" surely deserves a place in the history of science.

Varied as Leonardo's interests were, statistical analysis of his writings points to technology as the main subject. As was acutely pointed out by Bertrand Gille in a recent book, judging by the surviving original documents, Leonardo's métier was rather an engineer's than an artist's.

However we may feel about this opinion, it is disturbing to take an inventory of Leonardo's paintings, of which no more than half a dozen are unanimously authenticated by the world's leading experts.

Contrast this evident disinclination to paint with the incredible toil and patience Leonardo lavished on scientific and technical studies, particularly in the fields of geometry, mechanics, and engineering. Here his very indulgence elicited curious reactions from his contemporaries and in the minds of his late biographers. They regretted that a man endowed with such divine artistic genius should waste the precious hours of his life in such vain pursuits. And, of course, as the well-known episodes of his artistic career testify, this exposed him not only to criticism but also to serious inconveniences.

But were Leonardo's nonartistic activities truly marginal?

Documentary evidence proves that every official appointment refers to him not only as an artist but as an engineer as well.

At the court of Ludovico il Moro he was *Ingeniarius et pinctor.*[17] Cesare Borgia called him his most beloved *Architecto et Engengero Generale.*[18] When he returned to Florence he was immediately consulted as military engineer. . . . Louis XII called him *nostre chier et bien amé Léonard da Vincy, nostre paintre et ingenieur ordinaire.*[19] Even in Rome, despite the pope's famous remark on hearing of Leonardo's experiments with varnishes preparatory to beginning an artistic commission, Leonardo's duties clearly included technical work, as is documented by three rough copies of a letter to his patron Giuliano de' Medici. Nor was his position different when he went to France at the invitation of Francis I. The official burial document calls him *Lionard de Vincy, noble millanois, premier peinctre et ingenieur et architecte du Roy, mescanichien d'Estat, et anchien directeur du peincture du Duc de Milan.*[20]

We can thus see that Leonardo had a lively interest in the mechanical arts and engineering from his earliest youth, as evidenced by the oldest drawing in the Codex Atlanticus, to the end of his industrious life. Thousands of his drawings witness to it, from fleeting sketches (though always executed with the most uncanny bravura) to presentation projects finished in chiaroscuro wash. Often these sketches and drawings are accompanied by a descriptive text, comments, and discussion.

The drawings and writings of Leonardo on technical matters, though scattered throughout the notebooks and especially in the Codex Atlanticus (a true order probably never existed nor did the author attempt to make one), represent an important and unique source for the history of technology. . . .

It is far from my intention and beyond my possibilities to discuss Leonardo's technology as a whole on this occasion. Enough is said when we remember that there is hardly a field of applied mechanics where Leonardo's searching mind has left no trace in the pages of his notebooks. To illustrate Leonardo's methods I shall limit myself to discussing some little-known aspects of how he dealt with the main problem of technology, the harnessing of energy to perform useful work.

[17]Engineer and painter.—ED.

[18]Architect and Engineer-General.—ED.

[19]Our dear and well-loved Leonardo da Vinci, our painter and engineer ordinary.—ED.

[20]Leonardo da Vinci, Milanese nobleman, first painter and engineer and architect of the King, state technician, and former director of painting of the Duke of Milan.—ED.

At the time of Leonardo the waterwheel had been improved and in some favored places wind was used to grind corn or pump water. But the main burden of human industry still rested on the muscle power of man or animal. Little thought was given to how this should be used. Animals were attached to carts or traction devices; fortunately collar harness was already in use, multiplying by five the pulling strength of the horse. Men worked tools by hand, turned cranks, or operated treadmills. Of course, power could be gained, sacrificing time, with the help of levers, screws, gears, and pulleys. Little attention was given to the problems of friction, strength of materials, and to the rational development of power transmission. At least this is the picture suggested by studying the few manuscripts that precede Leonardo, devoted to technological matters.

Leonardo's approach was fundamentally different. He firmly believed that technological problems must be dealt with not by blindly following traditional solutions but according to scientific rules deduced from observation and experiment.

When Leonardo searched for the most efficient ways of using the human motor, the force of every limb, of every muscle, was analyzed and measured. Leonardo was the first engineer who tried to find a quantitative equivalent for the forms of energy available.

In MS H (written *ca.* 1494) on folios 43*v* and 44*r* (figs. 1 and 2) there are two beautiful sketches showing the estimation of human muscular effort with the help of a dynamometer. The force is mea-

Figure 1
MS H, fol. 43*v*.

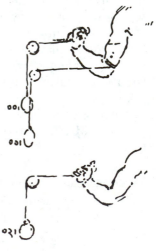

Figure 2
MS H, fol. 44*r*.

sured in pounds which represent the lifting capacity of the group of muscles under scrutiny. In figure 1 no less than six different cases covering the whole body are examined, while in figure 2 Leonardo tries to compare the force of the arm in different positions and points of attachment. Between the last two drawings a diagram shows the arm as a compound lever. In many other instances Leonardo compares the human body with a mechanical system, anticipating Borelli. We shall see one of them on folio 164*r, a* of the Codex Atlanticus. . . .

The interest of Leonardo in the maximum efficiency of muscle power is understandable. It was the only motor he could have used in a flying machine; a project that aroused his ambition as early as the year 1488 and in which he remained interested till the end of his life.

The efficiency of the human motor depends not only on its intrinsic strength but also on the ways the force is applied. Indeed, what is the greatest strength a man can generate, without the help of mechanical devices like levers, gears, or pulleys? In a very interesting passage of MS A, folio 30*v* (fig. 3), Leonardo answers the question:

> A man pulling a weight balanced against himself (as in lifting a weight with the help of a single block) cannot pull more than his own weight. And if he has to raise it, he will raise as much more than his weight, as his strength may be more than that of another man. The greatest force a man can apply, with equal velocity and impetus, will be when he sets his feet on one end of the balance and then leans his shoulders against some stable support. This will raise, at the other end of the balance, a weight equal to his own, and added to that, as much weight as he can carry on his shoulders.

Masterly executed marginal sketches illustrate the three different cases. The problem has been already touched on folio 90*v* of MS B, where the following suggestion is made beside a similar sketch: "See at the mill how much is your weight, stepping on the balance and pressing with your shoulders against something."

But Leonardo was always anxious to integrate theory with application. His own advice was: "When you put together the science of the motions of water, remember to include under each proposition its application and use, in order that this science may not be useless" (MS F, fol. 2*v*).

I should like to select, among many, a few cases in which Leonardo demonstrates the usefulness of his rules. One of them is pile driving for foundation work or the regulation of river banks. The simplest pile-driving machine consists of a movable frame, provided with a drop hammer raised by men pulling at a rope provided with hand lines. After being raised, the hammer is released by a trigger. The

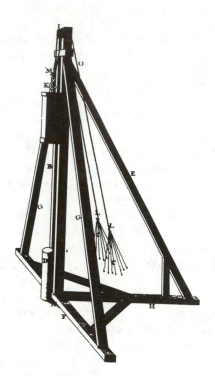

Figure 3
MS A, fol. 30*v*.

Figure 4
Belidor, *Architecture Hydraulique*, pt. 2,
p. 128, pl. 8.

operation is repeated until the pile has been sunk to the necessary depth. In Belidor's classic treatise we may see the figure of this age-old device (fig. 4).

Leonardo, often engaged in architectural and hydraulic projects, obviously had a more than theoretical interest in the operation. . . .

As for the practical improvements, I should like to present a group of notes on this subject, from the Leicester Codex, folio 28*v*, which so far as I know have never been reproduced, commented upon, or translated. Marginal drawings (figs. 5 and 6) illustrate the text.

The very best way to drive piles (*ficcare i pali a castello*) is when the man lifts so much of the weight of the hammer as is his own weight. And this shall be done in as much time as the man, without burden, is able to climb a ladder quickly. Now, this man shall put his foot immediately in the stirrup and he will descend with so much weight as his weight exceeds that of the hammer. If you want to check it thoroughly, you can have him carry a stone weighing a pound. He will lift so much

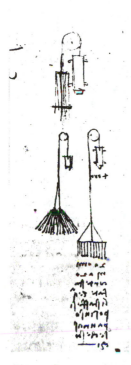

Figure 5
MS Leicester, fol. 28*v*.

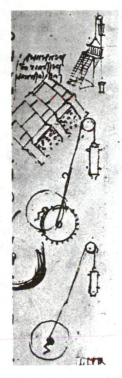

Figure 6
MS Leicester, fol. 28*v*.

weight as is his own on descending from the top of the ladder and the hammer will raise and remain on top, locked by itself, until the man dismounts the stirrup and again climbs the ladder. When you unlock the hammer with a string, it will descend furiously on top of the pile you want to drive in. And with the same speed the stirrup will rise again to the feet of the man. And this shall be done again and again. And if you want to have more men, take several ropes that end in one rope and several ladders to allow the men to reach the top of the ladders at the same time. Now, at a signal from the foreman, they shall put their feet in the stirrups and climb the ladder again. They will rest while descending and there is not much fatigue in climbing the ladders because it is done with feet and hands, and all the weight of the man that is charged on the hands will not burden the feet. But one man shall always give the signal.

Pile driving by raising the hammer by hand is not very useful, because a man cannot raise his own weight if he does not sustain it with his arms. This cannot be done unless the rope he is using is perpendicular to the center of his gravity. And this happens only to one of the men in a crowd who is pulling on the hammer.

We can further observe in the sketches of the Leicester Codex that Belidor's first two improvements had already been considered by Leonardo: the substitution of a large wheel for the block and use of a capstan or a winch. . . .

A last word on the pile driver of Leonardo. He spoke of a hammer that is locked and unlocked by itself. In the pile driver drawn on folio 289*r*, *e* of the Codex Atlanticus (fig. 7) we can observe the kind of mechanism Leonardo was hinting at. It is amazing to verify the identity of this device with that of the mentioned, improved pile driver of Belidor (fig. 8). According to the French author, the machine had been invented by Vauloue, a London watchmaker, and used at the construction of the famous Westminster bridge, that is, in 1738–1750. The story is recorded also by Desaguliers. Devices of this type are still used.

Many notes and sketches of Leonardo refer to the construction of canals, a subject that often turns up in the manuscripts. . . .

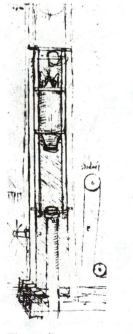

Figure 7
Codex Atlanticus, fol. 289*r*, *e*.

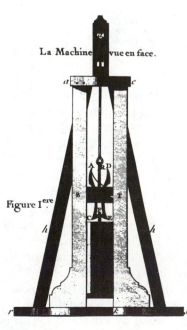

La Machine vue en face.

Figure Iere.

Figure 8
Belidor, *Architecture Hydraulique*.

He began by analyzing the best ways of disposing men to work if this had to be done by hand. For those calculations Leonardo even constructed a kind of chronometer on the nature of which Augusto Marinoni tells us more. He filled many sheets, extremely interesting in themselves, with calculations and sketches (e.g., C.A., fol. 210*r*, *a*), arriving at the conclusion that the only reasonable solution was to mechanize the whole operation. It was not only a matter of digging. The excavated material had to be cleared and transported a long way. For this purpose wheeled vehicles were considered next and rejected.

Leonardo did not underestimate wheeled vehicles. He notes that "the cart has the first place among all human inventions, particularly when it has the right proportions, although I have never seen such a one." But a cart is useful only on level ground; on steep runs the weight nullifies the effort of the animal. Besides, "to fill the carts requires more time than needed for the transport itself" (C.A., fol. 164*r*, *a*). . . .

The well-known folio 211*r*, *a* of the Codex Atlanticus shows the theoretical justification of this statement; less noticed are the beautiful sketches above the main drawing, where the influence of the relative thickness of the axle on the movement is measured by an amazingly modern-looking dynamometer. On folio 340*v*, *d*, of the same codex, a similar arrangement is suggested for the measurement of the force required in pulling a four-wheeled vehicle. Leonardo was to use the same type of apparatus to gauge the force of a waterfall (C. Fors. III, fol. 47*r*) and to determine the power requirement of a grain mill (*ibid.*, fol. 46*v*), anticipating the classic experiments of Smeaton.

After rejecting wheeled vehicles as unsuitable for excavation work and recognizing that a large and deep canal could not economically be dug by hand, Leonardo examined the possibility of substituting progressive hand shoveling from level to level by excavation machines combined with a system of cranes. Power was again his main concern.

To activate a crane, in addition to a horse-driven capstan, the only transportable motor available at the time would have been a treadmill, a machine that converts muscle power into rotary motion. . . .

Leonardo did not invent the external treadmill; there are older examples as far back as Vitruvius. But he was the first to use the principle rationally and in accordance with sound engineering principles. . . .

However, the increasing size of the complex machines created by the imagination of Leonardo required more power than that which could be supplied by the weight of a few men walking on a treadmill, even admitting the most rational mechanical arrangements. Leonardo was well aware of the situation, and wrote: "There you see the best of all motors, made by the ancient architects, that I cleaned from every fault and reduced to the ultimate perfection, with improvements that were not and could not be in its simple state. But I am still not satisfied and I intend to show a way of quicker motion of more usefulness and brevity" (C.A., fol. 370*v*, *c*). . . .

Still, the ultimate perfection had not yet been achieved. There was too much human work in filling and emptying the buckets and, particularly, in the excavation itself, the breaking up and the shoveling of the soil. Let us see how Leonardo the engineer tackled these problems.

Amazingly modern systems for the emptying of the buckets are described and shown on other pages of the Codex Atlanticus. The box is discharged by hitting the ground as in folio 363*r*, *a* (fig. 9), or by releasing the bottom with a string (C.A., fol. 344*r*, *a*), or it is

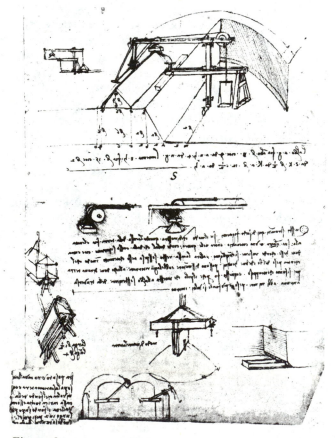

Figure 9
Codex Atlanticus, fol. 363*r*, *a*.

ingeniously overturned with the least possible effort as in folio 294*r*, *a*. As for the mechanization of the excavation itself, Leonardo offered several solutions that command the admiration of the modern engineer. He devised wheeled scrapers that with the aid of a horse could dig and remove the earth. Their design contains all the main features of modern tools (C.A., fols. 294*r*, *a*; 389*r*, *b*; 389*v*, *c*).

Leonardo's aim, however, was total mechanization. He declared emphatically that in the making of canals "the most useful method would be one by which the soil, removed, would jump by itself quickly on the instrument that will transport it" (C.A., fol. 164*r*, *a*; C. Ar., fol. 127*r–v*). . . .

A number of reasonable questions advanced by several authors will be echoed at this point. Those marvelously modern-looking projects of Leonardo, do they have reality or are they to be considered as the unfulfilled dreams of an inventor? Are they original or do they come from a long tradition of engineering experience?

These questions can be answered both ways. Leonardo did find ample inspiration in the deeds and writings of his predecessors in the technical arts, and some of his projects were so advanced that they could not have been carried out, for lack of adequate technical support. Others, even if brilliantly conceived, were based on faulty theories and would not work (e.g., the use of syphons more than 30 feet tall).

There can be no doubt, however, that most of Leonardo's technical ideas were grounded in firm and actual experience, even if the corresponding historical records are meager. His canal-building activity in the Romagnas, while in the service of Cesare Borgia, must have been successful in view of his immediate appointment by the Signoria of Florence in a similar capacity after the downfall of his frightful patron. Leonardo's innovations and inventions in the field of mechanical engineering can be traced in the writings of a number of sixteenth- and seventeenth-century authors, especially Cardan, Besson, Ramelli, Zonca, Castelli, Verantius, De Caus, etc. It is useless to speculate about the fact that Leonardo's manuscripts were hardly accessible to those writers: his technological ideas, like those related to the arts, were already incorporated in the common knowledge of the epoch.

But arts and techniques can be easily lost when genius is not understood and assimilated. The technology of the sixteenth and seventeenth centuries was much inferior to the standards set by Leonardo; only at the end of the seventeenth century was there a renewal that led to the beginning of modern engineering. A thorough study of Leonardo's technical activities and ideas, even if presented in the disorderly state of the mutilated and plundered heritage, points to him, as Feldhaus has correctly remarked, as the greatest engineer of all times.

Suggestions for Further Reading

There are two standard editions of Leonardo's notebooks, Leonardo da Vinci, *Notebooks,* tr. and ed. Edward McCurdy, 2 vols. (London: Cape, 1956), and *The Notebooks of Leonardo da Vinci,* ed. Jean Paul Richter, 2 vols. (New York: Dover, 1970), as well as a small collection of excerpts, Leonardo da Vinci, *Philosophical Diary,* tr. and ed. Wade Baskin (New York: Philosophical Library, 1959). There is also the recent *Leonardo on Painting: An Anthology of Writings by Leonardo da Vinci, with a selection of documents relating to his career as an artist,* ed. Martin Kemp (New Haven: Yale University Press, 1989). Of the many collections of his artistic works, one of the best is *Leonardo da Vinci* (New York: Reynal, 1956), the catalogue of the comprehensive Milan Leonardo Exposition of 1938. Another, relevant to the emphasis of this chapter, is *Leonardo da Vinci: Engineer and Architect* (Montreal: Museum of Fine Arts, 1987), the catalog of a major exhibit in 1987.

Two general works on Leonardo can be recommended—*Leonardo da Vinci: Aspects of the Renaissance Genius,* ed. Morris Philipson (New York: Braziller, 1966), a well-selected set of articles and special studies, and Cecil H. M. Gould, *Leonardo: the Artist and the Non-artist* (Boston: New York Graphic Society, 1975). Both these books recognize the two aspects of Leonardo's life and work that are generally dealt with, the scientific and the artistic. Of the works on Leonardo the artist, the best is Kenneth M. Clark, *Leonardo da Vinci: An Account of His Development as an Artist,* rev. ed. (Baltimore: Penguin, 1958); it may well be the best work on him of any sort. For Leonardo's mechanical engineering interests, the pioneer study is Ivor B. Hart, *The Mechanical Investigations of Leonardo da Vinci,* 2nd ed. (Berkeley: University of California Press, 1963 [1925]), and a later work by Hart updating the research, *The World of Leonardo: Man of Science, Engineer, and Dreamer of Flight* (New York: Viking, 1961). For Leonardo's anatomical studies, see Elmer Belt, *Leonardo the Anatomist* (New York: Greenwood, 1955) and Kenneth D. Keele, *Leonardo da Vinci's Elements of the Science of Man* (New York: Academic Press, 1983).

A special interest in Leonardo was stirred by two works of Sigmund Freud, *Leonardo da Vinci: A Study in Psychosexuality,* tr. A. A. Brill (New York: Random House, 1947), and *Leonardo da Vinci and a Memory of His Childhood,* tr. Alan Tyson (New York: Norton, 1964), in which Freud treated Leonardo as the subject of his most extensive attempt at psychohistory. The works are full of errors and not solidly based on research, but they thrust into the forefront of controversy about Leonardo the questions of his homosexuality and the paralyzing duality of his interests in science and art. There are two later important books in this controversy: Kurt R. Sissler, *Leonardo da Vinci: Psychoanalytic Notes on an Enigma* (New York: International Universities Press, 1961), and Raymond S. Stites, *The Sublimation of Leonardo da Vinci, with a Translation of the Codex Trivulzianus* (Washington: Smithsonian, 1970), the latter a large, detailed, and difficult book but an important revisionist study on Freud's tentative conclusions.

Although its assertions and research are now dated, students may still enjoy a famous historical novel, Dmitrii Merezhkovskii, *The Romance of Leonardo da Vinci*, tr. B. G. Guerney (New York: Heritage, 1938).

For the background to Leonardo's biography and the Renaissance, see Wallace K. Ferguson, *Europe in Transition, 1300–1520* (Boston: Houghton Mifflin, 1962), and Ernst Breisach, *Renaissance Europe, 1300–1517* (New York: Macmillan, 1973). And for an attractive and readable book on the Italy that formed Leonardo, see Lauro Martines, *Power and Imagination: City-States in Renaissance Italy* (New York: Knopf, 1979).

CHRISTOPHER COLUMBUS: ADMIRAL OF THE OCEAN SEA

c. 1451	Born
1492–93	First voyage
1493–96	Second voyage
1498–99	Third voyage
1502–04	Fourth voyage
1506	Died

Every schoolchild knows the name Christopher Columbus, the date 1492, and the fact that in that year Columbus discovered the New World. This alone assures Columbus a secure niche in history, for his was the most stupendous accomplishment of any discoverer-explorer. Never before had two entirely new and unsuspected continents been discovered. It is true that medieval Vikings touched the shores of North America and that Bristol fishermen may have worked the outer banks off Newfoundland. But neither left a permanent mark on the New World. That was the accomplishment of Christopher Columbus, who established the first permanent European settlement in the New World that quickly led to long-term colonization and conquest.

Yet, the supreme irony of the story of Columbus is that he himself never knew what he had discovered. He continued to believe, to the end of his life, that he had sailed to the coast of Asia. He was led to this conviction by the calculation of the circumference of the earth by contemporary cosmologists—ultimately going back to the ancient geographer Ptolemy—which was underestimated by some 25 percent. This shortfall was confirmed by the fact that Columbus's computation of a degree of longitude at the equator was 56.86 miles when in fact it is 69 miles. Moreover, Columbus had studied the works of Marco Polo, which indicated that the continent of Asia extended much farther to the east than it actually does. By Columbus's own calculations, then, when he made his first landfall on October 12, 1492, he had sailed 3,200 miles in just over 33 days and should have been off the coast of Japan. If he had even suspected the true distance to Asia, he probably would never have undertaken his great "enterprise."

The Ship's Log

CHRISTOPHER COLUMBUS

Columbus was a native-born Genoese but most of his mature life had been spent in Portugal, where he came to be involved in various Portuguese maritime adventures out of which grew his plan to reach the Orient by sailing to the west. For almost a decade, Columbus had tried to interest various European governments in supporting his plan. He had approached the Portuguese, the English, and the court of Spain, without success. Then, in 1492, he appealed again to Spain. This time he gained the ear of a great court official, Luis de Santangel, who not only interested the king and queen in Columbus's proposal but who himself provided a considerable part of the money to finance it. Under these circumstances, Ferdinand and Isabella agreed to underwrite the expedition, providing the ships, paying for the crews and supplies, setting out generous rewards for Columbus, and conferring upon him the title Admiral of the Ocean Sea. They also provided him with a letter of credence to the Great Khan.

The expedition sailed from Palos Friday, August 3, 1492. It consisted of three vessels, the Niña, *the* Pinta, *and the* Santa Maria, *Columbus's flagship. After a brief stop in the Canary Islands for fresh water and for rerigging the* Niña, *he sailed out to the west on his epochal voyage of discovery.*

In the course of that voyage Columbus, like the good sea captain he was, kept a detailed ship's log. On his triumphant return this log was presented to Queen Isabella. It has not survived. But the queen immediately had a copy made for Columbus, the "Barcelona copy," which remained among the papers of the Columbus family. This copy has also disappeared, but at some point before the disappearance, it came into the hands of Fray Bartolomé de las Casas. Las Casas was a great admirer of Columbus, a friend of the Columbus family, and the first major historian of the New World. In the course of collecting the materials for his own history, las Casas prepared an abstract of the "Barcelona copy" that seems to have been copied directly from "the formal words of the Admiral." This is the only surviving version of the Columbus log. Excerpts from it follow.

Wednesday, 10 October 1492

I held course to the WSW, running 7½ knots, and at times 9 knots, and for awhile 5¼ knots. Between day and night I made 177 miles. I

203

told the crew 132 miles, but they could stand it no longer. They grumbled and complained of the long voyage, and I reproached them for their lack of spirit, telling them that, for better or worse, they had to complete the enterprise on which the Catholic Sovereigns had sent them. I cheered them on as best as I could, telling them of all the honors and rewards they were about to receive. I also told the men that it was useless to complain, for I had started out to find the Indies and would continue until I had accomplished that mission, with the help of Our Lord.

Thursday, 11 October 1492

I sailed to the WSW, and we took more water aboard than at any other time on the voyage. I saw several things that were indications of land. At one time a large flock of sea birds flew overhead, and a green reed was found floating near the ship. The crew of the *Pinta* spotted some of the same reeds and some other plants; they also saw what looked like a small board or plank. A stick was recovered that looks man-made, perhaps carved with an iron tool. Those on the *Niña* saw a little stick covered with barnacles. I am certain that many things were overlooked because of the heavy sea, but even these few made the crew breathe easier; in fact, the men have even become cheerful. I sailed 81 miles from sunset yesterday to sunset today. As is our custom, vespers were said in the late afternoon, and a special thanksgiving was offered to God for giving us renewed hope through the many signs of land He has provided.

After sunset I ordered the pilot to return to my original westerly course, and I urged the crew to be ever-vigilant. I took the added precaution of doubling the number of lookouts, and I reminded the men that the first to sight land would be given a silk doublet as a personal token from me. Further, he would be given an annuity of 10,000 maravedies from the Sovereigns.

About 10 o'clock at night, while standing on the sterncastle, I thought I saw a light to the west. It looked like a little wax candle bobbing up and down. It had the same appearance as a light or torch belonging to fishermen or travellers who alternately raised and lowered it, or perhaps were going from house to house. I am the first to admit that I was so eager to find land that I did not trust my own senses, so I called for Pedro Gutiérrez, the representative of the King's household, and asked him to watch for the light. After a few moments, he too saw it. I then summoned Rodrigo Sánchez of Segovia, the comptroller of the fleet, and asked him to watch for the light. He saw nothing, nor did any other member of the crew. It was such an uncertain thing that I did not feel it was adequate proof of land.

The moon, in its third quarter, rose in the east shortly before midnight. I estimate that we were making about 9 knots and had gone some 67½ miles between the beginning of night and 2 o'clock in the morning. Then, at two hours after midnight, the *Pinta* fired a cannon, my prearranged signal for the sighting of land.

I now believe that the light I saw earlier was a sign from God and that it was truly the first positive indication of land. When we caught up with the *Pinta,* which was always running ahead because she was a swift sailer, I learned that the first man to sight land was Rodrigo de Tríana, a seaman from Lepe.

I hauled in all the sails but the mainsail and lay-to till daylight. The land is about 6 miles to the west.

Friday, 12 October 1492
(Log entry for 12 October is combined with that of 11 October)

At dawn we saw naked people, and I went ashore in the ship's boat, armed, followed by Martín Alonso Pinzón, captain of the *Pinta,* and his brother, Vincente Yáñez Pinzón, captain of the *Niña.* I unfurled the royal banner and the captains brought the flags which displayed a large green cross with the letters F and Y at the left and right side of the cross. Over each letter was the appropriate crown of that Sovereign. These flags were carried as a standard on all of the ships. After a prayer of thanksgiving I ordered the captains of the *Pinta* and *Niña,* together with Rodrigo de Escobedo (secretary of the fleet), and Rodrigo Sánchez of Segovia (comptroller of the fleet) to bear faith and witness that I was taking possession of this island for the King and Queen. I made all the necessary declarations and had these testimonies carefully written down by the secretary. In addition to those named above, the entire company of the fleet bore witness to this act. To this island I gave the name *San Salvador,* in honor of our Blessed Lord.

No sooner had we concluded the formalities of taking possession of the island than people began to come to the beach, all as naked as their mothers bore them, and the women also, although I did not see more than one very young girl. All those that I saw were young people, none of whom was over 30 years old. They are very well-built people, with handsome bodies and very fine faces, though their appearance is marred somewhat by very broad heads and foreheads, more so than I have ever seen in any other race. Their eyes are large and very pretty, and their skin is the color of Canary Islanders or of sunburned peasants, not at all black, as would be expected because we were on an east-west line with Hierro in the Canaries. These are tall people and their legs, with no exceptions, are quite straight, and none of them has a paunch. They are, in fact, well proportioned. Their hair is not kinky, but straight, and coarse like horsehair. They wear it short over the eyebrows, but they have a long hank in the back that they never cut. Many of the natives paint their faces; others paint their whole bodies; some, only the eyes or nose. Some are painted black, some white, some red; others are of different colors.

The people here called this land *Guanahaní*[1] in their language, and their speech is very fluent, although I do not understand any of it. They are friendly and well-dispositioned people who bare no arms except for small spears, and they have no iron. I showed one my sword, and through ignorance he grabbed it by the blade and cut himself. Their spears are made of wood, to which they attach a fish tooth at one end, or some other sharp thing.

I want the natives to develop a friendly attitude toward us because I know that they are a people who can be made free and converted to our Holy Faith more by love than by force. I therefore gave red caps to some and glass beads to others. They hung the beads around their necks, along with some other things of slight value that I gave them. And they took great pleasure in this and became so friendly that it was a marvel. They traded and gave everything they had with good will, but it seems to me that they have very little and are poor in everything. I warned my men to take nothing from the people without giving something in exchange.

This afternoon the people of San Salvador came swimming to our ships and in boats made from one log. They brought us parrots, balls of cotton thread, spears, and many other things, including a kind of dry leaf[2] that they hold in great esteem. For these items we swapped them little glass beads and hawks' bells.

Many of the men I have seen have scars on their bodies, and when I made signs to them to find out how this happened, they indicated

---

[1] The exact location of this first landfall is a subject of controversy. Following Morison, most modern scholars say it was Watling's Island in the Bahamas. But Fuson, following Dunn and Kelley, prefers Samana Cay.—Ed.

[2] This is the earliest reference to tobacco.—Ed.

that people from other nearby islands come to San Salvador to capture them; they defend themselves the best they can. I believe that people from the mainland come here to take them as slaves. They ought to make good and skilled servants, for they repeat very quickly whatever we say to them. I think they can easily be made Christians, for they seem to have no religion. If it pleases Our Lord, I will take six of them to Your Highnesses when I depart, in order that they may learn our language. . . .

If the weather permits, I shall depart this Cabo del Isleo and sail around Isabela until I find the king and see if I can get from him the gold which I hear that he wears. Then I shall sail for another great island which I strongly believe should be Japan, according to the signs made by the San Salvador Indians with me. They call that island *Colba,* where they say there are many great ships and navigators. And from that island I intend to go to another that they call *Bohío,* which is also very large. As to any others that lie in between, I shall see them in passing, and according to what gold or spices I find, I will determine what I must do. But I have already decided to go to the mainland and to the city of Quisay, and give Your Highnesses' letters to the Grand Khan and ask for a reply and return with it. . . .

Tuesday, 25 December 1492—Christmas Day

I sailed in a light wind yesterday from La Mar de Santo Tomás to Punta Santa, and at the passing of the first watch, 11 o'clock at night, I was 3 miles east of the point. I decided to lie down to sleep because I had not slept for two days and one night. Since it was calm, the sailor who was steering the ship also decided to catch a few winks and left the steering to a young ship's boy, a thing which I have always expressly prohibited throughout the voyage. It made no difference whether there was a wind or calm; the ships were not to be steered by young boys. . . .

Our Lord willed that at midnight, when the crew saw me lie down to rest and also saw that there was a dead calm and the sea was as in a bowl, they all lay down to sleep and left the helm to that boy. The currents carried the ship upon one of these banks. Although it was night, the sea breaking on them made so much noise that they could be heard and seen at a 3-mile distance. The ship went upon the bank so quietly that it was hardly noticeable. When the boy felt the rudder ground and heard the noise of the sea, he cried out. I jumped up instantly; no one else had yet felt that we were aground. Then the master of the ship, Juan de la Cosa, who was on watch, came out. I ordered him to rouse the crew, to launch the small boat we carry on our stern, and to take an anchor and cast it at the stern. The master and many others jumped into the small boat, and I assumed they were going to follow my orders. Instead, their only thoughts were to escape to the *Niña*, which was a 1½ miles to the windward. The crew of the *Niña* would not receive them, which was correct, and therefore they returned to the ship. But the boat from the *Niña* reached the ship before my own boat did!

When I saw that some of my own crew were fleeing and that the sea was becoming more shallow, with my ship broadside to it, I did the only thing I could. I ordered the mast cut and the ship lightened as much as possible, to see if it could be refloated. But the water became even more shallow, and the ship settled more and more to one side. Although there was little or no sea, I could not save her. Then the seams opened, though she remained in one piece.

I took my crew to the *Niña* for their safety, and as there was a light land breeze and still half the night ahead of us, and since I did not know how far the banks extended, I beat about till daybreak and then went inside the bank to the ship. I also dispatched Diego de Arana, master-at-arms of the fleet, and Pedro Gutiérrez, representative of the Royal Household, to take the small boat and go directly to the King that had last Saturday invited me to his village. I instructed them to beg the King to come to this harbor with his boats.

The village of this King is about 5 miles beyond this bank. My men told me that the King wept when he heard of the disaster. He sent all his people from the village with many large canoes to help us unload the ship. The King displayed great haste and diligence, and everything was unloaded in a very brief space of time. He himself personally assisted the unloading, along with his brothers and relatives, and guarded what was taken ashore in order that everything might be completely secure.

From time to time the King sent one of his relatives to me, weeping, to console me, and they said that I was not to be troubled or annoyed, for the King would give me whatever he possessed. I certify to Your Highnesses that in no part of Castile could things be so secure; not even a shoe string was lost! The King ordered everything placed near the houses, even emptying some in order that everything could be stored and guarded. He ordered armed men placed around the houses to guard everything all night. He, with all his people in the village, wept a great deal. They are an affectionate people, free from avarice and agreeable to everything. I certify to Your Highnesses that in all the world I do not believe there is a better people or a better country. They love their neighbors as themselves, and they have the softest and gentlest voices in the world and are always smiling. They may go naked, but Your Highnesses may be assured that they have very good customs among themselves, and the King maintains a most marvelous state, where everything takes place in an appropriate and well-ordered manner. It is a pleasure to see all of this. These people have good memories and want to see everything; they ask what things are and for what purpose they are used. . . .

The King was delighted to see me happy, and he understood that I desired a great deal of gold. He indicated by signs that he knew where there was a lot of it nearby and that I should be of good cheer, for he would give me as much of it as I desired. He told me all about this gold, specifically, that it is found in Japan, which they call *Cibao*. The people there have so much of it that they place no value on it and will bring it here. Also, the King told me, there is much gold here in the Isla Española, which they call Bohío, and in the province of Caribata. . . . I derived a great deal of pleasure and consolation from these things, and when I realized that this mitigated the trouble and affliction I had experienced by losing the ship, I recognized that Our Lord had caused me to run aground at this place so that I might establish a settlement here. And so many things came to hand here that the disaster was a blessing in disguise. Certainly, if I had not run aground here, I would have kept out to sea without anchoring at this place because it is situated inside a large bay containing two or three banks of shoals. Neither would I have left any of my people here on this voyage; even if I had desired to leave them, I could not have outfitted them well enough, nor given them enough ammunition, provisions, and materials for a fort. It is quite true that many of the people with me have pleaded with me to permit them to remain here.

Now I have ordered that a tower and a fortress be constructed, very well built, with a large moat. This is not because I believe this to be necessary with these Indians, for I am sure that I could subjugate the entire island—which I believe is larger than Portugal with twice the population—with the men that I have in my company. These Indians are naked, unarmed, and cowardly beyond help. But it is right that this tower be built, and what must be, must be. Since these Indians are so far from Your Highnesses, it is necessary that the people here know your people and what they can do, in order that the Indians may obey Your Highnesses with love and fear.

The men remaining have timbers with which to construct the fortress and provisions of bread and wine for more than a year, as well as seeds for sowing, and the ship's boat. I am leaving a caulker, a carpenter, a gunner, and a caskmaker among the many who desire zealously to serve Your Highnesses and who will please me greatly if they find the mine where the gold comes from. Thus, everything that has happened was for this purpose, that this beginning may be made. . . .

I hope to God that when I come back here from Castile, which I intend on doing, that I will find a barrel of gold, for which these people I am leaving will have traded, and that they will have found the gold mine, and the spices, and in such quantities *that within three years the Sovereigns will prepare for and undertake the conquest of the Holy Land. I have already petitioned Your Highnesses to see that all the profits of this, my enterprise, should be spent on the conquest of Jerusalem, and Your Highnesses smiled and said that the idea pleased them, and that even without this expedition they had the inclination to do it.* . . .

Tuesday, 8 January 1493

Because of a strong east and SE wind I did not start today, but I ordered the ships supplied with wood and water and everything necessary for the voyage. Although I wanted to sail this entire coast of the Isla Española, which I could do maintaining my course, my captains on the caravels are brothers, that is to say, Martín Alonso Pinzón and Vincente Yáñez Pinzón, and their followers are greedy and untrustworthy. They do not respect the honor I have shown them, and they have not and do not obey my commands. Rather, they have done and said many unjust things against me, and Martín Alonso left me from 22 November to 6 January, without cause or reason, but from disobedience. All this I have endured in silence, in order to finish my voyage successfully. On account of this, in order to escape such bad company, which I have to ignore, I have decided to return with the greatest possible haste and not to stop longer. Although there are many disobedient people among the crew, there are also many good men. Now is not the time to think about their punishment. . . .

Wednesday, 16 January 1493

Three hours before dawn I departed the gulf, which I have named the *Golfo de las Flechas*, first with a land breeze and then with a west wind. I turned the prow to the east by north, in order to go to the Isla de Caribe, where the people are whom the inhabitants of all these islands and countries fear so greatly. This is because the Caribes cross all these seas in their countless canoes and eat the men they are able to capture. One of the four Indians I took yesterday in the Puerto de las Flechas has shown me the course. After we had gone about 48 miles, the Indians indicated to me that the islands lay to the SE. I wanted to follow that course and ordered the sails trimmed, but after we had gone 6 miles the wind again blew very favorably for going to Spain. I noted that the crew were becoming dismayed because we had departed from a direct course for home; and as both ships were taking in a great deal of water, they had no help save that of God. I was compelled to abandon the course that I believe was taking me to the island; I returned to the direct course for Spain, NE by east, and held it until sunset, 36 miles. The Indians told me that on this course I would find the island of Matinino, which is inhabited only by women. I would like to carry five or six of them to the Sovereigns, but I doubt if the Indians know the course well, and I am not able to delay because of the danger with the leaking caravels. . . .

The danger was further increased by the fact that the ship was short of ballast, since the load had been lightened by the consumption of the provisions, water, and wine. I had not provided these in sufficient quantity, having hoped for favorable weather like I found in the islands, and having planned to take on ballast at the Island of Women. The solution I found for this problem, when I was able to do it, was to fill the empty water and wine casks with sea water; by this means I corrected the problem. . . .

Friday, 15 February 1493

Last night, after sunset, the skies commenced to clear toward the west, indicating that the wind was about to blow from that direction. I had the bonnet placed on the mainsail. The sea was still very high, although it was subsiding a little. I sailed to the ENE at a speed of 3 knots, and in 13 hours of the night I went 39 miles. After sunrise we saw land, off the prow to the ENE. Some said it was the island of Madeira; others, the Rock of Sintra in Portugal, near Lisbon. The wind changed and blew ahead from the ENE, and the sea came very high from the west. The caravel must have been 15 miles from land. According to my navigation I think we are off the Azores and believe the land ahead is one of those islands. The pilots and sailors believe that we are already off Castile.

From Success to Failure

Bartolomé de las Casas

Before the year was out Columbus had sailed on his second voyage, this time with a much larger and better provisioned fleet—seventeen ships carrying tools, seed, livestock, and more than a thousand colonists. His purpose was to settle the island of Hispaniola.

The expedition found the site of the first settlement deserted and its buildings destroyed. Columbus established a second settlement, which he named Isabela. He left his brother Diego in charge. Diego shortly abandoned Isabela for a more favorable location and the new town of Santo Domingo. Meanwhile Columbus himself had continued his exploration of the south coast of Cuba and discovered Jamaica. Early in 1496 he returned to Spain.

The king and queen were becoming somewhat disillusioned. Columbus had found only trifling amounts of gold and no spices, and there was muttering against him from the colony he had founded. Nevertheless, they supported a third voyage. This time Columbus discovered the coast of South America, which he took to be the mainland of Asia. But he found his colony in turmoil. To pacify the settlers, he was forced to parcel out the land—with the Indians as slave labor. Thus Columbus introduced into the New World the terrible repartimiento *system of plantation-slave agriculture, which had originally been developed in the Canary Islands.*

In the meantime the king and queen, disturbed by reports from the settlers in the New World, sent a new governor, Francisco de Bobadilla, to replace Columbus. When Columbus challenged his authority, Bobadilla had him arrested and sent back to Spain in irons.

Columbus had great difficulty in regaining the confidence of the king and queen, but they finally consented to support a fourth voyage, on the condition that he stay away from Santo Domingo. He left in the spring of 1502, with four ships; with him sailed his son Fernando, his brother Bartholomew, and many old shipmates. He did not, however, stay away from Santo Domingo, as ordered, but was refused permission to land by the new governor, Nicolas de Ovando, even in the face of an approaching hurricane. Columbus rode out the storm at sea and continued with his explorations. He explored the coast of Central America and lost two of his ships in battles with the native people, whom he called Indians. On the way back to Hispaniola Columbus's ships landed in Jamaica. After more than a year at

*sea the two remaining ships were rotting away and sinking under them:
Columbus ordered them beached.*

*It is at this desperate juncture in his fourth voyage that we turn to the
account of the final failure of what Columbus had called his* alto viaje,
"high voyage," that he was sure would rescue his fortunes.

The account is from the History of the Indies *by Fray Bartolomé de las
Casas. As we have seen, it was las Casas who abstracted and preserved the
log of Columbus's first voyage. In addition to admiring Columbus himself
and knowing Columbus's son Fernando, las Casas was present in the New
World and an eyewitness to many of the events he describes. He had come to
Hispaniola with Governor Ovando in 1502 and remained in the West
Indies until 1516, the first of several periods of residence in the New
World, culminating in his appointment as Bishop of Chiapas in Guatemala
in 1544. He went on to become a major figure of both the Spanish church
and court.*

*Las Casas began to write his history about 1527 and worked on it for
most of the rest of his life. His primary purpose was to defend the native
people from slavery and persecution by his fellow Spaniards. This became
the great work of las Casas's life and the theme not only of his history but of
all his voluminous writings. Despite his passion, however, las Casas remained a reliable reporter of historical events. His is the best contemporary
account of the later voyages of Columbus.*

We pick up his narrative of the alto viaje *as Columbus beached his ships
on the coast of Jamaica.*

Since the holds of the ships were drawing water, the admiral ran
aground safely away from the surf. The crew had orders to stay on
board and the Indians, a gentle people (don Hernando,[3] who was
there, actually said this), came in canoes to exchange food and other
objects for Castilian trinkets. To avoid inequities, disputes and
grudges, Columbus placed two persons in charge of trading and
distributing the goods equally among everyone, since all the food
supplies were gone, either eaten, rotten or lost in the hustle of departure from the Belén river. Don Hernando says the Lord guided them
to this island, then heavily populated and fertile, whose inhabitants
flocked from all the villages in their eagerness to trade with the
Spaniards.

For this reason, and to avoid Spanish misdemeanor on the island,
the admiral decided to rest and recover at sea because, as don
Hernando says, we are an uncouth lot of people and no manner of
order or punishment could prevent our men from stealing and mo-

---

[3]This is Columbus's son Fernando.—Ed.

lesting women if they went ashore, and this would greatly endanger our friendly relations with the Indians. We would be forced to fight for food and would find ourselves in a scrape. This was avoided because all the men remained assigned to their posts and could not leave ship except by special permission, which pleased the Indians. They brought us essential things at a very low cost to us: we traded an end strip of brass for one or two *hutías*, a rabbit-like animal; a handful of green or yellow glass beads for cassava bread, made of grated edible roots; and a rattle bell for something of more value. Sometimes, kings and nobles would receive a small looking glass, a colorful cap or a pair of scissors; thus these gifts relieved their misery and left them in good spirits. The admiral bought ten canoes for the crews of the grounded ships. In this manner the Spaniards were very well provided for and the Indians communicated with them.

The admiral held councils with his officers to discuss how the ships would be put to sail and at least reach Hispaniola. They were deprived of all human help and all hope of a rescue ship except by miracle, since everything, especially qualified officers, was lacking to start that journey again. They weighed advantages and disadvantages, ways and means and dangers involved over and over again for many days and concluded, by resolution of the admiral, to inform the governor general as well as Columbus's manager on Hispaniola of their plight and ask that a ship be sent to Jamaica with all the necessary equipment and a food supply. For this difficult enterprise, he named two persons whose faithfulness, courage and common sense could be relied upon. It was indeed a dangerous matter to cross a gulf which measures twenty or twenty-five leagues between Jamaica and Hispaniola without counting the thirty-five leagues they had to navigate along the coast of Jamaica from its eastern point, all this in frail canoes that are nothing but hollowed-out tree trunks.

There is a large rock called Navasa in that gulf, eight leagues from Hispaniola. Crossing the gulf was an exploit demanding great prowess and courage. Canoes are so shallow they turn over like pumpkins. This presents no danger to the Indians because they can swim and empty their canoes with gourds and climb in again; canoes do not sink when they are overturned. Of the men Columbus named, I knew one personally, Diego Méndez de Segura, chief clerk of the fleet and a very prudent, honorable, well-spoken man he was; the other was Bartolomé de Flisco, a Genoese worthy of this mission. Each took a canoe, six Spaniards and ten Indian oarsmen. Diego Méndez was told to embark for Castile from Santo Domingo and present letters and an account of the voyage to the King; Bartolomé Flisco was told to return to Jamaica with news of Diego Méndez's progress. Two hundred full leagues separated the admiral's ships from Santo Domingo.

I have a copy of the long letter Columbus wrote to the monarchs, in which he relates the anguish and the many adversities of his voyage, the new lands he had discovered, the richness of the Veragua[4] mines. He repeats the list of services he had rendered to the Spanish Crown by discovering the New World at the cost of much hardship, and he laments his fate and that of his brothers now made prisoners, their property confiscated, deprived of their honor and titles. Honor and titles he well deserved and well earned, for no services so famous were ever rendered to any other earthly King. The admiral did not write the last sentence; I am adding it because he is owed the praise.

Further in his letter, he asks for the restitution of his titles and satisfaction of his claims as well as for punishment of his accusers. He implores Heaven and earth to share his grief, saying: "Up to now I have cried alone; may Heaven take pity and may those on earth who are acquainted with charity, truth and justice cry with me!" and so on. He stresses his poverty, saying he has no roof of his own over his head, but instead must take to an inn when he needs to eat and sleep. After twenty years of extraordinary services, he and his brothers have acquired very little benefit. He misses the sacraments of the Church, especially since he is ill with the gout and fears death will overtake him in exile and isolation. He declares that he did not make this last voyage for personal fame and gains, as if to say he had these already, but sailed instead to serve the Crown with devotion and good intentions. Finally, he ends the letter by asking that, once back in Castile, he may be allowed to make a pilgrimage to Rome and other places, and entrusting the King to God, he signs his letter July 7, 1503, from Jamaica in the Indies.

Columbus also wrote a letter to the governor general of Hispaniola to notify him of his plight and recommend his two messengers for assistance in their mission, and not to forget the rescue ship. With these and other letters for Castile, Columbus dispatched Diego Méndez and Bartolomé Flisco with two canoes, with water, *ajes* and cassava bread for the Indians, and water, bread, and *hutías* or rabbits for the Spaniards which, though certainly not much, was all the canoes could hold. The ocean is always furiously rough near these islands; therefore, it was necessary to await the calming of the waves to enter the great gulf in such frail craft which, as I said, offer less danger to the Indians than our larger ships do to us. The admiral accompanied them to the tip of Jamaica, thirty leagues from where the ships had anchored, taking a few soldiers with him for the safety of his men in

---

[4]A site in Central America, near Panama, where substantial amounts of gold were indeed mined by the Indians. But it was never successfully exploited by the Spaniards.—Ed.

case of trouble with the Indians on the way. Then he returned slowly to his ships, visiting villages along his path and conversing joyfully with their inhabitants and leaving many friends behind.

A year later, the ship Diego Méndez had chartered arrived in Jamaica with a smaller caravel. Diego de Salcedo sailed it; he was Columbus's financial administrator I believe; and he brought with him a letter from the governor. Columbus complained a great deal about the governor's tardiness in sending help, accusing him of the deliberate intent to let him die there, since a whole year had passed without a sign of assistance. He said the governor finally relented only because people were talking in Santo Domingo and missionaries there were beginning to reprehend him in their sermons. Everyone, including Columbus, sailed from Jamaica on June 27, 1504. . . .

Columbus arrived in Santo Domingo on August 13, 1504. The governor and the whole city came to welcome him with great respect and celebration. The governor made Columbus a guest in his house and gave him excellent service. But Columbus was unhappy with the governor because underneath the friendliness and benevolence, there was a will at work to humiliate him, which made him believe that the governor's kindness was false. For example, the governor sent for Francisco de Porras,[5] whom Columbus kept imprisoned in the ship, unfettered him and freed him in the presence of Columbus. Also, the governor took it upon himself to punish those who had taken arms to defend the admiral, had participated in Porras's imprisonment, and had killed or wounded others, and he attempted to receive a full account from them of what had taken place in Jamaica. This right belonged only to the admiral since he was in general command of the fleet. Columbus gave advice and sentences that were not accepted or carried out because they said no one could understand him and all this I am told took place behind the admiral's back in mockery.

These vexations lasted until the ship they brought from Jamaica was repaired and they had equipped another for the return to Castile of Columbus, his brother, his son and his servants. The others stayed here and some went to San Juan to settle it or, rather, destroy it. They sailed September 12, 1504, losing a mast just as they came out of the river, which caused the admiral to proceed alone. They had good weather for one-third of their journey over the gulf, then a terrible storm broke out that greatly endangered them. On Saturday, the nineteenth of October, when the storm had ceased, the mast fell and

---

[5]Francisco de Porras and his brother Diego instigated a mutiny while the ships were beached in Jamaica, took the Indian canoes and tried to return to Santo Domingo. But rough seas forced them to return, and Columbus put them in irons.—ED.

broke into four pieces. But the admiral was a great sailor; despite an attack of gout, he repaired it by using the yard of a lateen sail, strengthening it in the middle with material from the forecastles undone for that purpose. Later, another storm broke the mizzenmast; indeed, it seemed the Fates were against the admiral, pursuing him relentlessly throughout his life with hardship and affliction. He navigated this way another 700 leagues until God willed he reach the port of San Lúcar de Barrameda, whence he went to Seville to rest a few days.

The End of the Admiral

SAMUEL ELIOT MORISON

For an account of Columbus's last years and an assessment of his achievements we turn to the greatest of modern authorities on him, the eminent American historian Samuel Eliot Morison. Morison not only mastered the sources and bibliography of Columbus's research, he actually navigated and sailed the routes of all Columbus's voyages. His Admiral of the Ocean Sea: A Life of Christopher Columbus, *2 vols. (1942) is the definitive biography. An abbreviated version is* Christopher Columbus, Mariner *(1955). The selection that follows is from his last major work touching the life and career of Columbus,* The European Discovery of America: The Southern Voyages A.D. 1492–1616 *(1974).*

The narrative begins with Columbus's return from his last voyage.

After this long and distressing voyage, Columbus expected at least to be summoned to court to tell his story, a favor accorded to almost every captain of an overseas voyage, however insignificant. But the report he had sent home by Diego Méndez did not make a good impression. This *Lettera Rarissima* is rambling and incoherent. It contains some interesting information, together with a superfluity of self-justification and numerous unconvincing "proofs" that he had been sailing along the Malay Peninsula or somewhere in the Far East.

By the time the Admiral reached Seville, 8 or 9 November, the Sovereigns were holding court at Segovia and the Queen was suffering an illness that turned out to be her last. She died on 26 November 1504, greatly to Columbus's grief and loss. Isabella had never sneered at him. She understood what he was trying to do, respected his rights, and protected him from envy and detraction. Ferdinand, too, had supported him, but the Indies were the Queen's overseas kingdom, not his.

The Admiral, now living in a hired house in Seville, was sick in heart and body, but not badly off in this world's goods. He retained a share of the gold acquired on the Fourth Voyage, and Carvajal had brought home a substantial sum for him in *Aguja*, which survived the hurricane of 1502. Two years later, Ovando delivered to him a chest of gold, and he claimed about $180,000 more, still at Hispaniola with his mark on it. But Columbus felt that he had been defrauded and repeatedly besought his son to obtain confirmation of what he called his tithes, eighths, and thirds. The tithe meant 10 per cent of the net exports from all lands that he discovered, as guaranteed by the original contract of 1492. Columbus complained that the government allowed him only a tenth of their fifth of the gold; that is, 2 instead of 10 per cent. The eighth meant the Admiral's guaranteed investment in one-eighth part of the lading of any vessel trading with the Indies. He complained that Bobadilla or Ovando impounded his eighth in sundry cargoes without payment. The third was preposterous. Columbus's grant as Admiral of the Ocean Sea stated that it carried "pre-eminences and prerogatives . . . in the same manner as . . . the Grand Admiral of Castile." Having ascertained that this Grand Admiral collected 33⅓ per cent tax on trade between Spain and the Canary Islands, Columbus claimed a similar cut on the entire inward and outward trade between Spain and the Indies! Obviously, if the crown had admitted that, little profit would have been left for anyone. As it was, even by collecting a mere 2 per cent of the gold, the Admiral was a rich man according to the standards of his day, and able to leave substantial legacies to his sons.

There is no evidence known to me to indicate that Columbus ever changed his cosmographical ideas, or realized the vast extent of the continent which he had discovered. Peter Martyr very early and Rodrigo Fernández de Santaella (the editor of the first Spanish edition of Marco Polo) in 1503, among others, questioned whether Columbus's Indies were the real Indies, but the Discoverer ignored them. He died believing that his *Otro Mundro* was but an extension of the Malay Peninsula for several hundred miles.

Even on his deathbed Columbus planned to finance a new crusade, and tried to provide for it in his last will and testament. He spent practically nothing on himself or on keeping up appearances, and he always intended to use the profits of his discoveries to recover the Holy Sepulchre from the infidel. But he also concerned himself over collecting pay for his seamen on the Fourth Voyage who had returned with him. Poor men with no other means of support, they now had two years' wages due. Thrice the Admiral begged the treasurer of Castile to pay them off, without result. They even sent a delegation to court to demand their back pay, with letters from the Admiral to his son and to other persons of influence backing them up, but for years nobody received anything.

Columbus now wisely concluded it was hopeless to expect to be sent back to Hispaniola as viceroy and governor; his poor health and "advanced age" of fifty-three made that impractical. So he concentrated on having the viceroyalty and admiralty conferred on his son Diego. That boy, a clever courtier, had made himself solid by marrying a lady of royal blood, Doña Maria de Toledo. And, three years after his father's death, Diego was appointed governor of Hispaniola and confirmed in some of his father's hereditary titles.

By the spring of 1505 Columbus felt well enough to travel, provided he could ride a mule; a horse's gait was too rough for him. The crown, under pressure by the horse breeders of Andalusia, had forbidden the use of mules for riding, so the Admiral had to beg for a special permit. That the King granted, and in May 1505 the Admiral started on his long journey to the court at Segovia, north of Madrid.

Ferdinand received him graciously and proposed that an arbitrator be appointed to settle his claims against the crown. Columbus refused because the King insisted that his viceroyalty and admiralty be adjudicated as well as the pecuniary claims, and he was too proud to arbitrate anything to which he had a clear legal title. The King then hinted that if he would renounce all titles, offices, and revenues, he would be granted a handsome estate with a fat rent roll. Columbus rejected that absolutely. He considered it dishonorable. He would have all or nothing, and nothing he got.

As the court moved to Salamanca and on to Valladolid, the Admiral painfully followed. A year passed, nothing happened, and in the meantime his arthritis grew worse, and he became bedridden. But he felt so certain of justice being done that he made a will providing legacies out of his expected revenues, such as a sinking fund for the crusade, a house in Genoa to be kept open perpetually for his descendants, a chapel in Hispaniola so endowed that daily Masses might be said for his soul forever. In his simplicity he seemed to feel that these pious bequests would attract the attention of the Almighty, who would compel the King to make them practicable.

Almost at the last moment of his life, Columbus had his hopes raised by the arrival in Spain of the Infanta Doña Juana to claim her mother's throne of Castile. She had been at court when Columbus first returned from the Indies, and looked wide-eyed at his artifacts and his Indians, so he hoped that she might confirm the favors granted by her sainted mother. He was too ill to move, so he sent brother Bartholomew to kiss the young sovereign's hands and bespeak her favor.

During Bartholomew's absence, the Admiral failed rapidly. On 19 May 1506 he ratified his final will, creating son Diego his principal heir and commending to his benevolence all other relatives, including Ferdinand's mother Beatriz de Harana. Next day he suddenly grew worse. Both sons, brother Diego, and a few faithful followers such as Diego Méndez and Bartolomeo Fieschi gathered at his bedside. A priest, quickly summoned, said Mass, and everyone in the devoted circle of relatives, friends, and domestics received the sacrament. After the concluding prayer, the Admiral, remembering the last words of his Lord and Saviour, murmured as his own, *In manus tuas, Domine, commendo spiritum meum*—"Into Thy hands, O Lord, I commend my spirit."

A poor enough funeral followed for the "Admiral of the Ocean Sea, Viceroy and Governor of the Islands and Mainlands in the Indies." The court sent no representative; no bishop, no great dignitary attended, and the official chronicle failed to mention either death or funeral. Columbus had the ill fortune to die at the moment when his discoveries were slightly valued and his personal fortunes and expectations were at their lowest ebb.

Little by little, as his life receded into history and the claims of others to be the "real" discoverers of America faded into the background, his great achievements began to be appreciated. Yet it is one of the ironies of history that the Admiral himself died ignorant of what he had really accomplished, still insisting that he had discovered a large number of islands, a province of China, and an "Other World"; but of the vast extent of that Other World, and of the ocean that lay between it and Asia, he had neither knowledge nor suspicion.

Now, more than five hundred years after his birth, when the day of Columbus's first landfall in the New World is celebrated throughout the length and breadth of the Americas, his fame and reputation may be considered secure, despite the efforts of armchair navigators and nationalist maniacs to denigrate him. A glance at a map of the Caribbean may remind you of what he accomplished: discovery of the Bahamas, Cuba, and Hispaniola on the First Voyage; discovery of the Lesser Antilles, Puerto Rico, Jamaica, and the south coast of Cuba on his Second, as well as founding a permanent European colony; discovery of Trinidad and the Spanish Main, on his Third; and on the Fourth Voyage, Honduras, Nicaragua, Costa Rica, Panama, and Colombia. No navigator in history, not even Magellan, discovered so much territory hitherto unknown to Europeans. None other so effectively translated his north-south experience under the Portuguese flag to the first east-west voyage, across the Atlantic. None other started so many things from which stem the history of the United States, of Canada, and of a score of American republics.

And do not forget that sailing west to the Orient was his idea, pursued relentlessly for six years before he had the means to try it. As a popular jingle of the 400th anniversary put it:

> What if wise men as far back as Ptolemy
> Judged that the earth like an orange was round,
> None of them ever said, "Come along, follow me,
> Sail to the West and the East will be found."

Columbus had his faults, but they were largely the defects of qualities that made him great. These were an unbreakable faith in God and his own destiny as the bearer of the Word to lands beyond the seas; an indomitable will and stubborn persistence despite neglect, poverty, and ridicule. But there was no flaw, no dark side to the most outstanding and essential of all his qualities—seamanship. As a master mariner and navigator, no one in the generation prior to Magellan could touch Columbus. Never was a title more justly bestowed than the one which he most jealously guarded—*Almirante del Mar Océano*—Admiral of the Ocean Sea.

Suggestions for Further Reading

There is a considerable body of Columbus's own writings—letters, journals, and the like. There are two comprehensive Spanish editions of these materials, but only two smaller collections available in English: *Select Documents Illustrating the Four Voyages of Columbus* 2 vols., ed. Cecil Jane (London: Hakluyt Society, 1930–33) and *Journals and Other Documents on the Life and Voyages of Christopher Columbus*, ed. and tr. Samuel Eliot Morison (New York: Heritage, 1964). There are several modern English translations of Columbus's log of his first voyage. For many years the standard edition was *The Journal of Christopher Columbus* (*During His First Voyage, 1492–93*), tr. and ed. Clement R. Markham (London: Hakluyt Society, 1893). Then there appeared *The Journal of Christopher Columbus*, tr. Cecil Jane, rev. by L. A. Vigneras (London: A. Blond, 1960), and a version of the log translated by Morison in his collection of documents (1964). The definitive contemporary edition is *The Diario of Christopher Columbus' First Voyage to America, 1492–1493*, ed. and tr. Oliver Dunn and James E. Kelley, Jr.

(Norman, Okla.: University of Oklahoma Press, 1987). This edition contains the Spanish text along with the translation and comprehensive notes. The text used for this chapter is based on the foregoing edition but is written in colloquial English and with some further refinements of terminology and extended notes, *The Log of Christopher Columbus*, tr. and ed. Robert H. Fuson (Camden, Maine: International Marine Publishing Co., 1987).

Columbus's achievements were described in detail by four contemporary writers who knew him well—Peter Martyr Anghiera, Gonzalo Fernández de Oviedo y Valdés, Fernando Colon (Columbus's son), and las Casas. Peter Martyr's *De orbe novo*, tr. and ed. F. A. MacNutt, 2 vols. (New York: Putnam, 1912) and *The Life of the Admiral Christopher Columbus by His Son Fernando*, tr. and ed. Benjamin Keen (New Brunswick, N.J.: Rutgers University Press, 1959) are translated into English. There is no definitive English translation of la Casas's *History of the Indies*. But Bartolomé de las Casas, *History of the Indies*, tr. and ed. Andrée Collard (New York, Evanston, and London: Torchbooks, 1971), excerpted for this chapter, is a partial translation.

The best modern biography of Columbus is Samuel Eliot Morison, *Admiral of the Ocean Sea: A Life of Christopher Columbus* (Boston: Little, Brown, 1942), in both one-volume and two-volume editions. Morison's *Christopher Columbus Mariner* (Boston and Toronto: Little, Brown, 1955) is an abridged edition of the foregoing. His *The European Discovery of America: The Southern Voyages A.D. 1492–1616* (New York: Oxford University Press, 1974) was his last major book dealing with Columbus and the one excerpted for this chapter.

The treatments of Columbus since Morison do not, on the whole, represent much of an improvement. Gianni Granzotto, *Christopher Columbus*, tr. Stephen Sartarelli (Garden City, N.Y.: Doubleday, 1985), is a fictionalized biography full of errors and misjudgments. Paolo Emilio Taviani, *Christopher Columbus: The Grand Design* (London: Orbis, 1985), while a larger book than Granzotto's, is not much more reliable: it is comprehensive without being critical. G. R. Crone, *The Discovery of America*, in the series "Turning Points in History" (New York: Weybright and Talley, 1969), is a competent but pedestrian survey. Hans Koning, *Columbus: His Enterprise* (New York and London: Monthly Review Press, 1976), starts out as a straightforward biography but quickly becomes a polemic against the Spanish exploitation of the New World and its people, which can hardly be blamed entirely on Columbus. There is one book that can be read with both pleasure and profit, Björn Landström, *Columbus* (New York: Macmillan, 1966), a handsome book and a popularized account of the best modern Columbus scholarship.

Two books of somewhat larger scope can be recommended: Carl Ortwin Sauer, *The Early Spanish Main* (Berkeley and Los Angeles: University of California Press, 1966), an account by a famous geographer of the conquest of the Caribbean rim, and *First Images of America: The Impact of the New World on the Old*, ed. Fredi Chiappelli (Berkeley: University of California Press, 1976).

MARTIN LUTHER: PROTESTANT SAINT OR "DEVIL IN THE HABIT OF A MONK"?

c. 1483	Born
1505	Entered Augustinian order
1517	The Ninety-five Theses
1521	Diet of Worms and trial of Luther
1525	Married Katherina von Bora
1546	Died

On a summer day in the year 1505, a young German law student was returning to the University of Erfurt after a visit home. He was overtaken by a sudden, violent thunderstorm and struck to the ground by a bolt of lightning. Terrified, he cried out, "St. Anne, help me! I will become a monk." Such vows were usually quickly forgotten, but not this one, for the student was Martin Luther, the man who was to bring about the most profound revolution in the history of the Christian faith. Within a matter of weeks, he disposed of his worldly goods, including his law books, and joined the order of the Augustinian Eremites in Erfurt. His father was furious; his friends were dismayed. And historians and theologians since the sixteenth century have speculated about the motives that compelled him. But this is only one of the questions about Martin Luther that have fascinated scholars and made him the subject of more writing than any other figure in European history.

There was seemingly nothing in his youth or adolescence to account for his decision to become a monk. But once that decision was made, Luther was swept by such a tidal wave of religious intensity that it troubled even his monastic superiors. He prayed for hours on end; he subjected himself to such ascetic rigors that he almost ruined his health; and he confessed his sins over and over again. He was assaulted by what one modern scholar has aptly called "the terror of

225

the holy." God was for him a terrible judge, so perfect and so righteous that sinful man could not even begin to deserve anything at His hands but eternal damnation. Martin Luther was beginning his search for "justification," the sense that somehow, against all odds, he might earn God's grace and escape damnation.

The terror of the holy remained, and the monastic life gave Luther no assurance that God's grace was close at hand. But the very religious disquiet that tormented the young monk also caused his superiors to single him out, for this was the stuff that the great figures of religion were made of—St. Francis, St. Bernard, St. Benedict. Moreover, Brother Martin, for all his inner turmoil, was a bright and capable young man and already well educated, a Master of Arts. Soon he was ordained priest. He was sent on a matter of chapter business to Rome. And his education was continued, but now in theology rather than law.

Then the Elector of Saxony, Frederick the Wise, approached the Erfurt Augustinians in search of faculty members for the newly founded university in his capital town of Wittenberg. Brother Martin was sent. In Wittenberg he taught the arts course, worked at his own studies, and assumed more than a fair share of the parish duties. By 1513 he earned his doctor's degree and began to teach theology. As he prepared a series of lectures on the Psalms, he began to gain new understanding of his texts. And then, while he was working out his lectures on the Epistles of St. Paul, he found meaning in the familiar passage from Romans 1:17 that he had never before perceived. "For therein is the righteousness of God revealed from faith to faith: as it is written, the just shall live by faith." Later Luther said, "This passage of Paul became to me a gate to heaven." Here was the "justification" he had sought so long in vain. People are justified by faith, by the simple act of belief in Christ, in a way that no amount of works, however pious and well intended, no amount of prayers or anguish or penance can insure. Justification by faith was to become the cardinal doctrine of a new religious sect.

But Luther's inward revelation might never have led to a separate sect, much less a Reformation, except for a chain of events external to him. It began with a particularly scandalous sale of indulgences in the neighboring lands of the Archbishop of Mainz. The doctrine of indulgences was the basis of the church's profitable traffic in "pardons," as they were sometimes called, remissions of the temporal penalties for sin. Although the doctrine was an outgrowth of the sacrament of penance, many religious were troubled by it. To Luther, the indulgences that had been bought across the border by some of his parishioners and the outrageous claims for their effectiveness that were being made by the indulgence preacher, the Dominican Johann

Tetzel, seemed a surpassingly bad example of the concept of "works," especially in light of his own increasing conviction that works cannot work salvation in people—only faith "sola fides." In response to this scandalous situation, Luther was led to propose his ninety-five theses against indulgences. The document was dated October 31, 1517, the most famous date in Protestantism. The theses were written in Latin, intended for academic disputation, but somehow they were translated into German and found their way into print. Despite their dry, scholarly prose and formal organization they became a popular, even an inflammatory manifesto. Ecclesiastical authorities, including the offended Archbishop of Mainz, complained to Luther's superiors and eventually to Rome. Luther was pressed to recant, but he refused. Instead, he clung stubbornly not only to his basic position on indulgences but to the ever more revolutionary implications of his belief in justification by faith. Within three years, he had come to reject much of the sacramental theory of the church, nearly all its traditions, and the authority of the pope. In 1520 he defied Pope Leo X's bull of condemnation; in the following year he defied the Emperor Charles V in the famous confrontation at the Diet of Worms. The Lord's good servant had become, in Charles's phrase, "that devil in the habit of a monk." The Catholic Luther had become the Protestant Luther.

The Protestant Luther

MARTIN LUTHER

The image of Luther the Protestant results most directly, of course, from Luther's deeds—his successful act of defiance against established church and established state, his uncanny ability not only to survive but to build around him a new political-religious community vital enough to maintain itself. Luther's Protestant image is also based upon the incredible quantity of his writings—tracts and treatises, sermons, commentaries, translations, disputations, hymns, and letters—nearly a hundred heavy volumes in the standard modern edition. But his image also rests upon an elaborate Protestant tradition that can be traced to Luther himself.

Luther was a voluble and expansive man. Even his formal treatises are rich in anecdotes from his own experience and filled with autobiographical detail. These qualities carried over into his talk, and Luther loved to talk. As the Reformation settled into a political and social reality and Luther married—for he rejected clerical celibacy along with the other doctrines of the old church—his kitchen table became the center of the Protestant world. In addition to his own large family, there were always people visiting— friends and associates, wandering scholars and ecclesiastics, professors and students, and religious refugees. After dinner, when the dishes were cleared and the beer steins passed around, they would talk, Luther usually taking the lead. He had opinions on practically everything—politics, people, theology, education, child raising—and he would reminisce about his own life as well.

Some of the guests took notes on these conversations, and a great many of them have been preserved—six volumes in the German Weimar edition— appropriately called the Tabletalk. *The following selections are from the* Tabletalk. *They are fragments of Luther's own recollections of his experiences of monasticism, his inward struggle to gain a sense of justification, and his defiance of the old church.*

He [Martin Luther] became a monk against the will of his father. When he celebrated his first mass and asked his father why he was angry about the step he took, the father replied reproachfully, "Don't you know that it's written, Honor your father and your mother" [Exod. 20:12]? When he excused himself by saying that he was so frightened by a storm that he was compelled to become a monk, his father answered, "Just so it wasn't a phantom you saw!" . . .

[Luther recalled] "later when I stood there during the mass and began the canon, I was so frightened that I would have fled if I hadn't been admonished by the prior. For when I read the words, 'Thee, therefore, most merciful Father,' etc., and thought I had to speak to God without a Mediator, I felt like fleeing from the world like Judas. Who can bear the majesty of God without Christ as Mediator? In short, as a monk I experienced such horrors; I had to experience them before I could fight them." . . . "I almost fasted myself to death, for again and again I went for three days without taking a drop of water or a morsel of food. I was very serious about it. I really crucified the Lord Christ. I wasn't simply an observer but helped to carry him and pierce [his hands and feet]. God forgive me for it, for I have confessed it openly! This is the truth: the most pious monk is the worst scoundrel. He denies that Christ is the mediator and highpriest and turns him into a judge."

"I chose twenty-one saints and prayed to three every day when I celebrated mass; thus I completed the number every week. I prayed especially to the Blessed Virgin, who with her womanly heart would compassionately appease her Son. . . ."

"When I was a monk I was unwilling to omit any of the prayers, but when I was busy with public lecturing and writing I often accumulated my appointed prayers for a whole week, or even two or three weeks. Then I would take a Saturday off, or shut myself in for as long as three days without food and drink, until I had said the prescribed prayers. This made my head split, and as a consequence I couldn't close my eyes for five nights, lay sick unto death, and went out of my senses. Even after I had quickly recovered and I tried again to read, my head went 'round and 'round. Thus our Lord God drew me, as if by force, from that torment of prayers. To such an extent had I been captive [to human traditions]. . . ."

"I wouldn't take one thousand florins for not having seen Rome because I wouldn't have been able to believe such things if I had been told by somebody without having seen them for myself. We were simply laughed at because we were such pious monks. A Christian was taken to be nothing but a fool. I know priests who said six or seven masses while I said only one. They took money for them and I didn't. In short, there's no disgrace in Italy except to be poor. Murder and theft are still punished a little, for they must do this. Otherwise no sin is too great for them." . . .

[As a young professor in Wittenberg] "the words 'righteous' and 'righteousness of God' struck my conscience like lightning. When I heard them I was exceedingly terrified. If God is righteous [I thought], he must punish. But when by God's grace I pondered, in the tower[1] and heated room of this building, over the words, 'He who through faith is righteous shall live' [Rom. 1:17] and 'the righteousness of God' [Rom. 3:21], I soon came to the conclusion that if we, as righteous men, ought to live from faith and if the righteousness of God should contribute to the salvation of all who believe, then salvation won't be our merit but God's mercy. My spirit was thereby cheered. For it's by the righteousness of God that we're justified and saved through Christ. These words [which had before terrified me] now became more pleasing to me. The Holy Spirit unveiled the Scriptures for me in this tower." . . .

"That works don't merit life, grace, and salvation is clear from this, that works are not spiritual birth but are fruits of this birth. We are not made sons, heirs, righteous, saints, Christians by means of works, but we do good works once we have been made, born, created such. So it's necessary to have life, salvation, and grace before works, just as a tree doesn't deserve to become a tree on account of its fruit but a tree is by nature fitted to bear fruit. Because we're born, created, generated righteous by the Word of grace, we're not fashioned, prepared, or put together as such by means of the law or works. Works merit something else than life, grace, or salvation—namely, praise, glory, favor, and certain extraordinary things—just as a tree deserves to be loved, cultivated, praised, and honored by others on account of its fruit. Urge the birth and substance of the Christian and you will at the same time extinguish the merits of works insofar as grace and salvation from sin, death, and the devil are concerned."

"Infants who have no works are saved by faith alone, and therefore faith alone justifies. If the power of God can do this in one person it can do it in all, because it's not the power of the infant but the power of faith. Nor is it the weakness of the infant that does it, otherwise that weakness would itself be a merit or be equivalent to one. We'd like to defy our Lord God with our works. We'd like to become righteous through them. But he won't allow it. My conscience tells me that I'm not justified by works, but nobody believes it. 'Thou art justified in thy sentence; against thee only have I sinned and done that which is evil in thy sight' [Ps. 51:4]. What is meant by 'forgive us our debts' [Matt. 6:12]? I don't want to be good. What would be easier than for a man to say, 'I am a sinful man' [Luke 5:8]? But thou art a righteous God. That would be bad enough, but we are our own tormentors.

---

[1]The tower was the "privy" of the cloister, and it was there that Luther suddenly saw the significance of justification by faith. Hence Lutheran scholarship refers to his *turmerlebnis,* or "tower experience."—ED.

The Spirit says, 'Righteous art thou' [Ps. 119:137]. The flesh can't say this: 'Thou art justified in thy sentence' [Ps. 51:4]." . . .

"God led us away from all this in a wonderful way; without my quite being aware of it he took me away from that game more than twenty years ago. How difficult it was at first when we journeyed toward Kemberg[2] after All Saints' Day in the year 1517, when I first made up my mind to write against the crass errors of indulgences! Dr. Jerome Schurff[3] advised against this: 'You wish to write against the pope? What are you trying to do? It won't be tolerated!' I replied, 'And if they have to tolerate it?' Presently Sylvester,[4] master of the sacred palace, entered the arena, fulminating against me with this syllogism: 'Whoever questions what the Roman Church says and does is heretical. Luther questions what the Roman Church says and does, and therefore [he is a heretic].' So it all began." . . .

"At the beginning of the gospel[5] I took steps only very gradually against the impudent Tetzel. Jerome, the bishop of Brandenburg, held me in esteem, and I exhorted him, as the ordinary of the place, to look into the matter and sent him a copy of my *Explanations*[6] before I published them. But nobody was willing to restrain the ranting Tetzel; rather, everybody ventured to defend him. So I proceeded imprudently while the others listened and were worn out under the tyranny. Now that I got into the matter I prayed to God to help me further. One can never pay the pope as he deserves."

The Catholic Luther

HARTMANN GRISAR

The traditional Catholic view of Luther is a hostile one. For Luther's Reformation set the new Protestantism against the old Catholicism with a bitterness and animosity that are apparent even to this day.

The following selection is from Martin Luther: His Life and Work, *by*

---

[2]A nearby monastery where, presumably, they were traveling on some routine parish business.—ED.

[3]A colleague of Luther's in the faculty of law.—ED.

[4]Sylvester Prierias, a papal official and a Dominican, the first dignitary in Rome to attack Luther.—ED.

[5]Luther often used this phrase for the beginning of the Reformation.—ED.

[6]The book Luther wrote explaining and defending his ninety-five theses.—ED.

the German Jesuit scholar Hartmann Grisar (1845–1932), a shorter and somewhat more pointed work based upon his more famous, six-volume Lu-ther. Although Grisar does abandon some of the more outrageous charges of the Catholic polemical tradition and displays an awesome knowledge of the detail of his subject, he is still openly partisan in his account and openly hostile in his interpretation. The passage below focuses on the last years of Luther the Catholic, the years at Wittenberg when Luther, as a young pro-fessor of theology, was struggling toward his understanding of justification by faith. Grisar insists that even then Luther was a "bad" Catholic. Instead of the frightened and solitary figure striving against "the terror of the holy," we find a truculent rebel, willfully distorting the rules of his own order and arrogantly preferring his own interpretation of scripture and ecclesiastical tradition to that of the church. Grisar makes Luther seem a selfish and overbearing man, neglectful of his proper religious duties. He finds him misled by his attraction to mysticism and excessive in his ascetic exercises. In short, what Grisar builds is a case for Luther's suffering from "a serious aberration."

The young professor of Sacred Scripture displayed a pronounced inclination toward mysticism. Mysticism had always been cultivated to a certain extent in the religious orders of the Catholic Church. The reading of Bonaventure had pointed Luther, even as a young monk, to the pious union with God at which Mysticism aims. Toward the close of his lectures on the Psalms, he became acquainted with certain works on Mysticism which he imbibed with great avidity. They were the sermons of Tauler and the tract *"Theologia deutsch."* They domi-nated his thoughts in 1515. Although these works were not designed to do so, they helped to develop his unecclesiastical ideas. His lively experience of the weakness of the human will induced him to hear-ken readily to the mystical voices which spoke of the complete relin-quishment of man to God, even though he did not understand them perfectly. His opposition to good works opened his mind to a falla-cious conception of the doctrines of those books of the mystical life. It appeared to him that, by following such leaders, his internal fears could be dispelled by a calm immersion in the Godhead. . . . In brief, he tried to transform all theology into what he called a theology of the Cross. Misconstruing Tauler's doctrine of perfection he would recog-nize only the highest motives, namely, reasons of the greatest perfec-tion for himself as well as for others. Fear of divine punishment and hope of divine reward were to be excluded.

These were extravagances that could not aid him, but, on the con-trary, involved great dangers to his orthodoxy; in fact, constituted a serious aberration. But he trusted his new lights with the utmost self-confidence. . . .

In the spring of 1515, Luther was elected rural vicar by his fellow Augustinians.

At stated times he visited the monasteries thus entrusted to him. There were eleven of them, including Erfurt and Wittenberg. After the middle of April, 1516, he made a visitation of the congregations of the Order at Dresden, Neustadt on the Orla, Erfurt, Gotha, Langensalza, and Nordhausen. The letters written by him during his term of office as rural vicar, which normally lasted three years, contain practical directions and admonitions concerning monastic discipline and are, in part, quite edifying. Some of his visitations, however, were conducted with such astonishing rapidity that no fruitful results could be expected of them. Thus the visitation of the monastery at Gotha occupied but one hour, that at Langensalza two hours. "In these places," he wrote to Lang, "the Lord will work without us and direct the spiritual and temporal affairs in spite of the devil." At Neustadt he deposed the prior, Michael Dressel, without a hearing, because the brethren could not get along with him. "I did this," he informed Lang in confidence, "because I hoped to rule there myself for the half-year."

In a letter to the same friend he writes as follows about the engagements with which he was overwhelmed at that time: "I really ought to have two secretaries or chancellors. I do hardly anything all day but write letters. . . . I am at the same time preacher to the monastery, have to preach in the refectory, and am even expected to preach daily in the parish church. I am regent of the *studium* [*i.e.*, of the younger monks] and vicar, that is to say prior eleven times over; I have to provide for the delivery of the fish from the Leitzkau pond and to manage the litigation of the Herzberg fellows [monks] at Torgau; I am lecturing on Paul, compiling an exposition on the Psalter, and, as I said before, writing letters most of the time. . . . It is seldom that I have time for the recitation of the Divine Office or to celebrate Mass, and then, too, I have my peculiar temptations from the flesh, the world, and the devil."

The last sentence quoted above contains a remarkable declaration about his spiritual condition and his compliance with his monastic duties at that time. He seldom found time to recite the Divine Office and to say Mass. It was his duty so to arrange his affairs as to be able to comply with these obligations. The canonical hours were strictly prescribed. Saying Mass is the central obligation of every priest, especially if he is a member of a religious order. If Luther did not know how to observe due moderation in his labors; if he was derelict in the principal duties of the spiritual life; it was to be feared that he would gradually drift away from the religious state, particularly in view of the fact that he had adopted a false Mysticism which favored the relaxation of the rule. As rural vicar, it is probable that he did not sustain among the brethren the good old spirit which the zealous Proles had introduced into the society. Of the "temptations of the flesh" which he mentions we learn nothing definite. He was not yet in conflict with his vows. His wrestlings with the devil may signify the fears and terrors to which he was subject. . . . At times, in consequence either of a disordered affection of the heart or of overwork, he was so distressed that he could not eat or drink for a long time. One day he was found seemingly dead in his cell, so completely was he exhausted as a result of agitation and lack of food. . . .

Did Luther subject himself to extraordinary deeds of penance at any period of his monastic life, as he frequently affirmed in his subsequent conflict with the papacy and monasticism, when he was impelled by polemical reasons to describe himself as the type of a holy and mortified monk, one who could not find peace of mind during his whole monastic career? Holding then that peace of mind was simply impossible in the Catholic Church, he arbitrarily misrepresents monasticism, in order to exhibit in a most glaring manner the alleged inherent impossibility of "papistic" ethics to produce the assurance of God's mercy. "I tormented my body by fastings, vigils, and cold. . . . In the observance of these matters I was so precise and superstitious, that I imposed more burdens upon my body than it could bear without danger to health." "If ever a monk got to heaven by monkery, then I should have got there." "I almost died a-fasting, for often I took neither a drop of water nor a morsel of food for three days." . . .

The above picture of singular holiness is produced not by early witnesses, but by assertions which Luther made little by little at a later period of life. The established facts contradict the legend. Perhaps his description is based partly on remembrances of his distracted days in the monastery, or on eccentric efforts to overcome his sombre moods by means of a false piety. His greatest error, and the one which most betrays him, is that he ascribes his fictitious asceticism to all serious-minded members of his monastery, yea, of all monasteries. He would have it that all monks consumed themselves in wailing and grief, wrestling for the peace of God, until he supplied the remedy. It is a rule of the most elementary criticism finally to cut loose from the distorted presentation of the matter which has maintained itself so tenaciously in Protestant biographies of Luther.

It may be admitted that, on the whole, Luther was a dutiful monk for the greatest part of his monastic life. "When I was in the monastery," he stated on one occasion, in 1535, "I was not like the rest of the men, the robbers, the unjust, the adulterous; but I observed chastity, obedience, and poverty."

Yet, after his transfer to Wittenberg, and in consequence of the applause which was accorded to him there, the unpleasant traits of his character, especially his positive insistence on always being in the right, began to manifest themselves more and more disagreeably. . . . His opposition to the so-called doctrine of self-righteousness caused him to form a false conception of righteousness; instead of attacking an heretical error, he combated the true worth of good works and the perfections of the monastic life.

Voluntary poverty, as practiced by the mendicants, was one of the foundations of his Order. The inmates of monastic houses were to live on alms according to the practice introduced by the great Saint Francis of Assisi and for the benefactions received were to devote themselves gratis to the spiritual needs of their fellowmen. Many abuses, it is true, had attached themselves to the mendicant system; self-interest, avarice, and worldly-mindedness infected the itinerant mendicants. But in his explanation of the Psalms Luther attacks the life of poverty *per se:* "O mendicants! O mendicants! O mendicants!" he pathetically exclaims, "who can excuse you? . . . Look to it yourselves," etc. He places the practice of poverty in an unfavorable light. In his criticism of the "self-righteousness" of his irksome enemies, he confronts them with the righteousness of the spirit that cometh from Christ. These people, whom he believed it his duty to expose, were guilty, in his opinion, of a Pharisaical denial of the true righteousness of Christ. His righteousness, and not our good works, effect our salvation; works generate a fleshly sense and boastfulness. These thought processes evince how false mysticism, unclear theological notions, a darkening of the monastic spirit, and passionate obstinacy conspired in Luther's mind. . . .

The germ of Luther's reformatory doctrine is plainly contained in this species of Mysticism. Step by step he had arrived at his new dogma in the above described manner. The system which attacked the basic truths of the Catholic Church, was complete in outline. Before giving a fuller exposition of it, we must consider the individual factors which cooperated in its development in Luther's mind.

Confession and penance were a source of torturing offense to the young monk. Can one obtain peace with God by the performance of penitential works? He discussed this question with Staupitz[7] on an occasion when he sought consolation. Staupitz pointed out to him that all penance must begin and end with love; that all treasures are hidden in Christ, in whom we must trust and whom we must love. . . . Nor was Staupitz the man who could thoroughly free Luther from his doubts about predestination, although Luther says he helped him. His general reference to the wounds of Christ could not permanently set the troubled monk aright. . . . Recalling Staupitz's exhortations, he says, in 1532: We must stop at the wounds of Christ, and may not ponder over the awful ministry. The only remedy consists in dismissing from our minds the possibility of a verdict of damnation. "When I attend to these ideas, I forget what Christ and God are, and sometimes arrive at the conclusion that God is a scoundrel. . . . The idea of predestination causes us to forget God, and the *Laudate* ceases and the *Blasphemate* begins." The part which these struggles had in the origin of his new doctrine, is to be sought in Luther's violent efforts to attain to a certain repose in the fact of his presumptive predestination. . . . In his interpretation of the Epistle of St. Paul to the Romans, given during the years 1515 and 1516, Luther completely unfolded his new doctrine.

Luther between Reform and Reformation

ERWIN ISERLOH

A phenomenon of the last generation or so of Luther scholarship has been the emergence of a new, more balanced, and more charitable Catholic view of him. The polemical tone has almost disappeared, the shortcomings of the old church have been recognized, and Luther himself is interpreted in ways other than simply as a bad Catholic and a worse monk, led by his own overweening hubris *to an inevitable apostasy.*

One of the best of the new Catholic critics is Erwin Iserloh, professor of church history at the University of Münster in Germany. The following selection is taken from his liveliest and most widely read book, The Theses

---

[7]Johann Staupitz was a superior of Luther and one of his most trusted friends and confidants. Though Staupitz remained Catholic and in orders, they remained friends for many years.—ED.

Were Not Posted: Luther Between Reform and Reformation. *It is, quite apart from its point of view, a stunning demonstration of how a thoughtful scholar may use a precise event to reach a general conclusion. The event in this case is the "primal image" of Luther nailing the ninety-five theses to the door of the Castle Church in Wittenberg, thereby defiantly proclaiming the beginning of his rebellion from the church. Iserloh presents evidence that this treasured picture appeared only after Luther's death, that it came not from Luther himself but from his younger associate Philipp Melanchthon, and that Melanchthon had not even witnessed the event. Iserloh goes on to point out that, far from an act of rebellion, Luther's handling of the matter of the theses shows him to have been, at this crucial point, both a good Catholic and a responsible theologian, in Iserloh's phrase, "an obedient rebel." Iserloh argues further that it was not necessary for Luther to have been driven to rebellion; he might well have been kept within the church to its great advantage, as well as his own.*

Our investigation of the sources and the reports concerning October 31, 1517, compels us to conclude that the drama of that day was notably less than what we would suppose from the jubilee celebrations which have been held since 1617 and from the Reformation Day festivals since their inception in 1668. In fact the sources rule out a public posting of the ninety-five theses.

Although October 31, 1517, lacked outward drama it was nevertheless a day of decisive importance. It is the day on which the Reformation began, not because Martin Luther posted his ninety-five theses on the door of the castle church in Wittenberg, but because on this day Luther approached the competent church authorities with his pressing call for reform. On this day he presented them with his theses and the request that they call a halt to the unworthy activities of the indulgence preachers. When the bishops did not respond, or when they sought merely to divert him, Luther circulated his theses privately. The theses spread quickly and were printed in Nürnberg, Leipzig, and Basel. Suddenly they were echoing throughout Germany and beyond its borders in a way that Luther neither foresaw nor intended. The protest that Luther registered before Archbishop Albrecht[8] and the inclusion of the theses with the letter eventually led to the Roman investigation of Luther's works.

Some will surely want to object: Is it not actually of minor importance whether Luther posted his theses in Wittenberg or not? I would answer that it is of more than minor importance. For October 31 was

[8]The Archbishop of Mainz, who had authorized the particular sale of indulgences.—ED.

a day on which the castle church was crowded with pilgrims taking advantage of the titular feast of All Saints. Luther's theses on the door would have constituted a public protest. If Luther made such a scene on the same day that he composed his letter to Archbishop Albrecht, then his letter loses its credibility, even when we take into account its excessive protestations of submissiveness and humility as conventions of the time.

Above all, if Luther did post his theses, then for the rest of his life he knowingly gave a false account of these events by asserting that he only circulated his theses after the bishops failed to act.

If the theses were not posted on October 31, 1517, then it becomes all the more clear that Luther did not rush headlong toward a break with the church. Rather, as Joseph Lortz has never tired of repeating, and as Luther himself stressed, he started the Reformation quite unintentionally. In the preface to an edition of his theses in 1538 Luther gave a detailed picture of the situation in 1517. It is as if he wanted to warn the Protestant world against dramatizing the start of the Reformation with false heroics. First he stresses how weak, reticent, and unsure he was; then he tells of his efforts to contact church authorities. This is something he knows his readers cannot appreciate, since they have grown used to impudent attacks on the broken authority of the pope. . . .

If Luther did turn first to the competent bishops with his protest, or better, with his earnest plea for reform, and if he did give them time to react as their pastoral responsibilities called for, then it is the bishops who clearly were more responsible for the consequences. If Luther did allow the bishops time to answer his request then he was sincere in begging the archbishop to remove the scandal before disgrace came upon him and upon the church. .

Further, there was clearly a real opportunity that Luther's challenge could be directed to the reform of the church, instead of leading to a break with the church. But such reform would have demanded of the bishops far greater religious substance and a far more lively priestly spirit than they showed. The deficiencies that come to light here, precisely when the bishops were called on to act as theologians and pastors, cannot be rated too highly when we seek to determine the causes of the Reformation. These deficiencies had far more serious consequences than did the failures in personal morality that we usually connect with the "bad popes" and concubinous priests on the eve of the Reformation. Archbishop Albrecht showed on other occasions as well how indifferent he was to theological questions, and how fully incapable he was of comprehending their often wide-ranging religious significance. For example, he expressed his displeasure over the momentous Leipzig debate of 1519 where famous professors were, as he saw it, crossing swords over minor points of no interest for true Christian men. This same Albrecht sent sizable gifts of money to Luther on the occasion of his marriage in 1525 and to Melanchthon after the latter had sent him a copy of his commentary on Romans in 1532.

A whole series of objections might arise here: Do not the indulgence theses themselves mark the break with the church? Do they not attack the very foundations of the church of that day? Or, as Heinrich Bornkamm wrote, do they not decisively pull the ground from under the Catholic conception of penance? Was a reform of the church of that day at all possible by renewal from within? Is not the Luther of the ninety-five theses already a revolutionary on his way inevitably to the Reformation as a division of the church?

Our first question must be whether Luther's indulgence theses deny any binding doctrines of the church in his day. And even if this be true, we cannot immediately brand the Luther of late 1517 a heretic. This would be justified only if he became aware of holding something opposed to the teaching of the church and then remained adamant in the face of correction. It is especially important to recall this in view of Luther's repeated assertions that the theses do not express his own position, but that much in them is doubtful, that some points he would reject, and no single one out of all of them would he stubbornly maintain. . . .

Still, a truly historical judgment on the theses will not consider their precise wording only. We must further ask in what direction they are tending and what development is already immanent in them. Luther's theses can only be understood in the context of late medieval nominalism. This theology had already made a broad separation of divine and human activity in the church. For God, actions in the church were only occasions for his saving action, with no true involvement of the latter in the former. Regarding penance and the remission of punishment, Luther simply carries the nominalist separation of the ecclesiastical and the divine to the extreme in that he denies that ecclesiastical penances and their remission even have an interpretive relation to the penance required by or remitted by God. I see here one root of Luther's impending denial of the hierarchical priesthood established by God in the church.

The theological consequences of the ninety-five theses were not immediately effective. The secret of their wide circulation and their electrifying effect was that they voiced a popular polemic. Here Luther touched on questions, complaints, and resentments that had long been smouldering and had often been expressed already. Luther made himself the spokesman for those whose hopes for reform had often been disappointed in a period of widespread dissatisfaction.

Theses 81–90 list the pointed questions the laity ask about indulgences. If the pope can, as he claims, free souls from purgatory, why then does he not do this out of Christian charity, instead of demanding money as a condition? Why does he not forget his building project and simply empty purgatory? (82) If indulgences are so salutary for the living, why does the pope grant them to the faithful but once a day and not a hundred times? (88) If the pope is more intent on helping souls toward salvation than in obtaining money, why is it that he makes new grants and suspends earlier confessional letters and indulgences which are just as effective? (89) If indulgences are so certain, and if it is wrong to pray for people already saved, why are anniversary masses for the dead still celebrated? Why is the money set aside for these masses not returned? (83) Why does the pope not build St. Peter's out of his own huge wealth, instead of with the money of the poor? (86) These are serious and conscientious questions posed by laymen. If they are merely beaten down by authority, instead of being met with good reasons, then the church and the pope will be open to the ridicule of their enemies. This will only increase the misery of the Christian people. (90)

Here Luther's theses brought thoughts out into the open that all had more or less consciously found troublesome. . . .

The rapid dissemination of his theses was for Luther proof that he had written what many were thinking but, as in John 7:13, they would not speak out openly "out of fear of the Jews" (WBr 1, 152, 17).

Luther regretted the spread of the theses, since they were not meant for the public, but only for a few learned men. Furthermore, the theses contained a number of doubtful points. Therefore he rushed the "Sermon on Indulgences and Grace" into print in March 1518 (W 1, 239–46) as a popular presentation of his basic point on indulgences, and he wrote the *Resolutiones* (W 1, 526–628 and LW 31, 83–252) as an extensive theological explanation of the theses. . . .

[The] prefatory statements accompanying the explanations of the theses have been singled out for a remarkable combination of loyal submissiveness, prophetic sense of mission, and an almost arrogant conviction of their cause. Meissinger saw here the maneuverings of a chess expert. This does not strike me as an adequate analysis. I see rather the genuine possibility of keeping Luther within the church. But for this to have happened the bishops who were involved, and the pope himself, would have to have matched Luther in religious substance and in pastoral earnestness. It was not just a cheap evasion when Luther repeated again and again in 1517 and 1518 that he felt bound only by teachings of the church and not by theological opinions, even if these came from St. Thomas or St. Bonaventure. The binding declaration Luther sought from the church came in Leo X's doctrinal constitution on indulgences, *"Cum postquam"* (DS 1447ff.), on November 9, 1518. . . .

The papal constitution declares that the pope by reason of the power of the keys can through indulgences remit punishments for sin by applying the merits of Christ and the saints. The living receive this remission as an absolution and the departed by way of intercession. The constitution was quite reticent and sparing in laying down binding doctrine. This contrasts notably with the manner of the indulgence preachers and Luther's attackers. . . .

Silvester Prierias, the papal court theologian, exceeded his fellow Dominican Tetzel in frivolity. For him, a preacher maintaining the doctrines attacked by Luther is much like a cook adding seasoning to make a dish more appealing. Here we see the same lack of religious earnestness and pastoral awareness that marked the bishops' reaction to the theses.

This lack of theological competence and of apostolic concern was all the more freighted with consequences, in the face of Martin Luther's zeal for the glory of God and the salvation of souls in 1517–18. There was a real chance to channel his zeal toward renewal of the church from within.

In this context it does seem important whether Luther actually posted his theses for the benefit of the crowds streaming into the Church of All Saints in Wittenberg. It is important whether he made such a scene or whether he simply presented his ninety-five theses to the bishops and to some learned friends. From the former he sought the suppression of practical abuses, and from the latter the clarification of open theological questions.

I, for one, feel compelled to judge Luther's posting of the ninety-five theses a legend. With this legend removed it is much clearer to what a great extent the theological and pastoral failures of the bishops set the scene for Luther to begin the divisive Reformation we know, instead of bringing reform from within the church.

Suggestions for Further Reading

Luther was himself a voluminous and powerful writer, and students should sample his writings beyond the brief excerpt from the *Tabletalk* presented in this chapter. The standard English edition of his works is in many volumes and sets of volumes, each edited by several scholars, elaborately cross-indexed and with analytical contents so that individual works are easy to find. Of particular interest should be the set *Martin Luther, Career of the Reformer,* vols. 31–34 (Philadelphia: Muhlenberg Press, 1957–1960). Some of the same works will be found in another edition, Martin Luther, *Reformation Writings*, tr. Bertram L. Woolf, 2 vols. (New York: Philosophical Library, 1953–1956).

The career of the young Luther, which is emphasized in this chapter, has been of particular interest to Luther scholars. Heinrich Boehmer, *Road to Reformation: Martin Luther to the Year 1521*, tr. John W. Doberstein and Theodore S. Tappert (Philadelphia: Muhlenberg Press, 1946), is the standard work by a great German authority. The same ground is covered by Robert H. Fife, *The Revolt of Martin Luther* (New York: Columbia University Press, 1957). DeLamar Jensen, *Confrontation at Worms: Martin Luther and the Diet of Worms. With a Complete English Translation of the Edict of Worms* (Provo, Utah: Brigham Young University Press, 1973), gives a detailed look at the terminal event in young Luther's career. Erik H. Erikson, *Young Man Luther: A Study in Psychoanalysis and History* (New York: Norton, 1958), is a famous and controversial book that students find provocative.

Of the many works on Luther's theology and thought, two especially are recommended. Heinrich Bornkamm, *Luther's World of Thought*, tr. Martin H. Bertram (St. Louis: Concordia, 1958), is one of the most influential works of modern Luther literature. It is fundamentally a theological rather than a historical work and is difficult but also important. Of particular interest to the background of the young Luther is Bengt R. Hoffman, *Luther and the Mystics: A Re-examination of Luther's Spiritual Experiences and His Relationship to the Mystics* (Minneapolis: Augsburg Press, 1976).

Of the many general biographical works, James Atkinson, *Luther and the Birth of Protestantism* (Baltimore: Penguin, 1968), places emphasis on his theological development. Probably the best and most readable of all the Luther biographies is Roland H. Bainton, *Here I Stand: A Life of Martin Luther* (Nashville: Abingdon Press, 1950). Three books are recommended for the broader topic of Luther and his age. Two are very large and comprehensive: Ernest G. Schwiebert, *Luther and His Times: The Reformation from a New Perspective* (St. Louis: Concordia, 1950), and Richard Friedenthal, *Luther: His Life and Times*, tr. John Nowell (New York: Harcourt, Brace, 1970). The third, A. G. Dickens, *The German Nation and Martin Luther* (New York: Harper & Row, 1974), is really an attractive, authoritative extended essay. Eric W. Gritach, *Martin—God's Court Jester: Luther in Retrospect* (Philadelphia: Fortress Press, 1983), while not a connected biography, is a study of aspects of Luther's life, personality, work, and influence by a great European authority. It is scrupulously based on Luther's own writings but reviews in a knowledgeable way the best modern scholarship. An attractive, up-to-date biography is Walther von Loewenich, *Martin Luther, The Man and His Work*, tr. Lawrence W. Denef (Minneapolis: Augsburg Publishing House, 1986).

For the still larger topic of Luther in relation to the Reformation, see
A. G. Dickens, *Reformation and Society in Sixteenth-Century Europe* (New
York: Harcourt, Brace, 1966); Lewis W. Spitz, *The Renaissance and Refor-
mation Movements,* vol. 2 (Chicago: Rand McNally, 1971); and Harold J.
Grimm, *The Reformation Era,* 2nd ed. (New York: Macmillan, 1973).
The new social history intrudes into Lutheran-Reformation studies
with Steven Ozment, *When Fathers Ruled: Family Life in Reformation
Europe* (Cambridge: Harvard University Press, 1983). A short book by
R. W. Scribner, *The German Reformation* (Atlantic Highlands, N.J.: Hu-
manities Press International, 1986), surveys the recent trends of Lutheran and Reformation scholarship and has an excellent annotated
bibliography.

ELIZABETH I,
THE ARMADA, AND
"THE BLACK LEGEND"

1533 Born
1558 Succeeded to the throne
1587 Execution of Mary Stuart
1588 Defeat of Spanish Armada
1603 Died

"She had a sharp tongue, a vile temper, almost no feminine delicacy, and little or no feminine modesty. Of personal loyalty and affection she seems to have commanded little or none."[1] The woman thus so unflatteringly described was Elizabeth I, Queen of England; the describer, Conyers Read, the most eminent American scholar of Tudor England. And yet Read goes on to point out, as he did in a dozen other works, that Elizabeth was "Good Queen Bess" to the great bulk of her subjects and that she has held an unrivaled place in the affections of the English since the end of the sixteenth century. Most other modern Elizabethan scholars would agree. They would also agree that despite their own learned assessments of the importance of one aspect or another of Elizabeth's reign—her management of the economy, her relations with Parliament, her domestic religious settlement—the most enduring of all Elizabethan traditions is that of Elizabeth and her England pitted against the Spain of Philip II, culminating in the dramatic English victory over the Spanish Armada in the late summer of the year 1588.

This hardy tradition has its origin in the Armada fight itself and in the events surrounding it. English hostility to Spain was growing for a number of reasons: sympathy for the beleaguered French Huguenots and the Protestants of Holland locked in their own desperate struggle

[1]Conyers Read, "Good Queen Bess," *American Historical Review* 31 (1926), 649.

with Philip; the undeclared sea war with Spain that English privateers and pirates had already been carrying on for a generation; as well as the gnawing fear of a domestic fifth column of Spanish spies and English Catholics ready to betray their country for the sake of their religion. Holinshed's famous *Chronicle*, for example, quotes a speech given by one "Maister Iames Dalton" in the year 1586 having to do with the designs of certain captive traitors and Spanish sympathizers, one of whom "vomited these prophane words out of his vncircumcised mouth; that it was lawfull for anie of worship in England, to authorise the vilest wretch that is, to séeke the death of hir highnese whose prosperous estate the italish préest and Spanish prince doo so maligne." Dalton goes on to decry "an inuasion long since pretended" and the popish threats "that would burn hir bones, and the bones of all such as loued hir, either alive or dead [and] that this was to de doone, when they held the sterne of gouernment; which shall be, when errant traitors are good subjects, and ranke knaues honest men."[2]

In the years immediately following the Armada, such sentiments were even more strongly voiced. Sir Walter Raleigh in his spirited account of "The Last Fight of the Revenge," written in 1591, spoke of "how irreligiously [the Spanish] cover their greedy and ambitious pretences with that veil of piety," and how they "more greedily thirst after English blood than after the lives of any other people of Europe, for the many overthrows and dishonours they have received at our hands, whose weakness we have discovered to the world, and whose forces at home, abroad, in Europe, in India, by sea and land, we have even with handfuls of men and ships over thrown and dishonoured."[3]

Thus by the end of the sixteenth century, the major elements of what modern Hispanic scholars have come to call "The Black Legend" were substantially formed: Spain was England's implacable enemy, cruel in victory, craven in defeat; Spaniards were treacherous and cowardly, made more so by their "popery"; and, though outmanned and out-gunned, English ships could either defeat Spanish ships or, if not, at least show how "beardless boys" could go to heroic death. The center of the legend was the Armada, which "more than any other event, implanted anti-Hispanism in the English consciousness."[4] And Queen Elizabeth became the exemplar of the virtues of her nation and the symbol of its hostility to Spain.

[2]*Holinshed's Chronicle* (London, 1808; rpt. New York: AMS Press, 1965), IV, 920.

[3]Sir Walter Raleigh, *Selected Prose and Poetry*, ed. Agnes M. C. Latham (London: University of London-Athlone Press, 1965), pp. 85, 87.

[4]William S. Maltby, *The Black Legend in England* (Durham, N.C.: Duke University Press, 1971), p. 84.

The Legendary Elizabeth

SIR FRANCIS BACON

Elizabeth's "Gloriana" image was a bit tarnished during the last years of her reign by grievances that had finally begun to surface, by the residue of unfulfilled hopes and unredeemed promises, and by a general restlessness after almost half a century of her rule. But the succession of her Stuart cousin James I shortly restored Elizabeth's luster. The Elizabethan Age and Elizabeth herself assumed heroic stature when compared with James I, "who feared his own shadow and manifested such unkingly habits as drivelling at the mouth, picking his nose, and closeting himself with pretty young men."[5] Yet it was not his personal habits, no matter how offensive, not even his penchant for playing at "kingcraft" or the muddle he made of the religious settlement that most alienated James's English subjects; it was his resolution to abandon the tradition of hostility to Spain, indeed to court a Spanish-Catholic alliance.

Sir Francis Bacon (1561–1626) was a functionary of James's court and one of the leading men of affairs in the new reign. But he had also been a figure of Elizabeth's court and a member of Parliament during the Armada. Though he had not advanced under Elizabeth as grandly as he thought his merits deserved, still, looking back to her reign, even the cold and analytical Bacon could not help being moved. In the summer of 1608, the year following his appointment by James as Solicitor General, Bacon wrote in Latin a memorial to Elizabeth that he titled "On the Fortunate Memory of Elizabeth Queen of England." He circulated the piece privately to a few friends but provided that it be published only after his death. Bacon was not only a stupendous genius but also a good judge of his own advantage.

"On the Fortunate Memory of Elizabeth Queen of England" is of considerable interest because it is the mature reflection of one who had been close to the center of events. The memorial is equally important because it shows a renewed interest in "the heroic Elizabeth" in the light of her unheroic successor and the new foreign and religious policies he was already considering. Bacon was writing a memorial not only to Elizabeth but to an age of giants now sadly past.

[5]Lacey Baldwin Smith, *The Elizabethan World* (Boston: Houghton Mifflin, 1967), pp. 204–5.

I account . . . as no small part of Elizabeth's felicity the period and compass of her administration; not only for its length, but as falling within that portion of her life which was fittest for the control of affairs and the handling of the reins of government. She was twenty-five years old (the age at which guardianship ceases) when she began to reign, and she continued reigning until her seventieth year; so that she never experienced either the disadvantages and subjection to other men's wills incident to a ward, nor the inconveniences of a lingering and impotent old age. . . .

Nor must it be forgotten withal among what kind of people she reigned; for had she been called to rule over Palmyrenes or in an unwarlike and effeminate country like Asia, the wonder would have been less; a womanish people might well enough be governed by a woman; but that in England, a nation particularly fierce and warlike, all things could be swayed and controlled at the beck of a woman, is a matter for the highest admiration.

Observe too that this same humour of her people, ever eager for war and impatient of peace, did not prevent her from cultivating and maintaining peace during the whole time of her reign. And this her desire of peace, together with the success of it, I count among her greatest praises; as a thing happy for her times, becoming to her sex, and salutary for her conscience. . . .

And this peace I regard as more especially flourishing from two circumstances that attended it, and which though they have nothing to do with the merit of peace, add much to the glory of it. The one, that the calamities of her neighbours were as fires to make it more conspicuous and illustrious; the other that the benefits of peace were not unaccompanied with honour of war,—the reputation of England for arms and military prowess being by many noble deeds, not only maintained by her, but increased. For the aids sent to the Low Countries, to France, and to Scotland; the naval expeditions to both the Indies, some of which sailed all round the globe; the fleets despatched to Portugal and to harass the coasts of Spain; the many defeats and overthrows of the rebels in Ireland;—all these had the effect of keeping both the warlike virtues of our nation in full vigour and its fame and honour in full lustre.

Which glory had likewise, this merit attached,—that while neighbour kings on the one side owed the preservation of their kingdoms to her timely succours; suppliant peoples on the other, given up by ill-advised princes to the cruelty of their ministers, to the fury of the populace, and to every kind of spoliation and devastation, received relief in their misery; by means of which they stand to this day.

Nor were her counsels less beneficent and salutary than her succours; witness her remonstrances so frequently addressed to the

King of Spain that he would moderate his anger against his subjects in the Low Countries, and admit them to return to their allegiance under conditions not intolerable; and her continual warnings and earnest solicitations addressed to the kings of France that they would observe their edicts of pacification. That her counsel was in both cases unsuccessful, I do not deny. The common fate of Europe did not suffer it to succeed in the first; for so the ambition of Spain, being released as it were from prison, would have been free to spend itself (as things then were) upon the ruin of the kingdoms and commonwealths of Christendom. The blood of so many innocent persons, slaughtered with their wives and children at their hearths and in their beds by the vilest rabble, like so many brute beasts animated, armed, and set on by public authority, forbade it in the other; that innocent blood demanding in just revenge that the kingdom which had been guilty of so atrocious a crime should expiate it by mutual slaughters and massacres. But however that might be, she was not the less true to her own part, in performing the office of an ally both wise and benevolent.

Upon another account also this peace so cultivated and maintained by Elizabeth is a matter of admiration; namely, that it proceeded not from any inclination of the times to peace, but from her own prudence and good management. For in a kingdom laboring with intestine faction on account of religion, and standing as a shield and stronghold of defence against the then formidable and overbearing ambition of Spain, matter for war was nowise wanting; it was she who by her forces and her counsels combined kept it under; as was proved by an event the most memorable in respect of felicity of all the actions of our time. For when the Spanish fleet, got up with such travail and ferment, waited upon with the terror and expectation of all Europe, inspired with such confidence of victory, came ploughing into our channels, it never took so much as a cockboat at sea, never fired so much as a cottage on the land, never even touched the shore; but was first beaten in a battle and then dispersed and wasted in a miserable flight with many shipwrecks; while on the ground and territories of England peace remained undisturbed and unshaken.

Nor was she less fortunate in escaping the treacherous attempts of conspirators than in defeating and repelling the forces of the enemy. For not a few conspiracies aimed at her life were in the happiest manner both detected and defeated; and yet was not her life made thereby more alarmed or anxious; there was no increase in the number of her guards; no keeping within her palace and seldom going abroad; but still secure and confident, and thinking more of the escape than of the danger, she held her wonted course, and made no change in her way of life.

Worthy of remark too is the nature of the times in which she flourished. For there are some times so barbarous and ignorant that it is as easy a matter to govern men as to drive a flock of sheep. But the lot of this Queen fell upon times highly instructed and cultivated, in which it is not possible to be eminent and excellent without the greatest gifts of mind and a singular composition of virtue. . . .

With regard to her moderation in religion there may seem to be a difficulty, on account of the severity of the laws made against popish subjects. But on this point I have some things to advance which I myself carefully observed and know to be true.

Her intention undoubtedly was, on the one hand not to force consciences, but on the other not to let the state, under pretence of conscience and religion, be brought in danger. Upon this ground she concluded at the first that, in a people courageous and warlike and prompt to pass from strife of minds to strife of hands, the free allowance and toleration by public authority of two religions would be certain destruction. Some of the more turbulent and factious bishops also she did, in the newness of her reign when all things were subject to suspicion—but not without legal warrant—restrain and keep in free custody. The rest, both clergy and laity, far from troubling them with any severe inquisition, she sheltered by a gracious connivency. This was the condition of affairs at first. Nor even when provoked by the excommunication pronounced against her by Pius Quintus (an act sufficient not only to have roused indignation but to have furnished ground and matter for a new course of proceeding), did she depart almost at all from this clemency, but persevered in the course which was agreeable to her own nature. For being both wise and of a high spirit, she was little moved with the sound of such terrors; knowing she could depend upon the loyalty and love of her own people, and upon the small power the popish party within the realm had to do harm, as long as they were not seconded by a foreign enemy. About the twenty-third year of her reign, however, the case was changed. And this distinction of time is not artificially devised to make things fit, but expressed and engraved in public acts.

For up to that year there was no penalty of a grievous kind imposed by previous laws upon popish subjects. But just then the ambitious and vast design of Spain for the subjugation of the kingdom came gradually to light. . . .

. . . It is true, and proved by the confession of many witnesses, that from the year I have mentioned to the thirtieth of Elizabeth (when the design of Spain and the Pope was put in execution by that memorable armada of land and sea forces) almost all the priests who were sent over to this country were charged among the other offices belonging to their function, to insinuate that matters could not long stay as they were, that a new aspect and turn of things would be seen shortly, and that the state of England was cared for both by the Pope and the Catholic princes, if the English would but be true to themselves. . . .

. . . This so great a tempest of dangers made it a kind of necessity for Elizabeth to put some severer constraint upon that party of her subjects which was estranged from her and by these means poisoned beyond recovery, and was at the same time growing rich by reason of their immunity from public offices and burdens. And as the mischief increased, the origin of it being traced to the seminary priests, who were bred in foreign parts, and supported by the purses and charities of foreign princes, professed enemies of this kingdom, and whose time had been passed in places where the very name of Elizabeth was never heard except as that of a heretic excommunicated and accursed, and who (if not themselves stained with treason) were the acknowledged intimates of those that were directly engaged in such crimes, and had by their own arts and poisons depraved and soured with a new leaven of malignity the whole lump of Catholics, which had before been more sweet and harmless; there was no remedy for it but that men of this class should be prohibited upon pain of death from coming into the kingdom at all; which at last, in the twenty-seventh year of her reign, was done. Nor did the event itself which followed not long after, when so great a tempest assailed and fell with all its fury upon the kingdom, tend in any degree to mitigate the envy and hatred of these men; but rather increased it, as if they had utterly cast off all feeling for their country, which they were ready to betray to a foreign servitude. . . .

The "New" Elizabeth

JAMES ANTHONY FROUDE

James Anthony Froude (1818–1894), for all the criticism he received—his Oxford rival E. A. Freeman called him "the vilest brute that ever wrote a book"[6]—was surely one of the most influential historians "that ever wrote a book." The book on which both his reputation and his influence most firmly rest is his massive, twelve-volume History of England from the Fall of Wolsey to the Defeat of the Spanish Armada. *Froude began work on*

[6]Quoted in F. Smith Fussner, *Tudor History and Historians* (New York: Basic Books, 1970), p. 55.

it about 1850, and it was published in two-volume installments roughly every other year between 1856 and 1870 to a rising chorus of popular acclaim. Ignoring the factual inaccuracies that bothered Froude's fellow scholars, the public was delighted by his preference for advocacy rather than objectivity. The people tended to agree with Froude that history proclaimed, or should proclaim, "the laws of right and wrong." Moreover, they agreed that right resided in the Church of England and wrong, more often than not, in the Church of Rome. If proof was needed for their prejudices—or his—it was abundantly available in the profusion of facts that crowded Froude's History *and gave it an unequalled sense of authenticity. For Froude was one of the first modern British historians to go extensively to the original sources for his research; he was aided by the fact that only in his lifetime was the great mass of English public documents of the Tudor age at last being systematically edited and published.*

Froude considered the Tudor age to be the pivot of all English history. The topical limits he set to his own great History *display his thesis. The fall of Wolsey and Henry VIII's break with Rome marked the start of the English Reformation; the defeat of the Spanish Armada marked the triumph of English Protestantism and the beginning of England's supremacy in the modern world. Like his life-long friend Carlyle, Froude was more impressed with people than with large economic or social forces. Heroic people accomplish heroic deeds. Henry VIII was Froude's hero, standing stalwart and unblinking at the beginning of his narrative. At the other end stood the most heroic deed in English history, the defeat of the Armada. Yet careful research revealed that Elizabeth, Henry's daughter, was—at least by Froude's standards—considerably less than heroic. Where Henry had been defiant, Elizabeth preferred to negotiate. Where Henry had carried the fight to the enemy, Elizabeth was suspicious of fighting and more than reluctant to throw her resources into the great national effort against Spain. Even when the fight was inevitable, she was stingy of her support and vacillating in her resolve. Worst of all, Froude found her, at the most charitable, to be a guarded and circumstantial Protestant, perhaps even a crypto-Catholic. If Henry VIII was Froude's hero, Elizabeth was his burden. In order to reconcile his low opinion of Elizabeth with the importance he attached to the Armada, Froude made the triumph over the Armada a victory "in spite of" Elizabeth, the product of the patient policy of her great Protestant advisers and the selfless heroism of her seamen.*

It may be charged that Froude, more than most historians, took his conclusions to his sources and then found them there. But this failing is surely not unique with him. Even his severest critics today admit that Froude's History *is "one of the great masterpieces of English historical literature,"*[7]

[7]Conyers Read, *Bibliography of British History: Tudor Period, 1485–1603,* 2nd ed. (Oxford: Clarendon Press, 1959), p. 30.

that it is "a classic"[8] *for its period, and that "more than any other nineteenth-century English historian James Anthony Froude set the nineteenth-century version of Tudor history."*[9] *An indispensable part of that version was Froude's equivocal image of the "new" Elizabeth.*

We turn now to the summation of Froude's account of Elizabeth and the Armada, from the conclusion of his History.

It had been my intention to continue this history to the close of Elizabeth's life. The years which followed the defeat of the Armada were rich in events of profound national importance. They were years of splendour and triumph. The flag of England became supreme on the seas; English commerce penetrated to the farthest corners of the Old World, and English colonies rooted themselves on the shores of the New. The national intellect, strung by the excitement of sixty years, took shape in a literature which is an eternal possession of mankind, while the incipient struggles of the two parties in the Anglican Church prepared the way for the conflicts of the coming century, and the second act of Reformation. But I have presumed too far already on the forbearance of my readers in the length to which I have run, and these subjects, intensely interesting as they are, lie beyond the purpose of the present work. My object, as I defined it at the outset, was to describe the transition from the Catholic England with which the century opened, the England of a dominant Church and monasteries and pilgrimages, into the England of progressive intelligence; and the question whether the nation was to pass a second time through the farce of a reconciliation with Rome, was answered once and for ever by the cannon of Sir Francis Drake. The action before Gravelines of the 30th of July, 1588, decided the largest problems ever submitted in the history of mankind to the arbitrement of force. Beyond and beside the immediate fate of England, it decided that Philip's revolted Provinces should never be reannexed to the Spanish Crown. It broke the back of Spain, sealed the fate of the Duke of Guise,[10] and though it could not prevent the civil war, it assured the ultimate succession of the King of Navarre.[11] In its remoter consequences it determined the fate of the Reformation in Germany; for had Philip been victorious the League must have been immediately triumphant; the power of France would have been on

[8]*Ibid.*

[9]Fussner, p. 55.

[10]The leader of the radical Catholic League in the French Wars of Religion.—ED.

[11]The sometime leader of the French Protestant Huguenots who became King Henry IV in 1594.—ED.

the side of Spain and the Jesuits, and the thirty years' war would either have never been begun, or would have been brought to a swift conclusion. It furnished James of Scotland with conclusive reasons for remaining a Protestant, and for eschewing for ever the forbidden fruit of Popery; and thus it secured his tranquil accession to the throne of England when Elizabeth passed away. Finally, it was the sermon which completed the conversion of the English nation, and transformed the Catholics into Anglicans. . . .

. . . The coming of the Armada was an appeal on behalf of the Pope to the ordeal of battle and the defeat of Spain with its appalling features, the letting loose of the power of the tempests—the special weapons of the Almighty—to finish the work which Drake had but half completed, was accepted as a recorded judgment of heaven. The magnitude of the catastrophe took possession of the nation's imagination. . . . Had the Spanish invasion succeeded, however, had it succeeded even partially in crushing Holland and giving France to the League and the Duke of Guise, England might not have recovered from the blow, and it might have fared with Teutonic Europe as it fared with France on the revocation of the Edict of Nantes. Either Protestantism would have been trampled out altogether, or expelled from Europe to find a home in a new continent; and the Church, insolent with another century or two of power, would have been left to encounter the inevitable ultimate revolution which is now its terror, with no reformed Christianity surviving to hold the balance between atheism and superstition.

The starved and ragged English seamen, so ill furnished by their sovereign that they were obliged to take from their enemies the means of fighting them, decided otherwise; they and the winds and the waves, which are said ever to be on the side of the brave. In their victory they conquered not the Spaniards only, but the weakness of their Queen. Either she had been incredulous before that Philip would indeed invade her, or she had underrated the power of her people: or she discerned that the destruction of the Spanish fleet had created at last an irreparable breach with the Catholic governments. At any rate there was no more unwholesome hankering after compromise, no more unqueenly avarice or reluctance to spend her treasure in the cause of freedom. The strength and resources of England were flung heartily into the war, and all the men and all the money it could spare was given freely to the United Provinces and the King of Navarre. The struggle lasted into the coming century. Elizabeth never saw peace with Spain again. But the nation throve with its gathering glory. The war on the part of England was aggressive thenceforward. One more great attempt was made by Philip in Ireland, but only to fail miserably, and the shores of England were never seriously threatened again. Portugal was invaded, and Cadiz burnt, Spanish commerce made the prey of privateers, and the proud galleons chased from off the ocean. In the Low Countries the tide of reconquest had reached its flood, and thenceforward ebbed slowly back, while in France the English and the Huguenots fought side by side against the League and Philip. . . .

[Yet] for Protestantism Elizabeth had never concealed her dislike and contempt. She hated to acknowledge any fellowship in religion either with Scots, Dutch, or Huguenots. She represented herself to foreign Ambassadors as a Catholic in everything, except in allegiance to the Papacy. Even for the Church of England, of which she was the supreme governor, she affected no particular respect. She left the Catholics in her household so unrestrained that they absented themselves at pleasure from the Royal Chapel, without a question being asked. She allowed the country gentlemen all possible latitude in their own houses. The danger in which she had lived for so many years, the severe measures to which she was driven against the seminary priests, and the consciousness that the Protestants were the only subjects she had on whose loyalty she could rely, had prevented her hitherto from systematically repressing the Puritan irregularities; but the power to persecute had been wanting rather than the inclination. The Bishops with whom she had filled the sees at her accession were chosen necessarily from the party who had suffered under her sister. They were Calvinists or Lutherans, with no special reverence for the office which they had undertaken; and she treated them in return with studied contempt. She called them Doctors, as the highest title to which she considered them to have any real right; if they disputed her pleasure she threatened to unfrock them; if they showed themselves officious in punishing Catholics, she brought them up with a sharp reprimand; and if their Protestantism was conspicuously earnest, they were deposed and imprisoned. . . .

To permit the collapse of the Bishops, however, would be to abandon the Anglican position. Presbytery as such was detestable to Elizabeth. She recognised no authority in any man as derived from a source distinct from herself, and she adhered resolutely to her own purpose. So long as her own crown was unsafe she did not venture on any general persecution of her Puritan subjects; but she checked all their efforts to make a change in the ecclesiastical system. She found a man after her own heart for the see of Canterbury in Whitgift; she filled the other sees as they fell vacant with men of a similar stamp, and she prepared to coerce their refractory "brethren in Christ" into obedience if ever the opportunity came.

On the reconciliation of the Catholic gentry, which followed on the destruction of the Spanish fleet, Elizabeth found herself in a position analogous to that of Henry IV of France. She was the sovereign of a nation with a divided creed, the two parties, notwithstanding, being at last for the most part loyal to herself.

Both she and Henry held at the bottom intrinsically the same views. They believed generally in certain elementary truths lying at the base of all religions, and the difference in the outward expressions of those truths, and the passionate animosities which those differences engendered, were only not contemptible to them from the practical mischief which they produced. On what terms Catholics and Protestants could be induced to live together peaceably was the political problem of the age. Neither of the two sovereigns shared the profound horror of falsehood, which was at the heart of the Protestant movement. They had the statesman's temperament, to which all specific religions are equally fictions of the imagination. . . .

To return to Elizabeth.

In fighting out her long quarrel with Spain and building her Church system out of the broken masonry of Popery, her concluding years passed away. The great men who had upheld the throne in the days of her peril dropped one by one into the grave. Walsingham died soon after the defeat of the Armada, ruined in fortune, and weary of his ungrateful service. Hunsdon, Knollys, Burghley, Drake, followed at brief intervals, and their mistress was left by herself, standing as it seemed on the pinnacle of earthly glory, yet in all the loneliness of greatness, and unable to enjoy the honours which Burghley's policy had won for her. The first place among the Protestant powers, which had been so often offered her and so often refused, had been forced upon her in spite of herself. "She was Head of the Name," but it gave her no pleasure. She was the last of her race. No Tudor would sit again on the English throne. . . . She was without the intellectual emotions which give human character its consistency and power. One moral quality she possessed in an eminent degree: she was supremely brave. For thirty years she was perpetually a mark for assassination, and her spirits were never affected, and she was never frightened into cruelty. She had a proper contempt also for idle luxury and indulgence. She lived simply, worked hard, and ruled her household with rigid economy. But her vanity was as insatiable as it was commonplace. No flattery was too tawdry to find a welcome with her, and as she had no repugnance to false words in others, she was equally liberal of them herself. Her entire nature was saturated with artifice. Except when speaking some round untruth Elizabeth never could be simple. Her letters and her speeches were as fantastic as her dress, and her meaning as involved as her policy. She was unnatural even in her prayers, and she carried her affectations into the presence of the Almighty. . . .

Vain as she was of her own sagacity, she never modified a course recommended to her by Burghley without injury both to the realm and to herself. She never chose an opposite course without plunging into embarrassments, from which his skill and Walsingham's were barely able to extricate her. The great results of her reign were the fruits of a policy which was not her own, and which she starved and mutilated when energy and completeness were needed. . . .

But this, like all other questions connected with the Virgin Queen, should be rather studied in her actions than in the opinion of the historian who relates them. Actions and words are carved upon eternity. Opinions are but forms of cloud created by the prevailing currents of the moral air. Princes, who are credited on the wrong side with the evils which happen in their reigns, have a right in equity to the honour of the good. The greatest achievement in English history, the "breaking the bonds of Rome," and the establishment of spiritual independence, was completed without bloodshed under Elizabeth's auspices, and Elizabeth may have the glory of the work. Many problems growing out of it were left unsettled. Some were disposed of on the scaffold at Whitehall, some in the revolution of 1688; some yet survive to test the courage and the ingenuity of modern politicians.

Elizabeth and the "Invincible" Armada

GARRETT MATTINGLY

Twentieth-century Elizabethan scholarship has largely forsaken the "standard" view of Elizabeth that, more than anyone else, Froude helped to frame. Froude's Elizabeth is both too simple and too doctrinaire: Elizabeth was neither. There have been literally hundreds of special studies and monographs on various aspects of Elizabeth's reign and even a number of biographies. But despite this profusion of writing, there is not yet a comprehensive general interpretation of her for our time or an entirely satisfactory biography.

The same cannot be said, however, of the Armada, for that great and popular adventure found its definitive twentieth-century interpretation in the work of Garrett Mattingly, professor of history at Columbia University until his death in 1962. In addition to the sources that Froude had used to such advantage, Mattingly had access to even more and better British sources, for the process of editing and publishing the public documents of the Tudor age had continued and new archives and collections had been opened. French and Netherlandish archives were available to him, as well as collections in Italy and Spain. Thus Mattingly had the advantage of a rounded collection of materials that earlier scholars, whether English or Spanish, had not had. And he had the disposition to write a balanced account, free of the special pleading and the special point of view that were ultimately Froude's greatest flaws.

The following excerpt is taken not from Mattingly's slim and elegant masterpiece, The Armada,[12] *but from a carefully abbreviated account that he prepared for the Folger Shakespeare Library monograph series, entitled* The "Invincible" Armada and Elizabethan England. *It was his last work.*

Not surprisingly, the work deals primarily with the Armada rather than with Elizabeth. But many elements of a contemporary view of Elizabeth—even though that view has not entirely coalesced—can be discovered. Mattingly admires Elizabeth's grasp of foreign policy, which reached beyond a simplistic hostility to Spain. He admires her courage to resist the opinions of her naval advisers that the war should be carried to Spanish waters, opinions that she seemed to be almost alone in opposing. The queen's courage was the greater when we realize, as Mattingly points out, that she was already past "the peak of her popularity and prestige." Finally, Mattingly admires the tenacity that enabled Elizabeth to maintain the peace, no matter how tenuously, for thirty years and that led her into war only when it could be fought on her terms. The victory over the Armada was indeed Elizabeth's victory, and, in the words of Froude, she may have the glory of it.

Probably no event in England's military history, not even the battles of Trafalgar and Waterloo, not even the battle of Hastings, has been so much written about, celebrated, and commented upon as the repulse of the Spanish Armada by English naval forces after nine days of dubious battle from the Eddystone to Gravelines in the summer of 1588. The repulse foiled decisively, as it turned out, the Spanish plan to invade England with the Duke of Parma's army of the Netherlands, covered and supported by a Spanish fleet, and reinforced by the troop transports and supply ships it convoyed. At first the significance of the repulse was by no means clear. As it became clearer, the chroniclers of both combatants tended to magnify, oversimplify, and distort the event. English writers, pamphleteers, and historians hailed the victory, first as a sign of God's favor to the champions of the Protestant cause, later as evidence of the manifest destiny of an imperial people. . . .

. . . By now, through the efforts of two generations of historians,

---

[12](Boston: Houghton Mifflin, 1959).

Spanish and English, most of the mistakes about the Armada campaign and the Anglo-Spanish naval war have been corrected and a more balanced emphasis restored. So far, however, no general account of the correction has been drawn up. Let us attempt one here.

We shall have to begin with the long period of uneasy peace, cold war, and "war underhand," undeclared and peripheral, before the actual outbreak of major hostilities. In general, historians both English and Spanish have tended to assume that since war was coming anyway the sooner it came the better, and that any policy that postponed its coming was feeble, shortsighted, and mistaken. Most English historians have been certain that Elizabeth should have unleashed her seadogs against the Spanish colossus long before she did and have blamed or excused her for feminine weakness, gullibility at the hands of smooth Spanish diplomats, and miserly reluctance to spend money. The chorus of blame begins in the correspondence of the leading Puritans of her own day. They were always bewailing to one another the Queen's vacillation, her stubborn refusal to subsidize Protestant leaders on the Continent as liberally as they would have liked to be subsidized, her obstinate belief that peace with the armies of Antichrist could still be preserved. The chorus of blame swelled through the centuries until it culminated in the thundering voice of James Anthony Froude, who could as little conceal his boundless, uncritical admiration for the male vigor of Henry VIII, who led England into one vainglorious, financially ruinous war after another, as he could his scorn for the feminine weakness of Henry's daughter Elizabeth, who preferred to save money and stay out of trouble. Since Froude, the chorus of blame has subsided somewhat, but its echoes are still distinctly audible. . . .

. . . Elizabeth . . . and her peace party had reasons more cogent (if any reasons can be more cogent) than prudence and economy. No ruler of this century was more sensitive to the economic interests of his subjects. She knew the importance of an outlet in the Netherlands—Antwerp for choice—for the vent of English cloth, on which, after agriculture, the prosperity of her realm depended. If there was a tradition of more than a hundred years of alliance with Spain, the tradition of alliance with Flanders, with "waterish Burgundy," was as old as any coherent English foreign policy at all. In Flanders, Zeeland, and Holland were the ports not only through which English goods could most cheaply and safely reach the Continent, but from which an invasion of England could be launched most quickly and easily. And on the frontier of Flanders lay France, divided for the moment by religious civil wars, but in area, population, productivity, and centralized power easily the greatest state in Europe. Somebody had to guard the Netherlands from France—if not Spain, then England.

Elizabeth preferred to have the Spanish bear the burden. . . .

There was still one tie between Elizabeth and Philip stronger than profitable trade, old alliances, or strategic necessities. That was the life of Mary Queen of Scots. For nearly twenty years Mary Stuart had been part guest, part prisoner of her cousin. Since she was a devout Catholic and the next in succession to the English throne, she had always been the center of plots by English Catholics. . . . But with each plot the outcry for Mary's life grew stronger, and at last Elizabeth could no longer resist the clamor. When in February, 1587, the ax fell, the die was cast. As soon as Philip heard the news and had taken his characteristic time to ponder the consequences, he began to put the creaky machinery of his painfully devised plans for the invasion of England into high gear.

His plans were further delayed by Drake's brilliant raid down the Spanish coast. On the whole that raid has been duly appreciated and well described, but perhaps for the sake of dramatic narrative the emphasis on its importance has been somewhat distorted. . . .

The real damage Drake did the Spaniards was afterward, by his operations off Cape St. Vincent. His mere presence there, though he found no one to fight with, kept the Spanish fleet from assembling. But more, he swept up along the coast a swarm of little coasting vessels, most of them laden with hoops and barrel staves ready to be made into casks for the food and drink of the invasion fleet. Without tight casks made of seasoned wood, provisions spoiled and wine and water leaked away. Drake burned the seasoned barrel staves. They were almost all the fleet at Lisbon was expecting, far more than it could ever collect again. This was the secret, mortal wound. Drake knew exactly what he was doing, but most of his biographers seem not to have appreciated it. . . .

After a description of the Spanish preparations for the Armada, Mattingly continues.

If Spanish historians have been too severe with their admiral and not critical enough of his sovereign, English historians have usually made the opposite mistake. From October, 1587, on, the English commanders by sea, Drake and Hawkins and finally even Lord Howard of Effingham, the Lord Admiral, had clamored to be let loose on the coast of Spain. If the smell of booty to be won by the sack of undefended Spanish towns had anything to do with their eagerness, they did not say so to the Queen. What they proposed was that they blockade the Spanish coast, fight the Spanish when they came out, perhaps prevent their sortie, or even destroy them in port. On the whole,

English naval historians have warmly approved their plan and condemned the Queen for squelching it. Perhaps they were thinking of Nelson's ships, or Collingwood's. Elizabethan ships had not the same sea-keeping qualities. If they had taken station off Lisbon in November, by April they would have been battered and strained, sails and spars and rigging depleted, crews decimated or worse by ship's fever and scurvy, and provisions exhausted. Even if none of them had foundered, and such foundering was not unlikely, the English fleet would have been in no condition to face an enemy for weeks, perhaps for months. And the cost in pounds, shillings, and pence would have been staggering. Elizabeth, who had kept a wary eye on naval accounts for forty years, knew this. What she probably did not know was that had the fleets met off the Spanish coast and the English adopted the same tactics they later used off the Eddystone, as they surely would have done, they would have fired every shot in their lockers before they had done the Spanish any appreciable harm, and would have been obliged to scuttle home in search of more munitions, while the Spanish could have marched grandly into the Channel. Partly by prudence and partly by luck, Elizabeth's preference that the battle, if there had to be one, should be fought in home waters was a major contribution to English victory. . . .

. . . About the strength and composition of the two fleets there is actually very little doubt. The Armada sailed from Lisbon with 130 ships. . . . Opposing this force, English lists show 197 ships. Actually, not all of these saw action; some of them, though not so many nor such large ships as in the Spanish fleet, were mere supply ships, practically noncombatants, and a good many, a slightly higher percentage than in the Armada, were under a hundred tons, incapable of carrying guns heavier than a six-pounder and useful mainly for scouting and dispatch work. The first line of the English fleet was twenty-one Queen's galleons of two hundred tons and upward, roughly comparable in size and numbers with the ten galleons of Portugal and ten galleons of the Indian Guard which made up the Spanish first line, but tougher, harder hitting, and, on the whole, bigger.

The myth of the little English ships and the huge Spanish ones has long since been refuted by naval historians, without, of course, being in the least dispelled. Taking the official tonnage lists of the two first lines, the biggest ship in either fleet is English, and the rest pair off in what seems like rough equality. . . . We do know that in comparison with their English adversaries the Spanish were seriously undergunned. . . . In such guns, especially the culverin type, firing round shot of from four to eighteen pounds for three thousand yards or more, the English were superior by at least three to one. . . .

There follows a detailed description of the battle, the stiff Spanish disci-
pline, the long-range gun battles that did little but deplete shot and pow-
der supplies, and the crucial failure of Parma to "come out" with his
barge-loads of soldiers to board the waiting fleet. They were blockaded by
the Dutch in the tidal waters, safe from the deep-water Spanish fleet.
Then came the English attack on the Armada mounted with fire ships
and fire power and finally the famous storm in the channel that permit-
ted the Armada to "escape" to the north and to its ultimate destruction,
sailing around the British Isles in a desperate and futile attempt to re-
turn home.

When, on the thirtieth anniversary of her reign, the Queen went in state to St. Paul's, where the captured Spanish banners had been hung up, the kneeling, cheering throngs hailed her as the victorious champion of her kingdom and their faith. The next few years were probably those of Elizabeth's greatest popularity, at least around London, and this was almost certainly due to her having come forward at last as the open champion of the Protestant cause, to her gallant conduct in the months of danger, and to the victory, by divine intervention almost everyone believed, which crowned her efforts. It is probable, too, that the victory gave a lift to English morale. It may be that a good many Englishmen, like a good many other Europeans, though not like Elizabeth's sea dogs, had doubted that the Spanish could ever be beaten. Now they knew that they could. The thoughtful and the well-informed understood, however, that England had not won a war, only the first battle in a war in which there might be many more battles. England was braced for the struggle.

Suggestions for Further Reading

To a considerable extent, the central problem of Elizabethan scholarship has been to disentangle the historical Elizabeth from the Elizabeth of legend. This chapter is really about an aspect of that process, for the defeat of the Spanish Armada was a powerful force in creating the Elizabeth legend. The historical Elizabeth still tends to elude scholars, but of all the books on her, the best modern work is still probably Sir John E. Neale, *Queen Elizabeth I* (London: J. Cape, 1961), reprinted a dozen times since it publication in 1934. Of the newer books on Elizabeth, the best by far is Lacey Baldwin Smith, *Elizabeth Tudor: Portrait of a Queen* (Boston: Little, Brown, 1975). But students may prefer Elizabeth Jenkins, *Elizabeth the Great* (New York: Coward, McCann and Geoghegan, 1958), a lively, personal-psychological biography, or the attractive, heavily illustrated Neville Williams, *The Life and Times of Elizabeth I* (New York: Doubleday, 1972). Two additional competent and straightforward biographies are also recommended: Joel Hurstfield, *Elizabeth I and the Unity of England,* "Teach Yourself History Library" (New York: Macmillan, 1960), and Paul Johnson, *Elizabeth I: A Biography* (New York: Holt, Rinehart and Winston, 1974). Jasper Ridley, *Elizabeth I: The Shrewdness of Virtue* (New York: Viking, 1988) is a readable, if somewhat superficial, biography, not too flattering to the queen. Students may find interesting Carolly Erickson, *The First Elizabeth* (New York: Summit Books, 1983), a general biography that has a tinge of contemporary feminism. Especially recommended is Alison Plowden, *Elizabeth Regina: The Age of Triumph, 1588–1603* (New York: Times Books, 1980), the culminating work in a series of books on Elizabeth, this one dealing precisely with the period of her life emphasized in this chapter.

Among the great monuments in modern Tudor scholarship are the studies of two of the men around Elizabeth by Conyers Read, *Mr. Secretary Walsingham and the Policy of Queen Elizabeth,* 3 vols. (Hamden, Conn.: Archon Books, 1967 [1925]), and *Mr. Secretary Cecil and Queen Elizabeth* (New York: Knopf, 1955) and its sequel *Lord Burghley and Queen Elizabeth* (New York: Knopf, 1960); these books are detailed and complex. Students may prefer the lighter and briefer Neville Williams, *All the Queen's Men: Elizabeth I and Her Courtiers* (New York: Macmillan, 1972). Two works on Elizabeth and her age are especially recommended: A. L. Rowse, *The England of Elizabeth: The Structure of Society* (New York: Macmillan, 1950), the first of two volumes on the Elizabethan age, the massive and lively work of a controversial and dynamic British scholar, and Lacey Baldwin Smith, *The Elizabethan World* (Boston: Houghton Mifflin, 1967). On the broader topic of Tudor England, the basic work is G. R. Elton, *England under the Tudors,* rev. ed. (London: Methuen, 1974); but students should see also A. J. Slavin, *The Precarious Balance: English Government and Society, 1450–1640* (New York: Knopf, 1973), an important revisionist study of the internal structure of Tudor England.

The standard work on the Armada is Garrett Mattingly, *The Armada* (Boston: Houghton Mifflin, 1959), eminently readable and exciting. Felipe Fernandez-Armesto, *The Spanish Armada: The Experience of the War in 1588* (Oxford and New York: Oxford University Press, 1988) is an up-to-date work that supplements Mattingly. For more detailed diplomatic history background, the best work is probably R. B. Wernham, *Before the Armada: The Emergence of the English Nation, 1485–1588* (New York: Harcourt, Brace and World, 1966), and for a closer look at the technical-naval aspects of the Armada, Michael A. Lewis, *The Spanish Armada* (New York: Crowell, 1960). An excellent revisionist account of the Armada is David A. Howarth, *The Voyage of the Armada,*

The Spanish Story (New York: Viking, 1981). For an account of the growth of the English anti-Spanish sentiment, see William S. Maltby, *The Black Legend in England: The Development of Anti-Spanish Sentiment, 1558–1660* (Durham, N.C.: Duke University Press, 1971). For Mary Queen of Scots, the diplomatic linchpin in the whole background of the Armada, see the large and thoroughly readable biography by Antonia Fraser, *Mary, Queen of Scots* (New York: Delacorte Press, 1969), and Alison Plowden, *Danger to Elizabeth: The Catholics Under Elizabeth I* (New York: Stein and Day, 1973), a work on a related topic.

THE CRIME
OF GALILEO

1564   Born
1592   Became professor of mathematics,
       University of Padua
1610   Invented Galilean telescope
1632   Published *A Dialogue Concerning the
       Two Chief World Systems*
1633   Condemned by Inquisition
1642   Died

In the opening years of the seventeenth century, Galileo Galilei was one of the most famous people in the world. Since 1592 he had been professor of mathematics at the great University of Padua, and in 1610 he became "first philosopher and mathematician" to the grand duke of Tuscany, Cosimo dei Medici, who had been his tutorial student. He was the familiar of princes, wealthy patricians, high officials of the church, and other scientists and mathematicians all over Europe. He was the principal advocate in Italy for the new natural philosophy, the usual name for the scientific interests that were beginning to become a passion with scientists and laymen alike.

In 1609 Galileo had heard about the development of a primitive perspective instrument by some Dutch spectacle makers that made distant objects appear larger and nearer. He built such an instrument himself and promptly improved its magnification so dramatically that it could be used for practical astronomical observation. He had invented the Galilean telescope. He observed the surface of the moon, the phases of Venus, the moons of Jupiter, the first hint of Saturn's rings, the phenomenon of sunspots, and that the Milky Way was actually a collection of enormously distant stars. In the following year, he published these observations in a little pamphlet volume entitled *Sidereus nuncius* [The Starry Messenger]. It was an instant sensation.

Even more exciting to Galileo than his astronomical discoveries was the support they clearly gave to the Copernican theory of the universe—that the sun and not the earth was its center and that the planets, including the earth, rotated around the sun, "the lamp that illumines the whole universe." Galileo had long believed in the validity of the rational and mathematical arguments that Copernicus had put forward in 1543 in his *De revolutionibus orbium coelestium.* Galileo had corresponded with his great German contemporary, the astronomer Johannes Kepler, also a dedicated Copernican, and had been free in letters to friends and colleagues in his espousal of the Copernican theory. He eagerly entered into a number of controversies with conservative academics who refused to accept the truth or consequences of his astronomical observations. In a dispute over the nature of sunspots in 1612, Galileo, in defending his own views on these phenomena, publicly and in print unequivocally endorsed the Copernican theory.

But by this time the Copernican theory was running into serious trouble, and so was Galileo. The Copernican theory was not simply a theory that one was free or not to accept—at least not in Catholic countries. For the church had long since accepted the older Ptolemaic model of the earth-centered universe, and it had become an integral part of the official Catholic theology. Thus the whole issue of Copernicanism became not merely an astronomical and mathematical proposition; it was a religious issue, and a dangerous one. The new Catholic attitude of the early seventeenth century was that of the Counter Reformation church, the revived and militant church prepared more than ever to defend its ancient truths. There was little disposition to accommodate radical new views that stood in opposition to established doctrine, and even less disposition to tolerate those who held such radical views. Moreover, from 1613 to 1615, in a series of published letters—actually treatises—Galileo had tried to defend the new sciences generally and the Copernican theory specifically in arguments that were as much theological as they were scientific. He was a loyal son of the church, and he wanted passionately to prevent its making a tragic error in this entire matter of the new theory of the universe.

But it became increasingly clear that the church was moving the other way. Galileo went himself to Rome early in 1615 to defend Copernicanism. He was courteously enough received by great churchmen, some of whom listened to him patiently and a few of whom supported his views. But then, on February 25, 1616, after a careful examination by a committee of theologians, the doctrine of Copernicus was formally condemned by the Congregation of the Index, summoned by Pope Paul V himself. It would have been condemned out of hand as heretical except for Galileo's friend, Cardinal Maffeo Barberini, who intervened to have it declared simply "erroneous in the faith." But what about Galileo? He was not only a vocal and celebrated advocate of the now condemned theory, but he had already been denounced to the Inquisition by a number of his enemies. At the pope's own order he was summoned, on the day following the decree, to appear before Cardinal Bellarmine, the chief theologian of the church, and told that he must neither "hold nor defend" the theory of Copernicus.

Galileo returned to Florence heartbroken. He kept silent on the issue for the next seven years and devoted himself to noncontroversial work. Then in 1623 Maffeo Barberini, his longtime friend and supporter, was elected Pope Urban VIII. Galileo hastened to Rome, confident that he could secure the revocation of the decree of 1616 and gain permission to write the great book he had long planned, "*On the System or Constitution of the World,* an immense design, full of philosophy, astronomy, and geometry."[1] He was wrong on both counts. The pope refused to reverse the condemnation of the Copernican theory. Moreover, failing totally to understand what Galileo really wanted, he would permit him to write about the constitution of the world only if he would write about both the Copernican system and the Ptolemaic and if he did not presume to choose between them.

Galileo agreed, and in 1632 he published his *Dialogue Concerning the Two Chief World Systems—Ptolemaic and Copernican.*

---

[1] From a letter to Belisario Vinta quoted in Galileo Galilei, *Dialogue on the Great World Systems,* ed. Giorgio de Santillana (Chicago: University of Chicago Press, 1953), Historical Introduction, p. xi.

The Two Chief World Systems

GALILEO GALILEI

The idea of a great, far-ranging work on the nature of the universe as seen in Copernican terms had long obsessed Galileo. He had mentioned it in 1597 in a letter to Kepler. In 1610, in the Starry Messenger, *he had referred to it as a forthcoming book. And references to it continued to crop up in his writings. But that was all changed by the pope's injunction of 1624. He would have to write a quite different book. He struggled with it, delayed by illness and family responsibilities. It was finally completed in January 1630, and he began the task of getting it licensed by the church to be printed. Rome delayed for almost two years and finally, under pressure from the Florentine ambassador, granted the imprimatur, with some trifling revisions to the title page. Florentine church authorities had already given their approval. The book, published in Florence on February 21, 1632, took the form of a dialogue with three participants. Filippo Salviati, a Florentine nobleman, friend, and supporter of Galileo, was represented as the advocate for Copernicanism. An imaginary character, Simplicio, was the defender of the Ptolemaic-Aristotelian traditional arguments. And the Venetian patrician Giovanni Sagredo, uncommitted to either view, was the audience to whom the other two addressed themselves. It was set in Sagredo's palace in Venice and ran through four days of conversation.*

The book was an immediate success despite its large size, its abstruse subject, and its formidable mathematics. Within five months every copy was sold. In large part it was successful because it was controversial. In clear and unmistakable violation of the ban of the church, Galileo defended the Copernican theory—and boldly said as much in his preface. In the dialogue itself, the arguments of Simplicio for the Ptolemaic view are systematically and enthusiastically demolished. At the very end of the dialogue, there is a weak and perfunctory admission by both disputants that no one can "limit and restrict the Divine power or wisdom to some particular fancy of his own" or really "discover the work of His hands." It was no more than the merest lip service to the demand that the pope had made of Galileo.

Here is Galileo's preface.

Several years ago there was published in Rome a salutary edict which, in order to obviate the dangerous tendencies of our present age, imposed a seasonable silence upon the Pythagorean opinion that the earth moves.[2] There were those who impudently asserted that this decree had its origin not in judicious inquiry, but in passion none too well informed. Complaints were to be heard that advisers who were totally unskilled at astronomical observations ought not to clip the wings of reflective intellects by means of rash prohibitions.

Upon hearing such carping insolence, my zeal could not be contained. Being thoroughly informed about that prudent determination, I decided to appear openly in the theater of the world as a witness of the sober truth. I was at that time in Rome; I was not only received by the most eminent prelates of that Court, but had their applause; indeed, this decree was not published without some previous notice of it having been given to me. Therefore I propose in the present work to show to foreign nations that as much is understood of this matter in Italy, and particularly in Rome, as transalpine diligence can ever have imagined. Collecting all the reflections that properly concern the Copernican system, I shall make it known that everything was brought before the attention of the Roman censorship, and that there proceed from this clime not only dogmas for the welfare of the soul, but ingenious discoveries for the delight of the mind as well.

To this end I have taken the Copernican side in the discourse, proceeding as with a pure mathematical hypothesis and striving by every artifice to represent it as superior to supposing the earth motionless—not, indeed, absolutely, but as against the arguments of some professed Peripatetics.[3] These men indeed deserve not even that name, for they do not walk about; they are content to adore the shadows, philosophizing not with due circumspection but merely from having memorized a few ill-understood principles. . . .

In the course of the third day, we find the most outspoken defense of Copernicus. Salviati is speaking:

. . . I have often seen Jupiter and Venus together, twenty-five or thirty degrees from the sun, the sky being very dark. Venus would appear eight or even ten times as large as Jupiter when looked at with the naked eye. But seen afterward through a telescope, Jupiter's disc would be seen to be actually four or more times as large as Venus. Yet the liveliness of Venus's brillance was incomparably greater than the pale light of Jupiter, which comes about only because Jupiter is very

[2]It was believed by Galileo, as earlier by Copernicus, that the ancient Greek heliocentric theory—probably actually first enunciated by Aristarchus—was one of the teachings of Pythagoras.—ED.

[3]The usual name for Aristotelians which is to say, in this context, defenders of the Ptolemaic theory. The term literally means "those who walk about."—ED.

distant from the sun and from us, while Venus is close to us and to the sun.

These things having been explained, it will not be difficult to understand how it might be that Mars, when in opposition to the sun and therefore seven or more times as close to the earth as when it is near conjunction, looks to us scarcely four or five times as large in the former state as in the latter. Nothing but irradiation is the cause of this. For if we deprive it of the adventitious rays we shall find it enlarged in exactly the proper ratio. And to remove its head of hair from it, the telescope is the unique and supreme means. Enlarging its disc nine hundred or a thousand times, it causes this to be seen bare and bounded like that of the moon, and in the two positions varying in exactly the proper proportion.

Next in Venus, which at its evening conjunction when it is beneath the sun ought to look almost forty times as large as in its morning conjunction, and is seen as not even doubled, it happens in addition to the effects of irradiation that it is sickle-shaped, and its horns, besides being very thin, receive the sun's light obliquely and therefore very weakly. So that because it is small and feeble, it makes its irradiations less ample and lively than when it shows itself to us with its entire hemisphere lighted. But the telescope plainly shows us its horns to be as bounded and distinct as those of the moon, and they are seen to belong to a very large circle, in a ratio almost forty times as great as the same disc when it is beyond the sun, toward the end of its morning appearances.

SAGR. O Nicholas Copernicus, what a pleasure it would have been for you to see this part of your system confirmed by so clear an experiment!

SALV. Yes, but how much less would his sublime intellect be celebrated among the learned! For as I said before, we may see that with reason as his guide he resolutely continued to affirm what sensible experience seemed to contradict. I cannot get over my amazement that he was constantly willing to persist in saying that Venus might go around the sun and be more than six times as far from us at one time as at another, and still look always equal, when it should have appeared forty times larger.

SAGR. I believe then that in Jupiter, Saturn, and Mercury one ought also to see differences of size corresponding exactly to their varying distances.

SALV. In the two outer planets I have observed this with precision in almost every one of the past twenty-two years. In Mercury no observations of importance can be made, since it does not allow itself to be seen except at its maximum angles with the sun, in which the inequalities of its distances from the earth are imperceptible. Hence such differences are unobservable, and so are its changes of shape, which must certainly take place as in Venus. But when we do see it, it would necessarily show itself to us in the shape of a semicircle, just as Venus does at its maximum angles, though its disc is so small and its brilliance so lively that the power of the telescope is not sufficient to strip off its hair so that it may appear completely shorn.

It remains for us to remove what would seem to be a great objection to the motion of the earth. This is that though all the planets turn about the sun, the earth alone is not solitary like the others but goes together in the company of the moon and the whole elemental sphere around the sun in one year, while at the same time the moon moves around the earth every month. Here one must once more exclaim over and exalt the admirable perspicacity of Copernicus, and simultaneously regret his misfortune at not being alive in our day. For now Jupiter removes this apparent anomaly of the earth and moon moving conjointly. We see Jupiter, like another earth, going around the sun in twelve years accompanied not by one but by four moons, together with everything that may be contained within the orbits of its four satellites.

SAGR. And what is the reason for your calling the four Jovian planets "moons"?

SALV. That is what they would appear to be to anyone who saw them from Jupiter. For they are dark in themselves, and receive their light from the sun; this is obvious from their being eclipsed when they enter into the cone of Jupiter's shadow. And since only that hemisphere of theirs is illuminated which faces the sun, they always look entirely illuminated to us who are outside their orbits and closer to the sun; but to anyone on Jupiter they would look completely lighted only when they were at the highest points of their circles. In the lowest part—that is, when between Jupiter and the sun—they would appear horned from Jupiter. In a word, they would make for Jovians the same changes of shape which the moon makes for us Terrestrials.

Now you see how admirably these three notes harmonize with the Copernican system, when at first they seemed so discordant with it. From this, Simplicio will be much better able to see with what great probability one may conclude that not the earth, but the sun, is the center of rotation of the planets. And since this amounts to placing the earth among the world bodies which indubitably move about the sun (above Mercury and Venus but beneath Saturn, Jupiter, and Mars), why will it not likewise be probable, or perhaps even necessary, to admit that it also goes around? . . .[4]

---

[4]The Copernican theory not only described the earth's planetary movement but its rotation. The Ptolemaic, of course, held that neither kind of motion existed.—ED.

SIMP. But what anomalies are there in the Ptolemaic arrangement which are not matched by greater ones in the Copernican?

SALV. The illnesses are in Ptolemy, and the cures for them in Copernicus. First of all, do not all philosophical schools hold it to be a great impropriety for a body having a natural circular movement to move irregularly with respect to its own center and regularly around another point?[5] Yet Ptolemy's structure is composed of such uneven movements, while in the Copernican system each movement is equable around its own center. With Ptolemy it is necessary to assign to the celestial bodies contrary movements, and make everything move from east to west and at the same time from west to east, whereas with Copernicus all celestial revolutions are in one direction, from west to east. And what are we to say of the apparent movement of a planet, so uneven that it not only goes fast at one time and slow at another, but sometimes stops entirely and even goes backward a long way after doing so? To save these appearances, Ptolemy introduces vast epicycles, adapting them one by one to each planet, with certain rules about incongruous motions—all of which can be done away with by one very simple motion of the earth. Do you not think it extremely absurd, Simplicio, that in Ptolemy's construction where all planets are assigned their own orbits, one above another, it should be necessary to say that Mars, placed above the sun's sphere, often falls so far that it breaks through the sun's orb, descends below this and gets closer to the earth than the body of the sun is, and then a little later soars immeasurably above it? Yet these and other anomalies are cured by a single and simple annual movement of the earth. . . .

At the end of the discourse of the fourth day, there occurs the weak disclaimer of both systems. Salviati is speaking again:

To you, Sagredo, though during my arguments you have shown yourself satisfied with some of my ideas and have approved them highly, I say that I take this to have arisen partly from their novelty rather than from their certainty, and even more from your courteous wish to afford me by your assent that pleasure which one naturally feels at the approbation and praise of what is one's own. And as you have obligated me to you by your urbanity, so Simplicio has pleased me by his ingenuity. Indeed, I have become very fond of him for his constancy in sustaining so forcibly and so undauntedly the doctrines of his master. And I thank you, Sagredo, for your most courteous motiva-

---

[5]Galileo was apparently unaware of his friend Kepler's theory about the elliptical orbits of the planets. But even if he did know about it, he never accepted the notion himself.—ED.

tion, just as I ask pardon of Simplicio if I have offended him sometimes with my too heated and opinionated speech. Be sure that in this
I have not been moved by any ulterior purpose, but only by that of
giving you every opportunity to introduce lofty thoughts, that I might
be better informed.

SIMP. You need not make any excuses; they are superfluous, and
especially so to me, who, being accustomed to public debates, have
heard disputants countless times not merely grow angry and get ex-
cited at each other, but even break out into insulting speech and
sometimes come very close to blows.

As to the discourses we have held, and especially this last one concerning the reasons for the ebbing and flowing of the ocean, I am
really not entirely convinced,[6] but from such feeble ideas of the matter as I have formed, I admit that your thoughts seem to me more
ingenious than many others I have heard. I do not therefore consider
them true and conclusive; indeed, keeping always before my mind's
eye a most solid doctrine that I once heard from a most eminent and
learned person, and before which one must fall silent, I know that if
asked whether God in His infinite power and wisdom could have
conferred upon the watery element its observed reciprocating motion
using some other means than moving its containing vessels, both of
you would reply that He could have, and that He would have known
how to do this in many ways which are unthinkable to our minds.
From this I forthwith conclude that, this being so, it would be excessive boldness for anyone to limit and restrict the Divine power and
wisdom to some particular fancy of his own.

SALV. An admirable and angelic doctrine, and well in accord with
another one, also Divine, which, while it grants to us the right to
argue about the constitution of the universe (perhaps in order that
the working of the human mind shall not be curtailed or made lazy)
adds that we cannot discover the work of His hands. Let us, then,
exercise these activities permitted to us and ordained by God, that we
may recognize and thereby so much the more admire His greatness,
however much less fit we may find ourselves to penetrate the profound depths of His infinite wisdom.

---

[6]Much of the argument of the day had been devoted to Galileo's theory that the
ocean tides were related to the rotation of the earth—a mistaken notion.—ED.

The Crime of Galileo

GIORGIO DE SANTILLANA

The pope was furious. He had every reason to believe he had been betrayed by Galileo's Dialogue. *Galileo's enemies were clamoring for his condemnation. The process of an inquiry by the Inquisition was begun, and in less than a year Galileo was summoned to Rome to stand trial. In June 1633 he was judged to have held and taught the Copernican theory, against the teachings of the church. This was the crime of Galileo. He was ordered to recant and did so. The normal sentence of life imprisonment was commuted to house arrest by the pope, and Galileo was permitted to return to his estate near Florence where he lived and worked for the remaining eight years of his life.*

His "crime" remains the center of the Galileo biography. Why did he do it? It was not an unwitting or accidental transgression. It was a clear and willful act of defiance. Was he courting martyrdom? Nothing in his behavior before or during his trial suggests it. One can only conclude that the vindication of his ideas was an important enough issue for the risk involved. And what risk did he take? He had obviously violated the spirit of the pope's instructions about the Dialogue, *but his book had been licensed by the pope's own censors in Rome and Galileo could claim that he had legally abided by the pope's instructions—no matter how badly.*

But there was another set of instructions, going back to the original condemnation of Copernicanism in 1616 and Galileo's interview with Cardinal Bellarmine. What had he been told or not told by the cardinal? It is clear that when the judgment of the Inquisition was finally made, Galileo was surprised and outraged at the severity of the sentence. Why? Because he had reason to believe he had stayed within the letter of the church's law on the matter. Two documents had turned up in the course of the trial, both having to do with the crucial interview with Bellarmine. One was in the Inquisition's file and was an official minute by its commissary general stating that he had been present at the interview and had personally warned Galileo not to hold or teach the theory of Copernicus "in any way whatsoever." Galileo claimed to know nothing about such a warning. And he, in turn, produced a certified copy of Cardinal Bellarmine's considerably milder charge to him. If the one document was a surprise to Galileo, the other was a surprise to the court. Bellarmine's certificate had not become a part of the record. Given this ambiguity, Galileo had reason to expect leniency, indeed, may have been promised leniency if he would simply recant. But the case had become as much a trial for the church as for Galileo, and he had to be made an example. Hence the severity of his sentence.

By most accounts, the crux of Galileo's trial and the charges against him was that now remote interview with Cardinal Bellarmine seventeen years before, and the conflicting documents. Many scholars have speculated about this matter. We excerpt opinions by two of the leading modern Galileo scholars. The first is that of Giorgio de Santillana from his book The Crime of Galileo.

What can be the conclusion concerning that famous injunction of 1616? It is, and will remain to the end, the kingpin of the case. With it, from the legal aspect, the trial stands or falls. It came to our notice how everything connected with it was being surrounded all along with a screen of vague, reticent, or misleading language so as to protect it from indiscreet curiosity.

Some curiosity is therefore in order. We are going to review the evidence, starting from the two critical documents. . . . One of them is the injunction; the other is Bellarmine's certificate.

"Friday, the twenty-sixth [of February]. At the palace, the usual residence of the Lord Cardinal Bellarmino, the said Galileo, having been summoned and being present before the said Lord Cardinal, was, in presence of the Most Reverend Michelangelo Segizi of Lodi, O.P., Commissary-General of the Holy Office, by the said Cardinal, warned of the error of the aforesaid opinion and admonished to abandon it; and immediately thereafter, before me and before witnesses, the Lord Cardinal being still present, the said Galileo was by the said Commissary commanded and enjoined, in the name of His Holiness the Pope and the whole Congregation of the Holy Office, to relinquish altogether said opinion that the Sun is the center of the world and immovable and that the Earth moves; nor further to hold, teach, or defend it in any way whatsoever, verbally or in writing; otherwise proceedings would be taken against him in the Holy Office; which injunction the said Galileo acquiesced in and promised to obey. Done at Rome, in the place aforesaid, in the presence of R. Bandino Nores and Agostino Mongardo, members of the household of said Cardinal, witnesses."

"We, Roberto Cardinal Bellarmino, having heard that it is calumniously reported that Signor Galileo Galilei has in our hand abjured and has also been punished with salutary penance, and being requested to state the truth as to this, declare that the said Signor Galileo has not adjured, either in our hand, or the hand of any other person here in Rome, or anywhere else, so far as we know, any opinion or doctrine held by him; neither has any salutary penance been imposed on him; but that only the declaration made by the Holy Father and published by the Sacred Congregation of the Index has been notified to him, wherein it is set forth that the doctrine attributed to Copernicus, that the Earth moves around the Sun and that the Sun is stationary in the center of the world and does not move from east to west, is contrary to the Holy Scriptures and therefore cannot be defended or held. In witness whereof we have written and subscribed these presents with our hand this twenty-sixth day of May, 1616."

. . . The first document looks gravely irregular both as to form and as to its place in the file; [and] the instructions of the Congregation to Bellarmine, as well as Bellarmine's subsequent report on what he had done that day, agree with his certificate and *not* with the injunction; and . . . there was in fact no allowable ground for an injunction as things stood.

We have seen further that in his most carefully considered piece of writing, the Preface to the *Dialogue,* Galileo deliberately mentions the famous audience as a signal distinction. He is actually calling the authorities to witness against the rumors that had been spread of a secret recantation. This would have been to provoke them foolishly if he had not been quite assured that things stood, in fact, so.

The natural supposition is that the record was hastily fabricated in 1632 when the authorities were trying to get a case against Galileo. . . .

Thus the matter stood for decades; it seemed suspended pending new evidence. This came eventually, not from any document, but from new physical means of analysis. In 1927 Laemmel, with the cooperation of the Vatican authorities, submitted the doubtful page first to soft X-rays and then to the much more rigorous test of the Hanau ultraviolet lamp. The result left no doubt on one point at least: the pages had never been tampered with. . . . The text is in exactly the same hand as other neighboring and certainly genuine documents; hence, it was written at or about the same time. To this we can add a clinching argument: the contemporary pagination shows that the original, if there ever was one, never got into the file; and therefore the decision to replace it with a falsification must have been taken then and there.

Still, there is something that remains hard to explain. The operation is curiously botched. The lack of an original alone might be construed as a mishap, for an inserted double sheet may drop out, but the wrong substitute job in the wrong place is painfully lasting evidence. A regular judge would have had to throw out the injunction on that evidence alone; even the judges of 1633 did not dare rely too much on it.

Should one see here plain cynical disregard for regularity? We would doubt it very much. Regularity was a fetish with the administration, and any such detectable irregularity always entailed a risk for its author. It would almost look as though the thing had been done by someone not in full control of events and having to make shift with what he had. Even so, from a Commissary-General able to arrange things at his will, one might expect more resourceful solutions. . . .

So there might remain a point of doubt. Let us check our conclusions as they stand by assuming the opposite to be true, namely, that things happened as written and that Galileo really stands guilty of violating his instructions. We would then have to say that the protocol was accidentally lost as soon as made out; that the official doing the pagination never noticed its absence; that someone noticed it soon afterward; and that it was deemed sufficient to insert a transcription which can only have been done from memory, for, if the original had been available somewhere, it would have been put back into place. It does not sound very convincing.

Thus we are led back perforce to our version, and the question why the operation was carried out so and not otherwise turns out to be simply a statement of the Commissary's best judgment, based upon what he thought could be done and could not be done. The straight fact that emerges is that it was not held to be quite essential to have the protocol—or, rather, that, following Bellarmine's audience, it was deemed better to have no protocol at all rather than an authentic version of that audience. And so we may be led to conclude that the Commissary simply decided to do without one. Regularity has its limits. But, it would seem, falsification has too.

We know that there had been a strong tension in 1616 between the higher authorities who had decided on diplomacy and the Dominicans, bent at that time on repression. Vatican quarters several times hinted to Guicciardini that "the monks" were relentless. We may then reconstruct as follows: The Commissary, as he watched the scene (we know he was present), was disgusted with the easy way in which Galileo was let off, and he decided to omit the protocol, although his instructions were clear, and the witnesses already designated, obviously by the Cardinal himself. On going back to his office, he told his assistant to arrange a more helpful minute of the proceedings. "And," he may have added, "make it stiff, just in case. What they don't know doesn't hurt them; when trouble arises, it is we who have to take it on." Or it may be, of course, that the assistant, Father Tinti, did the job on his own initiative. But it seems very unlikely. This theory would have the merit of explaining naturally why the protocol was omitted from the pagination as well as accounting for the other facts in the case.

To look at that silent sheet now, after three centuries, gives one a strange feeling, as though it were trying to tell us something. The first part, which reproduces the papal decree, is dealt out with well-practiced smoothness. As soon as it comes to the injunction, the lines get closer, and the writing becomes less legible, as though the writer were unconsciously trying to duck.

The falsification as such is, then, beyond doubt—truly, by modern standards, an exceedingly modest one. Father Segizi would never have dared forge a protocol. He had done a little something, the least he could do, in order to provide a toehold for prosecution if that were needed. . . .

Going back to Galileo, we can see that the course of events agrees with our previous conclusion. For not only, as we have shown, did Galileo feel completely confident that the officials were mistaken when the matter was finally revealed to him (and that would have been rather the time for him to grovel) but those very officials demonstrated, by their manner of handling the procedure of injunction when it was really necessary (viz., in order to summon Galileo to Rome), the elaborate context of rules in which such an act is framed. Here was a man who had patently fooled them, who was now subtly evading and challenging them; and yet a whole contraption had to be worked out in order to have something that would serve for an injunction without a previous refusal to motivate it. . . .

In the light of these later events it appears all the more incongruous that in 1616, when all was still clear, the Commissary should have sprung forward brandishing his threat *incontinenti,* as soon as Bellarmine had considerately informed Galileo that his theory had been found wrong, without even giving him the time to declare his acquiescence to the new ruling.

These problems really all reflect to the credit of the institution. In fear of its own absolute and unlimited powers, it had framed for itself such a rigid set of rules that, when the need came for cutting corners, it could not do so by merely stretching the interpretation. As a result, certain officials, who held the view that when a job has to be done it has to be done, did not shrink from altering the records without the acquiescence of their superiors. . . .

To maintain that Bellarmine himself was a party to the deceit ought to be out of the question. The operation seems to begin and end in the office of the Commissary-General of the time, Father Michelangelo Segizi, among those implacable Dominicans to whom Guicciardini alludes, "fired with holy zeal" [and] convinced that mathematicians are a tool of the Devil, who thought it an excellent precaution against the Adversary to put in this pretended registration. No one need be deceived by it if he did not want to, they thought; and, meanwhile, here was a trap to snare the Evil One in case of need. As it happened, it was Pope Urban and the Congregation who were to be snared in it. . . .

It might still be asked, finally: Why did Galileo in person never pronounce himself explicitly on the subject? He was the man to know. Well, we do have a fairly explicit statement from him—as explicit as he could make it without contempt of court. . . . He told the judges that he would not recite the formula of abjuration, even at the risk of dire penalties, *if it contained anything implying that he had ever deceived his censors and specifically in the matter of extorting a license.* And in fact it does not, although the sentence was built upon this specific accusation, and hence a penitential admission was in order. But, if he does *not* admit that he did "artfully and cunningly" refrain from telling about the injunction, then Galileo is saying as clearly as he can, in the face of the authorities, that the injunction never existed. And this ought to answer the question.

A Historical Speculation

STILLMAN DRAKE

Giorgio de Santillana argues in the foregoing passage that the injunction forbidding Galileo "to hold, teach, or defend . . . in any way whatsoever, verbally or in writing" the theory of Copernicus was a forgery, done by or at the bidding of Father Michelangelo Segizi, the commissary general of the Inquisition.

In the following excerpt, Stillman Drake, the principal translator of Galileo's writings and an acknowledged authority on Galileo, maintains that the disputed document is not a forgery. Rather, he sees it as a case of bureaucratic inertia, a notation routinely made, duly filed, and forgotten for seventeen years. He makes his case in what he calls "a historical speculation," a reconstruction of what must have happened in the background of "one of the most dramatic trials in history."

Two theories have long prevailed concerning the events of February 26, 1616, when Galileo was called before Cardinal Bellarmine and admonished to abandon the Copernican theory. Either theory has strong points in its favor and equally strong objections. One theory places Galileo in a good light and the Church in a bad one; the other reverses this. Competent scholars for nearly a century—that is, since all the known documents have been opened to examination and publication—have taken one side or the other, or have scrupulously withheld judgment. No real third alternative, to the best of my knowledge, has been put forth. . . .

. . . Everything seems to hinge upon the reliability of one crucial document, the copy of a supposed minute of the proceedings, bound into the official records used by the Inquisition at Galileo's trial in 1633. Advocates of the theory, which places Galileo in a good light, led in recent years by Professor Santillana, regard this document as a fabrication, a spurious account that includes events which never took place. This entails certain difficulties, for the minute has precisely the same authority as most of the documents which must be accepted in order to reconstruct the events. But this apparent disadvantage is not fatal, since the adversaries of this view labor under similar difficulties. In accepting the minute at its face value, they in turn are constrained to give a labored explanation of the existence or meaning of two or three documents of unquestioned authenticity. . . .

The two received theories appear to be poles apart, especially when considered in terms of the fundamental question whether the minute itself is true or false. Any third alternative may seem preposterous. Yet I shall advance the thesis that another theory is tenable; furthermore, that in the light of this theory, neither of the two prevalent interpretations is far from the truth, nor are they so far apart as they have previously seemed to be. . . .

In the winter of 1615–1616, Galileo debated often and publicly at Rome on the topic of the earth's motion. In these debates he succeeded in demolishing the position of his opponents, even if he did not win many converts to his own views. It was an inevitable consequence of his position that certain statements in the Bible would have to be reinterpreted. Now, freedom to interpret the Bible was a sore point with Catholic authorities at the time; this was one of the particular issues between them and the founders of various Protestant sects. Hence Galileo's plea that the Church continue to tolerate the teachings of Copernicus was one that could not be readily granted.

Though personally unsympathetic with the intellectuals of his time, Pope Paul V was cautious about alienating this influential group. Accordingly he consulted Cardinal Bellarmine, who was not only the leading theologian at Rome but was also an able administrator. As theologian, Bellarmine remarked that so long as astronomers took the idea of the earth's motion only hypothetically, there was no overt contradiction of the Bible; as administrator, he maintained that it was always a poor idea for the Church to take an official position on any matter where decision could be postponed or avoided. The Pope replied that he was aware of all this, but that Galileo was making an infernal nuisance of himself and had forced matters to a point where some official action had to be taken. In that event, answered Bellarmine, it would be necessary to stop all theological discussions of the earth's motion and to correct or suppress any books containing theological arguments in its favor. The proper procedure would be to submit the question to a duly constituted committee of theologians and to base official action on their ruling, the nature of which was easily predictable. Galileo, he was certain, would obey such an edict as a good Catholic; and since he alone was the present source of difficulty, the problem would be solved without the actual prohibition of Copernicanism. To make sure of this, however, he would undertake to test Galileo's obedience privately before the edict was published, and if there were any doubt about his cooperation, stronger measures could be applied. In view of the strong support Galileo enjoyed politically, intellectually, and in Church circles, it would be good to avoid the appearance of any personal or vindictive action in the matter.

Satisfied with Bellarmine's advice, the Pope appointed a council which duly reported its findings against the doctrine of the motion of the earth and stability of the sun. On the twenty-fifth of February, 1616, the Pope specifically instructed Bellarmine to call Galileo before him and admonished him to abandon these views as contrary to Scripture. If he refused, then the Commissary General of the Inquisition was to command him in the presence of a notary and witnesses to desist from such teachings, lest he be imprisoned. It is perfectly clear from the wording of this order that two separate actions were contemplated, the second to ensue only if the first failed; and it is equally clear that the presence of a notary and witnesses would be entirely out of place at the first action, which was to be informal and friendly in character.

Seghizzi, the Commissary General, was present when the Pope gave these instructions. He belonged to the Dominican order, which traditionally had charge of the Inquisition. He did not particularly like or trust the Jesuits, who had usurped the role of the Dominicans as leaders in Catholic education, and he was especially distrustful of the relatively liberal views of Bellarmine. Accordingly he decided to be personally present at Bellarmine's interview with Galileo, in order to make sure that if Galileo did object, Bellarmine would not reason with him and win him over rather than subject him to official action by the Inquisition. Thus on the morning of the twenty-sixth, shortly after Bellarmine had dispatched two of his familiars (special officers of arrest attached to the household of each Cardinal Inquisitor) to fetch Galileo, Seghizzi with a notary and some Dominican fathers paid a visit to Bellarmine's residence.

The visit was unusual, and Bellarmine quickly guessed its true purpose, which was personally offensive to him. At his age, and in his high position, he did not need any lesser officials present to see that he carried out his assignment properly. Still, there was no tactful way to get rid of them, and he could scarcely order them out of his house. Before long, the arrival of the officers with Galileo was announced. Bellarmine rose and went to the door of the audience chamber to greet Galileo, hat in hand, as was his custom with every guest of whatever condition. Indignant at Seghizzi's abuse of his hospitality and determined to render it pointless, he said in low tones to Galileo as they turned to enter, "His Holiness expects your precise obedience to what I am about to tell you." Then they returned together to the Cardinal's chair, and after seating himself, Bellarmine benignly announced to Galileo the decision of the council and admonished him to obey it.

Meanwhile, Seghizzi was thinking rapidly. He was no fool, and he guessed easily enough that Bellarmine had warned Galileo to voice no objection. Thus he had not only been outwitted, but by the very act of coming uninvited he had cut off any chance, however slight, that Galileo might be recalcitrant and that Bellarmine would turn him over to the Inquisition. Time was running out. There was only one way to save the day. When the Cardinal had finished his admonition, the Commissary was ready. Without allowing Galileo time for any reply, he proceeded to deliver his own stringent precept not to hold, defend, or teach Copernicanism in any way, orally or in writing, lest Galileo suffer imprisonment. The latter, forewarned, simply replied that as a good son of the Holy Church he would obey, perhaps adding that he was relieved to know that the matter had at last been settled by superhuman authority, and thanking the Cardinal for his having given him advance notice of the edict that would soon be published.

The notary, sublimely ignorant of the Pope's instructions, was faithfully recording these events, and had written that the Commissary "immediately and without holding back" had delivered his precept on the heels of the Cardinal's admonition. Bellarmine was astonished and exasperated at this further affront to his dignity and clear disobedience of the Pope's orders by the Commissary. But he knew precisely what to do. Taking Galileo by the arm and ushering him to the door, he said that he was pleased by his submission to the Church, and that at another time he wished to speak further with him, but that he had important business to discuss with the others and could not detain him longer that day. If Seghizzi tried to interrupt, the Cardinal quelled him with a glance. When Galileo was safely out of doors, he returned and asked the Commissary to confer with him privately.

Seghizzi may have begun the conference by angrily remonstrating against Galileo's having been permitted to leave without signing the notary's account of the interview. Bellarmine replied that it would have done little good for Galileo to sign this, since he himself had not the slightest intention of putting his name to a wholly illegal proceeding in direct violation of the Pope's orders. Seghizzi would do well to destroy this minute, he said. If the Pope were ever told precisely what had happened, he would be much incensed. . . .

Bellarmine gave his report to the Pope and the Cardinals of the Inquisition on March third precisely as if his own admonition were all that had been given to Galileo. Seghizzi, who was present, said not a word. The Pope then gave instructions for publication of the edict. . . .

In 1632, when the *Dialogue* was finally published and sent to Rome, the principal persons involved in the proceedings of 1616 were all dead except Galileo. The cardinals and officers of the Inquisition in 1633 had no reason whatever to doubt the authenticity of the copied minute as a faithful account of the instructions given to Galileo in 1616. Thus the rage of Pope Urban VIII, who had been Galileo's friend, is not hard to understand. It appeared to him that Galileo had persuaded him to permit publication of an "impartial" discussion of the Ptolemaic and Copernican theories, while concealing from him a specific injunction never to teach the latter theory in any way. On the other hand, Galileo was not aware of any misdeed, for he had faithfully followed Bellarmine's instruction to remember only his admonition, treating all else as if it had never happened. Nor did Galileo suspect that the official records belied this instruction, for Bellarmine had been a Cardinal of the Inquisition and presumably had had authority to keep the record consistent with his own affidavit.

Thus was the ground laid for one of the most dramatic trials in history. At its outset, both sides were acting in good faith. When Galileo was interrogated about the events of 1616, he gave precisely the account that Bellarmine had told him to give, and he produced a copy of Bellarmine's certificate in support of this, adding that he could produce the original if required. Considering that none of the inquisitors could possibly have suspected the existence of such a document, it must indeed have created a sensation in the mind of the new Commissary, Maculano. However, he calmly entered it in the record and proceeded with his examination. Galileo frankly admitted that some Dominican fathers were present on the occasion of the interview, but said he did not remember that any of them spoke to him. . . .

Maculano now pursued the question by asking whether, if he should read to Galileo what had actually been said at the time, Galileo would recall it. Galileo stood his ground resolutely, saying that he had frankly stated his recollection, and that he did not know that such a reading would alter his memory. Maculano then read to him the additional phrase "or teach in any way," and asked him if he remembered who had said this to him. Galileo reiterated that he did not recall anything having been said to him except by Cardinal Bellarmine. But for the first time, he now realized what the records must contain, and it was already too late for him to admit that anyone else had spoken to him. . . . Nor could Galileo's judges admit that he had been accused on the basis of a defective document in their own records.

Nevertheless, these men were judges and jurors of a strict tribunal, and they could not ignore the evidential value of Galileo's document. It is true that on April seventeenth, a committee of experts had found that Galileo had at least defended Copernicanism in the *Dialogue,* so that if the inquisitors were to drop the charge that he had been enjoined not to teach it in any way, he could still be found guilty of defending it. But no one wanted to drop the original charge at the cost of impugning the official records. . . .

It is apparent . . . that the trial was resumed only after Galileo had been induced to "cop a plea"; that is, had been promised a light sentence if he would cooperate by confessing to some lesser crime than that with which he was originally charged. It was a fair deal for both sides. Galileo could not hope to get off scot-free, and the inquisitors, with any kind of confession from him, could ignore the preponderance of the weight of Galileo's evidence over theirs on the crucial charge. Galileo's confession was duly handed in on April thirtieth. He said in effect that vanity had induced him to produce arguments of his own in favor of Copernicus without providing equally strong answers, but he insisted that there had been no wrong intention on his part. His defense, presented ten days later, explained the circumstances under which he had secured the affidavit from Bellarmine and stated that ". . . the two phrases in addition to 'hold' and 'defend,' which are 'teach' and 'in any way,' which I hear are contained in the command given to me and recorded, came to me as entirely new and [previously] unheard, and I do not think I should be doubted if in the course of fourteen or sixteen years they were lost to my memory. . . ."

At the end of April, the intention had been to make Galileo's punishment very light: probably a short term of imprisonment and some conventional religious penances. . . . But by the time the Cardinals of the Inquisition met again to pass sentence, at least one among them must have doubted the wisdom of letting him off lightly. . . . The only solution was to keep Galileo under physical arrest, while making the conditions of his detention easy for him. So long as he remained in the custody of the Inquisition, he would not dare breathe a word against that institution or in favor of Copernicanism, for the penalty against "relapsed heretics" was death.

Suggestions for Further Reading

There are two standard modern editions of Galileo's *Dialogue,* the one excerpted for this chapter, Galileo Galilei, *Dialogue Concerning the Two Chief World Systems—Ptolemaic and Copernican,* tr. and ed. Stillman Drake, foreword by Albert Einstein, 2nd ed. (Berkeley and Los Angeles: University of California Press, 1967), which is an entirely new translation and edition; and Galileo Galilei, *Dialogue on the Great World Systems,* in the Salusbury translation, rev. and ed. Giorgio de Santillana (Chicago: University of Chicago Press, 1953), which is a revised and annotated edition of the translation by the Englishman Thomas Salusbury in 1661. An anthology of Galileo's earlier writings, leading up to the *Dialogue,* is *Discoveries and Opinions of Galileo,* tr. and ed. Stillman Drake (New York: Doubleday, 1957). There are also two modern editions of Galileo's last major publication, *The Two New Sciences,* a treatise on mechanics and motion also written in dialogue form, which most authorities consider his most important scientific work. One is based on the definitive Italian national edition of 1913 by Antonio Favoro, *Dialogues concerning Two New Sciences,* tr. Henry Crew and Alfonso de Salvio (Evanston: Northwestern University Press, 1950); the other is a totally new edition and translation, Galileo Galilei, *Two New Sciences,* tr. and ed. Stillman Drake (Madison: University of Wisconsin Press, 1974). And there are recent editions of two of Galileo's earliest writings, both edited by Stillman Drake: *Cause, Experiment, and Science: A Galilean Dialogue Incorporating a New English Translation of Galileo's "Bodies That Stay Atop Water and Move in It"* (Chicago: University of Chicago Press, 1981) and *Telescopes, Tides, and Tactics: A Galilean Dialogue About the "Starry Messenger" and Systems of the World* (Chicago: University of Chicago Press, 1983). Most of the documents relative to Galileo's trial are either excerpted or reproduced in Karl von Gebler, *Galileo Galilei and the Roman Curia,* tr. Mrs. George Sturge (London: C. K. Paul, 1879; rpt. 1977).

Few figures have been so much revised and reappraised as Galileo. There are three works (among many) that have collected reflective essays on him: *Homage to Galileo,* Papers presented at the Galileo Quadricentennial, University of Rochester, October 8 and 9, 1964, ed. Morton F. Kaplon (Cambridge: M.I.T. Press, 1965); *Galileo Reappraised,* ed. Carlo L. Golino (Berkeley and Los Angeles: University of California

Press, 1966); and *Galileo, Man of Science,* ed. Ernan McMullin (New York and London: Basic Books, 1967).

The best treatment of Galileo as a scientist is Stillman Drake, *Galileo at Work: His Scientific Biography* (Chicago and London: University of Chicago Press, 1978). There is also a detailed critique of his *Dialogue on the Two World Sytems,* William R. Shea, *Galileo's Intellectual Revolution* (London: Macmillan, 1972). The best biography is probably still Giorgio de Santillana, *The Crime of Galileo* (Chicago: University of Chicago Press, 1955). But the best brief biography is surely Stillman Drake, *Galileo* "Past Masters Series" (New York: Hill and Wang, 1981). The slightly more general work by Ludovico Geymonat, *Galileo Galilei: A biography and inquiry into his philosophy of science,* tr. and ed. Stillman Drake (New York, Toronto, and London: McGraw-Hill, 1965), is also recommended. Pietro Redondi, *Galileo Heretic,* tr. Raymond Rosenthal (Princeton, N.J.: Princeton University Press, 1987) is a brilliant and exciting revisionist account of Galileo's "crime." Students may be interested in a book by the brilliant and provocative popularizer Arthur Koestler, *The Sleep Walkers: A history of man's changing vision of the universe* (New York: Macmillan, 1968 [1959]), which ends with an account and assessment of the work of Galileo and Newton.

LOUIS XIV:
"THE SUN KING"

1638	Born
1643	Succeeded to throne under a regency
1661	Beginning of Louis's personal government
1667–1668	War of Devolution
1689–1697	War of the Grand Alliance
1701–1714	War of the Spanish Succession
1715	Died

In 1661, on the death of the regent Cardinal Mazarin, the personal reign of Louis XIV of France began. Though he was just twenty-three years old, Louis had already been nominally the king for almost twenty years. And he was to rule for more than another half century, through one of the longest, most brilliant, most eventful, and most controversial reigns in the history of modern Europe.

It had been the aim of Cardinal Richelieu, the great first minister of Louis's father, "to make the king supreme in France and France supreme in Europe." And to an extent Cardinal Richelieu, as well as his successor, Cardinal Mazarin, had been successful. France was the richest and most populous nation in Europe. Its army had surpassed that of Spain as Europe's most formidable military machine. And the two wily cardinals had gained for France a diplomatic ascendancy to match her military might. It remained for Louis XIV to complete their work. In the process he became the archetype of divine-right monarchical absolutism, justifying later historians' labeling of the age that he dominated as the "Age of Absolutism." Louis took the sun as his emblem, as he himself wrote, for its nobility, its uniqueness, and "the light that it imparts to the other heavenly bodies," and as "a most vivid and a most beautiful image for a great monarch."[1]

---

[1]Louis XIV, . . . *Mémoires for the Instruction of the Dauphin*, Paul Sonnino, trans. (New York: Free Press, 1970), pp. 103–4

From the beginning of his personal rule, Louis XIV intended to make the other states of Europe—"the other heavenly bodies"—swing in the orbit of his sun. In 1667 he began the so-called War of Devolution to claim the disputed provinces of the Spanish Netherlands for his Spanish wife. He fought a series of wars with Spain and the Empire, the Dutch, and the English, culminating in the great European conflict, the War of the Spanish Succession (1701–1714), to set his grandson on the throne of Spain and create a Bourbon "empire" to dominate the continent. In the course of these wars, he gained the hostility of most of Europe and was finally brought to terms in 1715 at the Peace of Utrecht. Even though Louis was reported on his deathbed to have said, "I have loved war too much," he had, nevertheless, come closer to making France supreme in Europe than had any ruler before Napoleon.

Louis XIV disliked Paris. From early in his reign, he made increasing use of the royal estate of Versailles, some ten miles out of the city, as his principal residence and the locus of the court. Versailles grew in size and magnificence to become the most visible symbol of and the most enduring monument to Louis's absolutism. An English visitor, Lord Montague, sniffily called it "something the foolishest in the world," and thought Louis himself "the vainest creature alive."[2] But Versailles was far from foolish and, though vain indeed, Louis XIV was a consummate realist. Versailles was not simply a symbol of his absolutism; it was a working part of it. The function of Versailles was to help make the king supreme in France.

Royal supremacy was, in Louis's reign as before, most clearly threatened by the power and independence of the great nobility. On the very eve of Louis's personal rule, he, his mother, Mazarin, and the court had been faced with an uprising, called the Fronde, led by the great Princes of the Blood. Though it failed, Louis never forgot the Fronde. It became his deliberate policy to keep the great nobility at Versailles, separated from their provincial estates and the roots of their political power, and to redirect their interests and their energies. It may be argued that the elaborate court behavior that developed at Versailles with its perpetual spectacles and entertainments, its endless adulteries and affairs, its incredible tedium and banality—and its perpetual attendance upon the king—was really a device to neutralize the power of the great nobility while the king governed with the aid of a succession of ministers, appointed by him, answerable to him alone, and capable of being dismissed by him without question. It has

---

[2]Quoted in John C. Rule, "Louis XIV, Roi-Bureaucrate," in *Louis XIV and the Craft of Kingship,* ed. John C. Rule (Columbus: Ohio State University Press, 1969), p. 42.

been suggested by more than one scholar that Louis XIV was the archetype not only of the absolute monarch but of the "royal bureaucrat." The court life at Versailles was surely the most glittering sideshow ever staged. But it was a show that fascinated the very people who played their parts in it; and it has fascinated—and distracted—observers ever since.

The Memoirs

LOUIS, DUC DE SAINT-SIMON

The sources for the reign of Louis XIV are an embarrassment of riches—an enormous volume of public documents and official records, reports, and inventories and such a mass of royal correspondence that it still has not been completely edited. Many of the figures of the court wrote letters as prodigiously as the king, and almost as many wrote memoirs as well. Of these the most important are the memoirs of Louis de Rouvroy, Duc de Saint-Simon.

Saint-Simon was born at Versailles in 1675 and lived there for the next thirty years. Through much of that time—and throughout the rest of his long life—he kept his memoirs with a compulsive passion. In one edition, they run to forty-three volumes, and a complete text has yet to be published. Saint-Simon's memoirs are important not only for their completeness but also for the perspective they give on the age of Louis XIV. Saint-Simon fancied himself a chronicler in the tradition of Froissart or Joinville and saw his literary labor as preparing him in the knowledge of "great affairs" "for some high office." But preferment never came. Saint-Simon was never more than a minor figure of the court, moving on the fringes of the affairs that his memoirs so carefully record.

Saint-Simon blamed the king for his neglect—as he quite properly should have, for nothing happened at Versailles without the wish of the king, and the king simply disliked Saint-Simon. Saint-Simon also accused the king of demeaning the old aristocracy to which Saint-Simon so self-consciously belonged. This complaint is the nagging, insistent theme that runs like a leitmotif through the memoirs. Saint-Simon believed that Louis deliberately preferred "the vile bourgeoisie" to the aristocracy for high office and great affairs. Although the claim is somewhat exaggerated, it is indeed true that Louis preferred the lesser nobility for his bureaucrats because they had no separate power base beyond the king's preferment.

But while Saint-Simon hated his king, he was also fascinated by him, for, like it or not, Louis was the center of the world in which Saint-Simon lived. He set the fashion in dress, language, manners, and morals. Even his afflictions inspired instant emulation: after the king underwent a painful operation, no fewer than thirty courtiers presented themselves to the court surgeon and demanded that the same operation be performed on them.

Saint-Simon hated Versailles nearly as much as he hated the king, and he described it with the same malicious familiarity—its size, its vulgarity, its inconvenience and faulty planning. But he also described the stifling, debasing, desperate style of life that it dictated for the court nobility so grandly imprisoned there.

One modern scholar has called Saint-Simon "at once unreliable and indispensable."[3] We can correct his unreliability, however, by consulting other sources, and he remains indispensable for the picture he gives us of the "other side" of royal absolutism.

We turn now to Saint-Simon at Versailles *for Saint-Simon's appraisal of Louis XIV.*

He was a prince in whom no one would deny good and even great qualities, but he had many others that were petty or downright bad, and of these it was impossible to determine which were natural and which acquired. Nothing is harder to find than a well-informed writer, none rarer than those who knew him personally, yet are sufficiently unbiased to speak of him without hatred or flattery, and to set down the bare truth for good or ill.

This is not the place to tell of his early childhood. He was king almost from birth, but was deliberately repressed by a mother who loved to govern, and still more so by a wicked and self-interested minister, who risked the State a thousand times for his own aggrandisement. . . .

. . . After Mazarin's death, he had enough intelligence to realize his deliverance, but not enough vigour to release himself. Indeed, that event was one of the finest moments of his life, for it taught him an unshakable principle namely, to banish all prime ministers and ecclesiastics from his councils. Another ideal, adopted at that time, he could never sustain because in the practice it constantly eluded him. This was to govern alone. It was the quality upon which he most prided himself and for which he received most praise and flattery. In fact, it was what he was least able to do. . . .

. . . The King's intelligence was below the average, but was very capable of improvement. He loved glory; he desired peace and good government. He was born prudent, temperate, secretive, master of his emotions and his tongue—can it be believed?—he was born good and just. God endowed him with all the makings of a good and perhaps even of a fairly great king. All the evil in him came from without. His early training was so dissolute that no one dared to go near his apartments, and he would sometimes speak bitterly of those

[3]Peter Gay, in the introductory note to Louis, Duc de Saint-Simon, *Versailles, the Court, and Louis XIV*, ed. and trans. Lucy Norton (New York: Harper & Row, 1966), p. vii.

days and tell how they found him one night fallen into the fountain at the Palais Royal. He became very dependent on others, for they had scarcely taught him to read and write and he remained so ignorant that he learned nothing of historical events nor the facts about fortunes, careers, rank, or laws. This lack caused him sometimes, even in public to make many gross blunders.

You might imagine that as king he would have loved the old nobility and would not have cared to see it brought down to the level of other classes. Nothing was further from the truth. His aversion to noble sentiments and his partiality for his Ministers, who, to elevate themselves, hated and disparaged all who were what they themselves were not, nor ever could be, caused him to feel a similar antipathy for noble birth. He feared it as much as he feared intelligence, and if he found these two qualities united in one person, that man was finished.

His ministers, generals, mistresses, and courtiers learned soon after he became their master that glory, to him, was a foible rather than an ambition. They therefore flattered him to the top of his bent, and in so doing, spoiled him. Praise, or better, adulation, pleased him so much that the most fulsome was welcome and the most servile even more delectable. . . .

Flattery fed the desire for military glory that sometimes tore him from his loves, which was how Louvois[4] so easily involved him in major wars and persuaded him that he was a better leader and strategist than any of his generals, a theory which those officers fostered in order to please him. All their praise he took with admirable complacency, and truly believed that he was what they said. Hence his liking for reviews, which he carried to such lengths that he was known abroad as the "Review King," and his preference for sieges, where he could make cheap displays of courage, be forcibly restrained, and show his ability to endure fatigue and lack of sleep. Indeed, so robust was his constitution that he never appeared to suffer from hunger, thirst, heat, cold, rain, or any other kind of weather. He greatly enjoyed the sensation of being admired, as he rode along the lines, for his fine presence and princely bearing, his horsemanship, and other attainments. It was chiefly with talk of campaigns and soldiers that he entertained his mistresses and sometimes his courtiers. He talked well and much to the point; no man of fashion could tell a tale or set a scene better than he, yet his most casual speeches were never lacking in natural and conscious majesty.

[4]Michel Le Tellier, Marquis de Louvois (1641–1691), Louis's great minister of war.—ED.

He had a natural bent towards details and delighted in busying himself with such petty matters as the uniforms, equipment, drill, and discipline of his troops. He concerned himself no less with his buildings, the conduct of his household, and his living expenses, for he always imagined that he had something to teach the experts, and they received instruction from him as though they were novices in arts which they already knew by heart. To the King, such waste of time appeared to deserve his constant attention, which enchanted his ministers, for with a little tact and experience they learned to sway him, making their own desires seem his, and managing great affairs of State in their own way and, all too often, in their own interests, whilst they congratulated themselves and watched him drowning amidst trivialities. . . .

From such alien and pernicious sources he acquired a pride so colossal that, truly, had not God implanted in his heart the fear of the devil, even in his worst excesses, he would literally have allowed himself to be worshipped. What is more, he would have found worshippers; witness the extravagant monuments that have been set up to him, for example the statue in the Place des Victoires, with its pagan dedication, a ceremony at which I myself was present, and in which he took such huge delight. From this false pride stemmed all that ruined him. We have already seen some of its ill-effects; others are yet to come. . . .

The Court was yet another device to sustain the King's policy of despotism. Many things combined to remove it from Paris and keep it permanently in the country. The disorders of the minority[5] had been staged mainly in that city and for that reason the King had taken a great aversion to it and had become convinced that it was dangerous to live there. . . .

The awkward situation of his mistresses and the dangers involved in conducting such scandalous affairs in a busy capital, crowded with people of evey kind of mentality, played no small part in deciding him to leave, for he was embarrassed by the crowds whenever he went in or out or appeared upon the streets. Other reasons for departure were his love of hunting and the open air, so much more easily indulged in the country than in Paris, which is far from forests and ill-supplied with pleasant walks, and his delight in building, a later and ever-increasing passion, which could not be enjoyed in the town, where he was continually in the public eye. Finally, he conceived the idea that he would be all the more venerated by the multitude if he lived retired and were no longer seen every day. . . .

[5]A reference to the Fronde.—ED.

The liaison with Mme de La Vallière,[6] which was at first kept secret, occasioned many excursions to Versailles, then a little pasteboard house erected by Louis XIII when he, and still more his courtiers, grew tired of sleeping in a low tavern and old windmill, after long, exhausting hunts in the forest of Saint-Léger and still further afield. . . .

Gradually, those quiet country excursions of Louis XIV gave rise to a vast building project, designed to house a large Court more comfortable than in crowded lodgings at Saint-Germain, and he removed his residence there altogether, shortly before the death of the Queen.[7] Immense numbers of suites were made, and one paid one's court by asking for one, whereas, at Saint-Germain, almost everyone had the inconvenience of lodging in the town, and those few who did sleep at the château were amazingly cramped.

The frequent entertainments, the private drives to Versailles, and the royal journeys, provided the King with a means of distinguishing or mortifying his courtiers by naming those who were or were not to accompany him, and thus keeping everyone eager and anxious to please him. He fully realized that the substantial gifts which he had to offer were too few to have any continuous effect, and he substituted imaginary favours that appealed to men's jealous natures, small distinctions which he was able, with extraordinary ingenuity, to grant or withhold every day and almost every hour. The hopes that courtiers built upon such flimsy favours and the importance which they attached to them were really unbelievable, and no one was ever more artful than the King in devising fresh occasions for them. . . .

. . . He took it as an offence if distinguished people did not make the Court their home, or if others came but seldom. And to come never, or scarcely ever, meant certain disgrace. When a favour was asked for such a one, the King would answer haughtily, "I do not know him at all," or, "That is a man whom I never see," and in such cases his word was irrevocable. . . .

There never lived a man more naturally polite, nor of such exquisite discrimination with so fine a sense of degree, for he made distinctions for age, merit and rank, and showed them in his answers when these went further than the usual "*Je verrai*,"[8] and in his general bearing. . . . He was sometimes gay, but never undignified, and never, at any time, did he do anything improper or indiscreet. His smallest gesture, his walk, bearing, and expression were all perfectly becoming, modest, noble, and stately, yet at the same time he always seemed

[6]One of Louis's early mistresses.—ED.
[7]The Spanish princess Maria Theresa died in 1683.—ED.
[8]"We shall see."—ED.

perfectly natural. Added to which he had the immense advantage of a good figure, which made him graceful and relaxed.

On state occasions such as audiences with ambassadors and other ceremonies, he looked so imposing that one had to become used to the sight of him if one were not to be exposed to the humiliation of breaking down or coming to a full stop. At such times, his answers were always short and to the point and he rarely omitted some civility, or a compliment if the speech deserved one. The awe inspired by his appearance was such that wherever he might be, his presence imposed silence and a degree of fear. . . .

In everything he loved magnificently lavish abundance. He made it a principle from motives of policy and encouraged the Court to imitate him; indeed, one way to win favour was to spend extravagantly on the table, clothes, carriages, building, and gambling. For magnificence in such things he would speak to people. The truth is that he used this means deliberately and successfully to impoverish everyone, for he made luxury meritorious in all men, and in some a necessity, so that gradually the entire Court became dependent upon his favours for their very subsistence. What is more, he fed his own pride by surrounding himself with an entourage so universally magnificent that confusion reigned and all natural distinctions were obliterated.

Once it had begun this rottenness grew into that cancer which gnaws at the lives of all Frenchmen. It started, indeed, at the Court but soon spread to Paris, the provinces, and the army where generals are now assessed according to the tables that they keep and the splendour of their establishments. It so eats into private fortunes that those in a position to steal are often forced to do so in order to keep up their spending. This cancer, kept alive by confusion of ranks, pride, even by good manners, and encouraged by the folly of the great, is having incalculable results that will lead to nothing less than ruin and general disaster.

No other King has ever approached him for the number and quality of his stables and hunting establishments. Who could count his buildings? Who not deplore their ostentation, whimsicality and bad taste? . . . At Versailles he set up one building after another according to no scheme of planning. Beauty and ugliness, spaciousness and meanness were roughly tacked together. The royal apartments at Versailles are beyond everything inconvenient, with back-views over the privies and other dark and evil-smelling places. Truly, the magnificence of the gardens is amazing, but to make the smallest use of them is disagreeable, and they are in equally bad taste. . . .

But one might be for ever pointing out the monstrous defects of that huge and immensely costly palace, and of its outhouses that cost even more, its orangery, kitchen gardens, kennels, larger and smaller stables, all vast, all prodigiously expensive. Indeed, a whole city has sprung up where before was only a poor tavern, a windmill and a little pasteboard château, which Louis XIII built so as to avoid lying on straw.

The Versailles of Louis XIV, that masterpiece wherein countless sums of money were thrown away merely in alterations to ponds and thickets, was so ruinously costly, so monstrously ill-planned, that it was never finished. Amid so many state rooms, opening one out of another, it has no theatre, no banqueting-hall, no ballroom, and both behind and before much still remains undone. The avenues and plantations, all laid out artificially, cannot mature and the coverts must continually be restocked with game. As for the drains, many miles of them still have to be made, and even the walls, whose vast contours enclose a small province of the gloomiest, most wretched countryside, have never been completely finished. . . . No matter what was done, the great fountains dried up (as they still do at times) in spite of the oceans of reservoirs that cost so many millions to engineer in that sandy or boggy soil.

A Rationalist View of Absolutism

VOLTAIRE

Voltaire (1694–1778) was the preeminent figure of what modern scholars call the Enlightenment, or the Age of Reason. He was also one of the greatest and most influential of early modern historians. Among Voltaire's most important books was The Age of Louis XIV *(1751), which he conceived as one of the earliest instances of what we would nowadays call "cultural history." His intention in writing this book was to illuminate the great achievements of Louis's "age"—as the title announces—rather than the king himself. Indeed* The Age of Louis XIV *is usually published as part of his later* Essay on the Morals and the Spirit of Nations *(1756). But Louis the king was as impossible for Voltaire to ignore as he had been for Saint-Simon, and as he has been for historians of his age ever since.*

Voltaire knew and cultivated many of the survivors of Louis's court, some of them important figures. He collected their letters and memoirs and those of other contemporaries—in short, he had much of the equipment of modern historical research. Although Voltaire also had strong and independent

*views on the past, as on most other subjects, his portrait of Louis XIV is
surprisingly balanced. He does not evade Louis's faults, nor does he exploit
them. Indeed, Voltaire seems rather to have admired the king, both as a
person and as a ruler. We must remember, however, that, though a rationalist, Voltaire was not a revolutionary. He thought highly of what has come to
be called Enlightened Despotism. At the time he completed* The Age of
Louis XIV, *for example, Voltaire was in Berlin as the guest, tutor, and
"friend in residence" of Frederick the Great of Prussia.*

*We must remember, too, that Voltaire was a French patriot who shared
Louis XIV's love for the glory of France. We do not even find him denounc-
ing Louis's militarism, so often the target of more recent criticism. Voltaire
was especially mindful of the unprecedented domination of French culture
in Europe during the age of Louis XIV and of the extent to which Louis
himself exemplified that culture. Voltaire admired Louis's sound domestic
economy and the diligence with which he worked at his craft of kingship,
and he had considerable sympathy for his trials as a person. The picture
that Voltaire gives us of Louis XIV is altogether a very different one from
that created by Saint-Simon.*

Louis XIV invested his court, as he did all his reign, with such bril-
liancy and magnificence, that the slightest details of his private life
appear to interest posterity, just as they were the objects of curiosity to
every court in Europe and indeed to all his contemporaries. The
splendour of his rule was reflected in his most trivial actions. People
are more eager, especially in France, to know the smallest incidents of
his court, than the revolutions of some other countries. Such is the
effect of a great reputation. Men would rather know what happened
in the private council and court of Augustus than details of the conquests of Attila or of Tamerlane.

Consequently there are few historians who have failed to give an
account of Louis XIV's early affection for the Baroness de Beauvais,
for Mlle. d'Argencourt, for Cardinal Mazarin's niece, later married to
the Count of Soissons, father of Prince Eugene; and especially for her
sister, Marie Mancini, who afterwards married the High Constable
Colonne.

He had not yet taken over the reins of government when such
diversions occupied the idleness in which he was encouraged by Cardinal Mazarin, then ruling as absolute master. . . . The fact that his
tutors had allowed him too much to neglect his studies in early youth,
a shyness which arose from a fear of placing himself in a false position, and the ignorance in which he was kept by Cardinal Mazarin,
gave the whole court to believe that he would always be ruled like his
father, Louis XIII. . . .

In 1660, the marriage of Louis XIV was attended by a display of magnificence and exquisite taste which was ever afterwards on the increase. . . .

The king's marriage was followed by one long series of fêtes, entertainments and gallantries. They were redoubled on the marriage of *Monsieur,* the king's eldest brother, to Henrietta of England, sister of Charles II, and they were not interrupted until the death of Cardinal Mazarin in 1661.

The court became the centre of pleasures, and a model for all other courts. The king prided himself on giving entertainments which should put those of Vaux in the shade.

Nature herself seemed to take a delight in producing at this moment in France men of the first rank in every art, and in bringing together at Versailles the most handsome and well-favoured men and women that ever graced a court. Above all his courtiers Louis rose supreme by the grace of his figure and the majestic nobility of his countenance. The sound of his voice, at once dignified and charming, won the hearts of those whom his presence had intimidated. His bearing was such as befitted himself and his rank alone, and would have been ridiculous in any other. . . .

The chief glory of these amusements, which brought taste, polite manners and talents to such perfection in France, was that they did not for a moment detach the monarch from his incessant labors. Without such toil he could but have held a court, he could not have reigned: and had the magnificent pleasures of the court outraged the miseries of the people, they would only have been detestable; but the same man who gave these entertainments had given the people bread during the famine of 1662. He had bought up corn, which he sold to the rich at a low price, and which he gave free to poor families at the gate of the Louvre; he had remitted three millions of taxes to the people; no part of the internal administration was neglected, and his government was respected abroad. The King of Spain was obliged to allow him precedence; the Pope was forced to give him satisfaction; Dunkirk was acquired by France by a treaty honourable to the purchaser and ignominious to the seller; in short, all measures adopted after he had taken up the reins of government were either honourable or useful; thereafter, it was fitting that he should give such fêtes . . . that all the nobles should be honoured but no one powerful, not even his brother or *Monsieur le Prince*. . . .

Not one of those who have been too ready to censure Louis XIV can deny that until the Battle of Blenheim[9] he was the only monarch

---

[9]Marlborough's great victory (1704) for England and her allies in the War of the Spanish Succession.—ED.

at once powerful, magnificent, and great in every department. For while there have been heroes such as John Sobieski and certain Kings of Sweden who eclipsed him as warriors, no one has surpassed him as a monarch. It must ever be confessed that he not only bore his misfortunes, but overcame them. He had defects and made great errors, but had those who condemn him been in his place, would they have equalled his achievements? . . .

. . . It was the destiny of Louis XIV to see the whole of his family die before their time; his wife at forty-five and his only son at fifty; but a year later we witnessed the spectacle of his grandson the Dauphin, Duke of Burgundy, his wife, and their eldest son, the Duke of Brittany, being carried to the same tomb at Saint-Denys in the month of April 1712, while the youngest of their children, who afterwards ascended the throne, lay in his cradle at death's door. The Duke of Berri, brother of the Duke of Burgundy, followed them two years later, and his daughter was carried at the same time from her cradle to her coffin.

These years of desolation left such a deep impression on people's hearts that during the minority of Louis XV I have met many people who could not speak of the late king's bereavement without tears in their eyes. . . .

The remainder of his life was sad. The disorganisation of state finances, which he was unable to repair, estranged many hearts. The complete confidence he placed in the Jesuit, Le Tellier, a turbulent spirit, stirred them to rebellion. It is remarkable that the people who forgave him all his mistresses could not forgive this one confessor. In the minds of the majority of his subjects he lost during the last three years of his life all the prestige of the great and memorable things he had accomplished. . . .

On his return from Marli towards the middle of the month of August 1715, Louis XIV was attacked by the illness which ended his life. His legs swelled, and signs of gangrene began to show themselves. The Earl of Stair, the English ambassador, wagered, after the fashion of his country, that the king would not outlive the month of September. The Duke of Orleans, on the journey from Marli, had been left completely to himself, but now the whole court gathered round his person. During the last days of the king's illness, a quack physician gave him a cordial which revived him. He managed to eat, and the quack assured him that he would recover. On hearing this news the crowd of people that had gathered round the Duke of Orleans diminished immediately. "If the king eats another mouthful," said the Duke of Orleans, "we shall have no one left." But the illness was mortal. . . .

Though he has been accused of being narrow-minded, of being too harsh in his zeal against Jansenism,[10] too arrogant with foreigners in his triumphs, too weak in his dealings with certain women, and too severe in personal matters; of having lightly undertaken wars, of burning the Palatinate and of persecuting the reformers—nevertheless, his great qualities and noble deeds when placed in the balance eclipse all his faults. Time, which modifies men's opinions, has put the seal upon his reputation, and, in spite of all that has been written against him, his name is never uttered without respect, nor without recalling to the mind an age which will be forever memorable. If we consider this prince in his private life, we observe him indeed too full of his own greatness, but affable, allowing his mother no part in the government but performing all the duties of a son, and observing all outward appearance of propriety towards his wife; a good father, a good master, always dignified in public, laborious in his study, punctilious in business matters, just in thought, a good speaker, and agreeable though aloof. . . .

The mind of Louis XIV was rather precise and dignified than witty; and indeed one does not expect a king to say notable things, but to do them. . . .

Between him and his court there existed a continual intercourse in which was seen on the one side all the graciousness of a majesty which never debased itself, and on the other all the delicacy of an eager desire to serve and please which never approached servility. He was considerate and polite, especially to women, and his example enhanced those qualities in his courtiers; he never missed an opportunity of saying things to men which at once flattered their self-esteem, stimulated rivalry, and remained long in their memory. . . .

It follows from what we have related, that in everything this monarch loved grandeur and glory. A prince who, having accomplished as great things as he, could yet be of plain and simple habits, would be the first among kings, and Louis XIV the second.

If he repented on his death-bed of having lightly gone to war, it must be owned that he did not judge by events; for of all his wars the most legitimate and necessary, namely, the war of 1701, was the only one unsuccessful. . . .

His own glory was indissolubly connected with the welfare of France, and never did he look upon his kingdom as a noble regards his land, from which he extracts as much as he can that he may live in luxury. Every king who loves glory loves the public weal; he had no

---

[10]A sect named after the Flemish theologian Cornelis Jansen that was, though Catholic, rather Calvinistic in many of its views. Jansenism was bitterly opposed by the Jesuits who finally persuaded Louis XIV to condemn it.—Ed.

longer a Colbert[11] nor a Louvois, when about 1698 he commanded each comptroller to present a detailed description of his province for the instruction of the Duke of Burgundy. By this means it was possible to have an exact record of the whole kingdom and a correct census of the population. . . .

The foregoing is a general account of what Louis XIV did or attempted to do in order to make his country more flourishing. It seems to me that one can hardly view all his works and efforts without some sense of gratitude, nor without being stirred by the love for the public weal which inspired them. Let the reader picture to himself the condition to-day, and he will agree that Louis XIV did more good for his country than twenty of his predecessors together; and what he accomplished fell far short of what he might have done. The war which ended with the Peace of Ryswick[12] began the ruin of the flourishing trade established by his minister Colbert, and the war of the succession completed it. . . .

. . . Nevertheless, this country, in spite of the shocks and losses she has sustained, is still one of the most flourishing in the world, since all the good that Louis XIV did for her still bears fruit, and the mischief which it was difficult not to do in stormy times has been remedied. Posterity, which passes judgment on kings, and whose judgment they should continually have before them, will acknowledge, weighing the greatness and defects of that monarch, that though too highly praised during his lifetime, he will deserve to be so for ever, and that he was worthy of the statue raised to him at Montpellier, bearing a Latin inscription whose meaning is *To Louis the Great after his death.*

Louis XIV
and the Larger World

PIERRE GOUBERT

The historiography of Louis XIV is almost as vast as the original sources and almost as intimidating. Few figures in European history have been more variously or more adamantly interpreted. As W. H. Lewis has said,

---

[11]Jean Baptiste Colbert, Louis's great minister of finance (d. 1683).—ED.
[12]The War of the League of Augsburg (1688–1697).—ED.

"To one school, he is incomparably the ablest ruler in modern European History; to another, a mediocre blunderer, pompous, led by the nose by a succession of generals and civil servants; whilst to a third, he is no great king, but still the finest actor of royalty the world has ever seen."[13] *And such a list does not exhaust the catalog of Louis's interpreters.*

There is at least one contemporary revisionist school that has turned again to "the world of Louis XIV," not the limited world that Saint-Simon saw—the world of the court and the hated prison of Versailles—but the larger world of economic and social forces beyond the court. One of the best exponents of this school is the French historian Pierre Goubert, from whose Louis XIV and Twenty Million Frenchmen *the following selection is taken. Goubert is essentially an economic historian, occupied with such things as demographic trends, price and wage fluctuations, gross national products, and the like. In this book he is concerned with Louis XIV as an able bureaucratic manager rather than as strictly an autocrat; as a king whose foreign policy was often governed not by his own absolutist theories, but by the realities of economics, and whose domestic policies were limited by the dragging, inertial resistance to change of the inherited institutions of his own nation.*

As early as 1661, as he declared in his *Mémoires,* Louis meant to have sole command in every sphere and claimed full responsibility, before the world and all posterity, for everything that should happen in his reign. In spite of constant hard work, he soon found he had to entrust the actual running of certain departments, such as finance or commerce, to a few colleagues, although he still reserved the right to make major decisions himself. There were, however, some aspects of his *métier de roi* to which he clung absolutely and persistently, although his persistence was not invariably absolute. Consequently, it is permissible to single out a kind of personal sphere which the king reserved to himself throughout his reign, although this sphere might vary, while the rest still remained, as it were, under his eye.

As a young man, Louis had promised himself that his own time and posterity should ring with his exploits. If this had been no more than a simple wish, and not an inner certainty, it might be said to have been largely granted.

As a hot-headed young gallant, he flouted kings by his extravagant gestures and amazed them by the brilliance of his court, his entertainments, his tournaments and his mistresses. As a new Augustus he could claim, for a time, to have been his own Maecenas. Up to the

[13]W. H. Lewis, *The Splendid Century: Life in the France of Louis XIV* (New York: Doubleday, 1957), p. 1.

year 1672, all Europe seems to have fallen under the spell of his various exploits and his youthful fame spread even as far as the "barbarians" of Asia. For seven or eight years after that, the armies of Le Tellier and Turenne[14] seemed almost invincible while Colbert's youthful navy and its great admirals won glory off the coast of Sicily. Then, when Europe had pulled itself together, Louis still showed amazing powers of resistance and adaptability. Even when he seemed to be ageing, slipping into pious isolation amid his courtiers, he retained the power to astonish with the splendours of his palace at Versailles, his opposition to the Pope and the will to make himself into a "new Constantine," and later by allying himself with Rome to "purify" the Catholic religion. When practically on his death bed, he could still impress the English ambassador who came to protest at the building of a new French port next door to the ruins of Dunkirk. . . .

For precisely three centuries, Louis XIV has continued to dominate, fascinate and haunt men's minds. "The universe and all time" have certainly remembered him, although not always in the way he would have wished. From this point of view, Louis' personal deeds have been a great success. Unfortunately, his memory has attracted a cloud of hatred and contempt as enduring as that which rises from the incense of his worshippers or the pious imitations of a later age.

In his personal desire to enlarge his kingdom, the king was successful. The lands in the north, Strasbourg, Franche-Comté and the "iron belt"[15] are clear evidence of success. In this way Paris was better protected from invasion. But all these gains had been made by 1681 and later events served only to confirm, rescue or reduce them. . . .

As absolute head of his diplomatic service and his armies, from beginning to end, he was well served while he relied on men who had been singled out by Mazarin or Richelieu but he often made a fool of himself by selecting unworthy successors. He was no great warrior. His father and his grandfather had revelled in the reek of the camp and the heady excitement of battle. His preference was always for impressive manoeuvres, parades and good safe sieges rather than the smoke of battle, and as age grew on him he retreated to desk strategy. Patient, secretive and subtle in constructing alliances, weaving intrigues and undoing coalitions, he marred all these gifts by ill-timed displays of arrogance, brutality and unprovoked aggression. In the last analysis, this born aggressor showed his greatness less in triumph

---

[14]Le Vicomte Henri de Turenne (d. 1675), one of Louis's generals. A holdover from Louis's father's reign, Turenne was the French hero of the Thirty Years War and the war against Spain.—ED.

[15]A reference to the fortifications—the *frontiére de fer*—of the Marquis de Vauban (1663–1707), Louis's master military and siege engineer.—ED.

than in adversity but there was never any doubt about his effect on his contemporaries whose feelings towards him were invariably violent and uncompromising. He was admired, feared, hated and secretly envied. . . .

More often than not, and permanently in some cases, administrative details and the complete running of certain sectors of the administration were left to agents appointed by the king and responsible to him. Louis rarely resorted to the cowardly expedient of laying the blame for failure on his subordinates. Not until the end of his life, and notably in the case of the bishops, did he indulge in such pettiness. Everything that was done during his reign was done in his name and Louis' indirect responsibility in matters he had delegated was the same as his direct responsibility in his own personal spheres. Moreover, the two sectors could not help but be closely connected.

A policy of greatness and prestige demanded an efficient and effective administration as well as adequate resources, both military and financial. . . .

In order to disseminate the king's commands over great distances and combat the complex host of local authorities, a network of thirty intendants had been established over the country. These were the king's men, dispatched by the king's councils and assisted by correspondents, agents and *subdélégués* who by 1715 were numerous and well organized. By this time the system was well-established and more or less accepted (even in Brittany). It met with reasonable respect and sometimes obedience. Sometimes, not always, since we only have to read the intendants' correspondence to be disabused swiftly of any illusions fostered by old-fashioned textbooks or history notes. The difficulties of communications, the traditions of provincial independence, inalienable rights and privileges and the sheer force of inertia, all died hard. Lavisse used to say this was a period of absolutism tempered by disobedience. In the depths of the country and the remote provinces, the formula might almost be reversed. Nevertheless, there is no denying that a step forward had been made and that the germ of the splendid administrative systems of Louis XV and of Napoleon was already present in the progress made between 1661 and 1715. . . .

In one adjacent but vital field, ministers and jurists laboured valiantly to reach a unified code of French law, giving the king's laws priority over local custom and simplifying the enormous tangled mass of statute law. . . .

The navy, rescued from virtual oblivion by Colbert who gave it arsenals, shipwrights, gunners, talented designers, its finest captains and fresh personnel obtained by means of seaboard conscription, distinguished itself particularly from 1672 to 1690. . . .

The greatest of all the king's great servants were those who helped him to build up an army, which in size and striking force was for the most part equal to all the other armies of Europe put together. They were first Le Tellier and Turenne and later, Louvois and Vauban. Many others of less fame, such as Chamlay, Martinet, Fourilles and Clerville would also deserve a place in this unusually lengthy roll of honour if the historian's job were the awarding of laurels, especially military ones. The fighting strength was increased at least fourfold, discipline was improved, among generals as well as officers and men, and a civil administration superimposed, not without a struggle, on the quarrelsome, short-sighted and in many cases incompetent and dishonest military one. New ranks and new corps were introduced; among them the artillery and the engineers, as well as such new weapons as the flintlock and the fixed bayonet, and a new military architect, Vauban, all helped to make the army more efficient. Most important of all, the army at last possessed a real *Intendance* with its own arsenals, magazines, and regular staging posts. Uniforms became more or less general, providing employment for thousands of workers. The first barracks were an attempt to put an end to the notorious custom of billeting troops on civilian households. The Hôtel des Invalides[16] was built, on a grand scale. The instrument which these invaluable servants placed at their master's disposal was almost without parallel in their time, a genuine royal army, growing ever larger and more diversified, modern and disciplined. . . .

An ambition to astonish the world with magnificence and great armies is all very well so long as the world is prepared to be astonished.

At the beginning of his reign, when Louis surveyed the rest of Europe, he saw nothing but weakness and decline. Some of his observations, as regards Spain and Italy, were perfectly correct. In others, he was mistaken. He stupidly underestimated the United Provinces, as though a small, bourgeois and Calvinist population were an inevitable sign of weakness. Yet another observation was swiftly belied by the changes which occurred in two highly dissimilar entities; England and the Empire.

Louis XIV found himself baulked at every turn by the diplomacy and dogged courage, as well as by the seapower and the immense wealth of the United Provinces. It is no longer fashionable to believe that the "Golden Age" of the Dutch was over in 1661. For a long time after that, their Bank, their Stock Exchange, their India Company, their fleets and their florins remained as powerful as ever. The invasion of 1672 weakened them only temporarily and even in 1715 . . .

---

[16]Now a military museum and the site of Napoleon's tomb but originally intended as an old soldiers' home.—ED.

their wealth, currency and bankers remained powerful and respected and often decisive. Their policy was not yet tied directly to England's. It was simply that they no longer enjoyed undivided supremacy: another nation's economy had reached the same level and was about to overtake them.

Louis XIV always did his best to ignore economic factors but they would not be denied and they took their revenge. . . .

Louis found other forces of opposition within the borders of his kingdom . . . the ancient, traditional and heavily calculated weight of inertia possessed by that collection of "nations," *pays, seigneuries,* fiefs and parishes which together made up the kingdom of France. Each of these entities was accustomed to living independently, with its own customs, privileges and even language, snug in its own fields and within sound of its own bells. The king consecrated at Rheims was a priest-king to be revered and almost worshipped, but from afar. . . .

If, dazzled by the splendours of Versailles, we let ourselves forget the constant presence of these seething undercurrents, we will have understood nothing of the France of Louis XIV and of the impossible task which the king and his ministers had set themselves, or of the massive inertia which made it so difficult. . . .

For some years now, younger historians of a certain school have tended to ignore the bustle of individuals and events in favour of what they call revealing, measuring, defining and illustrating the great dominant rhythms which move world history as a whole. These rhythms emerge as largely economic. . . . From 1600 onwards, the quantities of silver reaching Spain from America grew less and less until by 1650 the imports were only a fifth of what they had been in 1600. A probable revival of the mines of central Europe was insufficient to make up the deficit. First gold, and then silver, grew scarce, giving rise to hoarding. Copper from Sweden or Japan (via Holland) tended to take their place but it was a poor substitute. The whole age of Louis XIV was an age that Marc Bloch has called "monetary famine.". . .

Historians and economists have long been aware that the seventeenth century as a whole and the period from 1650–90 in particular, or even 1650–1730, was marked by a noticeable drop in the cost of basic foodstuffs as well as of a great many other things—a drop quite separate from annual "accidents." Landed incomes, offices and possible moneylending, all seem to have been affected by the same general reduction. . . .

There remains a strong impression that the period of Louis' reign was one of economic difficulties, suffering both from sudden, violent crises and from phases of stagnation and of deep depression. It is not easy to govern under such conditions especially when, like the king and most of his councillors, one is unaware of them. But what they tried to do and sometimes, despite such obstacles, achieved, remains nonetheless worthy of interest and even admiration.

It is possible, therefore, that France under Louis XIV may have been unconsciously subject to powerful economic forces which are still much disputed and not fully understood. Social, demographic, mental and other factors, wholly or partly incomprehensible to the rulers, may have played their part also. . . .

About the great mass of French society and its slow, ponderous development we know almost nothing, only a few glimmers here and there. . . .

It is true that Louis XIV, like most men who grew up between 1640 and 1660, was incapable of rising beyond the limits of his education, let alone of taking in, at one glance, the whole of the planet on which he lived, to say nothing of infinite space. A king to the depths of his being, and a dedicated king, he had a concept of greatness which was that of his generation: military greatness, dynastic greatness, territorial greatness and political greatness which expressed itself in unity of faith, the illusion of obedience and magnificent surroundings. He left behind him an image of the monarchy, admirable in its way, but already cracking if not outworn at the time of his death.

Suggestions for Further Reading

The best biography of Louis XIV is John B. Wolf, *Louis XIV* (New York: Norton, 1968), a comprehensive, analytical, and persuasive book. Another work, by an eminent French historian, Pierre Gaxotte, *The Age of Louis XIV,* tr. Michael Shaw (New York: Macmillan, 1970), can also be recommended, but it is not as readable as Nancy Mitford, *The Sun King* (New York: Harper & Row, 1966), a handsome book on Louis and the daily life at Versailles—the court intrigues and decisions of government—a lively and witty, if somewhat superficial, book by a popular British novelist and biographer. Three brief biographies can also be recommended: Maurice Ashley, *Louis XIV and the Greatness of France,* "Teach Yourself History Library" (New York: Macmillan, 1948), Vincent Buranelli, *Louis XIV,* "Rulers and Statesmen of the World" series (New York: Twayne, 1966), and Olivier Bernier, *Louis XIV: A Royal Life* (New York et al.: Doubleday, 1987).

Louis XIV, no matter how he is judged, is the central figure in seventeenth-century Europe. Some works on that century and the age of Louis XIV are therefore necessary to an understanding of the

Sun King. David Ogg, *Europe in the Seventeenth Century*, 8th rev. ed. (London: Macmillan, 1961), and G. N. Clark, *The Seventeenth Century*, 2nd ed. (Oxford, England: Clarendon Press, 1961), have long been the standard works of respectively, the narrative and institutional history of the period. A famous interpretive book, somewhat like Clark, is W. H. Lewis, *The Splendid Century: Life in the France of Louis XIV* (New York: Doubleday, 1957 [1953]), but it is more lively and entertaining. More comprehensive and much more far-ranging in subject is Maurice Ashley, *The Golden Century: Europe 1598–1715* (New York: Praeger, 1969). Of the same sort, but more popular, is Ragnhild Hatton, *Europe in the Age of Louis XIV* (New York: Harcourt, Brace and World, 1969). J. B. Wolf, *Toward a European Balance of Power, 1620–1715* (Chicago: Rand McNally, 1970), deals almost entirely with the central role of Louis XIV's France in the evolution of that important political-diplomatic concept. Students interested in the intellectual history of Louis's France should consult the small but well-done work by Edward John Kearns, *Ideas in Seventeenth-Century France: The Most Important Thinkers and the Climate of Ideas in which They Worked* (New York: St. Martin's Press, 1979).

Through the last generation or so, seventeenth-century studies, and the study of Louis XIV, have passed through a major crisis of revision. One of the early works reflecting this is J. B. Wolf, *The Emergence of the Great Powers, 1685–1715*, "Rise of Modern Europe" series (New York: Harper & Row, 1951), a brilliant synthesis of narrative, analysis, and modern research. Students should read more extensively in the important work, Pierre Goubert, *Louis XIV and Twenty Million Frenchmen*, tr. Anne Carter (New York: Pantheon, 1970), excerpted in this chapter. Students interested in this sort of work might be interested in the vast, two-volume compendium of French institutional history by the great French authority, Roland E. Mousnier, *The Institutions of France under the Absolute Monarchy, 1598–1789*, vol. 1 *Society and the State*, tr. Brian Pearce (Chicago and London: University of Chicago Press, 1979), vol. 2 *The Organs of State and Society*, tr. Arthur Goldhammer (Chicago and London: University of Chicago Press, 1984). There are three sets of readings that represent much of the newer research and interpretation of Louis XIV: *Louis XIV and the Craft of Kingship*, ed. John C. Rule (Columbus: Ohio State University Press, 1969), *Louis XIV and Absolutism*, ed. Ragnhild Hatton (Columbus: Ohio State University Press, 1976), and *Louis XIV and Europe*, ed. Ragnhild Hatton (Columbus: Ohio State University Press, 1976). An important revisionist book is Roger Mettam, *Power and Faction in Louis XIV's France* (Oxford and New York: Blackwell, 1988) which argues that Louis was actually an ineffective king in terms of his domestic policy. Finally, students may be interested in an important thesis book on the so-called general crisis of the seventeenth century: Theodore K. Rabb, *The Struggle for Stability in Early Modern Europe* (New York: Oxford University Press, 1975), in which Rabb argues that the crisis was a search for a principle of authority.

Acknowledgments (continued from p. iv)

SOCRATES: From *The Clouds* by Aristophanes, translated by William Arrowsmith. Copyright © 1962 by William Arrowsmith. All rights reserved. Reprinted by permission of New American Library, a division of Penguin Books USA. From "The Apology" from *The Dialogues of Plato* translated by Benjamin Jowett, third edition, 1892. Reprinted by permission of Oxford University Press. "The Image of Socrates" from *Heroes and Gods* by Moses Hadas and Morton Smith. Copyright © 1965 by Moses Hadas and Morton Smith. Reprinted by permission of Harper & Row, Publishers, Inc.

ALEXANDER: *The Campaigns of Alexander* by Arrian, translated by Aubrey de Selincourt (Penguin Classics, 1958). Copyright © the Estate of Aubrey de Selincourt, 1958. Reprinted by permission of Penguin Books Ltd. Reprinted by permission of the Loeb Classical Library from Strabo: *Geography*, Vol. I, Horace L. Jones, translator, Cambridge, Mass.: Harvard University Press, 1917. Reprinted by permission of the Loeb Classical Library from Plutarch: *Moralia*, Vol. IV, Frank C. Babbitt, translator, Cambridge, Mass.: Harvard University Press, 1936. Reprinted by permission of the Loeb Classical Library from Plutarch: *The Parallel Lives,* Vol. VII, B. Perrin, translator, Cambridge, Mass.: Harvard University Press, 1919. W. W. Tarn, "Alexander the Great and the Unity of Mankind," by permission of the British Academy, *Proceedings of the British Academy, Volume XIX, 1933.* N. G. L. Hammond, *Alexander the Great: King, Commander and Statesman.* 2nd revised edition (The Bristol Press 1989).

JULIUS CAESAR: From *The Lives of The Twelve Caesars,* Suetonius, edited and translated by Joseph Gavorse. Copyright 1931 and renewed 1959 by Modern Library, Inc. Reprinted by permission of Random House, Inc. From *The History of Rome* by Theodore Mommsen, published by Charles Scribner's Sons. From Ronald Syme, *The Roman Revolution,* published in 1939. Reprinted by permission of Oxford University Press.

ST. AUGUSTINE: From *The Confessions of St. Augustine,* translated by Rex Warner. Copyright © 1963 by Rex Warner. Reprinted by permission of New American Library, a division of Penguin Books USA. From *The Christian Philosophy of St. Augustine* by Etienne Gilson, translated by L. E. M. Lynch. Copyright © 1960 by Etienne Gilson. Reprinted by permission of Random House, Inc. Peter Brown, *Augustine of Hippo: A Biography,* University of California Press, pages 158–175. Copyright © 1967.

CHARLEMAGNE: From *The Life of Charlemagne* by Einhard, translated by Samuel Epes Turner, University of Michigan Press, 1960. Reprinted by permission of the Medieval Academy of America from: Heinrich Fichtenau, *The Carolingian Empire* (Medieval Academy Reprints for Teaching, Vol. 1), pp. 25–29, 31–34 and 44–46. Published by the University of Toronto Press in association with the Medieval Academy of America. Reprinted by permission from *Speculum: A Journal of Medieval Studies,* vol. 24 (1949) pp. 523–27.

ELEANOR OF AQUITAINE: From *William Archbishop of Tyre: A History of Deeds Done beyond the Sea,* Vol. II, translated by E. A. Babcock and A. C. Krey, Columbia University Press, 1943. From *The Historical Pontificals of John of Salisbury,* edited and translated by Marjorie Chinball, 1956, pp. 52–53. Reprinted by permission of Oxford University Press. Reprinted by permission of the publishers

314

from *Eleanor of Aquitaine and the Four Kings* by Amy Kelly, Cambridge, Mass.: Harvard University Press, Copyright © 1950 by the President and Fellows of Harvard College, © 1978 by Margaret Malcolm. From *Eleanor of Aquitaine* by Marion Meade. Copyright © 1977 by Marion Meade. A Hawthorne book. Reprinted by permission of Dutton Books, an imprint of New American Library, a division of Penguin Books USA.

PETER ABELARD: Reprinted by permission of the publishers from *The Renaissance of the Twelfth Century* by Charles Homer Haskins, Cambridge, Mass.: Harvard University Press, Copyright © 1927 by Charles Homer Haskins, © 1955 by Clare Allen Haskins. Excerpts from pp. 121–130 of *The Evolution of Medieval Thought* by David Knowles, copyright © 1962. Reprinted by permission of Helicon Press, Inc.

LEONARDO DA VINCI: From *Lives of the Most Eminent Painters, Sculptors, and Architects.* Vol. IV, by Giorgio Vasari, translated by Gaston C. DeVere. Reprinted by permission of the Medici Society Ltd. From "The Place of Leonardo da Vinci in the Emergence of Modern Science" by John Herman Randall, Jr., published in *Journal of the History of Ideas,* 14 (1935). Reprinted by permission of *Journal of the History of Ideas.* Ladislao Reti, "The Problem of the Prime Movers" from *Leonardo's Legacy: An International Symposium,* edited by C. D. O'Malley. Published by the University of California Press. Pages 69–81, 83–84, 99–100. Copyright © 1969 The Regents of the University of California.

CHRISTOPHER COLUMBUS: Reprinted, with permission, from book number 60660, *The Log of Christopher Columbus,* by Robert Fuson. Copyright © 1987 by Robert H. Fuson. Published by International Marine Publishing Company, a division of TAB Books/McGraw Hill, Blue Ridge Summit, PA 17294 (1–800–233–1128 or 717–794–2191). Excerpt from *History of the Indies* by Bartolomé de las Casas, translated and edited by Andree Collard. Reprinted by permission of Harper & Row, Publishers, Inc. From *The European Discovery of America: The Southern Voyages 1492–1616* by Samuel Eliot Morison. Copyright © 1974 by Samuel Eliot Morison. Reprinted by permission of Oxford University Press, Inc.

MARTIN LUTHER: Reprinted from *Luther's Works,* Vol. 54, edited and translated by Theodore G. Tappert, copyright © 1967 Fortress Press. Used by permission of Augsburg Fortress. Excerpts from pp. 58–64 of *Martin Luther, His Life and Work* by Hartmann Grisar, S. J., adapted from the second German edition by F. J. Eble. Edited by A. Preuss. Copyright by Newman Press. From *These Theses Were Not Posted* by Erwin Iserloh. Copyright © 1966, English Translation, by Jared Wicks, S. J. Reprinted by permission of Beacon Press.

ELIZABETH I: From *On the Fortunate Memory of Elizabeth Queen of England* by Sir Francis Bacon. From *History of England from the Fall of Wolsey to the Defeat of the Spanish Armada* by James Anthony Froude. Excerpts from *The Invincible Armada and Elizabethan England* by Garrett Mattingly. Copyright © 1963 by the Folger Shakespeare Library. Reprinted by permission of Associated University Presses.

GALILEO GALLILEI: Galileo Gallilei. *Dialogue Concerning the Two Chief World Systems: The Ptolemaic and Copernican. 2nd revised edition,* translated and edited by Stillman Drake. Published by the University of California. Pages 5–6, 338–342, 463–464. Copyright © 1962 The Regents of the University of California. From *The Crime of Galileo* by Giorgio de Santillana. Copyright 1955 by The University of Chicago Press. Reprinted by permission. From "The Galileo-Pellarme Meeting: A Historical Speculation," Appendix A in Ludvico Seymonat, *Galileo Gallilei,* translated by Stillman Drake. Reprinted by permission.

LOUIS XIV: From *Saint-Simon of Versailles* selected and translated from the *Memoirs of M. le Duc de Saint-Simon* by Lucy Norton. Copyright © 1958 by Hamish Hamilton Ltd. Reproduced by permission of Hamish Hamilton Ltd. From *The Age of Louis XIV* by Voltaire, translated by Martyn P. Pollack. An Everyman's Library Edition. Published in the United States by E. P. Dutton & Co, Inc. From *Louis XIV and Twenty Million Frenchmen* by Pierre Goubert, translated by Anne Carter. Reprinted by permission of Pantheon Books, a Division of Random House, Inc. Copyright © 1970 by Anne Carter.